Tableau for Salesforce

Visualise data and generate insights with the leading platforms for data analytics

Damiana Spadafora
Lars Malmqvist

www.bpbonline.com

First Edtion 2024

ISBN: 978-93-55519-245

Distributors:

BPB PUBLICATIONS
20, Ansari Road, Darya Ganj
New Delhi-110002
Ph: 23254990/23254991

DECCAN AGENCIES
4-3-329, Bank Street,
Hyderabad-500195
Ph: 24756967/24756400

MICRO MEDIA
Shop No. 5, Mahendra Chambers,
150 DN Rd. Next to Capital Cinema,
V.T. (C.S.T.) Station, MUMBAI-400 001
Ph: 22078296/22078297

To View Complete BPB Publications Catalogue Scan the QR Code:

Published by Manish Jain for BPB Publications, 20 Ansari Road, Darya Ganj, New Delhi-110002 and Printed by him at Manipal Technologies, Manipal

www.bpbonline.com

Dedicated to

Our parents, who taught us the importance of working together, and to our Children, that they may learn it themselves

About the Authors

- **Damiana Spadafora** is a highly experienced and accomplished analytics professional with a strong background in driving Tableau rollouts at top-tier organizations. With a wealth of experience gained at Europe's top Tableau partner, the *Information Lab*, Damiana has a proven track record of successfully implementing Tableau solutions at organizations such as the *Financial Times, Schroder's,* and *Virgin Atlantic.*

  Currently, Damiana serves as the Head of Financial Crime Data at a large Nordic bank, where she has been instrumental in driving analytics and Tableau usage across financial crime and compliance. Damiana is a well-established expert in data analytics, data management and data governance. She holds MSc degrees in Management and Economics as well as a postgraduate degree in data science. She is also a Tableau Certified professional.

- **Lars Malmqvist** has spent the past 13 years working as an architect and CTO within the Salesforce ecosystem. He has worked on over 40 Salesforce implementations, ranging from simple out-of-the-box scenarios to advanced, bespoke, multi-cloud solutions for large global brands. He is a 29-time certified Salesforce CTA with degrees in anthropology, mathematics, and technology management, an MBA from the University of Cambridge, and a Ph.D. in computer science from the University of York. Currently, he is a partner at *Implement Consulting Group.*

About the Reviewers

- **Naresh Kumar Miryala** is a highly experienced engineering leader with nearly 20 years of industry experience and a strong background in cloud, platform engineering, and artificial intelligence. He has been leading high-performing cloud data platforms teams in his current role at *Meta Platforms, Inc.* He has a proven track record of cloud transformations, infrastructure implementation, database management, ERP solutions, and DevOps deployments. His expertise spans multiple domains such as database systems, large-scale backend infrastructure, security, multi-cloud deployments, cloud infrastructure, DevOps, and Artificial Intelligence.

  Naresh has contributed to esteemed organizations such as Oracle Corp and Computer Sciences Corporations, where he played a pivotal role in migrating and implementing enterprise technologies for Fortune 500 companies across the globe. His impact spans various industries worldwide, including pharmaceuticals, retail, banking, and gold mining companies.

  Naresh's experience in cloud migrations, particularly involving relational, open-source, and NoSQL databases, middleware, and applications, has granted him a comprehensive understanding of multi-faceted technical and business challenges in the modern world and developing innovative solutions across the industry to solve large-scale data transformation and security problems using Artificial Intelligence.

- **Santosh Chitalkar** is a seasoned Salesforce Technical Architect, currently working with *Cognizant*, with over 13 years of dedicated experience in the field. His expertise spans the spectrum of Salesforce implementation, Lightning Web Component (LWC) development, CRM analytics, and seamless integrations. Throughout his career, Santosh has demonstrated a keen ability to design and execute innovative solutions tailored to meet the unique needs of diverse clients. With a meticulous approach to problem-solving and a deep understanding of Salesforce's capabilities, he has consistently delivered transformative outcomes that drive business success. Santosh's passion for harnessing technology to empower organizations has earned him a reputation as a trusted advisor in the Salesforce ecosystem. His commitment to excellence and continuous learning underscores his status as a leader in the field of Salesforce architecture.

Acknowledgement

There are a few people we would like to thank who helped make this book a reality. First and foremost, our families for being always supportive of our ambitions. Next, our children, their refusal to sleep has not made writing this book any faster, but their bright spark has given meaning to this and all our endeavours.

Our gratitude also goes to the team at BPB Publication for their infinite patience as we tried our best but still came short of meeting all our deadlines. We would also like to acknowledge the work of Santosh Chitalkar and Naresh Miryala whose kind input has made this work better in every way.

Preface

Tableau is a powerful data visualization tool, and Salesforce CRM is the most successful customer relationship management software. Companies often use these two tools to analyze data and create visualizations. However, many barriers prevent them from working together. This book will teach you how to bridge Tableau and Salesforce CRM to deliver cutting-edge data analysis and visualization.

After reading this book, the reader will have the knowledge to start using both tools to analyze real-world CRM data and create CRM Analytical dashboards that generate value for their companies.

This book is divided into 10 chapters. It starts with an introduction to both Tableau and Salesforce CRM. It then goes on to show you how you can connect Tableau with Salesforce CRM to link the two tools. Then, it walks through some of the key features of this connection that allow for seamless data analysis and visualization. It then moves on to advanced use cases combining Salesforce and Tableau for advanced analytics and decision making. The details are listed below:

Chapter 1: Introducing Salesforce and Tableau – This chapter will provide an overview of the history and key features of Salesforce and Tableau, and explore the benefits of integrating the two tools for Customer Relationship Management (CRM) analytics.

Chapter 2: Setting Up Salesforce with Tableau – This chapter will provide a step-by-step guide on setting up a Salesforce org with CRM analytics and integrating it with Tableau.

Chapter 3: Building and Integrating Data Pipelines – This chapter will focus on different methods for connecting to data in Tableau as well as data cleaning and transformation capabilities.

Chapter 4: Exploring Charts, Graphs, and Dashboards – This chapter will provide guidance on creating simple visualizations of Salesforce CRM data in Tableau.

Chapter 5: Extracting Deeper Insights with Funnels, Maps, and Hybrid Visualisations – This chapter will delve deeper into the topic of Tableau visualizations. Intermediate-level visualizations like donut charts and funnels, which are particularly useful when analyzing CRM data, will be explained. Maps and Tableau geographical features will also be introduced.

Chapter 6: Dealing with Complex Visualisations, Customisations, and APIs – This chapter will deal with advanced visualisations that can be used to unlock deeper insight from CRM data. It will show the full extent of Tableau's visualisations capabilities and the endless ways in which a chart can be customised.

Chapter 7: Integration, Authentication, and Tableau Viz LWC – This chapter will provide a comprehensive guide on integrating Tableau with Salesforce through the Tableau Viz LWC component.

Chapter 8: Blending Tableau with Traditional CRM Analytics – This chapter will introduce the concept of CRM Analytics and its importance in understanding and improving customer relationships.

Chapter 9: Exploring Einstein AI and Advanced Analytics – This chapter will focus on the concept of advanced analytics and its applications in Tableau and Salesforce. It will provide guidance on how to create a combined analytical use case across Tableau and Salesforce, leveraging the strengths of both platforms for enhanced data analysis and decision making.

Chapter 10: Troubleshooting, Tricks, and Best Practices – This chapter will summarize why Tableau and Salesforce are such a powerful combination, with an emphasis on their capabilities for data analysis, visualization and decision making. Additionally, it will provide tips on how to get started using Tableau and Salesforce, with guidance on best practices and useful resources. It will also contain guidance on troubleshooting common issues. Lastly, it will explain how to continue the learning journey, including recommended further reading.

Tableau Files and Coloured Images

Please follow the link to download the
Tableau Files and the *Coloured Images* of the book:

https://rebrand.ly/qp3z52n

The Tableau files for the book are hosted on GitHub at
https://github.com/bpbpublications/Tableau-for-Salesforce.
In case there's an update to the files, it will be updated on the existing GitHub repository.

We have code bundles from our rich catalogue of books and videos available at **https://github.com/bpbpublications**. Check them out!

Errata

We take immense pride in our work at BPB Publications and follow best practices to ensure the accuracy of our content to provide with an indulging reading experience to our subscribers. Our readers are our mirrors, and we use their inputs to reflect and improve upon human errors, if any, that may have occurred during the publishing processes involved. To let us maintain the quality and help us reach out to any readers who might be having difficulties due to any unforeseen errors, please write to us at :

errata@bpbonline.com

Your support, suggestions and feedbacks are highly appreciated by the BPB Publications' Family.

Piracy

If you come across any illegal copies of our works in any form on the internet, we would be grateful if you would provide us with the location address or website name. Please contact us at **business@bpbonline.com** with a link to the material.

If you are interested in becoming an author

If there is a topic that you have expertise in, and you are interested in either writing or contributing to a book, please visit **www.bpbonline.com**. We have worked with thousands of developers and tech professionals, just like you, to help them share their insights with the global tech community. You can make a general application, apply for a specific hot topic that we are recruiting an author for, or submit your own idea.

Reviews

Please leave a review. Once you have read and used this book, why not leave a review on the site that you purchased it from? Potential readers can then see and use your unbiased opinion to make purchase decisions. We at BPB can understand what you think about our products, and our authors can see your feedback on their book. Thank you!

For more information about BPB, please visit **www.bpbonline.com**.

Join our book's Discord space

Join the book's Discord Workspace for Latest updates, Offers, Tech happenings around the world, New Release and Sessions with the Authors:

https://discord.bpbonline.com

Table of Contents

Chapter 1
Introducing Salesforce and Tableau

Introduction

This chapter will provide an overview of the history and key features of Salesforce and Tableau, it will also explore the benefits of integrating the two tools for **Customer Relationship Management (CRM)** analytics. This chapter will begin by discussing the origins and evolution of Salesforce as a CRM platform and the emergence of Tableau as a leading data visualization and business intelligence tool. It will then delve into the specific functions and capabilities of each tool. Then, we will discuss why using analytics tools can provide businesses with a powerful and flexible solution for gaining insights from customer data and thereby driving business value. Finally, the chapter will explore the advantages of using Salesforce and Tableau specifically, such as the ability to make more informed decisions, improve customer satisfaction, and drive growth.

Structure

The chapter covers the following topics:

- History of Salesforce and Tableau
- Defining Salesforce
- Defining Tableau
- Driving value with analytics

- Need for CRM analytics
- Advantages of using Tableau and Salesforce together

Objectives

After completing this chapter, learners will be able to describe the history and evolution of Salesforce and Tableau as leading tools for CRM and data visualization respectively. They will learn how to explain the specific functions and capabilities of Salesforce and Tableau. The readers will know how to analyze the benefits of using analytics tools for gaining insights from customer data and driving business value. This chapters will help the readers evaluate the advantages of integrating Salesforce and Tableau for CRM analytics and identify ways in which using Salesforce and Tableau can lead to more informed decision-making, improved customer satisfaction, and business growth.

History of Salesforce and Tableau

Salesforce is the world's top enterprise software company. Founded in 1999 by a group of former *Oracle* executives, Salesforce has been on a journey of growth and innovation. Due to its innovative **Software-as-a-Service (SaaS)** approach, all but unknown at the time, Salesforce quickly gained traction, and by 2002, it had amassed over 1,000 customers. Despite being affected by the dot-com bubble in the early 2000s, Salesforce continued to push through and saw its revenue skyrocket from $5.4 million in 2001 to over $100 million in 2003.

Salesforce initially focused on CRM applications and services but has since expanded its services to include a variety of cloud-based solutions. In 2005, Salesforce launched its AppExchange platform, allowing users to customize and share applications built on the Salesforce platform. This was followed by the introduction of Force.com, a **Platform-as-a-Service (PaaS)** offering that allowed customers to quickly create and deploy custom applications and, in 2009, *Service Cloud,* its first foray into areas outside the traditional Sales CRM space.

Over the years, Salesforce has continued to evolve and expand its offerings, launching new products in more than 20 different areas of enterprise software, such as marketing, digital commerce, integration, collaboration, AI, and industry clouds. It has also grown by acquiring companies like Heroku, MuleSoft, Slack, and, most importantly for this book, Tableau, the world-leading analytics platform.

According to research firm *Gartner*, Salesforce has held the top spot in their *Magic Quadrant for Sales Force Automation* for 16 years running, a testament to the company's ability to deliver on its vision and execute its strategy. Salesforce's CRM platform is used by a wide range of businesses, from small and medium-sized enterprises to large enterprise organizations. The following figure shows the Magical Quadrant for Sales Force automation.

Figure 1.1: *Gartner Magic Quadrant for Sales Force Automation 2022*

In addition to its dominance in the CRM space, Salesforce has also made strides in other areas of enterprise software. *Gartner* has placed Salesforce in the leader's quadrant in Magic Quadrants related to customer service, marketing automation, and digital commerce, recognizing the company's capabilities in broader digital transformation.

In terms of market share, Salesforce holds a significant portion of the CRM market, with industry analysts estimating that the company has a market share of around 23.8%, significantly larger than its closest competitors. Additionally, Salesforce has a growing presence in other areas of enterprise software, such as marketing automation, customer service, and e-commerce.

In 2022, Salesforce reported second-quarter earnings of $7.72 billion, surpassing SAP to become the world's largest enterprise software vendor. Through all of these changes and challenges, Salesforce has remained committed to its mission of delivering a platform that helps companies connect with their customers in a whole new way.

Tableau started as a Ph.D. dissertation by *Chris Stolte* under *Professor Hanrahan*. This was the culmination of his six years of research work in the analysis of multidimensional data at Stanford. Nor was he a stranger to the world of visualization, as prior to Tableau, Chris had founded *BeeLine Systems*, a mapping and visualization software that would then be bought by *Vicinity Corporation.*

Professor Pat Hanrahan currently serves as a Professor of Computer Science and Electrical Engineering at *Stanford* and has been covering the field of visualization and computer graphics since the late 90s.

Christian Chabot, the company's third founder, who would go on to become Tableau's CEO and eventually its chairman, was in the dissertation room where Stolte discussed his research. This was not by chance, as Christian was BeeLine Systems' co-founder, together with *Chris Stolte.*

From this academic start came software that would be used by Fortune 500 companies and millions of people in the corporate and not-for-profit world, Tableau.

In 2013, Tableau went public with an IPO on the New York Stock Exchange, which raised more than $250M. This 10-digit figure is perhaps not surprising when considering that as of 31 December 2012, Tableau could count on more than 10,000 customers and had achieved an 8-digit profit for the third year in a row.

Salesforce's 2019 acquisition of Tableau for $15.7 billion was hailed as a highly strategic move for the company, and a significant step towards fulfilling its goal of providing a comprehensive, 360-degree view of the customer. With this purchase, Salesforce not only gained access to an enthusiastic data community but also acquired an enterprise-standard visualization tool. By integrating Tableau with its existing platform and technology, such as Einstein, the joint company is in a position to offer a powerful data stack for enterprises. The decision to acquire Tableau was made after Salesforce CEO *Marc Benioff* heard so much positive feedback from customers that he decided to OK the deal. The following figure shows the Magical Quadrant for Business Analytics Platforms.

Source: Gartner (February 2021)

Figure 1.2: *Gartner Magic Quadrant for Business Analytics Platforms 2021*

Tableau has continued to run as a separate business in many ways after the acquisition, but the products have been ever more tightly integrated. In 2022, Tableau celebrated 10 years as a Leader in the Gartner Magic Quadrant for Business Intelligence platforms.

Defining Salesforce

We noted above that Salesforce has products in more than twenty different enterprise software areas. That means a comprehensive overview of all the functionality provided by the company would easily run to a book in its own right. However, a good way to familiarize ourselves with Salesforce is to look at the architecture of its core platform, called the **Lightning Platform**.

The lightning platform rests on a multi-tenant **Software-as-a-Service (SaaS)** platform that ensures high availability, scalability, and performance of the applications running on top.

The platform layer also handles database management, a compilation of custom code, and management of the metadata that represents the configuration of the unique customer environment. This figure shows an overview of the lightning platform.

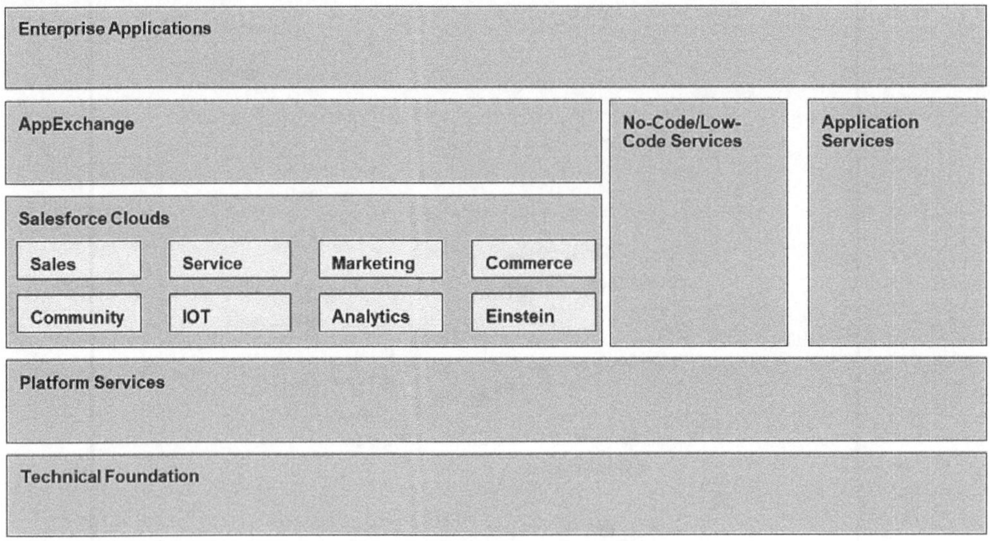

Figure 1.3: *Lightning Platform Overview*

The ability to customize almost everything via point-and-click tools is one of the strongest features in Salesforce and that ability is based on the fact that, everything is represented as metadata that is only compiled into a final application at runtime. The platform provides a range of core services that all applications make use of. These include security, internationalization, mobility, collaboration, and compliance. On top of these basic platform services, there are powerful building blocks that are used to assemble functionality into working applications.

First, there are tools to customize the data model. Within Salesforce you find both a standard data model with common objects and fields for instance to represent contacts or accounts. But you also have full flexibility to create a custom data model that meets your requirements.

Second, you have extensive automation capabilities that allow you to define custom processes and workflows. These can be triggered as part of business processes from the user interface or using scheduled data. They can use integrations to create cross-platform automation and increasingly incorporate AI to handle advanced processing.

Third, you have a large palette of no-code tools that you can use to customize the user experience. This includes for instance creating list views, pages, and page layouts, and branding the user experience to your company's identity.

While the configuration of the data model, automation, and user experience gives you a lot of flexibility, sometimes you need to go even further.

By combining these capabilities, you can achieve a high level of unique functionality without having to invest in large amounts of custom code.

Defining Tableau

The Tableau software ecosystem contains a number of different elements that together provide an unparalleled data analytics experience.

The following diagram shows the general overview:

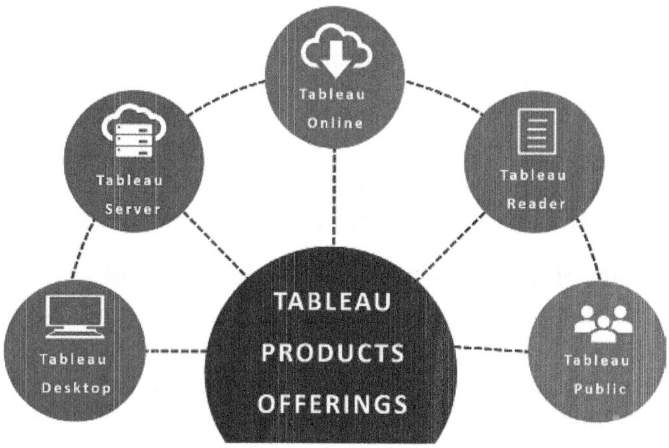

Figure 1.4: *Tableau product overview*

Tableau Desktop is a drag-and-drop analytics and data visualization software that allows you to connect to a wide range of data sources, create ad hoc analyses, build cohesive dashboards, and share views with others.

Tableau Public, a free version of Tableau Desktop, is suitable for non-proprietary data analysis and allows users to connect to limited data sources like Microsoft Excel.

Tableau Server is a central repository managed by organizations that store all published workbooks, shared data sources, and/or Tableau Prep workflows.

Tableau Online, a hosted version of Tableau Server, has nearly all the same functionalities.

Tableau Reader is a free desktop application that enables users to view and interact with packaged workbooks from Tableau Desktop. Finally, Tableau Mobile is a free mobile app that allows users to view and interact with analyses published on Tableau Server or Tableau Online.

Finally, *Tableau Prep Builder* is a user-friendly data engineering software that enables you to connect to various data sources and clean, aggregate, pivot, and merge data before publishing it to a central repository for others to use. With *Tableau Prep Conductor,* an add-on in Tableau's Data Management, you can schedule and automate data engineering flows developed in Tableau Prep Builder.

In this book, we will focus mainly on Tableau Desktop to do the analysis of Salesforce data. However, we will also be getting acquainted with Tableau Prep, Tableau Server, and Tableau Online, particularly as we discuss some of the more advanced use cases for combining Salesforce and Tableau in the later chapters of the book.

Driving value with analytics

Analytics is the process of using data to make informed decisions, uncover hidden patterns and trends, and gain insights into a particular area of interest. This process involves the collection, processing, analysis, and interpretation of data, using statistical and computational methods to identify and extract meaningful information.

Businesses use analytics to solve a wide range of problems, from optimizing processes and increasing efficiency to understanding customer behavior and improving marketing strategies. By leveraging data analytics, companies can gain a deeper understanding of their operations and customers, improve performance, and drive revenue growth.

One of the key benefits of analytics is that it can help businesses identify patterns and trends that would be difficult or impossible to detect manually. For example, a retailer may use data analytics to understand which products are selling well, what types of customers are buying those products, and how often they are making purchases. By analyzing this data, the retailer can adjust their inventory and pricing strategies to better meet customer demand and increase sales.

Another way that analytics can add value is by enabling businesses to optimize their operations and reduce costs. For instance, a logistics company may use data analytics to track shipments, identify bottlenecks in the supply chain, and optimize delivery routes to minimize transportation costs. By using analytics to improve efficiency, the company can reduce operational expenses, increase profits, and improve customer satisfaction.

In addition to these benefits, analytics can also be used to improve customer engagement and retention. For example, a media company may use data analytics to understand which types of content resonate with their audience and use this information to create more targeted and engaging content. By using analytics to better understand their customers' preferences, the company can increase engagement, attract new subscribers, and increase advertising revenue.

One important point to note is that data analytics is not just a tool for large enterprises. Small and medium-sized businesses can also benefit from analytics by using data to gain insights into their operations and customer behavior. For example, a local coffee shop may use data analytics to track sales, identify popular menu items, and understand which marketing channels are most effective at driving foot traffic. By using analytics to better understand their customers' preferences, the coffee shop can increase sales, reduce waste, and improve customer loyalty.

Overall, analytics is a powerful tool that businesses can use to drive insights and value. By leveraging data to identify patterns and trends, optimize operations, and improve customer engagement, companies can make more informed decisions and drive revenue growth. Whether you are a small business or a large enterprise, analytics can help you gain a competitive edge in your industry and achieve your business goals.

Need for CRM analytics

Customer Relationship Management (CRM) analytics is a crucial tool for businesses looking to enhance their sales and customer service capabilities. It involves collecting and analyzing data on customer interactions, preferences, behaviors, and demographics to develop insights that can be used to improve decision-making, drive revenue, and gain a deeper understanding of the customer. In the following sections, we will explore the benefits of CRM analytics for businesses, focusing on analytics for sales and service.

Empowering users to make better decisions faster

One of the primary benefits of CRM analytics is that it empowers users to make better decisions faster. By leveraging data and analytics, businesses can gain a better understanding of their customers, identify trends, and develop insights that can be used to inform strategic decisions. This means that businesses can make more informed decisions about product development, marketing campaigns, sales strategies, and customer service initiatives.

For example, consider a retail business that wants to improve its customer experience. By analyzing customer data, the business may discover that customers are unhappy with the current checkout process. Armed with this insight, the business can implement changes to the checkout process, such as introducing new payment methods or redesigning the checkout flow, to improve customer satisfaction.

Driving revenues and closing more deals

Another key benefit of CRM analytics is that it can drive revenues and help businesses close more deals. By analyzing customer data, businesses can identify potential sales opportunities and develop targeted sales and marketing campaigns to capitalize on them. This means that businesses can more effectively reach out to customers with the right message at the right time, increasing the chances of converting leads into sales.

For example, consider a business that sells software products. By analyzing customer data, the business may discover that a particular customer has been using a trial version of their software but has not yet made a purchase. The business can then use this insight to reach out to the customer with a targeted sales offer, such as a discount or a personalized demo, to encourage them to make a purchase.

Gaining a deeper understanding of your customer

Finally, CRM analytics can help businesses gain a deeper understanding of their customers. By analyzing customer data, businesses can identify patterns and trends that can be used to develop insights into customer behavior, preferences, and needs. This means that businesses can better understand what their customers want and need and develop products and services that meet those needs.

For example, consider a healthcare provider that wants to improve the patient's experience. By analyzing patient data, the healthcare provider may discover that patients are unhappy with the current wait times for appointments. Armed with this insight, the healthcare provider can implement changes to the appointment scheduling process, such as introducing an online booking system or adding more staff, to improve patient satisfaction.

CRM analytics is a crucial tool for businesses looking to enhance their sales and customer service capabilities. By empowering users to make better decisions faster, driving revenues closing more deals, and gaining a deeper understanding of the customer, businesses can gain a competitive edge in today's market. By leveraging data and analytics, businesses can develop insights that can be used to inform strategic decisions, improve customer's experience, and drive business growth.

Advantages of using Tableau and Salesforce together

The combination of Salesforce and Tableau creates a powerful analytics solution that offers numerous benefits to companies. This goes beyond the value of either solution on its own. In the following sections, we will explore how you can leverage the combined power of these world-leading platforms.

Unlocking Salesforce data with Tableau's visualization capabilities

Tableau's visualization capabilities enable users to create rich and interactive visualizations that allow them to easily explore and analyze Salesforce data. This includes the ability to create detailed dashboards, and interactive reports, and even embed visualizations directly within Salesforce objects. The result is a more intuitive and user-friendly experience that makes it easier to extract insights and identify trends.

In addition to its advanced visualization capabilities, Tableau also allows companies to blend Salesforce data with other business data for increased visibility and a deeper understanding of their customers. This means that users can combine data from multiple sources, including ERP systems, marketing automation platforms, and other business applications, to gain a more complete picture of their customers and operations.

By providing finance, operations, channel teams, and executives with secure, customized, and up-to-date views of their data, Tableau enables organizations to make data-driven decisions with ease. For example, a sales team could use Tableau to gain insights into customer behavior, including purchase history, preferences, and buying patterns. With this information, the team can identify potential sales opportunities, optimize their sales funnel, and increase revenue.

Empowering users by bringing Tableau dashboards into Salesforce CRM environments

Integrating Tableau dashboards into Salesforce CRM environments can be a game-changer for businesses. It empowers users by providing them with powerful data visualization tools that enable them to spot trends and patterns that may have otherwise gone unnoticed. This integration allows users to work more efficiently and effectively, providing insights that help predict outcomes.

Tableau's Dashboard Starters for Salesforce is a valuable tool that allows companies to quickly create actionable data analysis. This feature provides users with pre-built dashboards that are specifically designed to provide insights into Salesforce data. The dashboard starters are customizable, allowing companies to tailor them to their specific needs, such as sales forecasting, customer service analytics, and marketing campaign analysis.

One of the key benefits of integrating Tableau dashboards into Salesforce CRM workflows is the seamless integration it provides. By integrating with Salesforce CRM workflows, users can view and analyze their data without having to leave the CRM platform. This means that users can make data-driven decisions in real time, providing them with a competitive advantage in the marketplace.

For example, consider a sales team that is looking to identify new sales opportunities. By integrating Tableau dashboards into Salesforce, the sales team can analyze data on customer behavior, preferences, and past purchases to identify potential sales opportunities. With Tableau's data visualization tools, the sales team can quickly identify patterns and trends, making it easier to develop targeted sales campaigns and close more deals.

Bringing Tableau dashboards to the next level with advanced insights from Einstein AI

Salesforce's Einstein AI models can be easily set up with no coding necessary, allowing companies to connect analytics to the next action to take. With Data Cloud for Tableau, users can unlock their customer data and deliver actionable insights at scale. By natively connecting to integrated, unified data from any source, including their Salesforce instance, Data Cloud for Tableau enables users to discover customer insights and make data-driven decisions.

Tableau's integration with Salesforce also includes **CRM Analytics (CRMA)**, a fully native analytics solution built on Salesforce's platform. CRMA combines Salesforce's sales, service, and marketing data with Tableau's data visualization capabilities to provide companies with comprehensive insights into their operations. With CRMA, companies can identify trends and predict outcomes, spot anomalies, and improve their customer experience.

In summary, the combination of Salesforce and Tableau unlocks customer data, empowers users to work more efficiently, and provides advanced insights through Einstein AI and Data Cloud for Tableau. Furthermore, Tableau CRM offers a fully native analytics solution built on Salesforce's platform, allowing companies to achieve comprehensive insights into their operations. By leveraging Tableau's data visualization capabilities and Salesforce's extensive customer data, companies can make data-driven decisions and improve their overall performance.

Conclusion

This chapter has provided an overview of Salesforce and Tableau and explored the benefits of integrating these two powerful tools for CRM analytics. We discussed the origins and evolution of Salesforce and Tableau, as well as the specific functions and capabilities of each tool. By using analytics tools, businesses can gain insights from customer data and drive business value.

We also discussed the advantages of using Salesforce and Tableau specifically, including the ability to make more informed decisions, improve customer satisfaction, and drive growth. By mastering the topics covered in this chapter, you should now have a better understanding of, how Salesforce and Tableau can be used together to gain insights that will help them make better business decisions and drive success.

In our next chapter, we will move on to discuss how to set up the software and tools needed for the rest of the book.

Join our book's Discord space

Join the book's Discord Workspace for Latest updates, Offers, Tech happenings around the world, New Release and Sessions with the Authors:

https://discord.bpbonline.com

CHAPTER 2
Setting Up Salesforce with Tableau

Introduction

This chapter will provide a step-by-step guide on setting up a Salesforce org with **Customer Relationship Management (CRM)** analytics integrating it with Tableau, and highlighting the key features and configuration options for enabling CRM analytics. Next, we are going to cover the steps for setting up Tableau Desktop and Tableau Online, including installing the software and creating an account.

Structure

This chapter covers the following topics:

- Setting up a Salesforce org with CRM Analytics
- Setting up Tableau Desktop
- Getting started with Tableau Public

Objectives

By the end of this chapter, learners will have gained a comprehensive understanding of how to set up a Salesforce organization, including its primary features and configuration options tailored for CRM analytics. Additionally, they will become familiar with the procedures to establish Tableau Desktop and Tableau Online, encompassing both the software installation and the process of account creation. Moreover, the chapter offers insights on how to configure Tableau Public for complimentary access to Tableau tools. Armed with this knowledge, readers will be well-prepared to delve into the connection between Salesforce and Tableau in the upcoming chapter.

Setting up a Salesforce org with CRM Analytics

The first thing you will need to set up to follow the examples in this book is an Analytics enabled Salesforce Org. This differs from a regular Salesforce Developer Org by having CRMA enabled out of the box, along with data you can explore to learn its functionality. We will be using this environment throughout the following chapters.

To create a new Salesforce Analytics Enabled Developer org, follow these steps:

1. Navigate to **developer.salesforce.com/promotions/orgs/analytics-de**. This will take you to the sign-up form:
2. Fill in the required fields in the form and click **Sign me up >,** as can be seen in the following figure. This will initiate the process of provisioning an org.

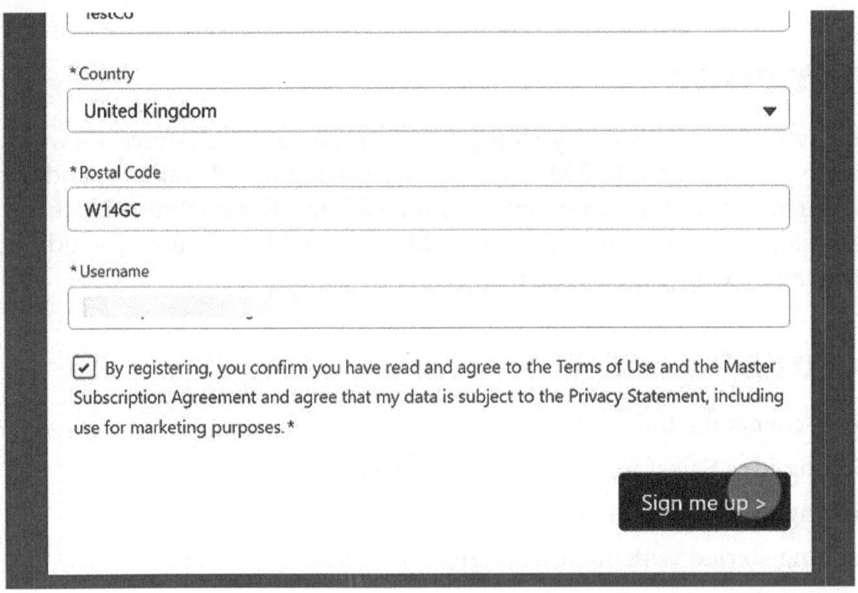

Figure 2.1: *Filled in Sign-up form*

3. You will now receive an email telling you the org has been created. This can sometimes take a few minutes. Click the button in the email to verify your account, as shown in the following figure:

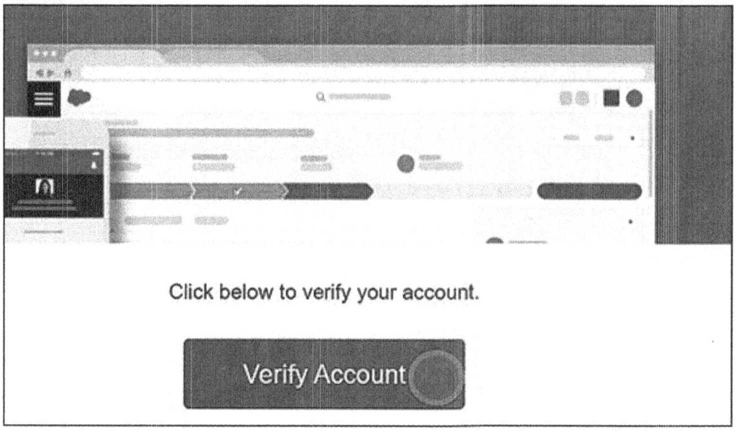

***Figure 2.2:** Verify account*

4. Enter the password you want to use for your new org and your security question and answer. Click **Change Password** to save and finish the provisioning process, as shown in *Figure 2.3*:

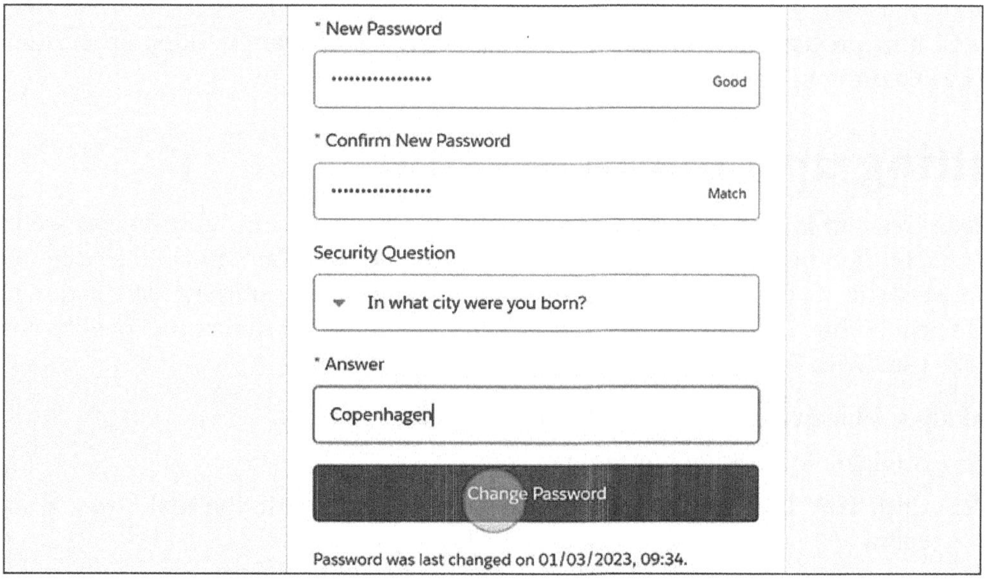

***Figure 2.3:** Change password*

5. You have now created a ready-to-use Salesforce environment for this book.

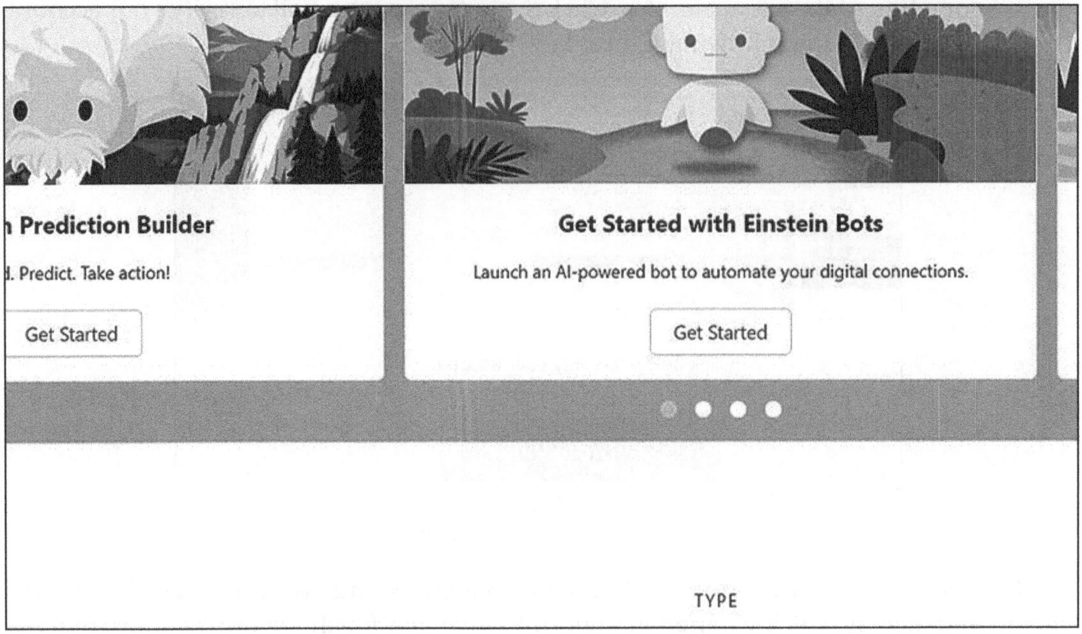

Figure 2.4: *Salesforce environment created*

We will now proceed with installing Tableau Desktop, the main desktop application we will be exploring in this book.

Setting up Tableau desktop

Tableau Desktop is an application you need to download and install from the web. You can get a 14-day trial for free, but you must first sign up for a Tableau Online Account and create a test site. If you need more than 14 days for your learning journey, you can download the Tableau Public Desktop application, which has almost the same functionality but can only be used with Tableau Public, described below.

To set up a Tableau Online account, follow these steps:

1. Navigate to **https://www.tableau.com/**
2. Click **TRY TABLEAU FOR FREE**. This will send you to the trial form, as shown below:

***Figure 2.5:** Tableau trial sign-up*

3. Fill in the required information in the form and click the **Request Free Trial** button:

***Figure 2.6:** Requesting a free trial*

4. You will now receive an email with a link to create a new Tableau Site. Click on that link.
5. Click **CREATE OR LOG IN TO TABLEAU** (*Figure 2.6*):

***Figure 2.6:** Create Tableau Online site*

6. Click **CREATE AN ACCOUNT** (*Figure 2.7*):

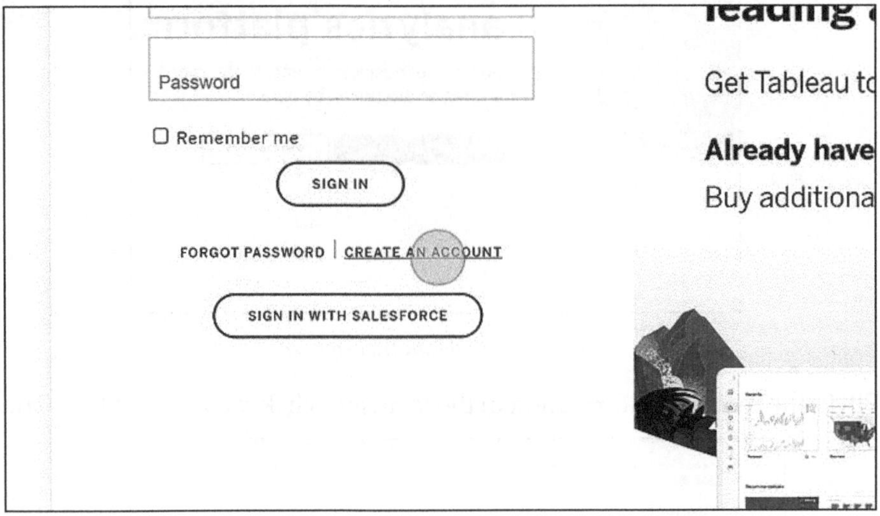

***Figure 2.7:** Account creation form*

7. Fill in the form and click **CREATE MY ACCOUNT**, as can be seen in the following figure:

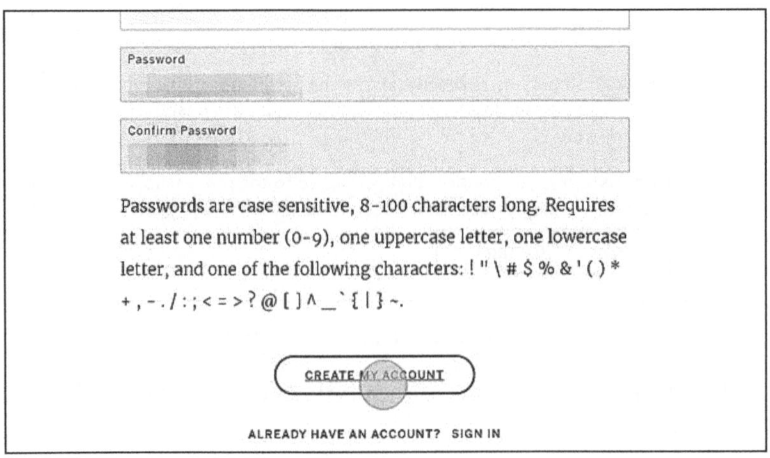

***Figure 2.8:** Create account*

8. Now sign in with your new credentials, as shown in the following figure:

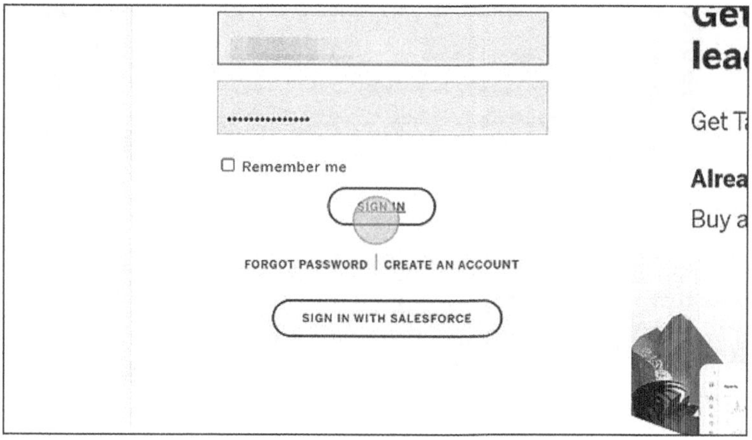

Figure 2.9: *Sign-in form*

9. Fill out the information about your test site. Pick the site location nearest to you. Click **ACTIVATE NOW** when you are done, as shown in the following figure:

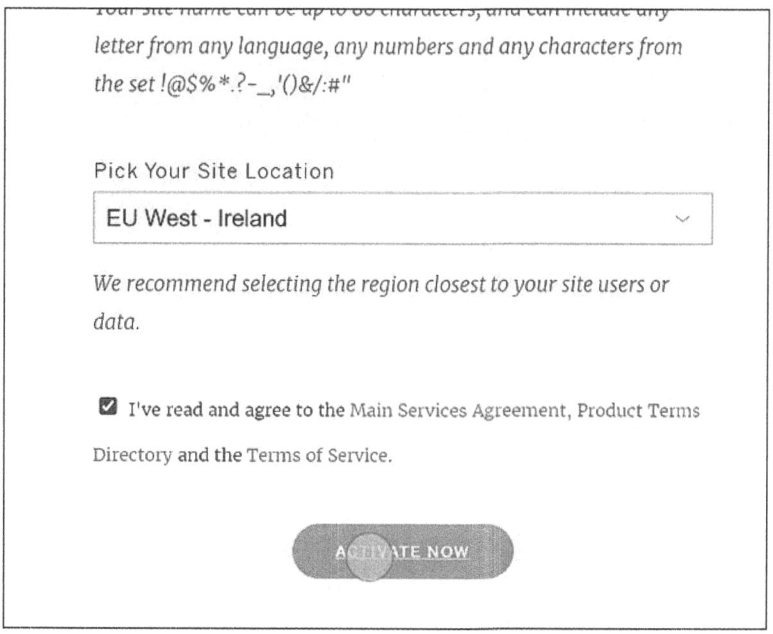

Figure 2.10: *Activate Tableau Online site*

10. You have now created your Tableau account and test site. You can close any pop-ups that appear without any actions, as per the following figure.

Figure 2.11: Close down pop-up

You can now proceed to download and install Tableau Desktop. To do so, follow these steps:

1. From your Tableau site, click the link **Download Tableau Desktop**, as shown in the following figure:

Figure 2.12: Download Tableau Desktop

2. Click the link to view the current version. Refer the following figure:

Figure 2.13: Go to current version

3. Click the link to download Tableau Desktop. Take a look at the following figure:

Figure 2.14: Download Tableau Desktop

4. Pick the version for Windows or Mac, depending on what platform you use, as shown in the following figure:

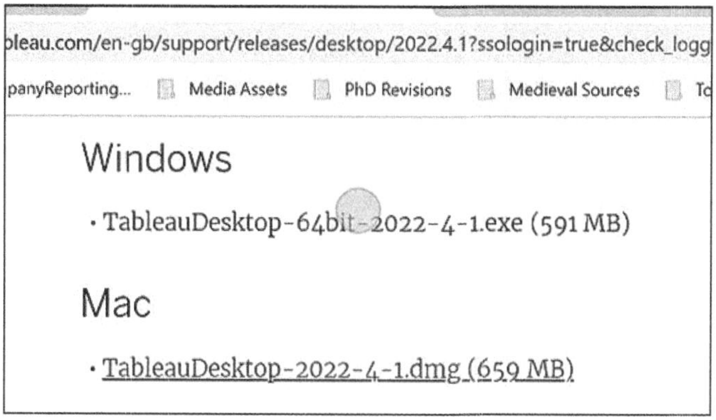

***Figure 2.15:** Pick the right version for your environment*

5. Open the downloaded file to start the installation, as shown in the following figure:

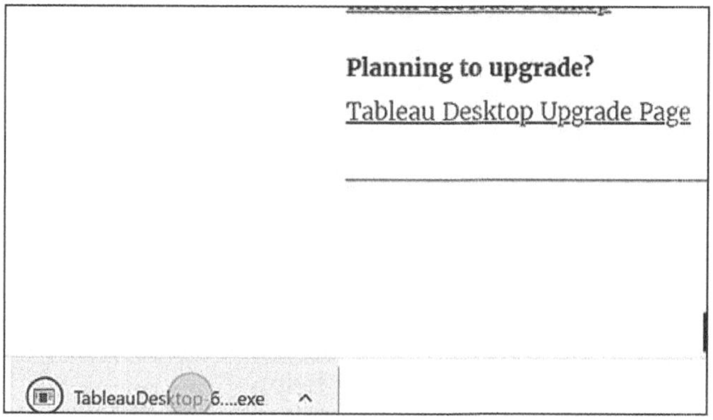

***Figure 2.16:** Start installation of Tableau Desktop*

6. Click to accept the license agreement, then click Install. Refer the following figure:

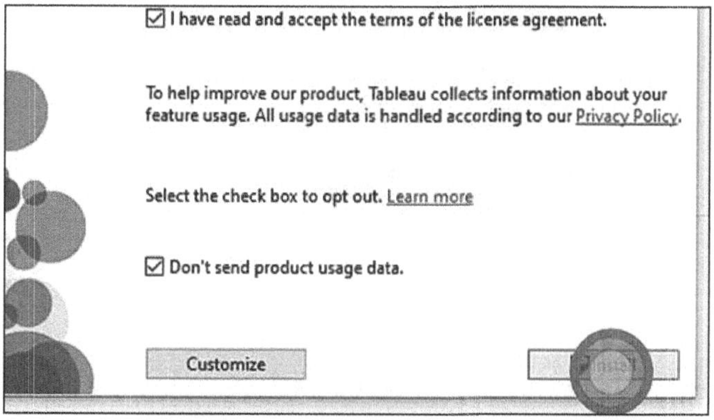

***Figure 2.17:** Install Tableau Desktop*

7. Once the installation is complete, fill in the form and click Start Trial Now. Take a look at the following figure:

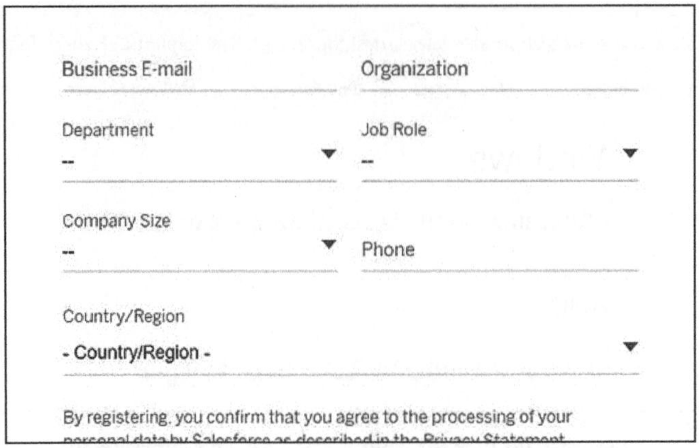

Figure 2.18: Start Tableau Desktop Trial

You have now successfully installed Tableau Desktop, and we just have one final hurdle to complete before we can check that everything works, creating an account for Tableau Public.

Getting started with Tableau Public

Tableau Public is a free site for sharing data visualizations. By working in this space and downloading the free version of Tableau Desktop for use with Tableau Public, you get the opportunity to continue your learning journey beyond the initial 14-days trial.

To sign up for Tableau Public, follow the steps below:

1. Navigate to **https://public.tableau.com/app/discover**
2. Click **Sign Up for Tableau Public**, as per the following figure:

Figure 2.19: Sign up for Tableau Public

3. Fill in the form, answer the captcha, and click **Create My Account**. This will result in an email being sent for you to verify your email, as shown in the following figure:

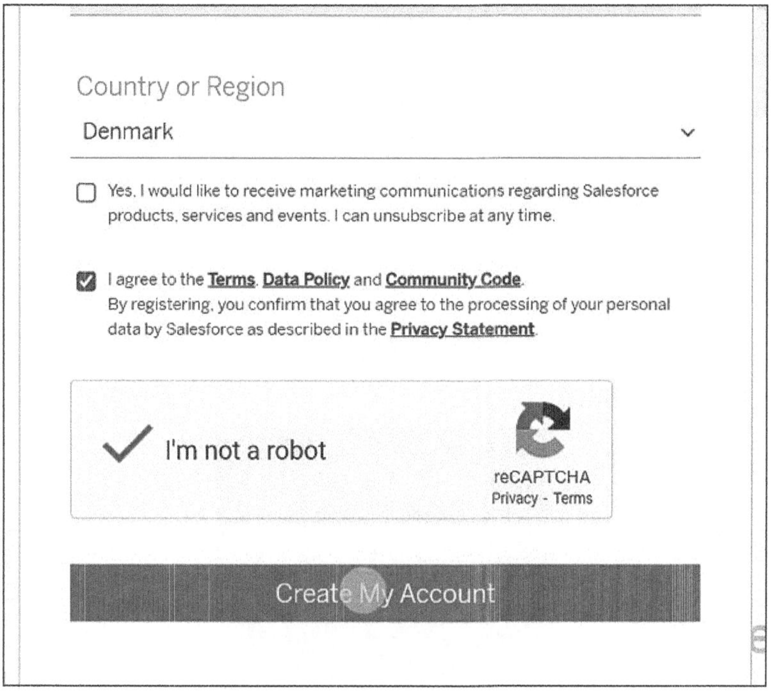

Figure 2.20: Create a Tableau Public account

4. On the ensuing popup, click **Skip to profile**, and you have successfully signed up for Tableau Public. Take a look at the following figure:

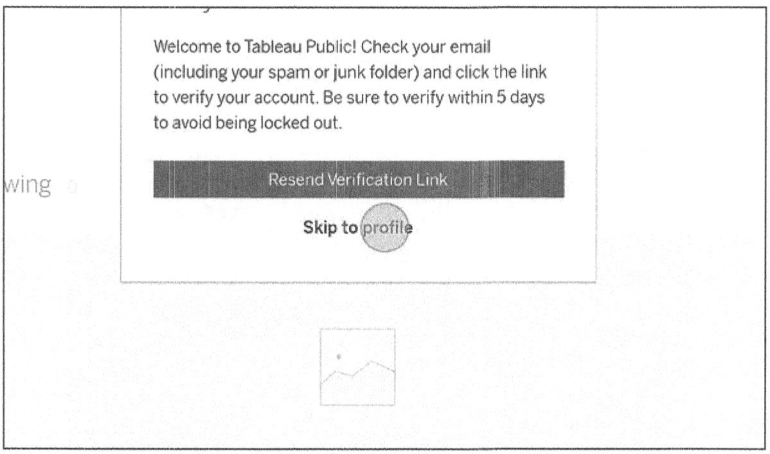

Figure 2.21: Skip to profile

5. Remember to verify your account by clicking the link in the email you have received.

You have now successfully installed or signed up for all the key components required for this book. Now, let us make sure it all works together by creating a "Hello World" example to check that everything works.

Now, it is time to put the tools together in an example that demonstrates that we are ready to move forward to the next chapter. We do that by connecting our Tableau Desktop instance to our CRMA Developer Org and creating a simple test chart based on data from that org.

To accomplish that task, follow these steps:

1. Open Tableau Desktop.
2. Expand the connections by clicking **More** under Connect | **To a Server**, as shown in the following figure:

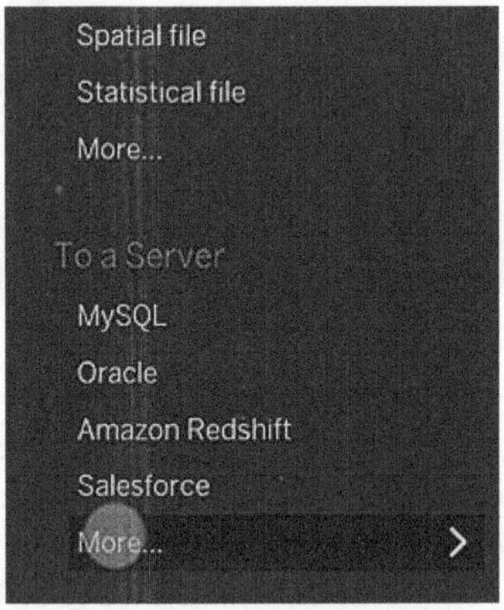

Figure 2.22: Connection to Salesforce

3. Click on **Salesforce** (*Figure 2.23*). This will start the connection to a Salesforce Data Source:

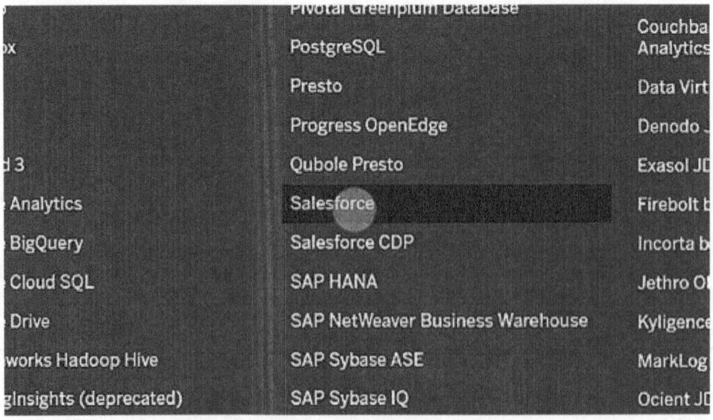

Figure 2.23: Pick the right connector

4. Login with your Salesforce credentials, as shown in the following figure:

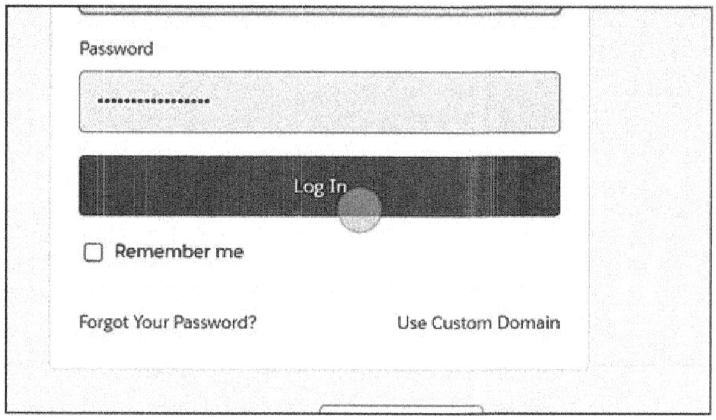

Figure 2.24: *Enter Salesforce credentials*

5. Click **Allow** to finish the authentication, as can be seen in the following figure:

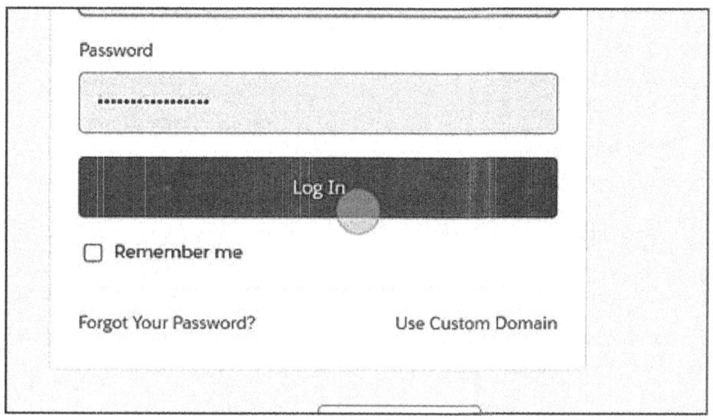

Figure 2.25: *Allow access for Tableau*

6. Back in Tableau Desktop, drag the **Accounts** object to the canvas on the right, as shown in the following figure:

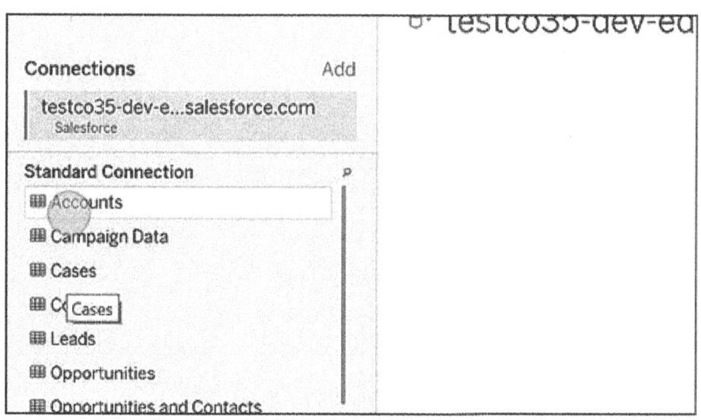

Figure 2.26: *Drag Accounts object*

7. Double-click Accounts, select the dropdown option for **Record Type**, and click **Remove**. Take a look at the following figure:

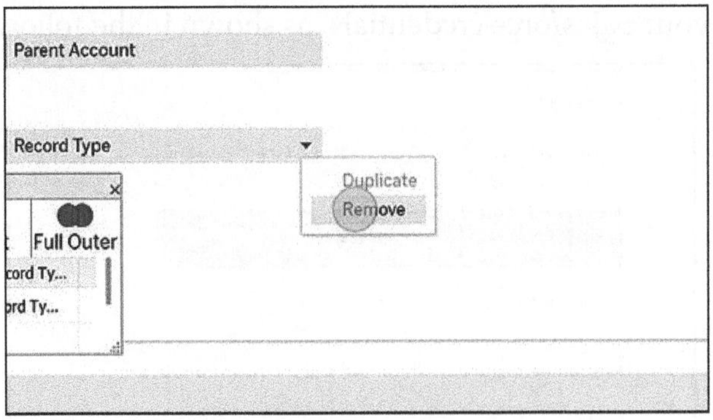

Figure 2.27: *Remove Record Type*

8. Click **Sheet 1** to go to the worksheet, as shown in the following figure:

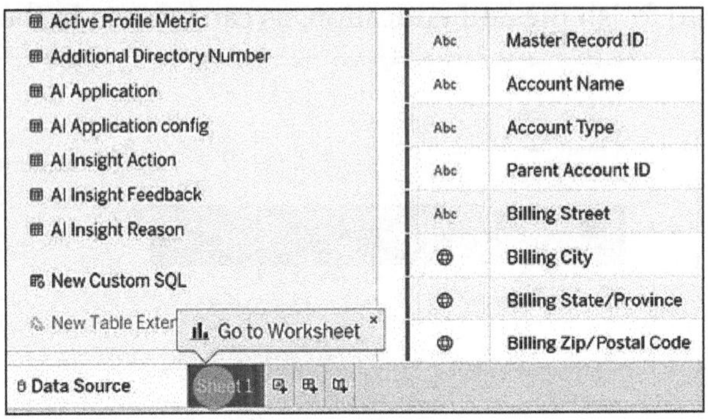

Figure 2.28: *Go to worksheet*

9. Click **Accounts**, as per the following figure:

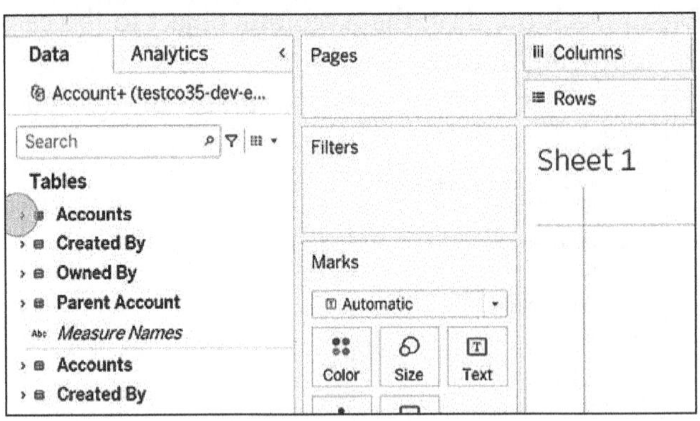

Figure 2.29: *Look at accounts*

10. Drag the fields **Billing Country** and **Account Name** to the Columns bar, as shown in the following figure:

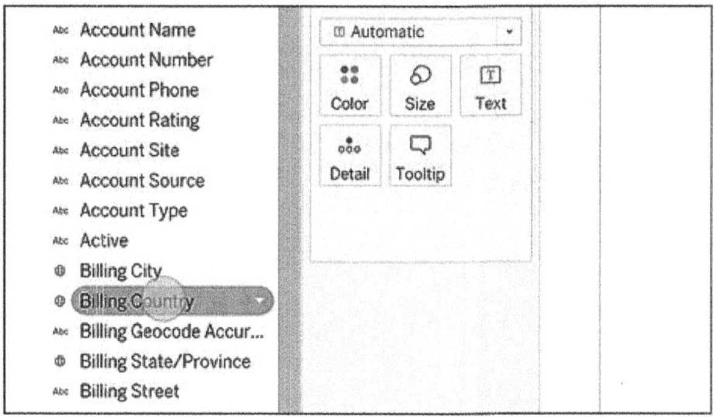

Figure 2.30: Add Billing Country

11. Click **Add all members** in the ensuing pop-up, as can be seen in the following figure:

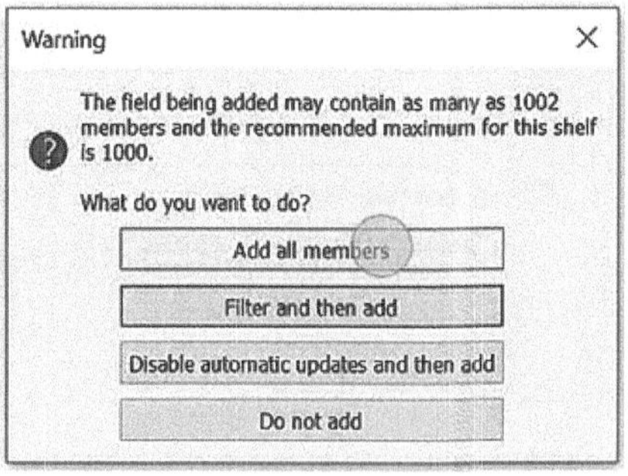

Figure 2.31: Add all members

12. Expand the options under **Account Name**, as shown in the following figure:

Figure 2.32: Account Name

13. Click **Measure** | **Count (Distinct)**, as shown in the following figure:

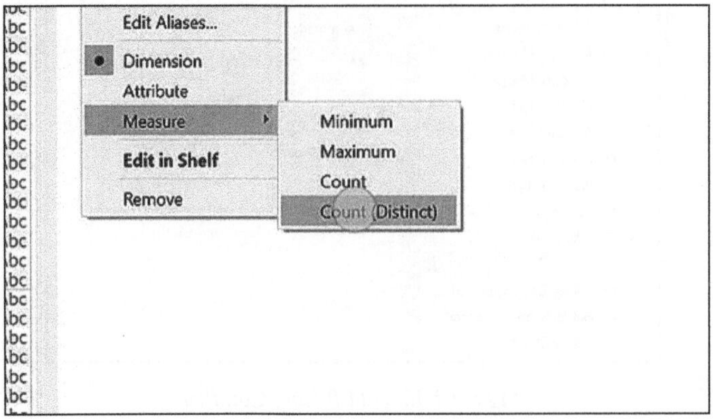

Figure 2.33: Select Count(Distinct)

14. Click the Sheet 1 text and type in **`Accounts by Country,`** and click OK:

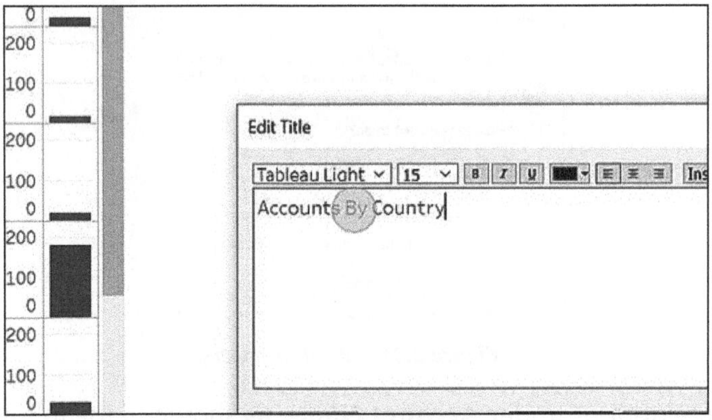

Figure 2.34: Change Title

15. You now have a very basic chart of the number of Accounts in Salesforce grouped by country, as shown in the following figure:

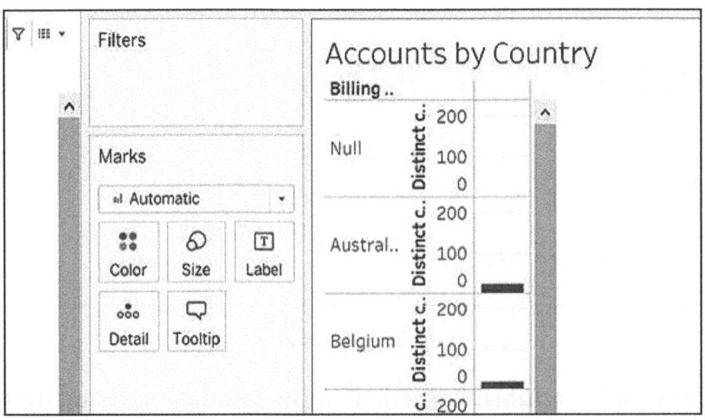

Figure 2.35: Basic chart

We have now confirmed that everything is set up correctly and that we can start with the real learning journey of the book. Before we move on to *Chapter 3, Dynamic developer environment*, where we will learn more about ingesting data in Tableau, let us conclude and summarize our learning for this chapter.

Conclusion

In this chapter, we provided a step-by-step guide on setting up a Salesforce org with CRM analytics and integrating it with Tableau. We began by walking through the process of setting up a Salesforce org and highlighting the key features and configuration options for enabling CRM analytics. We then covered the steps for setting up Tableau Desktop and Tableau Online, including software installation and account creation.

We also explained how to connect to Tableau Public by providing a detailed guide on how to set up and get started with the platform. By following the steps outlined in this chapter, you should now be able to successfully set up a Salesforce org with CRM analytics and be ready to integrate it with Tableau. You will learn how to manage this connection between Tableau and Salesforce in the next chapter.

We will now move on to the start of our real learning journey as we tackle the key task of ingesting data with Tableau.

CHAPTER 3

Building and Integrating Data Pipelines

Introduction

This chapter will focus on different methods for connecting to data in Tableau as well as data cleaning and transformation capabilities. The chapter explains how to connect to data in Salesforce via the Salesforce Connector, including the authentication and configuration steps required to establish the connection. Next, the chapter will cover connecting data exported to an SQL database and discuss how this method may be useful in certain scenarios. Tableau also allows you to manipulate data in several ways, such as pivot, join, and split, once the data is loaded in the software. The chapter will then move on to managing data sources in Tableau, including options for connecting to multiple data sources, creating data source filters, and calculating fields.

Structure

The chapter covers the following topics:

- Introduction to Tableau's data capabilities
- Connecting to Salesforce data with Salesforce connector
- Connecting to data in SQL databases

- Data manipulation in Tableau
- Managing data sources in Tableau

Objectives

By the end of this chapter, learners will be able to understand the importance of connecting to data in Tableau and the software's data cleaning and transformation capabilities. They will do so by learning how to connect to Salesforce data using the Salesforce Connector, including the authentication and configuration steps required for a successful connection, and how to connect to data that has been exported to a SQL database and recognize scenarios where this method may be beneficial. They will also acquire the ability to manipulate data in Tableau using various techniques, such as pivot, join, and split, once the data is loaded into the software. Finally, they will develop skills in managing data sources in Tableau, including connecting to multiple data sources, creating data source filters, and crafting calculated fields and apply the knowledge gained from this chapter to effectively connect to, clean, and transform data in Tableau for enhanced data analysis and visualization.

Introduction to Tableau

Tableau can connect to a variety of data sources, both locally, like .csv and Excel files, and online sources, such as SQL databases, but also Hadoop clusters and files held on cloud storage, such as Google Drive and OneDrive.

For Salesforce data, there are two options:

1. Connecting via Tableau's Salesforce connector
2. Connecting to the database where the Salesforce data is held (usually a SQL database)

We will now examine each option in detail.

Connecting via Tableau Salesforce connector

The steps below will guide you toward connecting to Salesforce data via the Salesforce connector:

1. Upon opening Tableau, you should see the option to connect to Salesforce already, as shown in *Figure 3.1:*

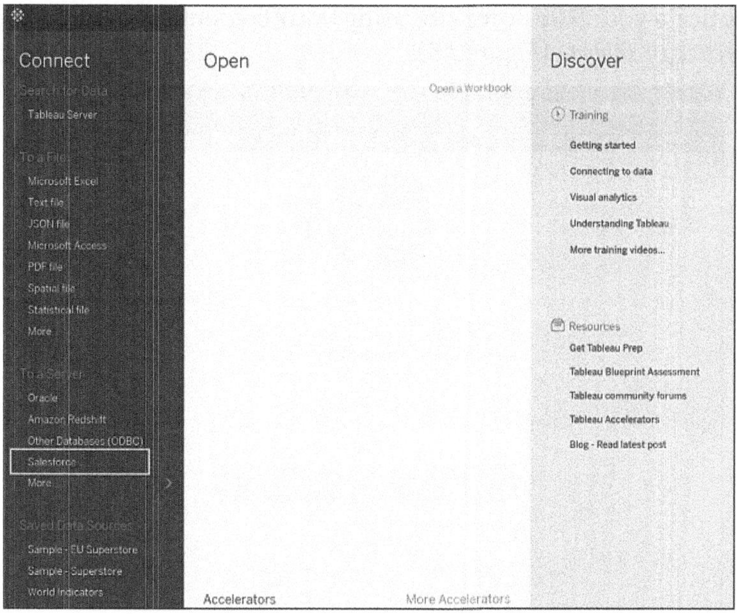

Figure 3.1: Connector pane in Tableau showing Salesforce as a connection option

2. If that option is not available to you, click on **More** to open the full list of connection possibilities in Tableau as can be seen in *Figure 3.2*. You will see Salesforce in the list, which is helpfully organized alphabetically.

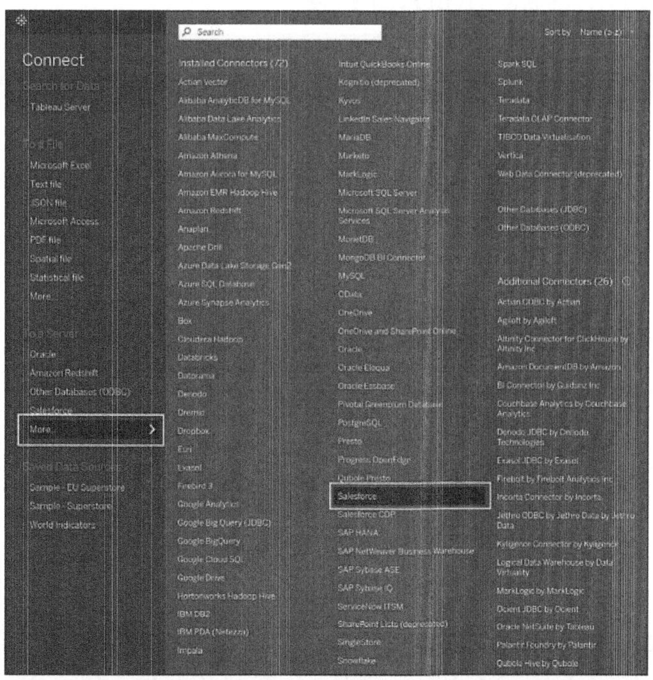

Figure 3.2: Full list of data connection options in Tableau, with Salesforce listed alphabetically

3. Authenticate your Salesforce site using your credentials as in *Chapter 2, Setting Up Salesforce with Tableau* (*Figure 3.3*).

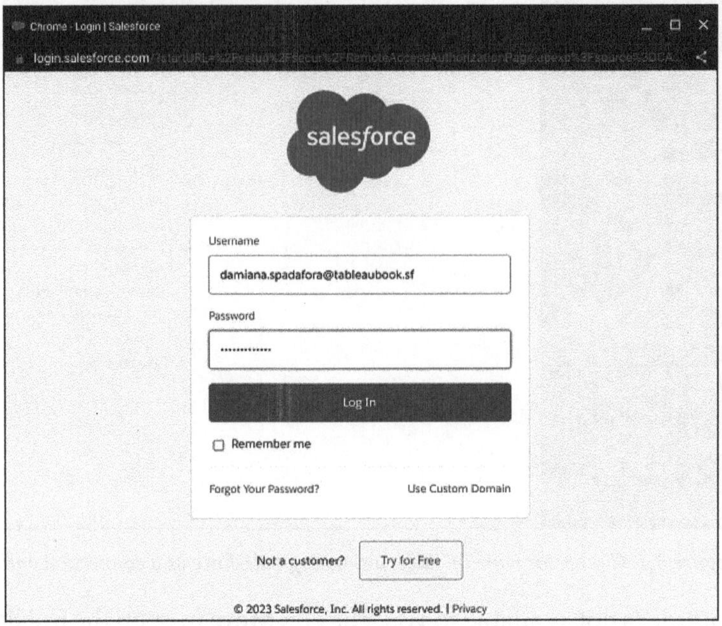

Figure 3.3: *Authenticating to Salesforce using login credentials*

4. Click on **Allow**, as shown in *Figure 3.4*:

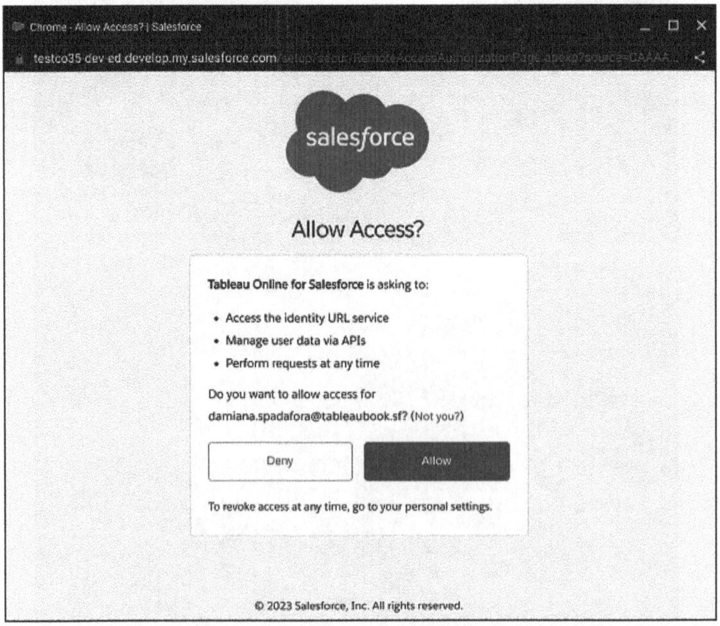

Figure 3.4: *Allowing Tableau access to Salesforce data*

If the previous steps have been successful, you will now see, on the left side of your screen, all the different Salesforce objects available for your analysis.

If you are using Tableau Cloud, you can also configure your Salesforce environment in Tableau using the following steps:

1. On your Tableau Cloud homepage, click on **Settings** in the bottom left corner of your screen.
2. Click on **Integrations**, as shown in *Figure 3.5*:

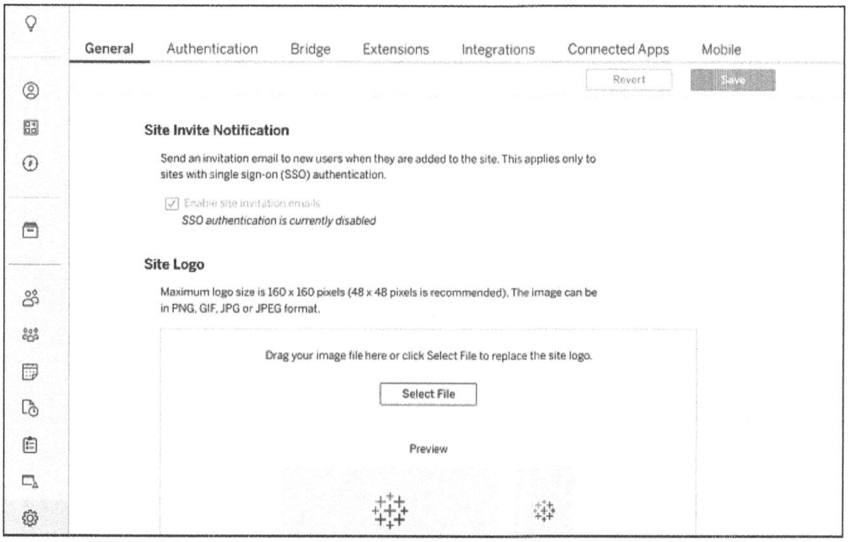

Figure 3.5: *Settings menu in Tableau Online*

3. Click on **Connect to Salesforce**, as shown in *Figure 3.6*:

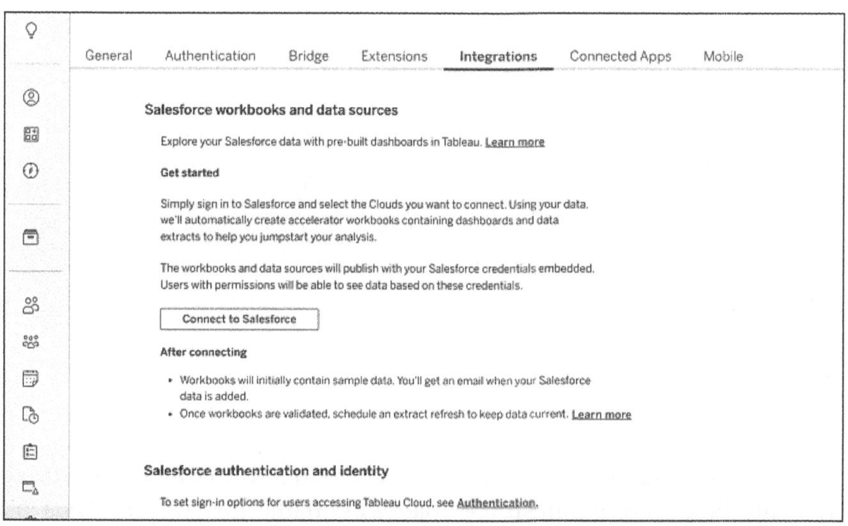

Figure 3.6: *Connecting Tableau Online to Salesforce*

4. Follow the same steps as before to authenticate and allow Tableau Online access to your Salesforce data.

Connecting to your Salesforce data in SQL

Salesforce can be stored on a variety of SQL-based databases. The steps below were performed using a SQLite database, but they can be applied to all SQL databases shown in the new data source menu in Tableau. From the welcome screen, follow the below-mentioned steps:

1. Click on **More** under the **To A Server** menu.
2. Select the kind of database you are using. As we are using SQLite, we will be choosing **Other Databases (ODBC)**, as shown in *Figure 3.7*:

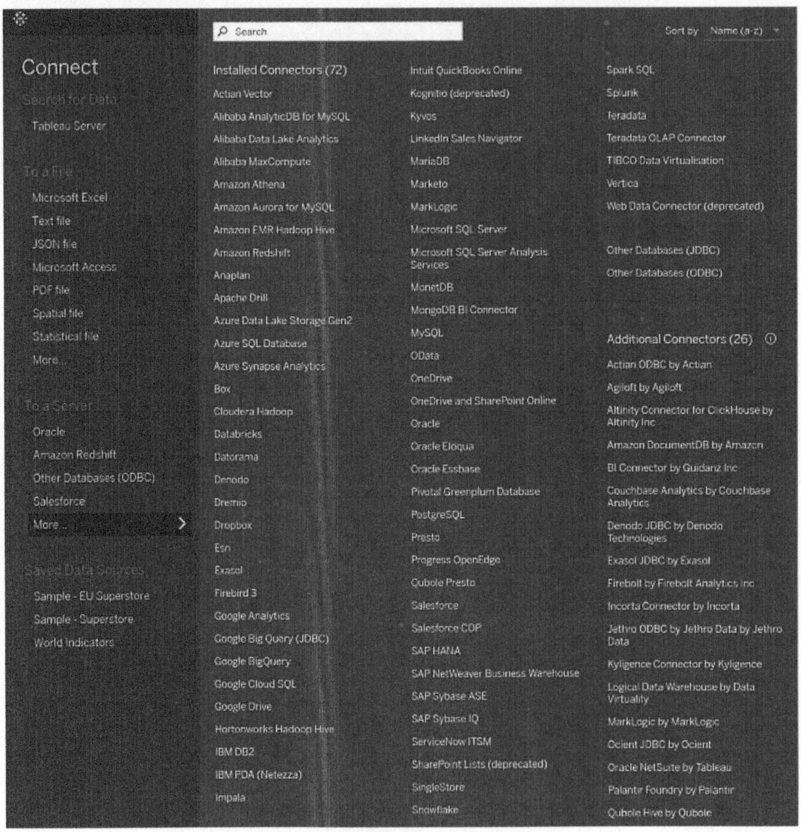

Figure 3.7: Overview of Connections

3. Follow the prompts to authenticate to your database.

Just as before, if the previous steps have been successful, you will now see on the left side of your screen all the different Salesforce objects available for your analysis, as shown in *Figure 3.8*:

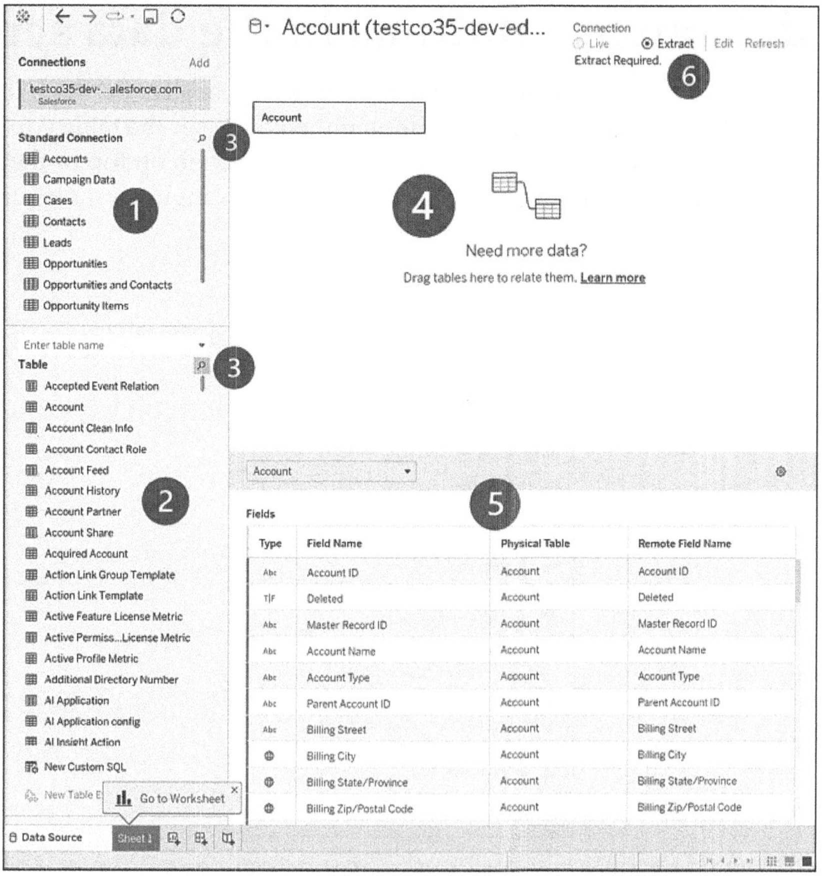

Figure 3.8: Salesforce data objects available for analysis in Tableau after a successful connection

Data source screen in Tableau

Congratulations on managing to connect to your Salesforce data! You are now in your data tab, and these are its components:

1. **Standard Connection list:** If you are using the Salesforce connector, here you will be able to see a list of the most used data feeds.
2. **Table list:** This is the list of all the tables available in Salesforce for your analysis.
3. **Search function:** By clicking on this icon and starting to type, Tableau will filter the table list until you see the one you need.
4. **Main data area:** This is where you will drag your tables and create your dataset.
5. **Data preview area**: Once you have dragged a table, this is where you will see the list of fields in your table and related information.
6. **Connection:** Here, you can choose to use a live connection or an extract.

Basic data manipulations in the data screen

To start working with your data, simply choose any of the objects on the left side of the screen and drag it to the main area. If you cannot immediately see the table you are looking for on the left side of the screen, you can use the search function on top of the list of table names. Simply start typing, and the list will be filtered accordingly, as shown in *Figure 3.9*:

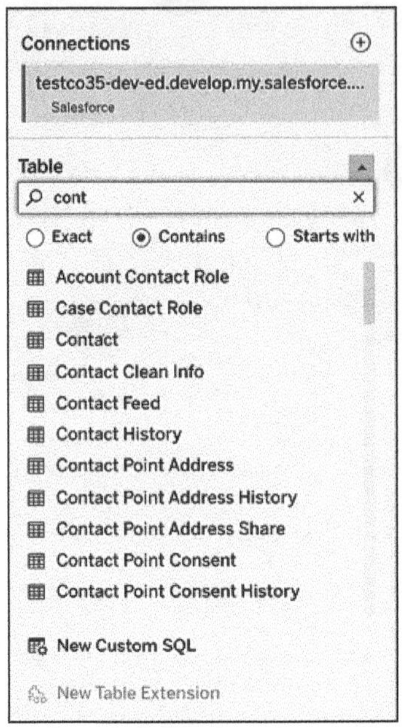

Figure 3.9: *Using the search function in Tableau to filter the list of tables*

On the lower part of your screen, you should now see more information about the table you just added. In particular, the following information should be available (as shown in *Figure 3.10*):

- **Data type**: Tableau will look at your data and decide how to categorize it among the following data types:
    - o **String**: For text fields.
    - o **Numeral (integer)**: For whole numbers without decimals.
    - o **Numeral (decimal)**: For numbers with decimals.
    - o **Geographical value**: This is the type of data that allows Tableau to create maps and store geographical information. More about this in the maps section of this book.
    - o **Date & time**: For date fields, which also contain times.
    - o **Date**: For date fields without times.
- **Field Name**: The name of the field as it is read by Tableau.

- **Physical table**: The name of the table in which the field is stored, useful when working with more than one table.
- **Remote Field Name**: The field's "original" name in the table. Useful in case a field has been renamed or an alias is used.

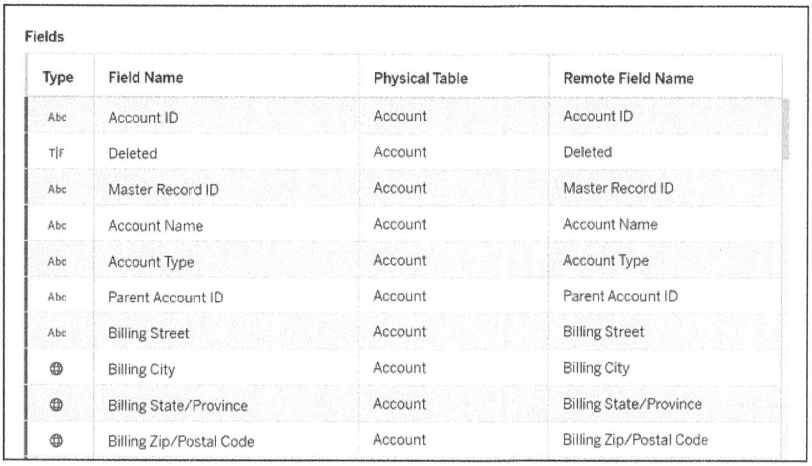

Fields

Type	Field Name	Physical Table	Remote Field Name
Abc	Account ID	Account	Account ID
T|F	Deleted	Account	Deleted
Abc	Master Record ID	Account	Master Record ID
Abc	Account Name	Account	Account Name
Abc	Account Type	Account	Account Type
Abc	Parent Account ID	Account	Parent Account ID
Abc	Billing Street	Account	Billing Street
	Billing City	Account	Billing City
	Billing State/Province	Account	Billing State/Province
	Billing Zip/Postal Code	Account	Billing Zip/Postal Code

Figure 3.10: *Tableau interpreting and categorizing data types*

Already on this screen, it is possible to fix some issues that may be present in the data.

To rename a field:

1. Click on the field you want to rename. You will notice a caret on the right of the field's name.
2. Click on the caret, then choose **Rename** in the menu that will open, as shown in *Figure 3.11*:

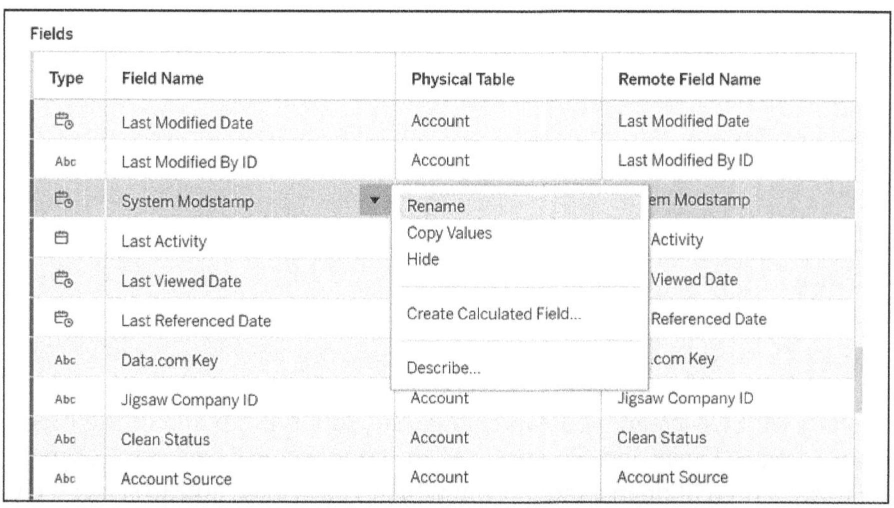

Fields

Type	Field Name	Physical Table	Remote Field Name
	Last Modified Date	Account	Last Modified Date
Abc	Last Modified By ID	Account	Last Modified By ID
	System Modstamp		em Modstamp
	Last Activity		Activity
	Last Viewed Date		Viewed Date
	Last Referenced Date		Referenced Date
Abc	Data.com Key		.com Key
Abc	Jigsaw Company ID	Account	Jigsaw Company ID
Abc	Clean Status	Account	Clean Status
Abc	Account Source	Account	Account Source

Figure 3.11: *Renaming a field by clicking the caret icon in Tableau*

3. You will now be able to type the new name directly in the name field, as shown in *Figure 3.12*:

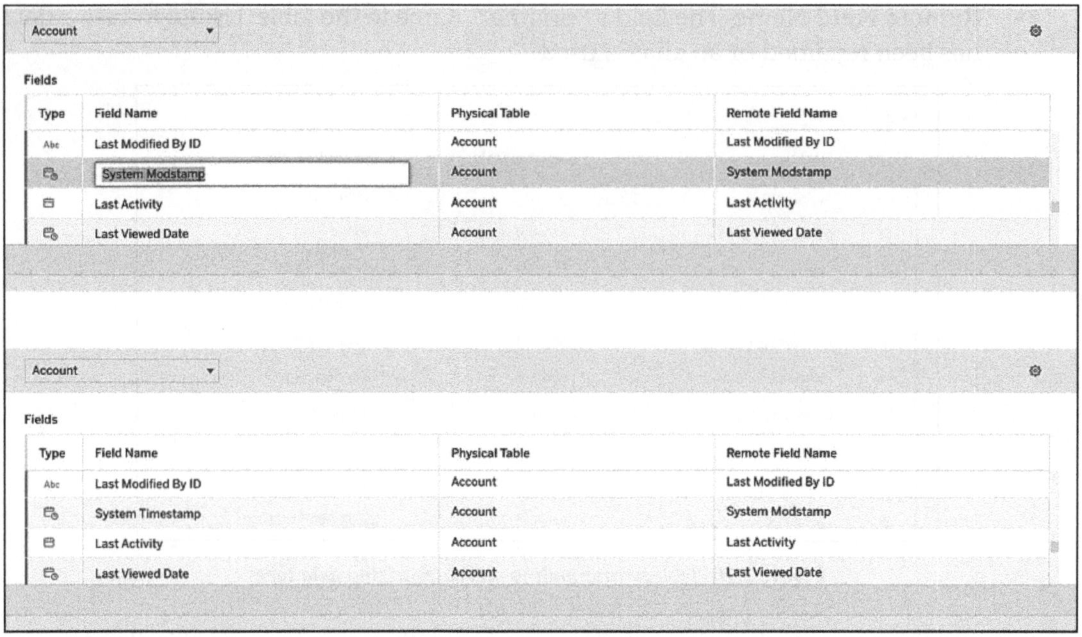

Figure 3.12: *Entering a new name directly in the name field.*

In this initial screen, you can also assign a variable to have a geographic or an image role (available as of Tableau 2022.4), which will allow you to create maps or bring image assets into your dashboard.

To assign one of these roles, click on the icon showing which data type every data field falls under. This will open a menu from where you will be able to choose whether to assign a geographic or an image role to the field, as shown in *Figure 3.13*:

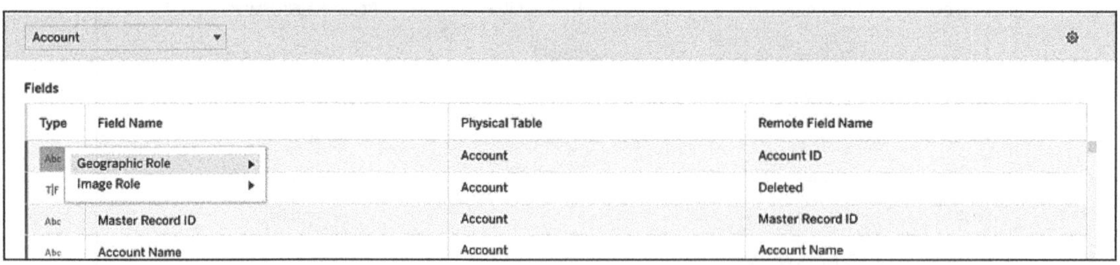

Figure 3.13: *Assigning a geographic or image role to a variable using the data type icon menu*

Finally, already on this screen, you can change the data type to any of the types listed in the previous section. The process is similar to the geographic / image role, where clicking on the data type icon will open a menu from which you will be able to select the right data type.

In this screen, you can also start fixing some data quality issues. If, for example, the values for a specific field are scattered across different columns, you can solve the problem by following these steps:

1. Select all the columns containing the data you need.
2. On the last column you select, click on the **caret**.
3. Select **Merge Mismatched Fields**.
4. Tableau will now merge the columns and keep only non-null values.
5. Beware that if there are more values for the same row, Tableau will keep only the leftmost one.

At the same time, if you have several values in one column that should be separate, you can also address this issue in this screen with these steps:

1. Select the column containing the data.
2. Click on the **caret**.
3. Click on **Split** from the menu that opens. Tableau will split the data into several columns automatically.
4. If the automatic split does not work as required, follow the same steps as before, but click on **Custom Split**.
5. From this menu, specify the separators(s) in your field and whether Tableau should split all the columns, only the first, or only the last.

If you are struggling with variations in spelling or similar issues that would affect the quality of your data, you can create a group to capture all different values under one label. In order to create a group, follow these steps:

1. Select the field of interest
2. Click on the **caret**.
3. Select **Create Group**. This option will only be available for string fields.
4. A menu will open.
5. Select all the values you wish to group.
6. Click on **Group**.
7. Tableau will create a Group automatically.
8. Write the desired name from the group.
9. Press *Enter*.

All Groups can be edited at any point in time. You can tell if a data field is a group by its icon. All groups have a paperclip in their data type icon. To edit a group:

1. Right-click on its name either in the data or the visualization screen.
2. Click on **Edit Group**.
3. The same menu as before will open.

4. Make your changes as shown before.
5. It is possible to make several adjustments in the same group.

Choosing between Live or Extract data

On the top right of your screen, you will see a live or extract option, as shown in *Figure 3.14*. If you are connecting using the Salesforce connector, that option will be greyed out, as it is not possible to connect to live Salesforce data via the connector.

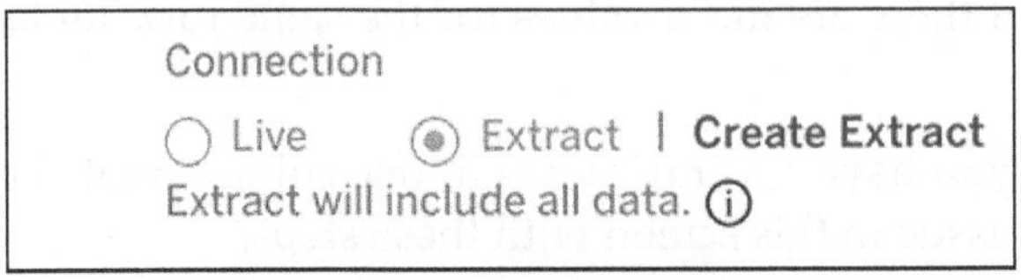

***Figure 3.14:** Create Extract*

If, instead, you are connecting to the database on which your Salesforce data is stored, you will be able to choose whether to use an extract or live data. But what is the difference between live and extracted data?

If you choose live data, no data is stored locally on your machine. Tableau will only store the connection details and will send a query to your database for each action you perform in Tableau. This has the advantage of not needing storage on your machine, and it gives you the certainty that you are always working with the latest available version of the data, but it requires a fast connection in order to avoid frustration.

An extract instead is a copy of the data that is stored on your machine and needs to be manually refreshed to be kept up to date with the master data. As all the data is stored locally, no time is spent waiting for a query to be sent to your database and back to your machine, but it requires enough storage space for all your data (which may easily be gigabytes), and the initial wait for the extract to be created could be even a few hours for large extracts. Furthermore, the result of your analysis may not be as relevant if your data is stale.

If you decide to use an extract, there are still options to reduce the size of the data, such as reducing the number of fields or aggregation. We will discuss these options later and explain why they may work for you or cause you frustration.

Bringing additional tables

One table may be enough to start your analysis, but often, you will need more than one object to retrieve the information you need. Tableau's data visualization capabilities are such that you may start with one or two tables. Still, they will quickly add more as your analysis journey progresses and you ask yourself more questions.

There are several ways to connect different data sources in Tableau:

- **Joins**: These function like traditional SQL joins.
- **Relationships**: Introduced in Tableau 2020.2, they are an easier way to combine different data.
- Blends.
- Unions.

Joins

Tableau makes it easy to join different tables by working out whenever it can on which fields the tables should be joined.

To start joining tables, follow these steps:

1. Drag a table from the left side of the screen.
2. Double-click on the table name, and a small menu will open.
3. Drag the second table you wish to join.
4. If Tableau has enough information, it will automatically select an inner join on all the fields found in both tables. If this is correct, you do not need to make any changes.
5. If Tableau cannot find a link, it will highlight the problem with an empty Venn Diagram and a red exclamation mark, as shown in *Figure 3.15*:

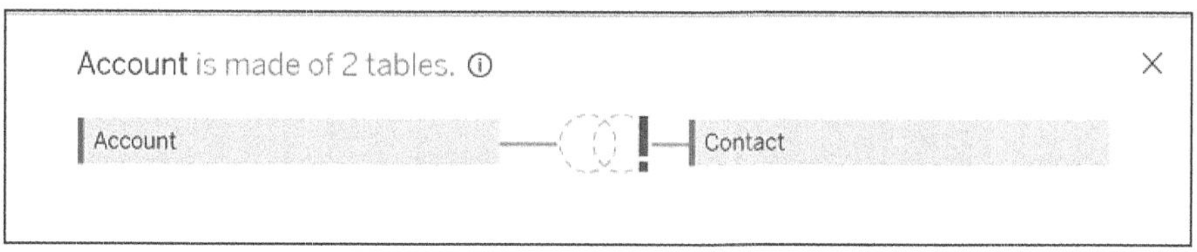

***Figure 3.15:** Tableau indicating it cannot automatically join two tables*

6. In the cases where Tableau cannot automatically join the tables or if the default option is not the one you need, please follow the steps below:
   a. Click on the join icon to open the join menu. From here, you can select the following options:
      - The field on the left side table to use in the join.
      - The type of join, which can be an inner join, a left outer join, a right outer join, or a full join. These kinds of join work exactly as they would in SQL.
      - The field in the right-side table to use in the join.
      - A calculated field can also be used in a join. To create one, click on **"Create Join Calculation"** and proceed to create the field you need. More information on calculated fields will come in a separate section.

In the case below shown in *Figure 3.16,* the join is configured so that Tableau can use the table **Account** with the table **Contact** by using the field **Account ID** present in both tables but labeled as **Account ID (Contact)** in the **Contact** table.

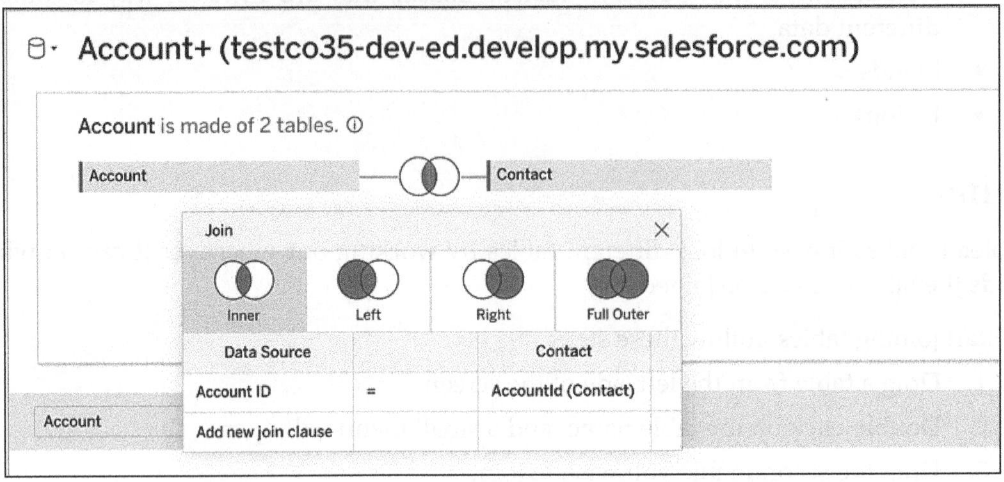

Figure 3.16: *Manually defining the join in Tableau using the join menu*

As you can see, the red exclamation mark has disappeared and the two tables are now joined. This process can be repeated on as many objects as necessary. Simply drag any additional table into the join area, as shown in *Figure 3.17,* and proceed with the steps defined above.

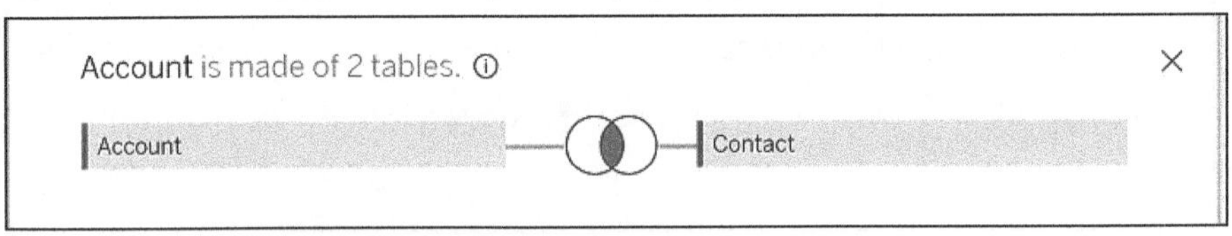

Figure 3.17: *Multiple tables successfully joined in Tableau*

To remove a table, follow these steps:

1. Hover on the table name
2. Click on the caret on the left side of the table name. A menu will open, as shown in *Figure 3.18:*

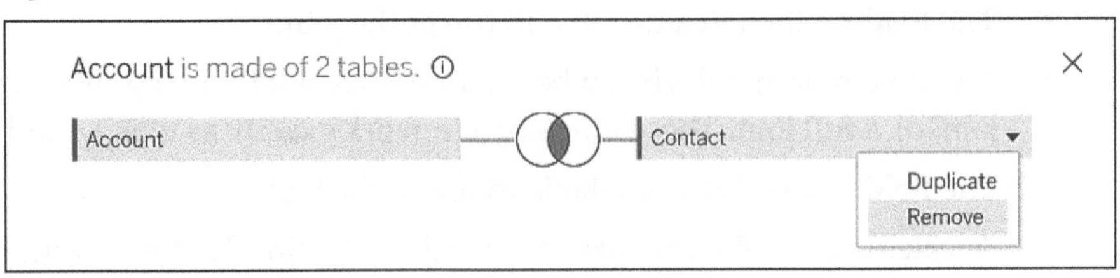

Figure 3.18: *Removing a table from the join in Tableau*

- Click on **Remove.**

The table has now been removed from the join. You can see that the number of tables in **Account** has changed from 2 to 1, as shown in *Figure 3.19*:

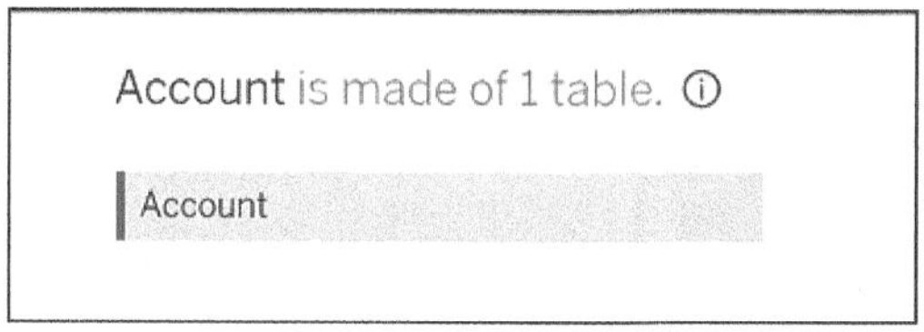

Figure 3.19: *The join table count is decreasing after removing a table*

Relationships

Introduced in 2020.2, relationships are a new way of connecting different data objects. While joins happen on the physical layer of the data source, relationships happen at the logical layer. This means that there is no new data source created, and Tableau will automatically handle duplicates and null values.

Relationships are the default way used by Tableau to connect data objects. Therefore, the process of using relationships requires fewer steps than joins. To start using relationships with your tables, follow these steps:

1. Drag a table from the left side of the screen.
2. Drag the second table you wish to join from the left side of the screen.
3. If Tableau has enough information, it will set up an automatic relationship.
4. If Tableau cannot establish a relationship automatically, it will highlight the problem just as it finds a link. It will highlight the problem with a triangle, as shown in *Figure 3.20*:

Figure 3.20: *Tableau indicating it cannot automatically create a relationship between two tables*

5. If that is the case, you can use the menu at the bottom of your screen to specify which fields should be used to establish the relationship.
6. Just as before, the join is configured so that Tableau can use the table **Account** with the table **Contact** by using the field **Account ID** present in both tables but labeled as **Account ID (Contact)** in the **Contact** table, as shown in *Figure 3.21*.

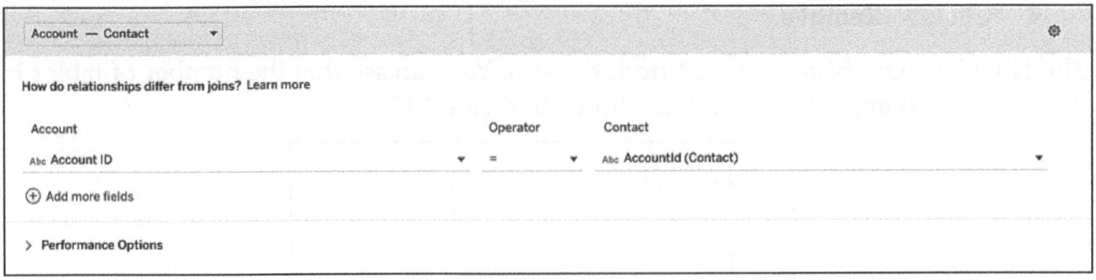

***Figure 3.21:** Manually defining the relationship in Tableau using the relationship editor*

7. As you can see, the red triangle mark has disappeared, and the two tables are now joined. This process can be repeated on as many objects as necessary. Simply drag any additional table into the join area, as shown in *Figure 3.22*, and proceed with the steps defined above.

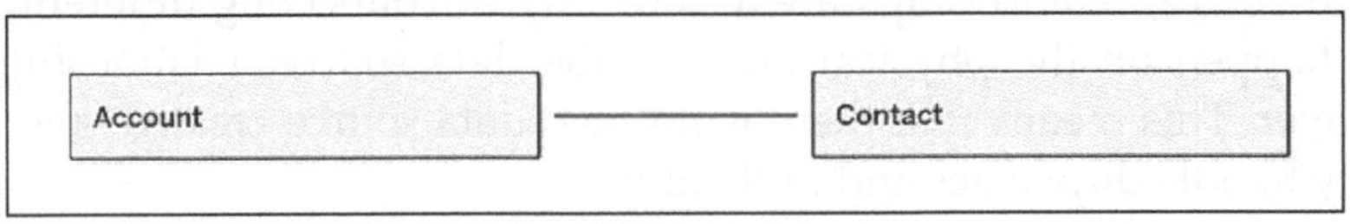

***Figure 3.22:** Multiple tables successfully related in Tableau*

To remove a table, follow the same steps outlined in the *Joins* section.

Joins versus relationships

At first glance, it may seem that relationships and joins are quite similar, if not identical. However, there are differences in their substance and behaviors worth understanding to decide which option to use.

The obvious advantage of relationships is that they do not require any prior understanding of SQL-like join behavior, which makes them a great option for beginner users. Advanced users, however, may prefer the additional degree of flexibility that comes from defining which type of join to employ and which fields to use.

It is also worth mentioning that relationships may not work as intended for data where the quality is exceptionally poor and may cause performance issues if large quantities of data are needed.

Blends

Data blends are useful in the case of data sources that have a limited relationship to each other and are used together for only some parts of the analysis and are kept separate for the remainder.

To blend a data source, follow these steps:

1. Add a data object to the main area.

2. Go to your visualization sheet.
3. Click on the **Data** menu at the top of your screen, as shown in *Figure 3.23*.

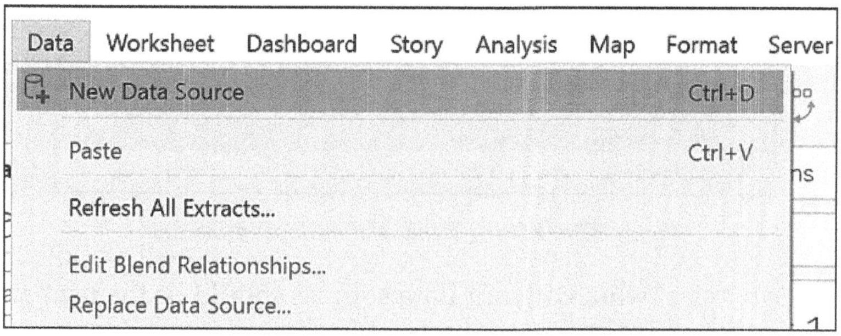

Figure 3.23: *Accessing the Data menu in Tableau*

4. Click on **New Data Source**.
5. Select the desired data source type and follow the prompts. For this example, we have chosen the Salesforce Superstore data, as shown in *Figure 3.24*:

Figure 3.24: *Adding a new data source in Tableau*

6. You will now see two different data sources in the top left corner of your data menu, as shown in *Figure 3.25*:

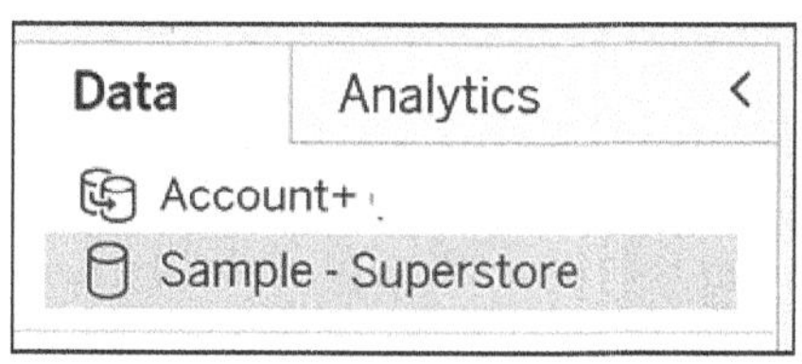

Figure 3.25: *Two different data sources are visible after adding a new one*

It is now time to define how the data sources should be blended. In order to do so:

1. Click on the **Data** menu at the top of your screen.
2. Click on **Edit Blend Relationships**. A menu will now open, as shown in *Figure 3.26*:

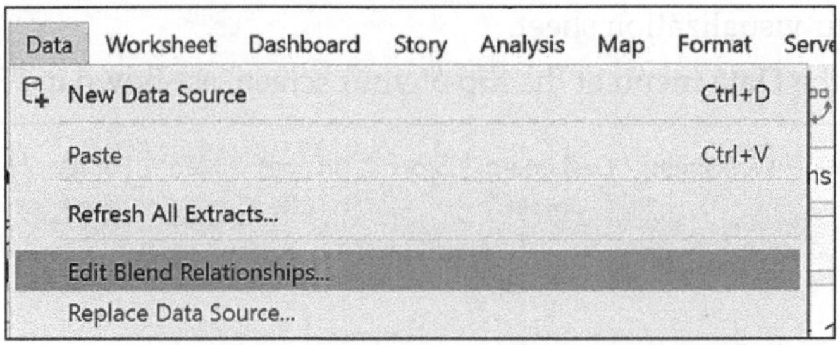

***Figure 3.26:** Editing blend relationships in Tableau*

3. In the menu, select which of your data sources should be the primary one. A good rule of thumb is the data source from which you will be taking the most fields, as shown in *Figure 3.27*:

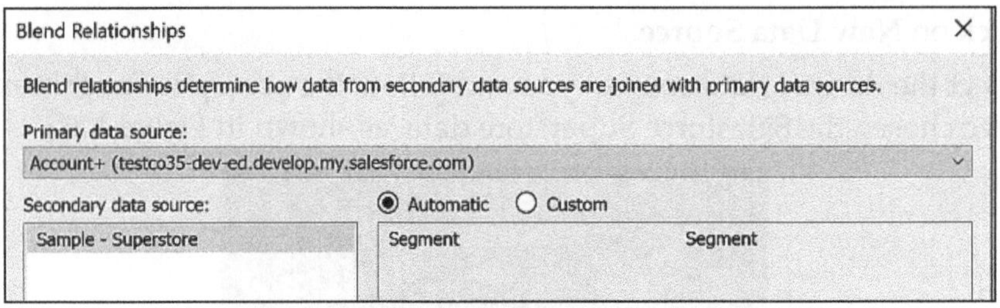

***Figure 3.27:** Selecting the primary data source for a blend in Tableau*

4. Below the primary data source selector, you will see a list of fields.

   Tableau will try to populate those whenever possible. However, if these fields are incorrect or missing, you can adjust them by following these steps, as shown in *Figure 3.28*:

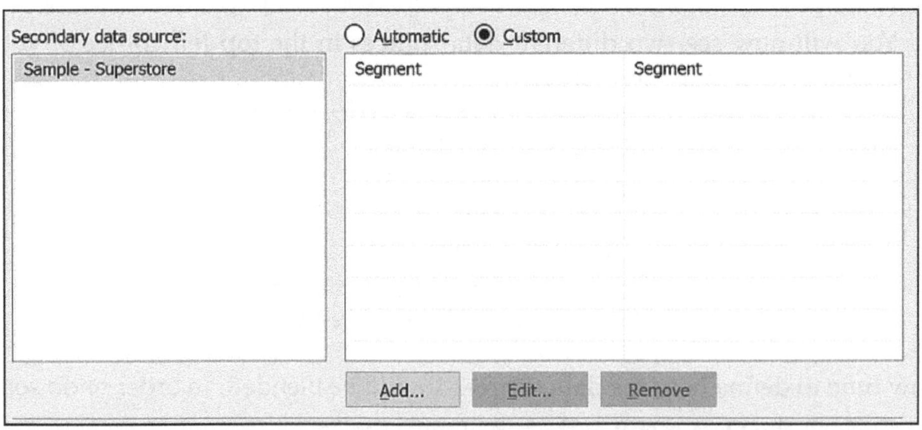

***Figure 3.28:** Defining relationships between fields in a Tableau data blend*

5. Select **Custom** from the Automatic/Custom selector.
6. Click on a field (if present).

7. Choose one of the options in the menu at the bottom:
   - **Add**: To establish a relationship between two fields.
   - **Edit**: To edit the relationship between two fields.
   - **Remove**: To remove the relationship between two fields.
8. Clicking on any of these options will open a menu from where you can pick a field from the primary data source list and its counterpart in the secondary data source field
9. In this case, we have added the Billing State / Province from Salesforce and matched it with State/Province in the Salesforce data. We have also kept the Segment to Segment match, as shown in *Figure 3.29*:

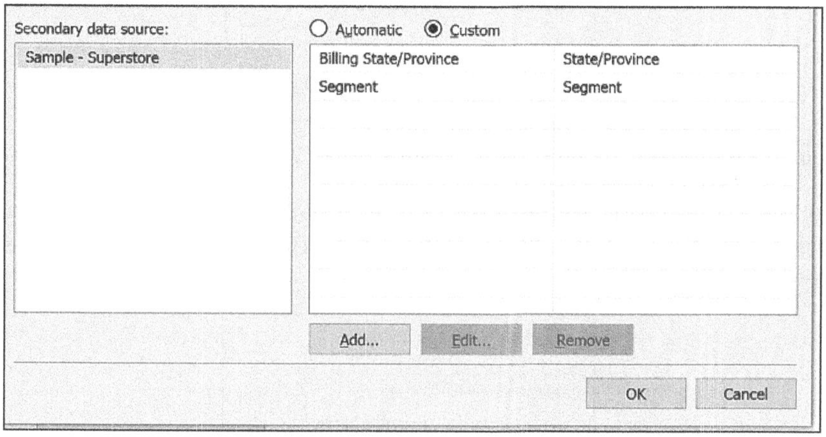

***Figure 3.29:** Mapping fields between two data sources to create a Tableau data blend*

10. Click on **OK**.
11. If your blend is successful, you will notice the following changes:
    - Your primary data source has a blue tick next to its name.
    - Your secondary data source has an orange tick to its name, as shown in *Figure 3.30*:

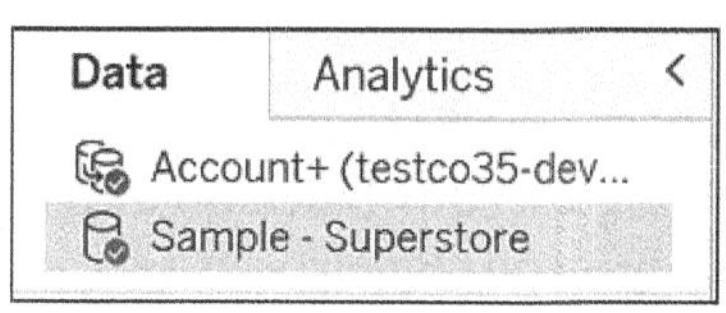

***Figure 3.30:** Indicators of a successful Tableau data blend*

- The field(s) used for the blend have a chain icon next to their name.

You can turn the blend on and off by clicking the chain icon. Two linked chain rings indicate that the blend is currently active, and a barred chain icon indicates a currently inactive blend, as shown in *Figure 3.31*:

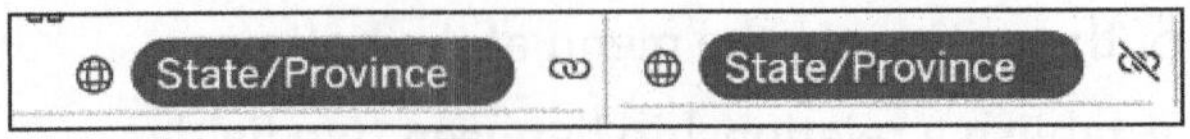

Figure 3.31: Chained versus barred chain icons indicating blend status

Troubleshooting tip

If you cannot see the changes, start dragging fields into the main visualization area. Tableau will treat the data source containing the first field you will use in the visualization as the primary one. For example, here, we have started by dragging the Industry field from the Salesforce data and only afterward added the Segment field from Superstore. So now you can see a blue tick next to Salesforce, as shown in *Figure 3.32*:

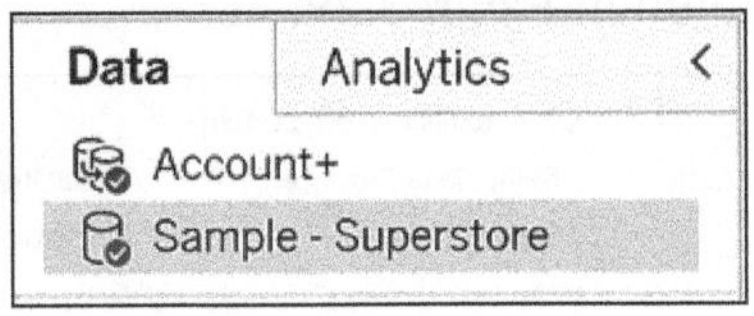

Figure 3.32: Tableau interpreting the first visualized field's data source as primary in a blend

In this case, we started with the Superstore data and dragged Salesforce data afterward. The blue tick is now on the Superstore data, and the orange is on Salesforce, as shown in *Figure 3.33*:

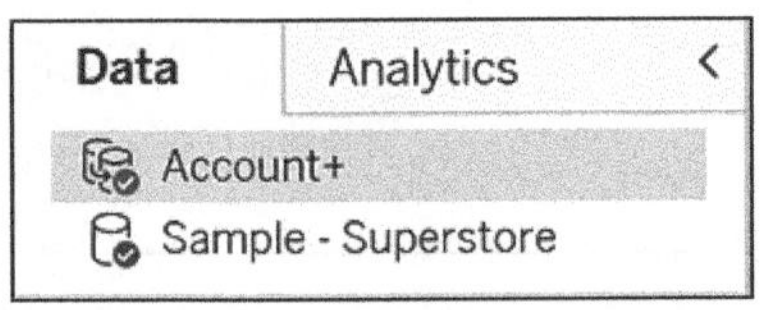

Figure 3.33: Tableau interpreting the first visualized field's data source as primary in a blend[1]

Blends work regardless of the data source type, as you can see in this case, where the Salesforce data is being blended with the standard Tableau Superstore data, which comes as an Excel `.xls` file. They are a good solution when dealing with different data types, as in this case, but can quickly encounter performance issues.

Unions

It is not possible to union data using the Salesforce connector, so the steps below will only be available if you are connecting to your Salesforce data via a database connection as shown in the section Connecting to your Salesforce data in SQL.

A union works differently from the methods shown above in that, rather than adding columns from different data sources, it adds rows to existing data. In order for unions to work, all data objects must have the same structure.

1 Disclaimer: You may not be able to see the color of the ticks change if you have brought a paperback version of the book. However, you can access the colored version of the image at the link given at the beginning of the book.

The steps to perform in this case are the following:

1. Connect to the database as shown in the section Connecting to your Salesforce data in SQL.
2. Drag the **New Union** button to the main data area, as shown in *Figure 3.34*:

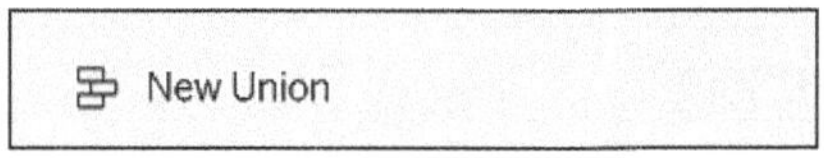

***Figure 3.34:** Adding a new union in Tableau*

3. A menu will open, as shown in *Figure 3.35*:

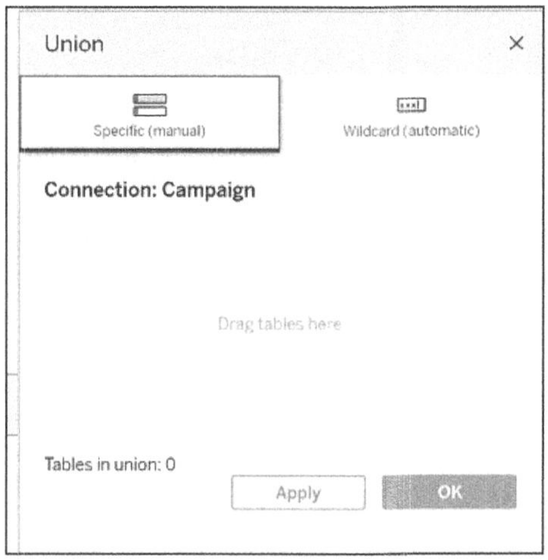

***Figure 3.35:** Creating union*

4. Drag here all the objects to be unioned. Tableau will read the structure of the first object and expect all objects to follow the same structure, as shown in *Figure 3.36*:

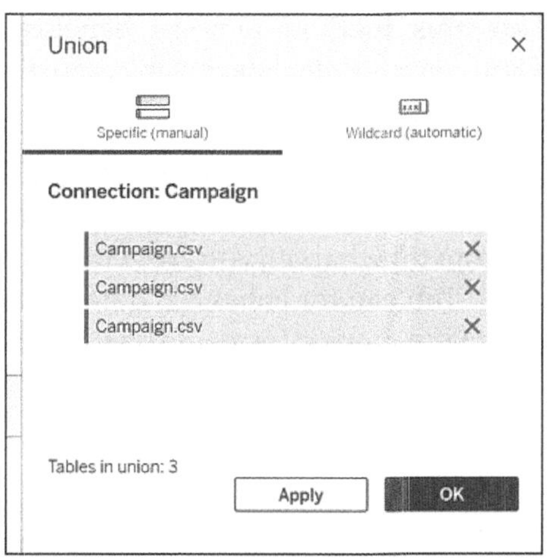

***Figure 3.36:** Selecting data sources to union in Tableau*

5. If Tableau encounters no problem in unioning the data, you will see the final dataset at the bottom of your screen.
6. You can always add or remove objects by clicking on the caret on your union and clicking **Edit Union**, as shown in *Figure 3.37*:

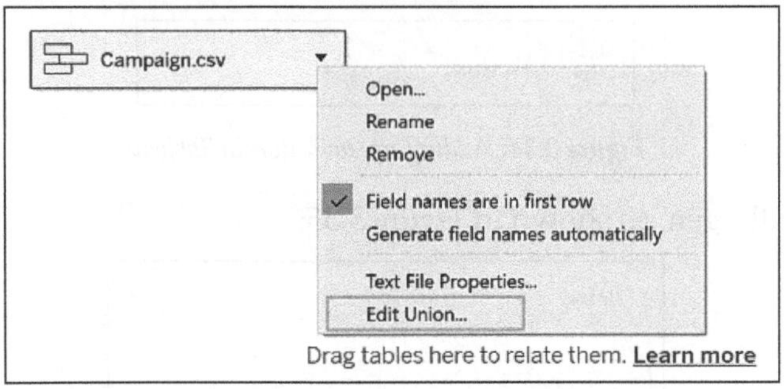

***Figure 3.37**: Final unioned dataset shown in Tableau*

7. The same menu will open. From this same menu you can specify whether the field names are in the first row of your data or whether Tableau should generate field names automatically. The option to choose will depend on how your data is structured.

Conclusion

In this chapter, we have explored various methods for connecting to data in Tableau and delved into the software's data cleaning and transformation capabilities. You have learned how to connect to Salesforce data using the Salesforce Connector and how to authenticate and configure the connection successfully.

We also discussed connecting to data that has been exported to an SQL database and highlighted scenarios where this method may be beneficial. Furthermore, we have equipped you with the skills to manipulate data in Tableau using techniques such as pivot, join, and split once the data is loaded into the software.

In addition, we have covered managing data sources in Tableau, including connecting to multiple data sources, creating data source filters, and crafting calculated fields. With the knowledge and skills gained from this chapter, you are better prepared to effectively connect to, clean, and transform data in Tableau for enhanced data analysis and visualization. This will ultimately enable you to make more informed decisions and drive impactful insights from your data.

In the next chapter, we will delve into the core functionality that makes Tableau such a powerful visualization tool.

CHAPTER 4
Exploring Charts, Graphs, and Dashboards

Introduction

This chapter will provide guidance about visualizing Salesforce CRM data in Tableau. We will start with a section on things to remember when visualizing Salesforce data, such as understanding CRM data and the types of analysis you may want to perform. The chapter will then cover the basics of creating visualizations in Tableau, such as using the Show Me menu and creating simple charts.

Structure

The chapter covers the following topics:

- Fundamentals of creating visualizations in Tableau
    - Using 'Show Me' menu and bar charts
    - Line charts in Tableau
    - Tables in Tableau
    - Pie charts in Tableau
    - Treemaps in Tableau
    - Scatterplots in Tableau
- Bringing all your insights together in a dashboard

Objectives

By the end of this chapter, learners will be able to understand why and how CRM data is crucial for data analysis and decision-making. Specifically, they will be able to recognize different types of analyses that can be performed on Salesforce CRM data, how these might dictate different visualization approaches, and comprehend the factors to consider when visualizing CRM data, including strategies to avoid common visualization pitfalls. They will also familiarize themselves with the key functionalities of Tableau's **"Show Me"** menu and basic chart creation techniques. Finally, they will be able to create meaningful visualizations using Salesforce CRM data in Tableau and develop the skills necessary to interpret visualizations effectively, drawing out actionable insights from data presented in visual form.

Fundamentals of creating visualizations in Tableau

This section aims to equip you with the fundamental knowledge and techniques needed to navigate Tableau's interface and leverage its capabilities to create compelling visualizations. Starting with the Data Source screen and moving into the creation of various chart types, we will explore key concepts such as Sheets, Dashboards, Dimensions, Measures, and more. By understanding these foundational elements, you will be well on your way to effectively visualizing your data, from basic charts to more complex analyses. Whether you are analyzing customer data, tracking campaign performance, or exploring financial metrics, this guide provides a step-by-step approach to harnessing Tableau's potential to uncover valuable insights hidden within your data.

Now that you have fixed your data to the best possible quality, it is time to start visualizing it. From the Data Source screen, click on **Sheet 1**. This is the working space where you will create your visualizations. Before we start, it is useful to get acquainted with the following terminology:

- **Sheet/Worksheet:** A sheet is a container for each chart in Tableau. Each chart requires a different sheet. We will use the terms sheet and worksheet interchangeably.
- **Dashboard:** A collection of sheets displayed at the same time covering related information.
- **Dimensions:** These are the categorical variables or the fields you will want to use to slice and dice your data. An example of a dimension can be color, country, name, or surname. Dimensions in Tableau, are blue.
- **Measures:** These are the numerical variables, that is, the actual numbers you want to show. For example, sales, number of customers, or profit. Measures in Tableau are green.

- **Field:** It is either a dimension or a measure. This word will be used when the dimension/measure distinction does not matter.
- **Mark:** Every single point in your visualization is a mark. Each bar in your bar chart, each dot in a scatter plot, and each value in a table is a mark.

Now that we have clarified the basics let us take a look at some of the areas in *Figure 4.1:*

1. **Data**: This shows the data source being used currently. When you start using several data sources across several sheets, it is always a good idea to check that the one you are using in each sheet is correct.
2. **Fields area**: This lists all your dimensions and values, which you will use to create your visualizations. At the top, there is a handy filter box for searching a specific field.
3. **Columns/Rows**: This is where you will drag your fields to create your visualizations. Different dimensions and measures in different columns/rows arrangements give different charts.
4. **Filters**: Every field you use to filter your data, will be shown in this area.
5. **Marks**: Here is where you control the aspect of your charts. From here, you can select color, size, and how your labels should look. This area will become increasingly useful as we look into intermediate and advanced charts.
6. **Show me**: This is the menu helping beginner users create their charts. Once you stop relying on this menu, you know you will have succeeded in the task of learning to use Tableau.
7. **New Worksheet/Dashboard/Story**: Clicking on each of these buttons will create new sheets/dashboard/stories.
8. **Chart area**: This is where you will see your visualization. You can also drop fields in this area rather than in the columns/rows area to create charts.

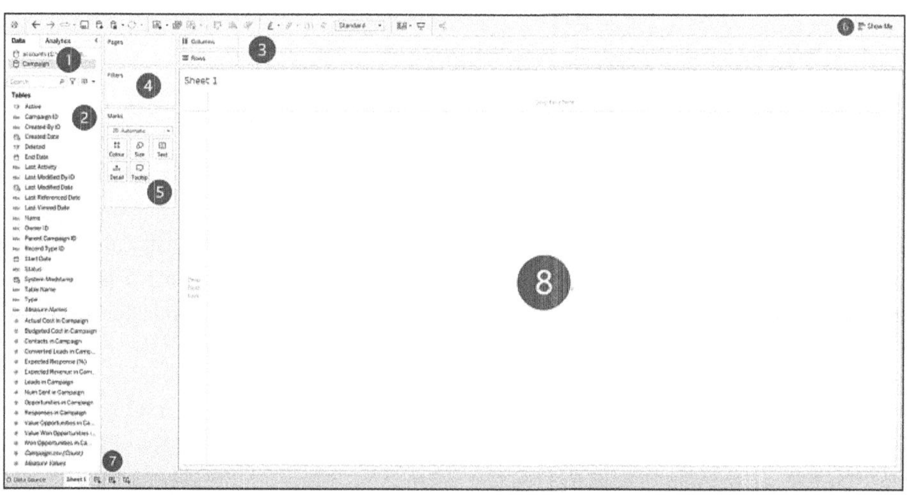

Figure 4.1: *Chart area: Visualize and create charts by dropping fields in this area*

Using 'Show Me' menu and bar charts

The quickest way for a beginner to start creating visualizations in Tableau is to use the **Show Me** menu, which will showcase a range of ready-made charts and the combinations of Dimensions and Measures you will need to create *Figure 4.2*:

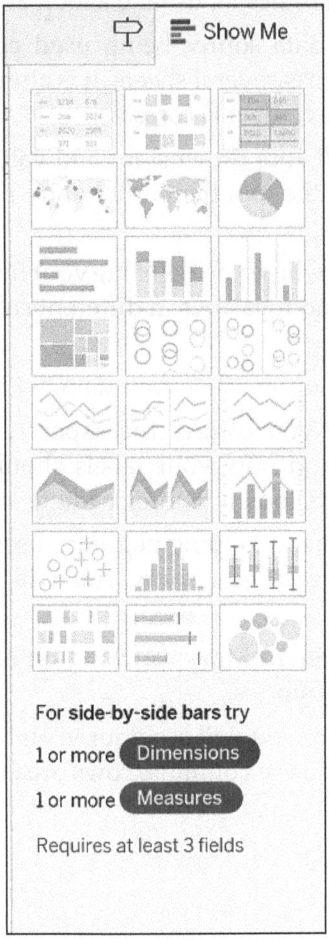

Figure 4.2: *A beginner's guide: Explore Tableau's Show Me menu for effortless chart creation*

For example, to answer a question like who my largest customer is, you can select **Account Name,** hold *CTRL,* and select **Annual Revenue,** then click on **Horizontal Bars** in the **Show Me** menu, as shown in *Figure 4.3:*

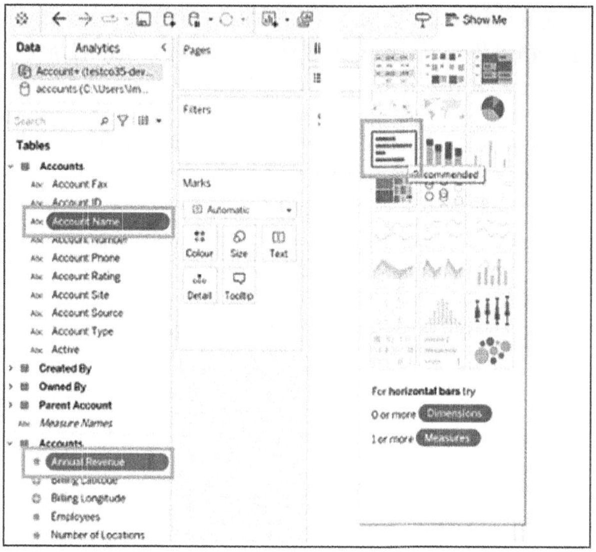

Figure 4.3: Selecting account name and annual revenue, then choose horizontal bars

Tableau will recommend which chart to use with a border. This time, we will agree with the recommendation.

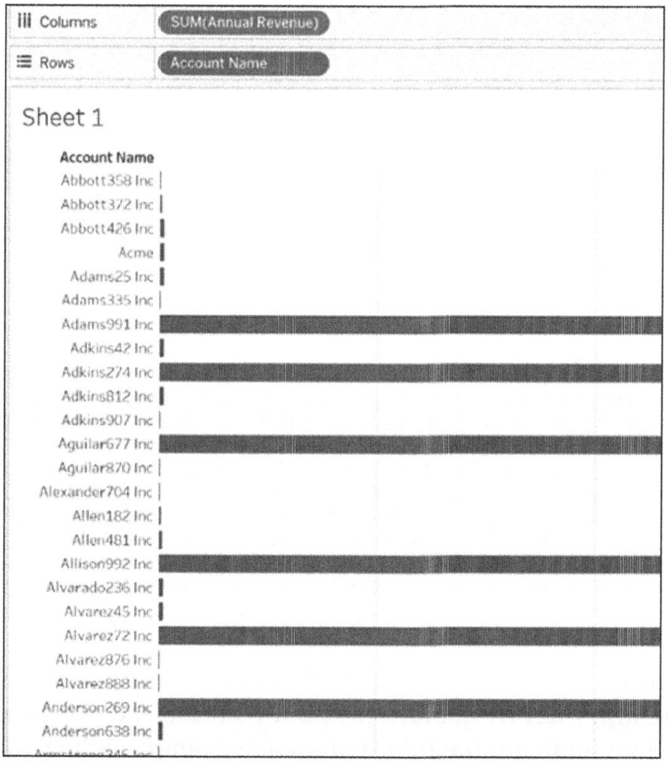

Figure 4.4: *Tableau chart*

So, this is your first Tableau chart (*Figure 4.4*). It looks strange, but we wanted to know who our largest customers were. To do that, we need to sort our chart so that the customers with the largest revenue are at the top.

There are several ways to do that; for now, we will click on the Sort button above the columns / rows area, as shown in *Figure 4.5*:

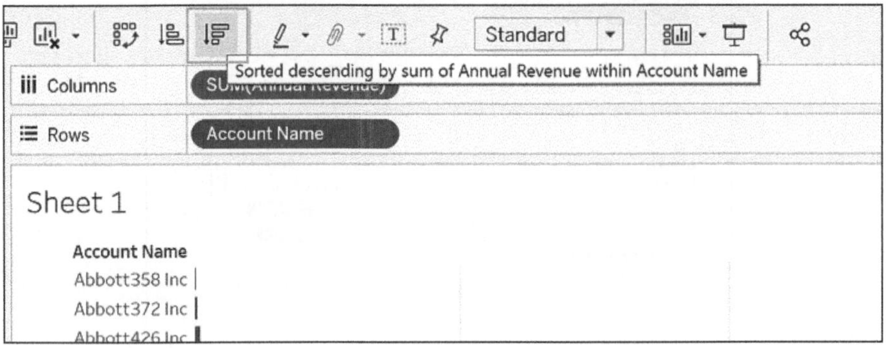

***Figure 4.5:** Clicking on the sort button to organize columns/rows*

Our chart looks as shown in *Figure 4.6*:

***Figure 4.6:** Account chart*

It seems that we have a lot of customers with the same level of revenue, so this is probably not the most insightful chart we could create. But with Tableau, we are never more than a few clicks away from finding more information. For example, which industries bring the largest revenue?

To answer that question, we will select the **Industry** field and drag it on top of the **Account Name** field in the Rows panel.

We now have a much better-looking chart as shown in *Figure 4.7*:

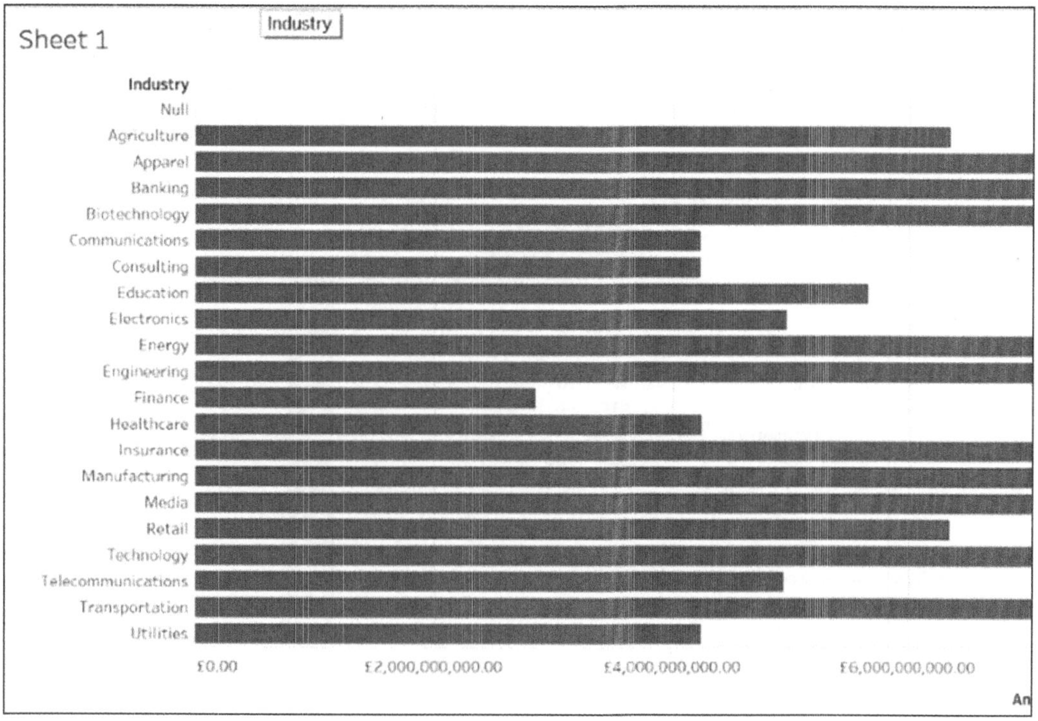

***Figure 4.7:** Better chart*

After sorting it in descending order as we did before, this is what our chart looks as shown in *Figure 4.8:*

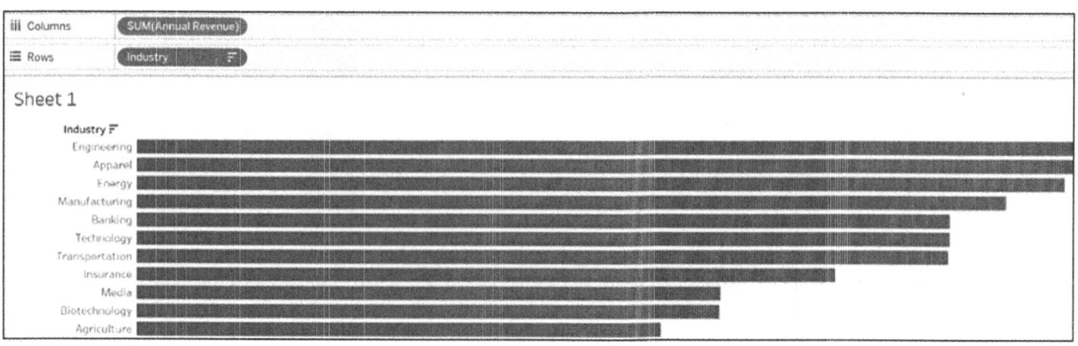

***Figure 4.8:** Descending sorted chart.*

We now know that **Engineering** and **Apparel** are the largest industries by revenues, with Energy being a distant third.

Line charts in Tableau

Another simple use case for Tableau and Salesforce is to track campaigns over time. In this specific example, we would like to track how much we spent on our campaigns versus the budget we set. To do so we will start by selecting **Actual Cost in Campaign** from our **Measures** list and drag it into **Rows** as shown in *Figure 4.9*:

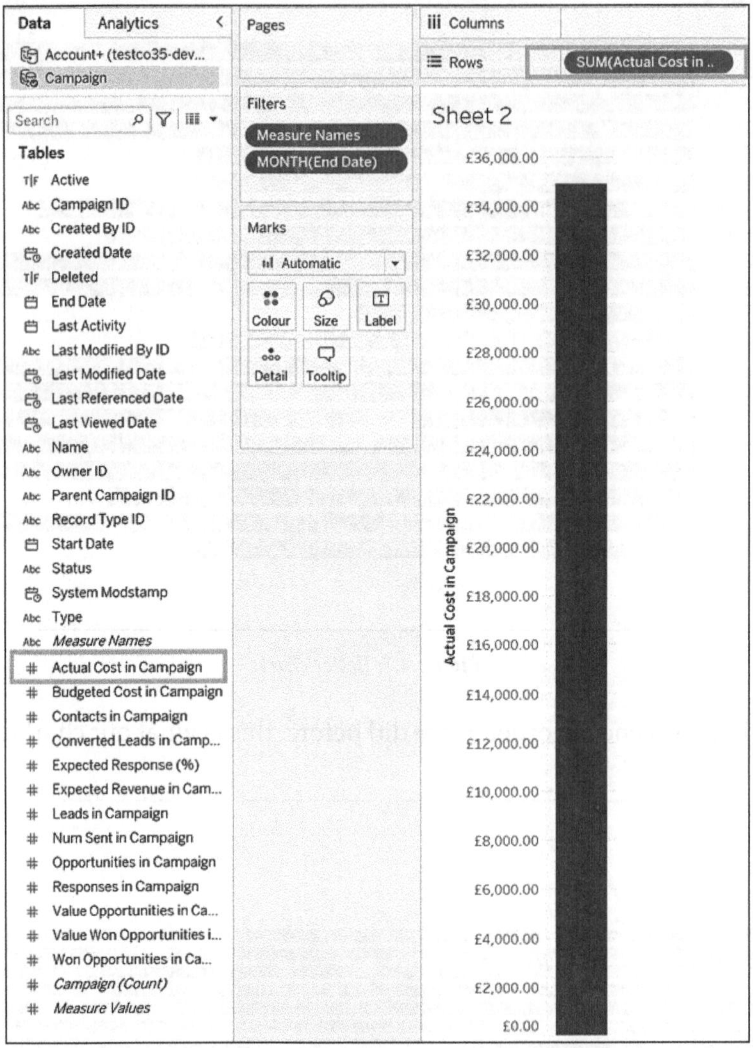

Figure 4.9: *Tracking campaign costs compared to budget using Tableau and Salesforce*

This has now created a vertical bar chart. And while we now know that we have spent almost £35,000 on our campaigns, we need more information. Therefore, we will now select **Budgeted Cost in Campaign** and drag it on the **Actual Cost in Campaign** axis. The cursor will change to show two green bars, as shown in *Figure 4.10*:

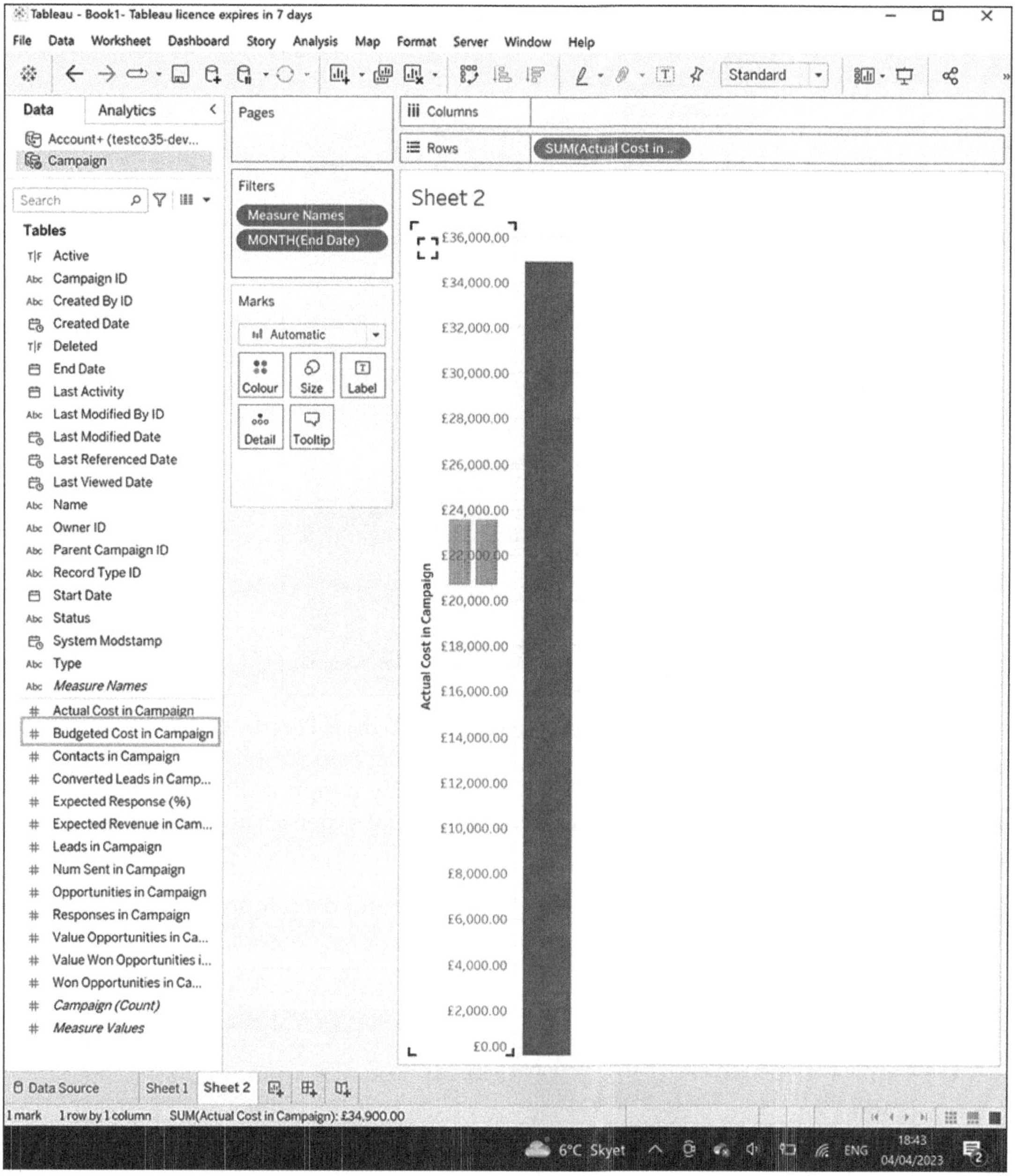

***Figure 4.10:** A vertical bar chart comparing Budgeted Cost and Actual Cost in Campaign*

We will now drop our field onto the axis, and Tableau will add this measure to the visualization so that we will now see the **Actual Cost** and the **Budgeted Cost** side by side in two bars as shown in *Figure 4.11*:

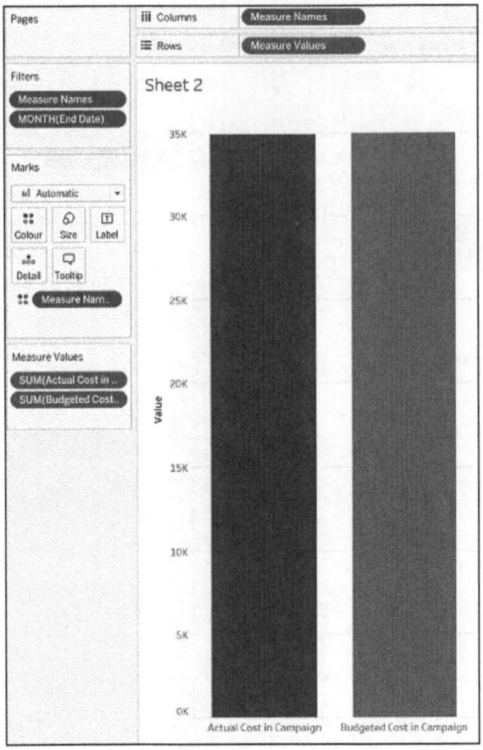

Figure 4.11: *Side-by-side bars showing Actual Cost and Budgeted Cost*

To facilitate comprehension, Tableau will automatically assign a different color to each measure. So now we know that our budgeted and actual expenses align, but was that the case throughout the campaigns?

To answer this final question, we will select **End Date** and drop it on top of the **Measure Names** pill in **Columns** as shown in *Figure 4.12*:

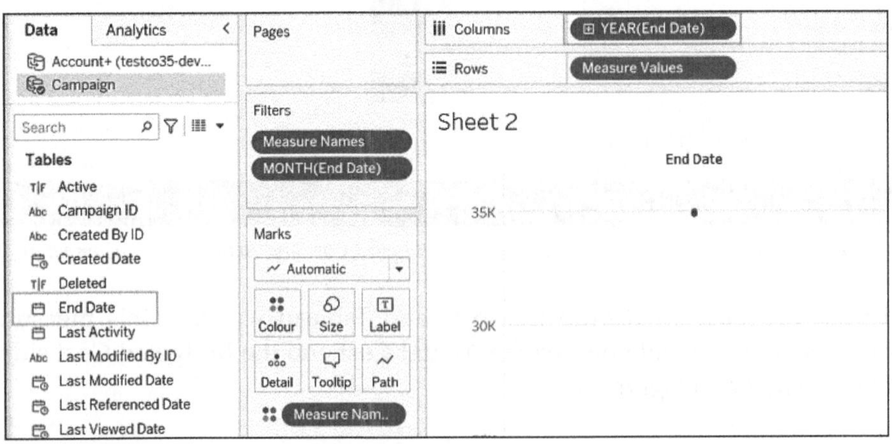

Figure 4.12: *End Date dropped onto Measure Names in Columns for final question resolution.*

Tableau will by default choose to display the year of the date of our choice. It may make sense in some cases, but not in this one. Therefore, we will click on the **End Date** blue pill and select the second month on the list as shown in *Figure 4.13*:

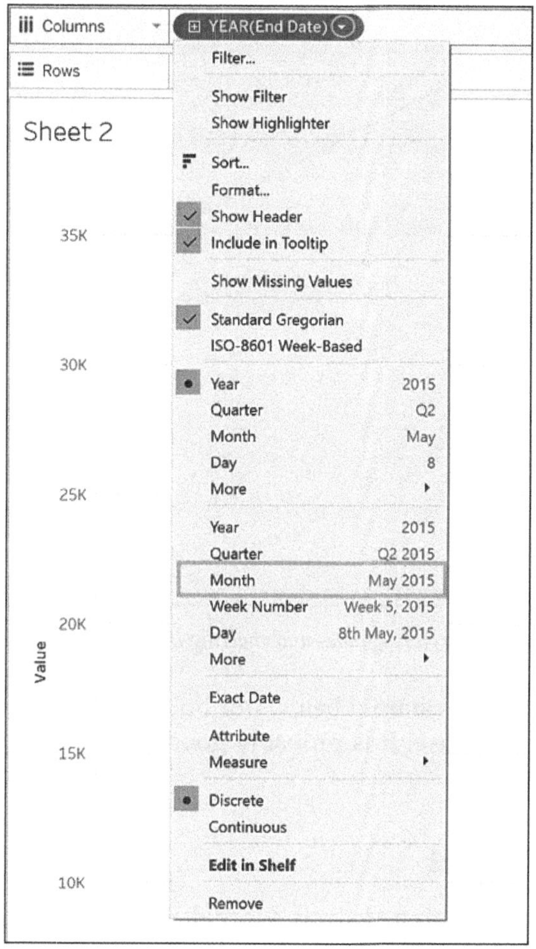

***Figure 4.13:** Choosing the second month on the End Date blue pill in Tableau.*

We will discuss dates in Tableau in the next chapters, where we will go through more complex visualizations. After you have selected the correct date, your chart will look as in *Figure 4.14*:

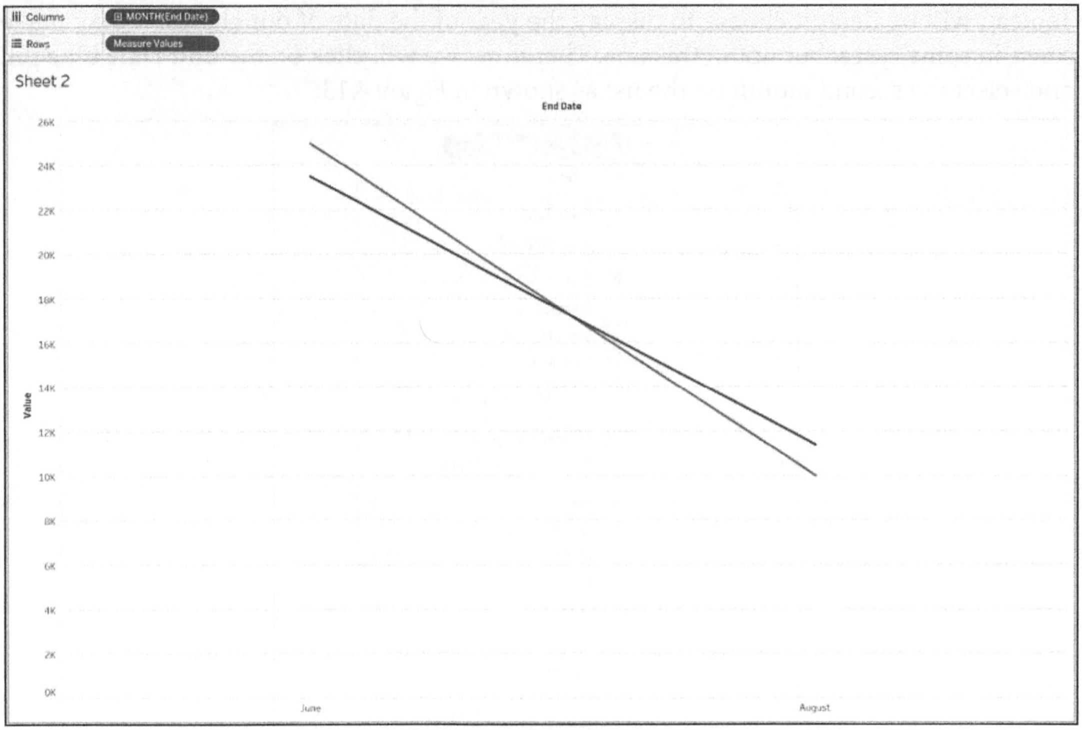

Figure 4.14: Exploring dates and charting in Tableau's next chapters

We can now see that while we started below our budget, as the campaign progressed, we went over our planned expense. It is probably good that our campaigns did not run for long.

Tables in Tableau

As we proceed with our campaign analysis, we may want to understand specifically which campaigns ran over budget. In cases like this, a table may provide some useful insights. To create a table:

1. Select **Name** from the list of dimensions and drag it onto **Rows** as shown in *Figure 4.15*:

Figure 4.15: Dragging the 'Name' dimension from the list.

2. Select **Actual Cost in Campaign** and drag it onto **Text** in the **Marks** area as shown in *Figure 4.16*:

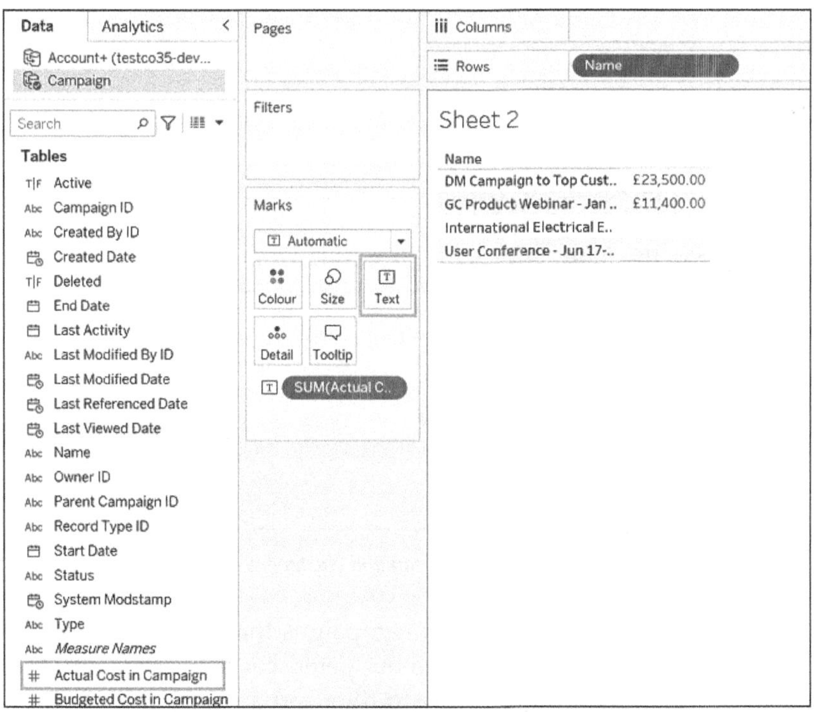

Figure 4.16: Adding Actual Cost to Text in the Marks area

3. Select **Budgeted Cost in Campaign** and drop it onto the table's numbers. The cursor will change and say **Show Me** as shown in *Figure 4.17*:

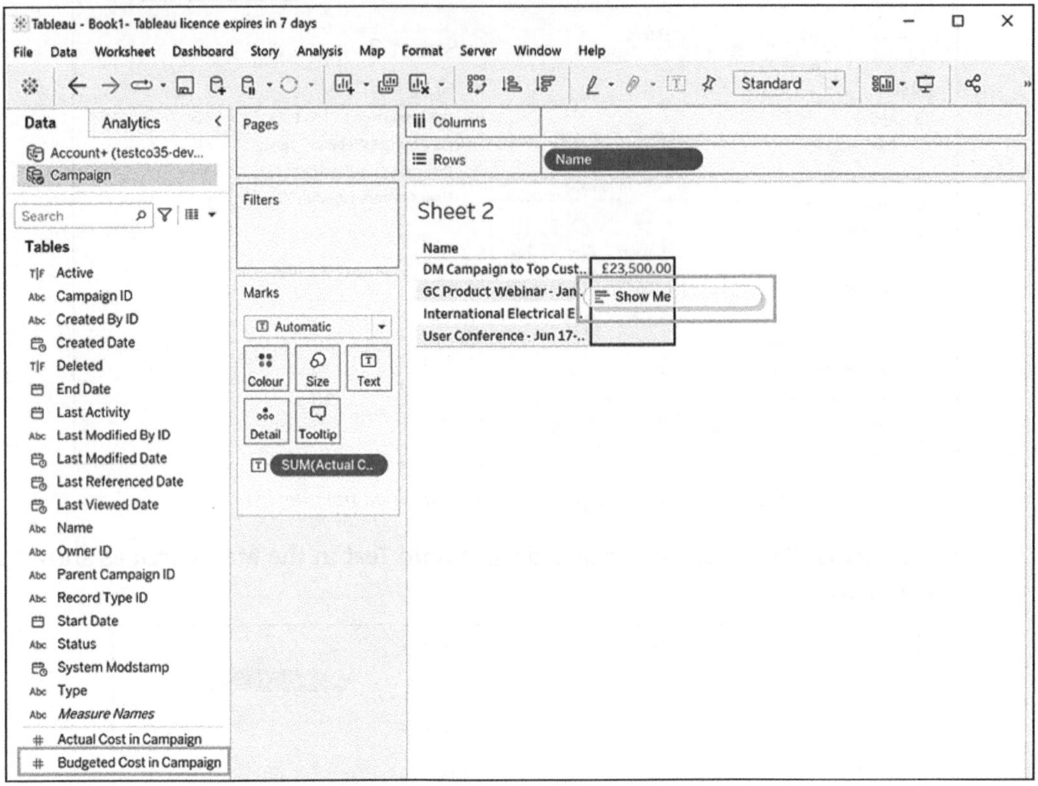

Figure 4.17: Selecting Budgeted Cost in Campaign and using "Show Me"

4. Once you drop the field, your table should look as shown in *Figure 4.18*:

Sheet 2

Name	Actual Cost in Campaign	Budgeted Cost in Ca..
DM Campaign to Top Cust..	£23,500.00	£25,000.00
GC Product Webinar - Jan ..	£11,400.00	£10,000.00
International Electrical E..		£50,000.00
User Conference - Jun 17-..		£100,000.00

Figure 4.18: Clean and clutter-free

We can now see that it was only one of our campaigns that ran over budget. We can also see that for some campaigns, we only have budgeted costs and no actual costs. We will therefore filter them out. The quickest way to filter out a single entry is to right-click on the name you wish to filter out and select **Exclude** from the menu that opens up as shown in *Figure 4.19*:

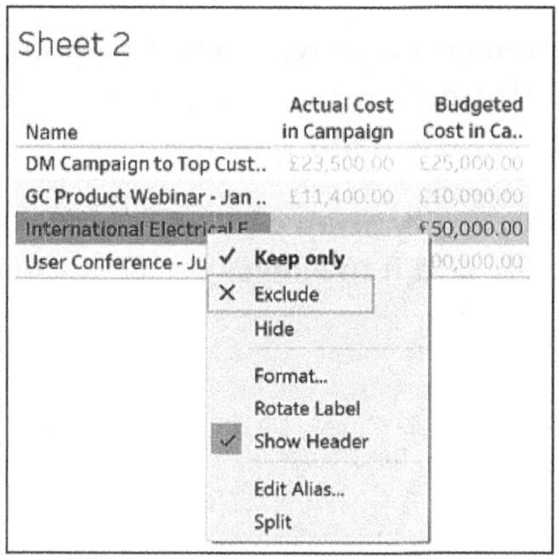

Figure 4.19: *Filtering out campaigns with budgeted costs only*

You can also press *CTRL* and select multiple elements, then right-click on any of them and choose **Exclude** from the menu that opens up. This is what our campaign details looks like after filtering out the campaigns for which we have no actual expenditure amount as shown in *Figure 4.20*:

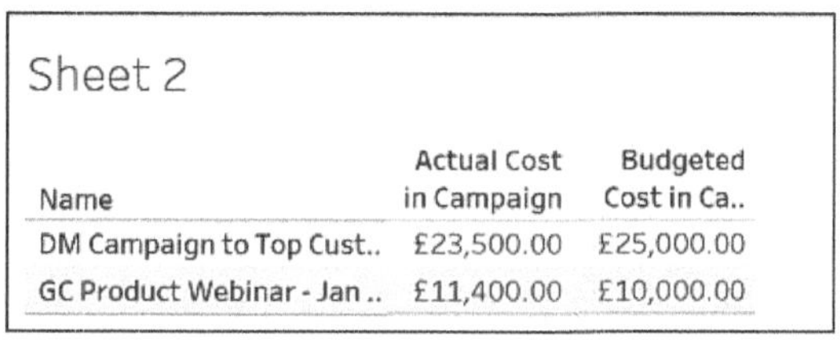
Sheet 2

Name	Actual Cost in Campaign	Budgeted Cost in Ca..
DM Campaign to Top Cust..	£23,500.00	£25,000.00
GC Product Webinar - Jan ..	£11,400.00	£10,000.00

Figure 4.20: *Filtered campaigns without actual expenditure amount*

Pie charts in Tableau

The easiest way to create pie charts and tree maps in Tableau is to use the **Show Me** menu (an alternative way to create pie charts will be discussed in the next chapter). For this example, we will be using the **Opportunities** data which can be found under the **Standard Connection** tab in the data menu as shown in *Figure 4.21*:

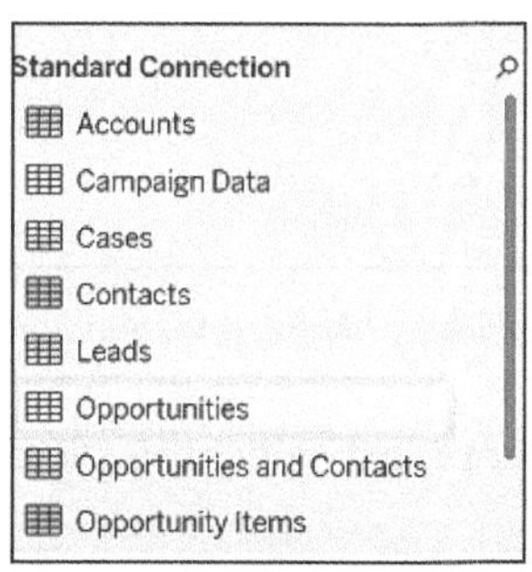

Figure 4.21: *Tableau's Show Me menu simplifies the creation of diagrams*

Disclaimer: Pie charts become hard to read when they are split into more than two categories, and the same information can be represented in other charts, which take up less screen space, so please use them sparingly.

To start, double-click on **Opportunity Source** in the **Dimensions** menu as shown in *Figure 4.22*. Tableau will automatically add it to **Rows.**

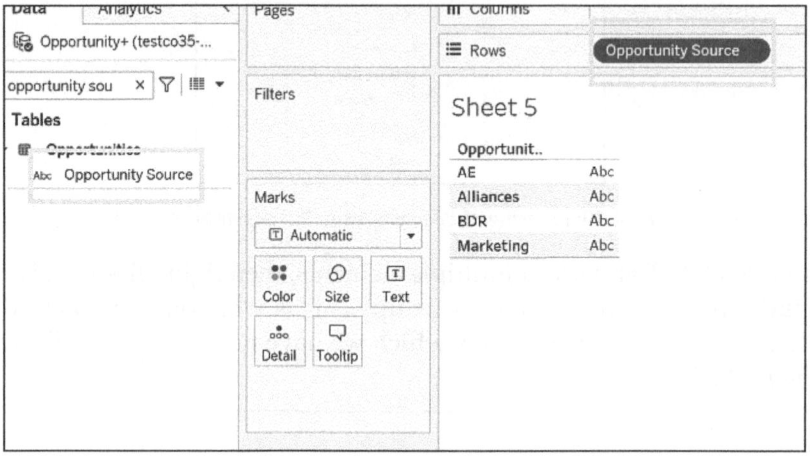

Figure 4.22: Opportunity source

Next, double-click on **Expected Amount**. Tableau will automatically add it to the Label mark as shown in *Figure 4.23*:

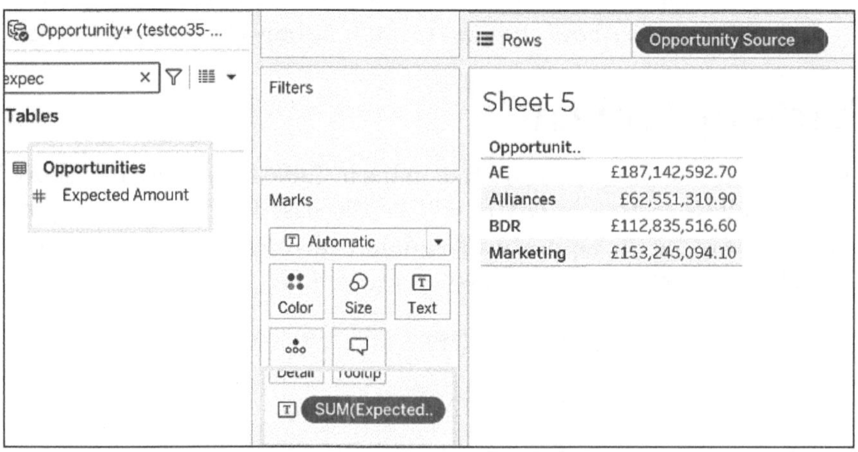

Figure 4.23: Tableau adds Expected Amount to Label mark.

Finally, click on the **Show Me** menu and select the pie chart visualization from the menu as shown in *Figure 4.24*:

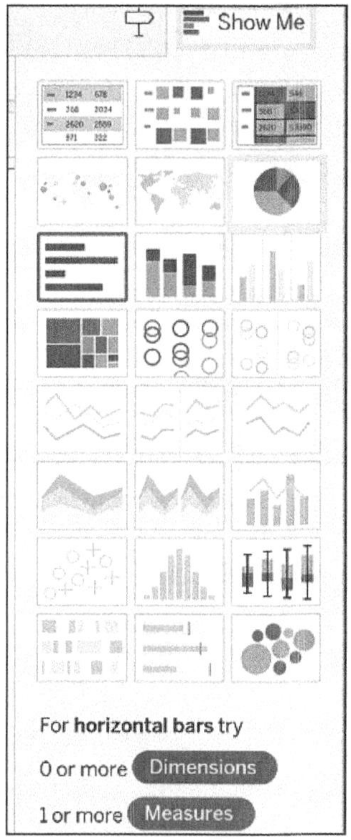

***Figure 4.24:** Choosing the pie chart from the Show Me menu*

Tableau will now create a pie chart for you, as shown in *Figure 4.25*:

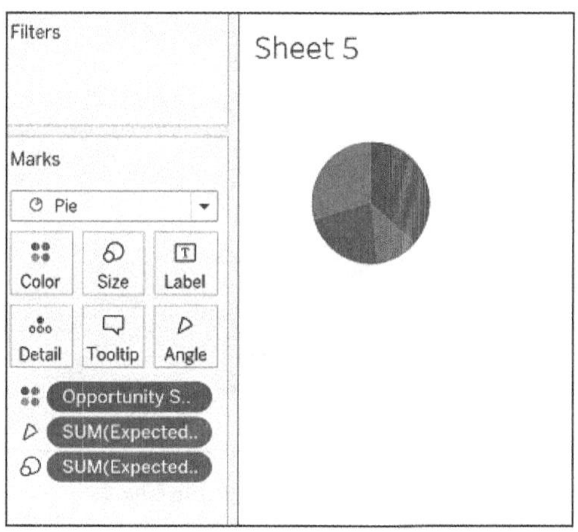

***Figure 4.25:** Tableau effortlessly creates a pie chart*

However, this pie chart is not very informative, so let us try and add more information. Clicking on the **Size** mark will allow us to resize the pie chart as shown in *Figure 4.26*:

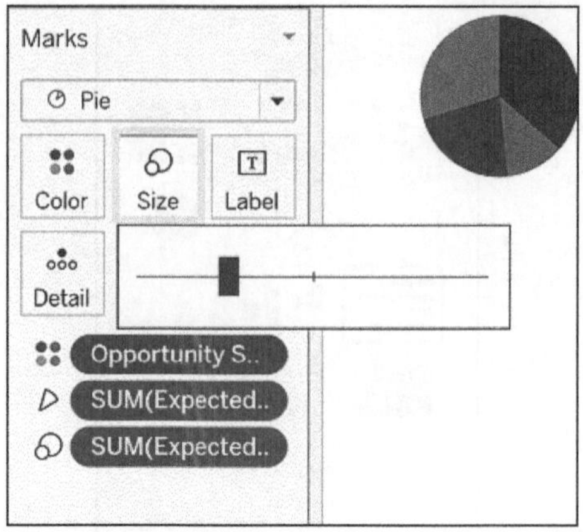

***Figure 4.26:** Enhancing pie chart by resizing to convey more information*

We chose to make it bigger as shown in *Figure 4.27*:

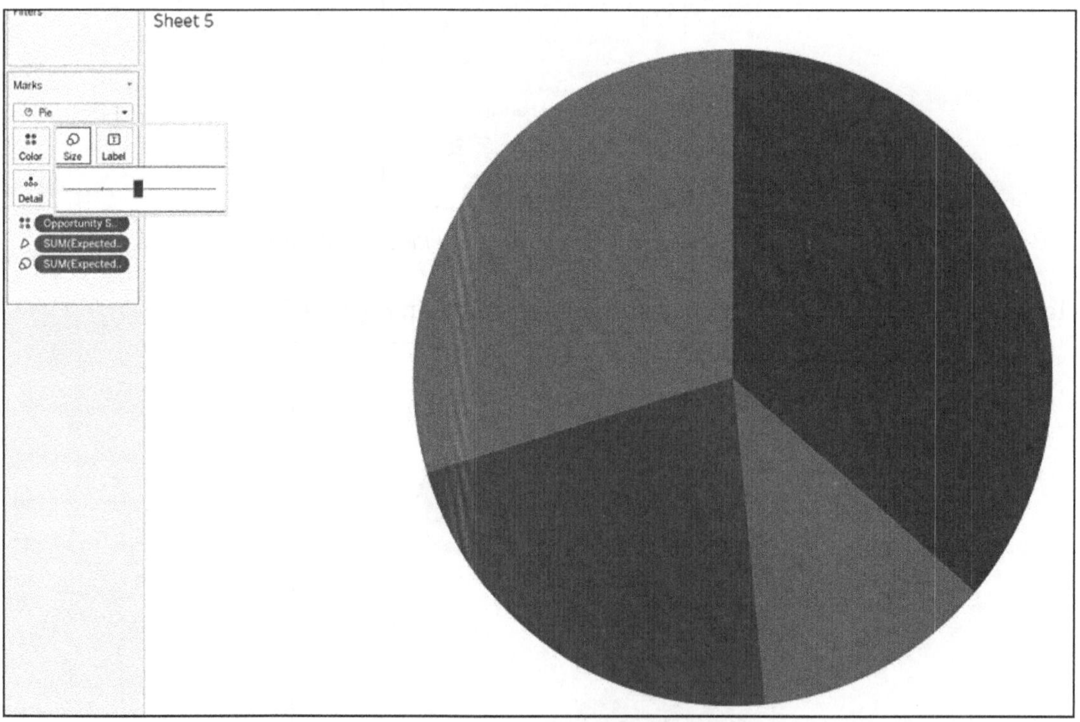

***Figure 4.27:** Enhanced Pie Chart*

Next, we dragged **Opportunity Source** and **Expected Amount** to the **Label** mark so that both fields are shown in the chart in *Figure 4.28*:

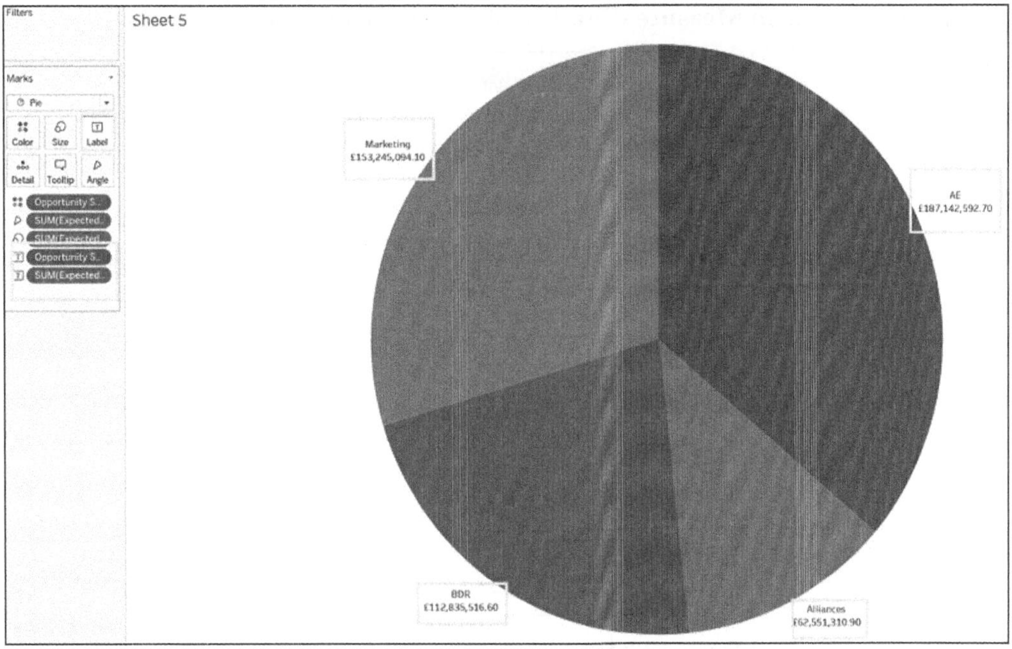

Figure 4.28: Chart displaying the next steps

On second thought, the average Expected Amount may be more informative than the total Expected Amount. Click on the first green pill in the **Marks** menu to change the chart from the total to the average as shown in *Figure 4.29*:

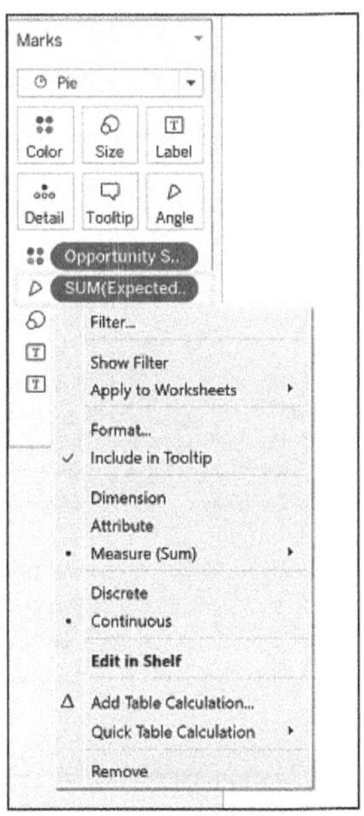

Figure 4.29: The importance of average Expected Amount for better insights

From the menu, click on **Measure (Sum),** as shown in *Figure 4.30*:

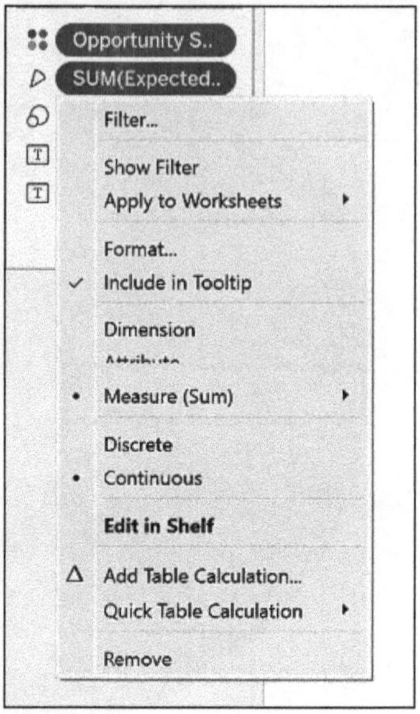

***Figure 4.30:** Select Measure (Sum) from the menu*

Choose **Average** from the list as shown in *Figure 4.31*:

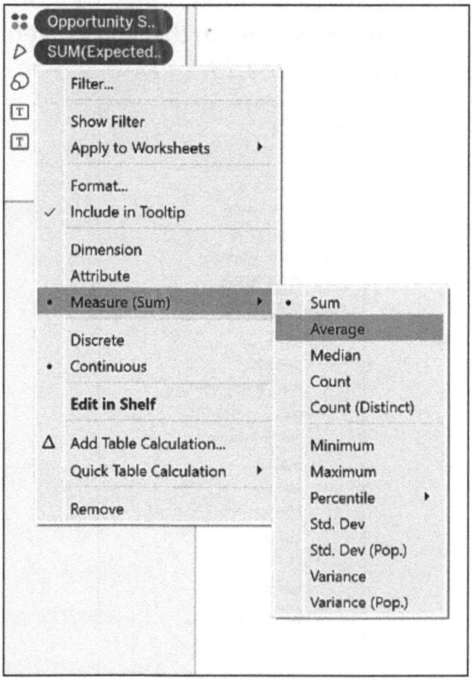

***Figure 4.31:** Select 'Average' option from the list*

Repeat for all your measures as shown in *Figure 4.32*:

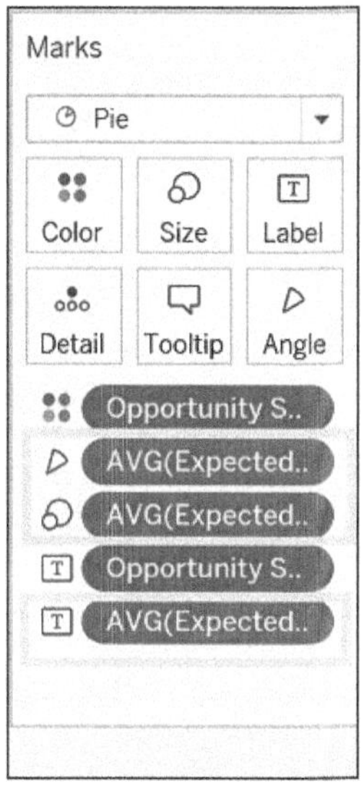

***Figure 4.32:** Precision and efficiency in every step*

The pie chart looks much different from before as shown in *Figure 4.33*:

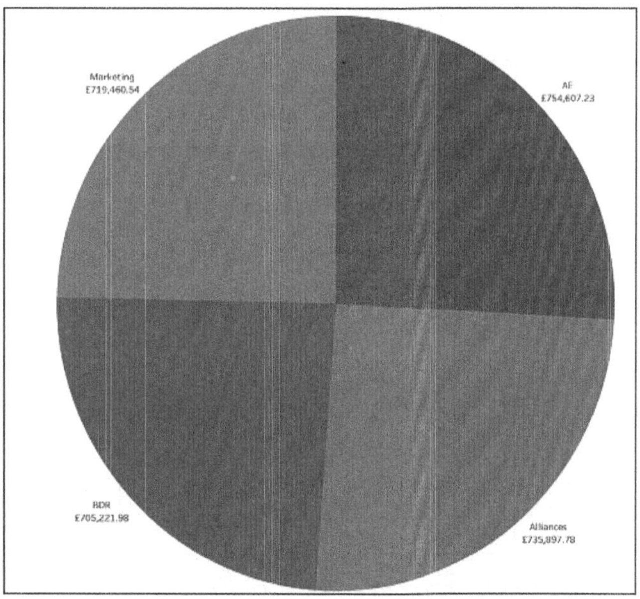

***Figure 4.33:** Updated pie chart introduces significant changes*

For added context, we will also add the total **Expected Amount** to the chart. To do so, drag Expected Amount to the **Label** mark as shown in *Figure 4.34*:

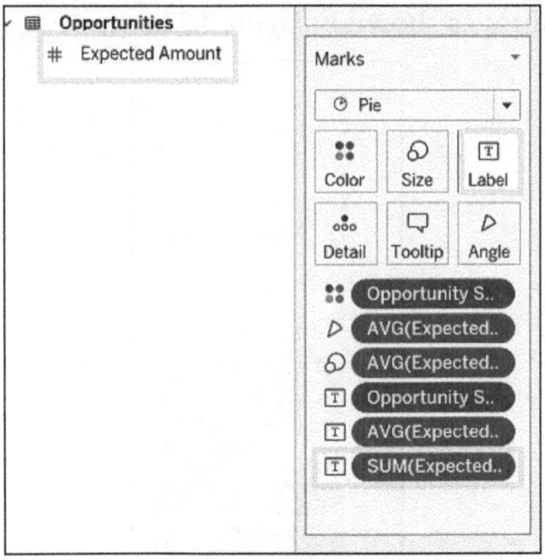

Figure 4.34: Drag Expected Amount to the Label mark for added context

However, while it may be clear to the dashboard creator what the chart shows, another user may need more information. We will therefore write what each number represents. To do so, click on the **Label** mark as shown in *Figure 4.35*:

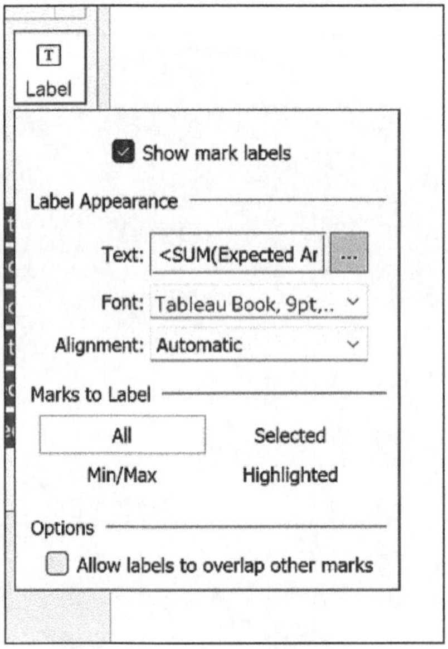

Figure 4.35: Clarify chart details by clicking on the Label mark

Click on the three horizontal dots next to **Text** as shown in *Figure 4.36:*

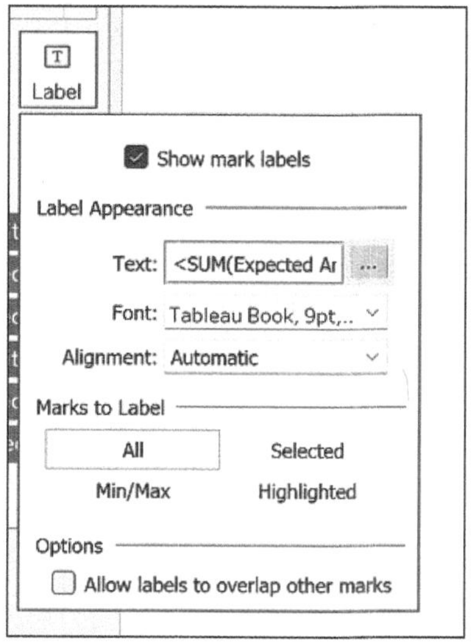

***Figure 4.36:** Options menu icon allows access to additional functions*

A menu will open, from which you can choose how to format your text. However, you can also add more information. Here we have added in bold the definitions for all the fields shown in *Figure 4.37*:

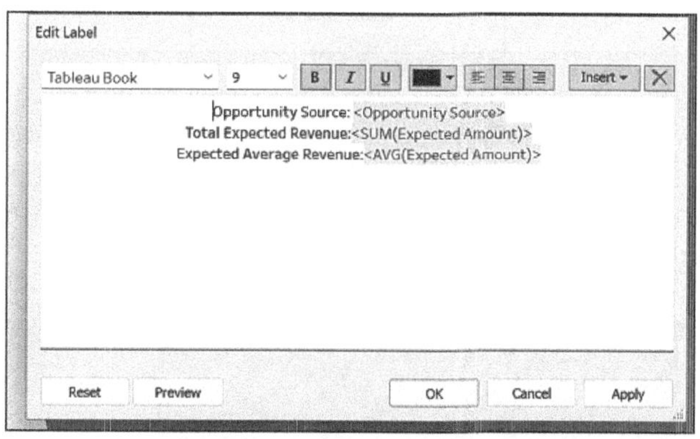

***Figure 4.37:** Text formatting and field definitions displayed on a menu interface*

We now understand that there is not a great difference in the average expected amount that can be attributed to each source, but some sources seem to be generating more opportunities than others.

Treemaps in Tableau

The process to create treemaps in Tableau using the **Show Me** menu is the same as for creating pie charts. The only difference is that rather than clicking on the pie chart icon, you should click on the treemaps icon as shown in *Figure 4.38*:

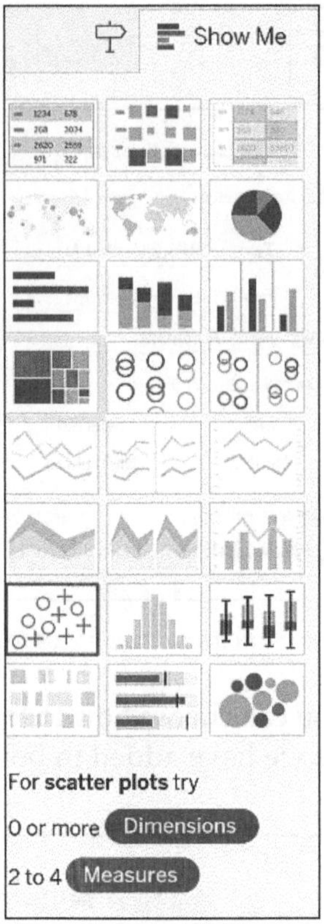

Figure 4.38: *Creating treemaps in Tableau is just like creating pie charts, but with a treemaps icon*

In this case, rather than using Expected Amount, we will be using Amount. Following the same steps as before, this is the final chart, as shown in *Figure 4.39*:

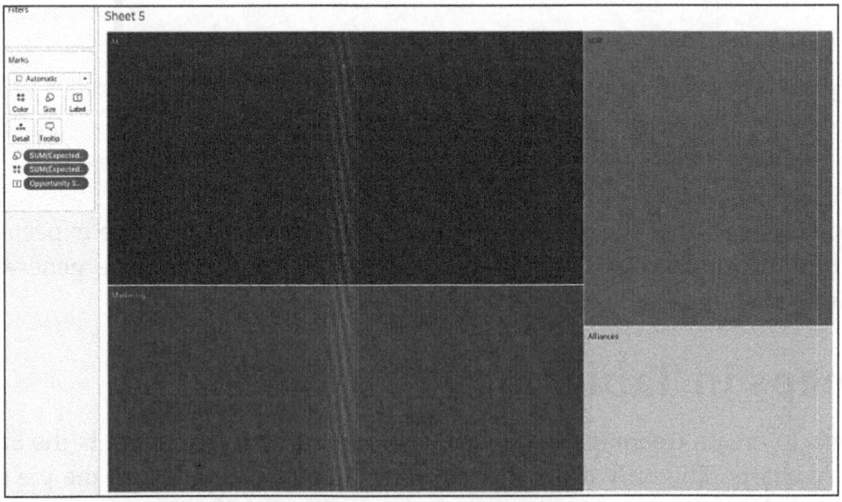

Figure 4.39: *Final chart showing the usage of "Amount" instead of "Expected Amount"*

Just as before, we will change from the total amount to the average amount and add more information to the chart to benefit the reader. The final result is shown in *Figure 4.40*:

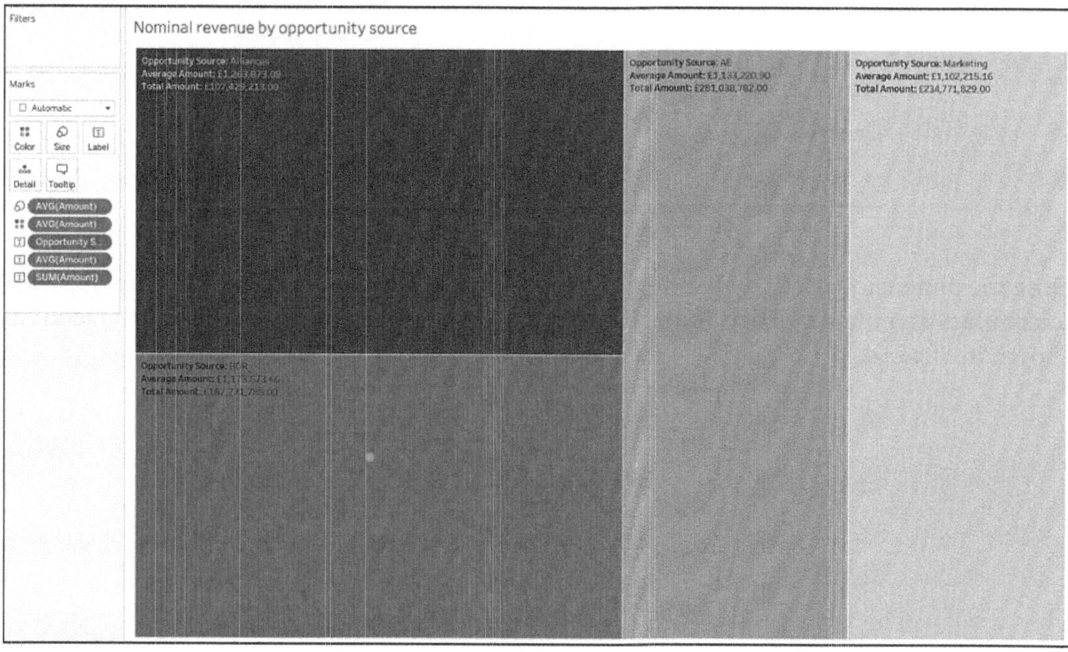

***Figure 4.40:** Chart displaying total and average amounts, enhanced with additional information*

Just as in the previous case, it would seem that average amount is the same, but some sources generate more opportunities.

Scatterplots in Tableau

Looking at **Opportunities** Source gave us some insights, but we want to understand more about where our revenues are coming from, so we will look at Lead Source instead and compare expected revenues with nominal revenues in a scatter plot.

To create a scatter plot in Tableau, start by dragging one of your measures to **Rows** as shown in *Figure 4.41*:

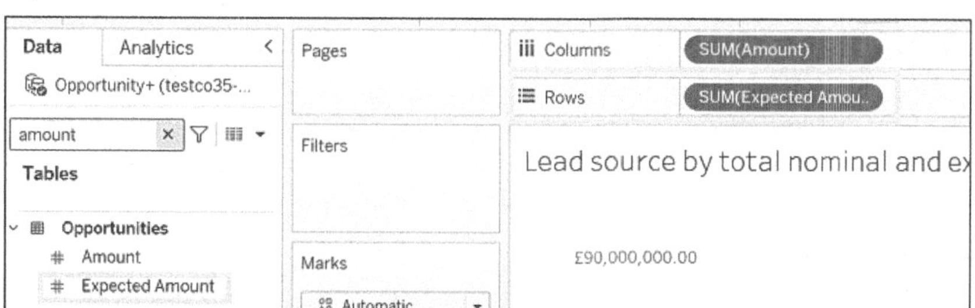

***Figure 4.41:** Scatter plot creation in Tableau: Dragging a measure to Rows*

Drag the other measure to **Columns** as shown in *Figure 4.42*:

***Figure 4.42:** Drag the measure to Columns*

Drag the dimension used to breaking down your measures to **Detail**. In this case, we want to compare revenues by **Lead Source**, so **Lead Source** is the field we will add to **Detail** as shown in *Figure 4.43*:

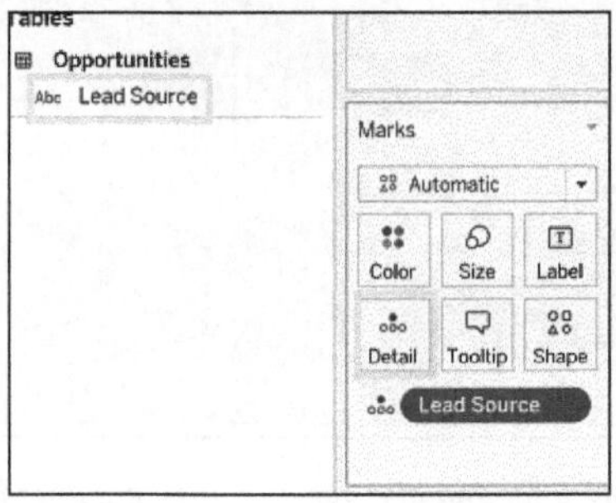

***Figure 4.43:** Breaking down measures by Lead Source in a dimension drag*

You now have your scatterplot as shown in *Figure 4.44*:

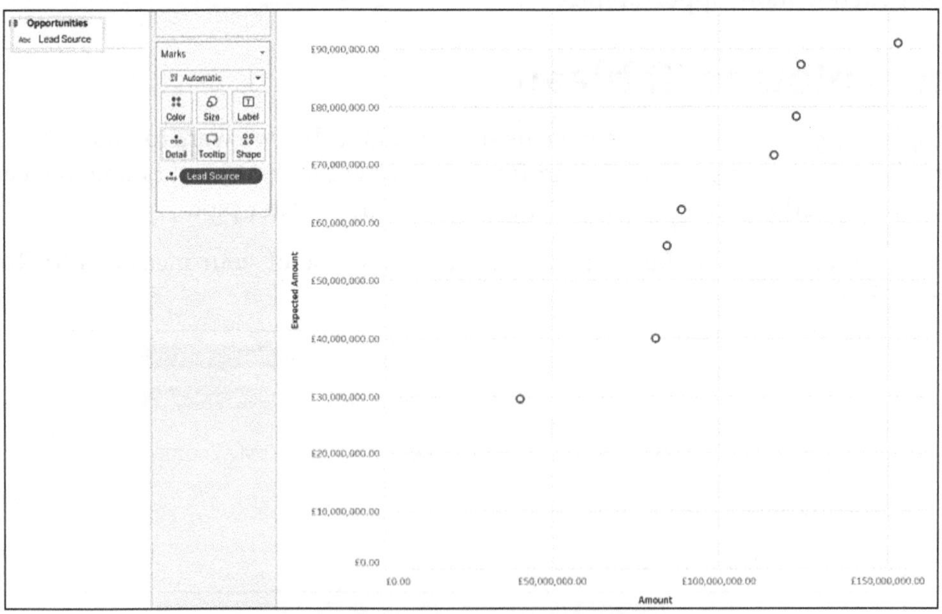

***Figure 4.44:** Visualization of the scatterplot*

Just as before, to better aid comprehension, the chart can be customized. To add the name of the lead source to the chart, drag **Lead Source** to the **Label** mark as shown in *Figure 4.45*:

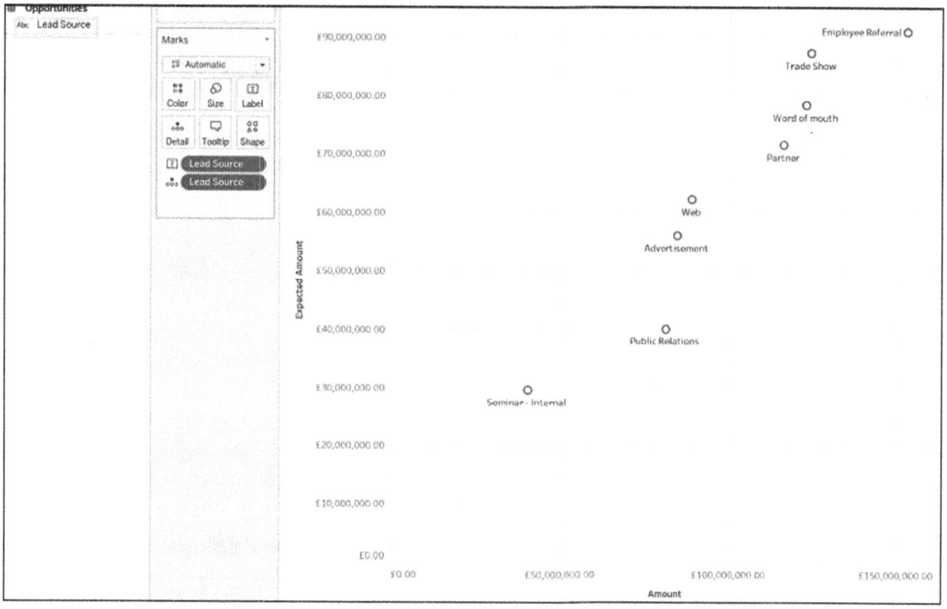

***Figure 4.45:** Adding lead source to the chart for better comprehension*

To further differentiate, drag **Lead Source** to the **Color** mark. Each circle now has a different color as shown in *Figure 4.46:*

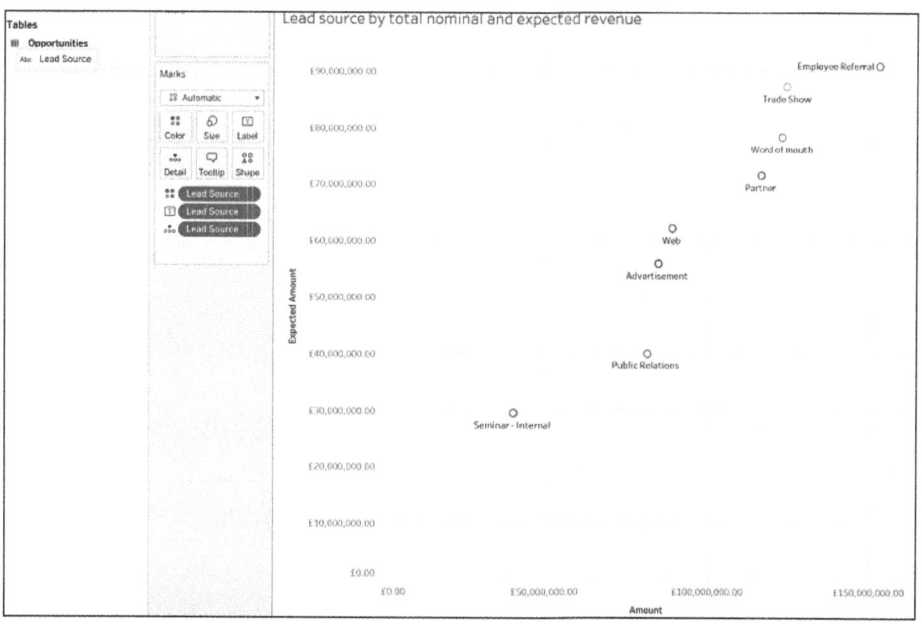

***Figure 4.46:** Differentiating lead sources by dragging to the mark, resulting in varying circle colors*

It is also possible to choose which shape to display in the chart. To do so, click on the **Shape** mark. You will now see a selection of shapes from which you can choose your favorite as shown in the *Figure 4.47*:

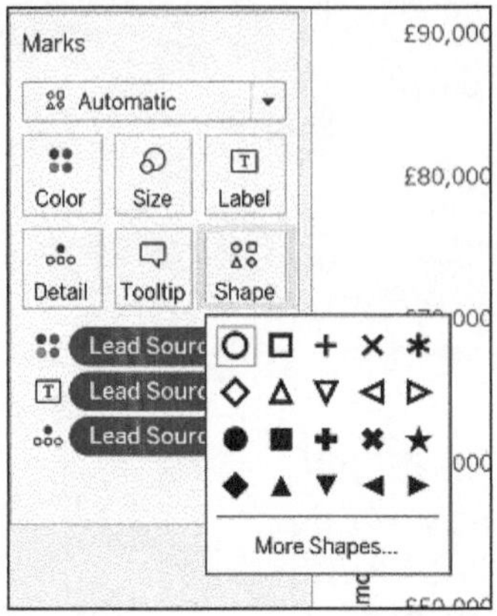

Figure 4.47: *Choosing a shape for the chart*

Here, we chose to replace circles with dots as shown in *Figure 4.48*:

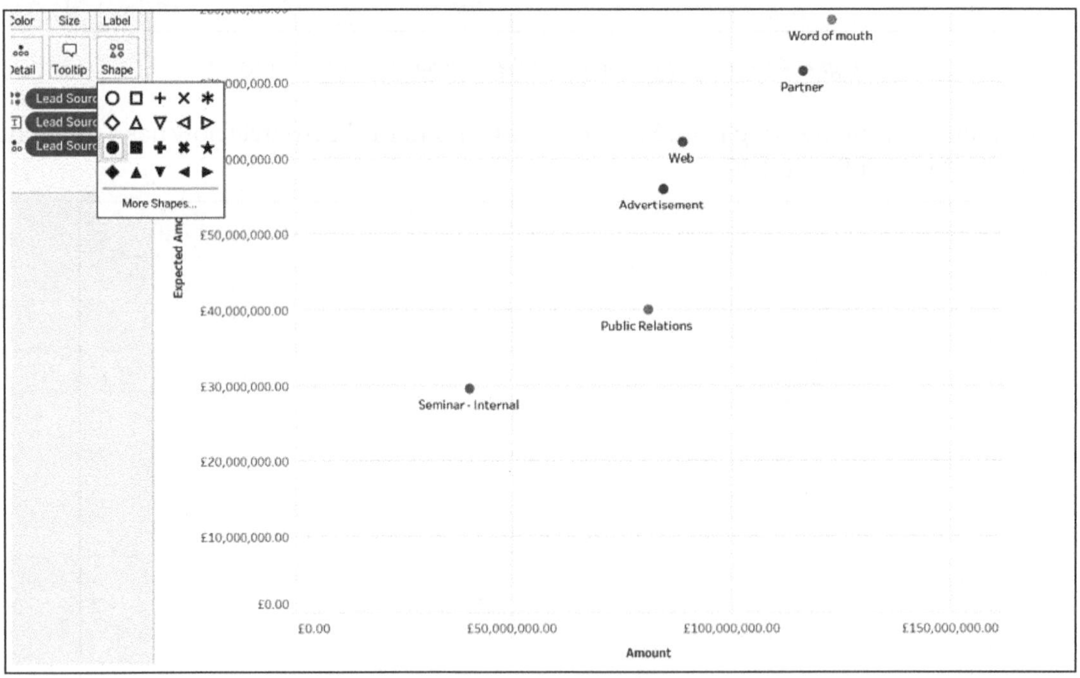

Figure 4.48: *Circular shapes transformed into dots*

When comparing totals, unsurprisingly, there is a strong positive correlation between expected revenues and nominal revenues, so the higher the amount in our pipeline, the higher the amount we expect to convert into actual revenues. We can further confirm this by adding a trend line to the chart. To add a trend line, click on the **Analysis** menu as shown in *Figure 4.49*:

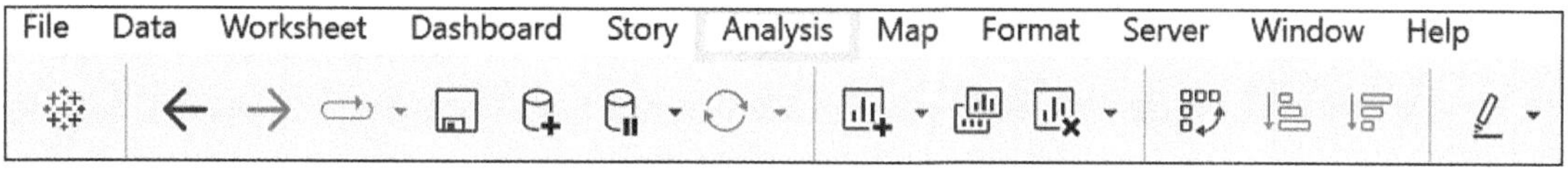

Figure 4.49: *Analysis menu*

Hover on **Trend Lines** as shown in *Figure 4.50*:

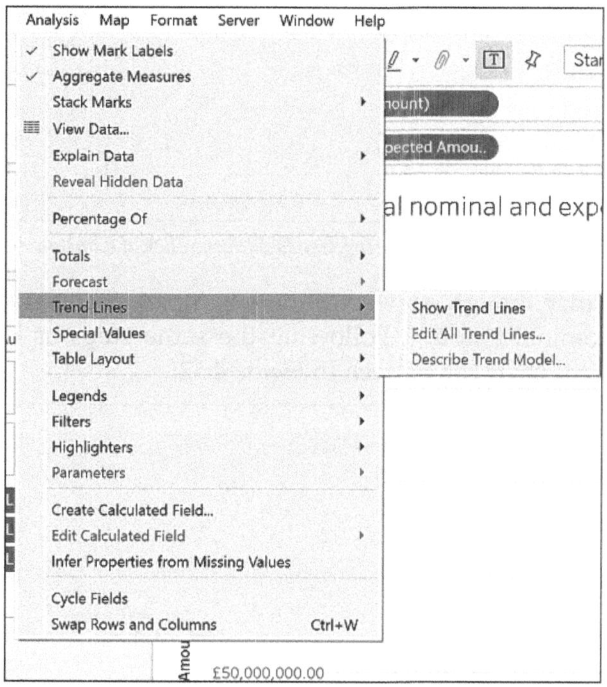

Figure 4.50: *Visualizing trends*

Click on **Show Trend Lines** as shown in *Figure 4.51*:

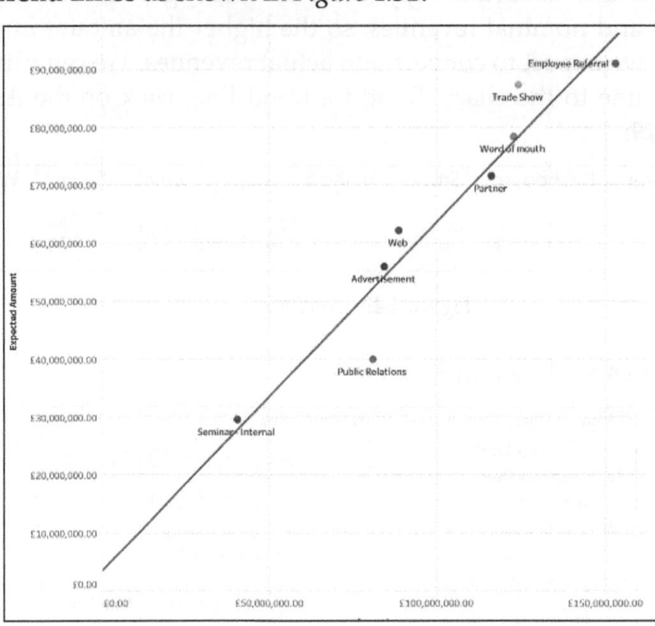

Figure 4.51: *Analyzing trends with the click of a button*

This is not the full story though, so we will now compare the average expected amount with the average nominal amount. Following the same steps as before, including the customization, the final chart can be seen in *Figure 4.52*:

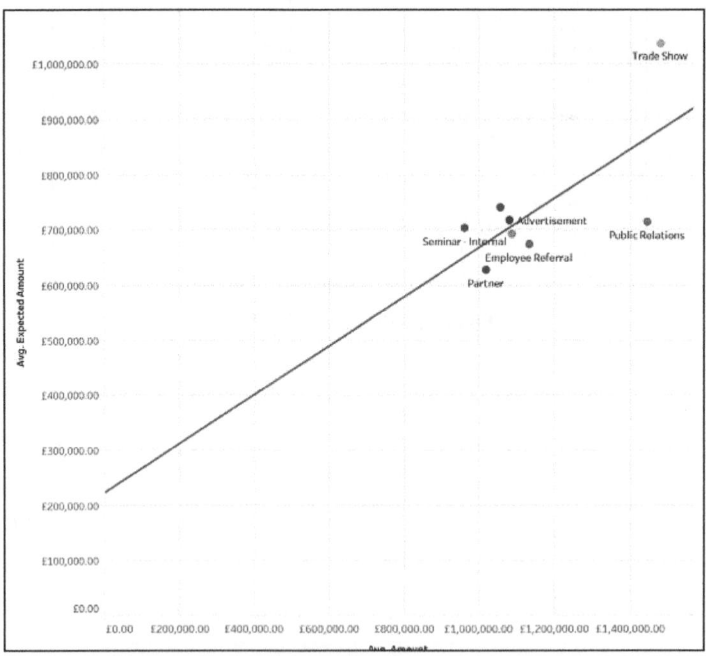

Figure 4.52: *Comparing average expected and nominal amounts*

Comparing these two charts reveals that some sources bring in higher quality opportunities than others. For example, the two sources that bring in the largest amounts of opportunities, tell a different story when comparing averages. Trade shows bring in more opportunities which are also more likely to realize as concrete revenues. However, opportunities brought in via employee referrals, while many, are less likely to close than they should be. Finally, opportunities brought in via Public Relations are fewer and less likely to close, so we may want to review our strategy there.

Bringing all your insights together in a dashboard

The previous example shows that sometimes the full extent of our analysis can only be achieved by comparing several charts. However, we would not want our users to keep switching back and forth between tabs to follow our conclusions. This is where Tableau's dashboard functionality comes in handy.

To create a dashboard, click on the **New Dashboard** button as shown in *Figure 4.53*:

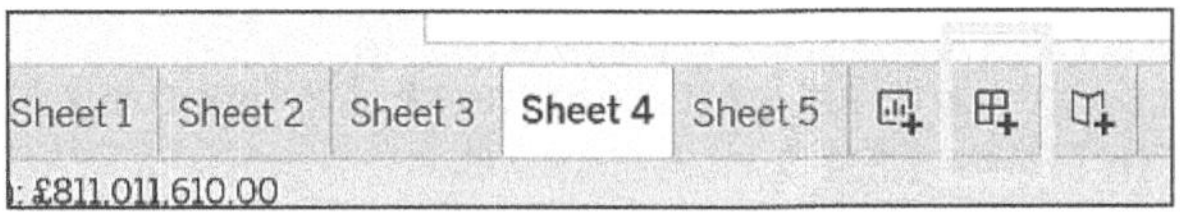

Figure 4.53: *Clicking on 'New Dashboard' button to create a dashboard*

This is the dashboard area. It displays the following as shown in *Figure 4.54*:

1. **Preview menu:** This menu allows you to see how your dashboard will look on different devices.
2. **Size:** From here, you can choose your dashboard size among a list of preset ones or define your own.
3. **Sheets:** From here, you can choose which sheets to drag to the dashboard.
4. **Objects:** From here, you can choose additional objects like images and text boxes to add to the dashboard.
5. **Layout:** The layout tab allows you to finetune the way your dashboard looks.
6. **Dashboard:** It is the actual dashboard, your canvas on which you will add your charts.

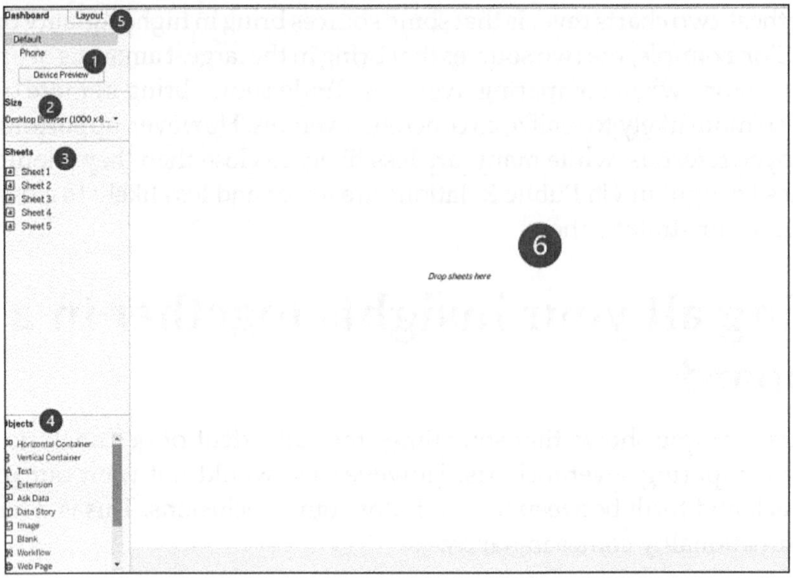

Figure 4.54: Turning data into visual insights on your dashboard

To add a sheet to the dashboard, select it from the sheets list, drag it, and drop it onto the dashboard as shown in *Figure 4.55*:

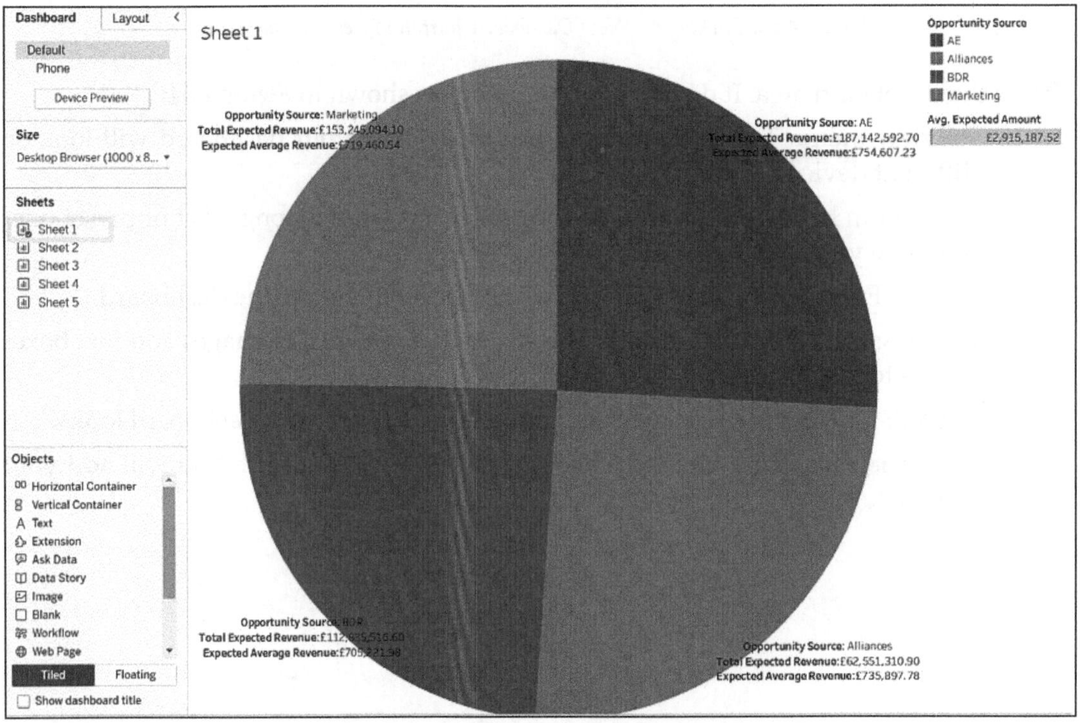

Figure 4.55: Adding a sheet to the dashboard by dragging and dropping from the sheets list

As you can see, Tableau has added the chart so that it takes the entire dashboard and added on the right a color and size legend. Now add the second chart on the right of the first one. Tableau will grey out the area which will be covered by your chart as you drag it as shown in *Figure 4.56*:

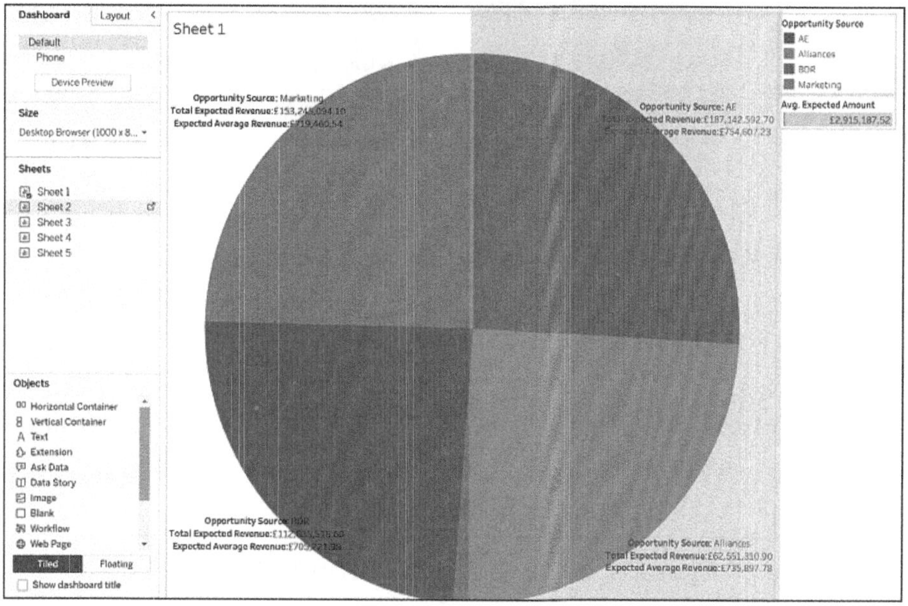

Figure 4.56: Tableau dashboard with enlarged chart and size legend, ready for placement of second chart

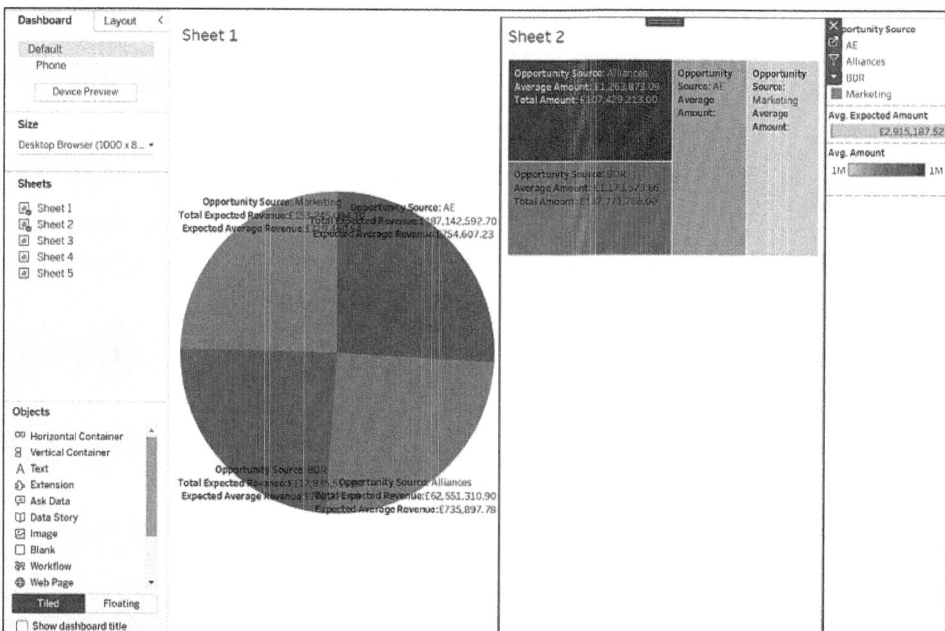

Figure 4.57: Second chart

Next, add your third chart underneath the first one (*Figure 4.57*) as shown in *Figure 4.58*:

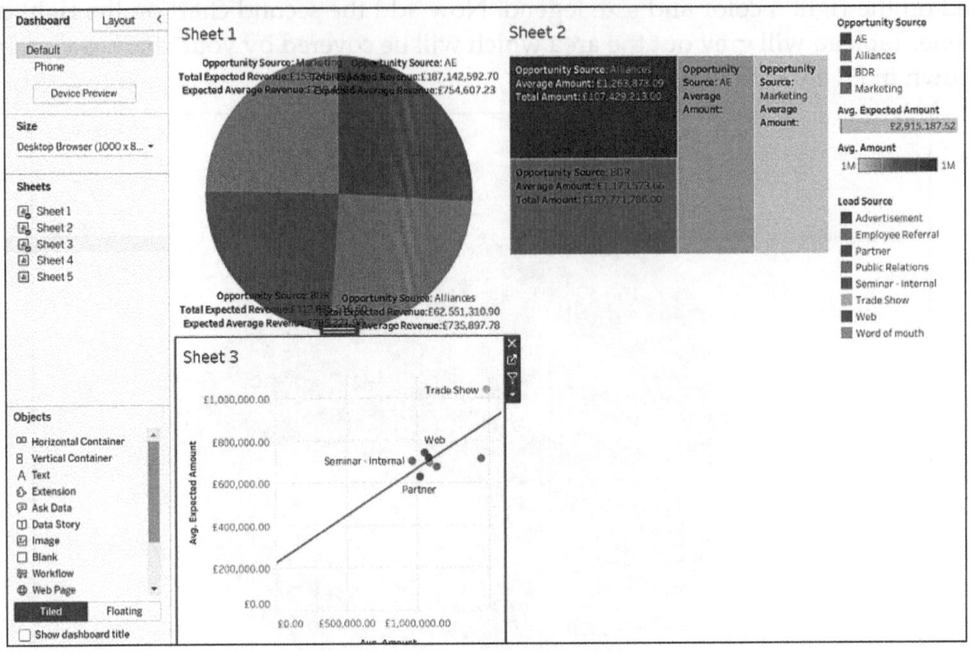

***Figure 4.58:** The third chart is added below the first chart*

Finally, add your last chart, in the bottom right quadrant as shown in *Figure 4.59*:

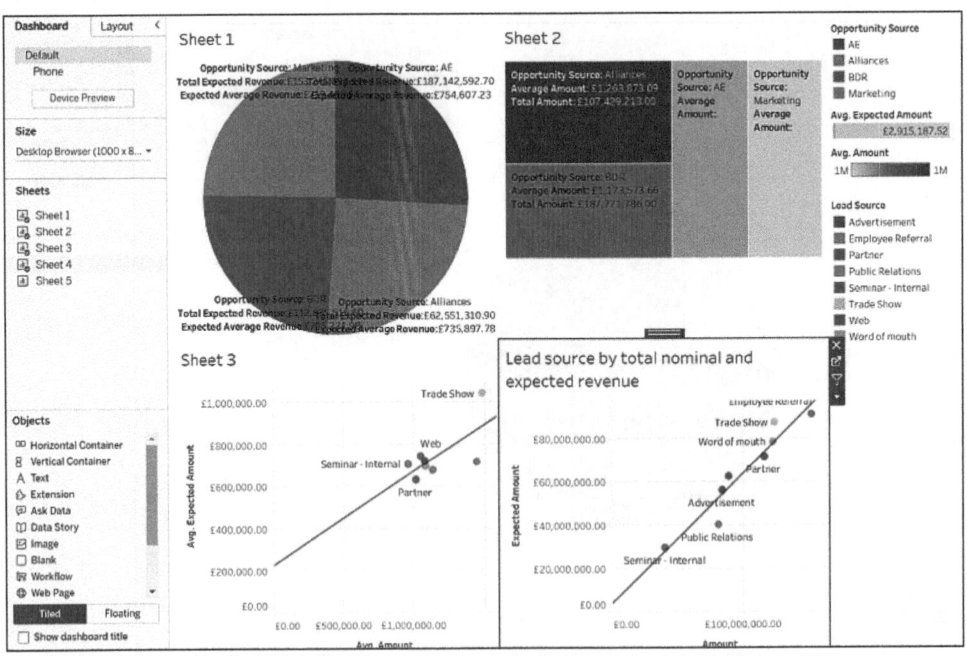

***Figure 4.59:** Bottom right quadrant chart added as final touch*

This dashboard is not particularly informative therefore some adjustments are required. First, the size should be increased to obtain more space to work with. To change size, click on the **Size** menu as shown in *Figure 4.60*:

***Figure 4.60:** Adjusting dashboard size for enhanced working space*

Click on **Desktop Browser (1000 x 800)** as shown in *Figure 4.61*:

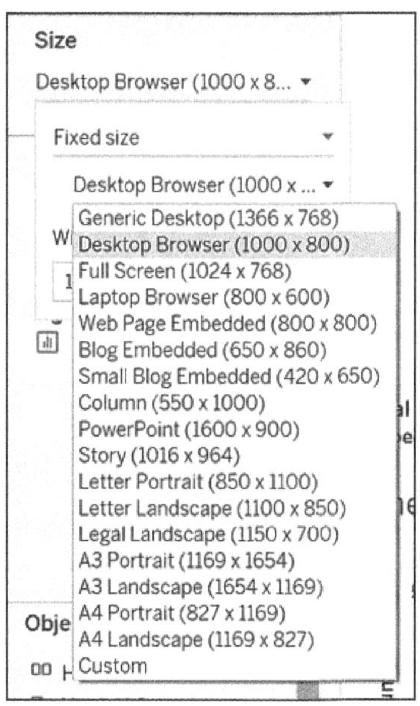

***Figure 4.61:** A desktop browser displayed on a screen*

Choose your preferred size. Here, we have chosen **Generic Desktop**, as shown in *Figure 4.62*:

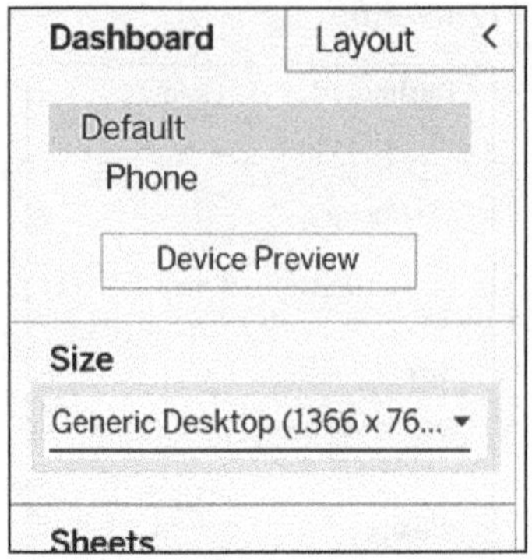

***Figure 4.62:** Selecting Generic Desktop size for customized experience*

You can also alter the **Width** and **Height** values directly to your preferred values, as shown in *Figure 4.63*:

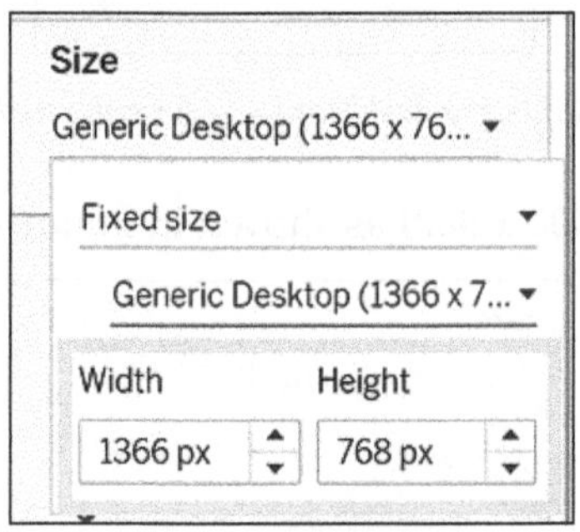

***Figure 4.63:** Customize dimensions effortlessly by directly inputting preferred Width and Height values*

Next, we will add the dashboard title by clicking on the **Dashboard** menu as shown in *Figure 4.64*:

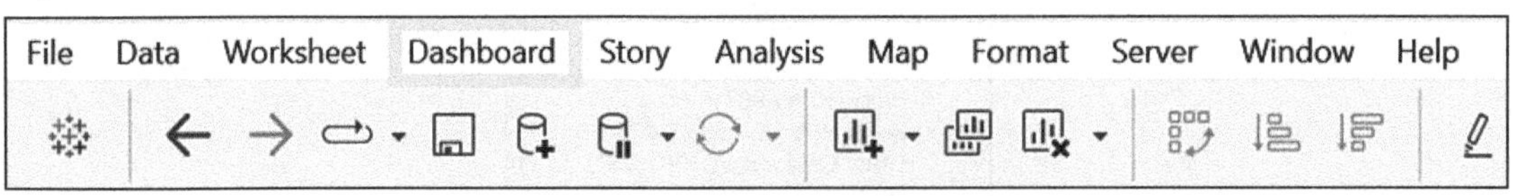

***Figure 4.64:** The Dashboard title is added by clicking on the Dashboard Menu*

And we will click on **Show Title** as shown in *Figure 4.65:*

Figure 4.65: *Click "Show Title"*

Dashboard 1 is not a very insightful title. To change a title, double-tap on it, to open a menu as shown in *Figure 4.66*:

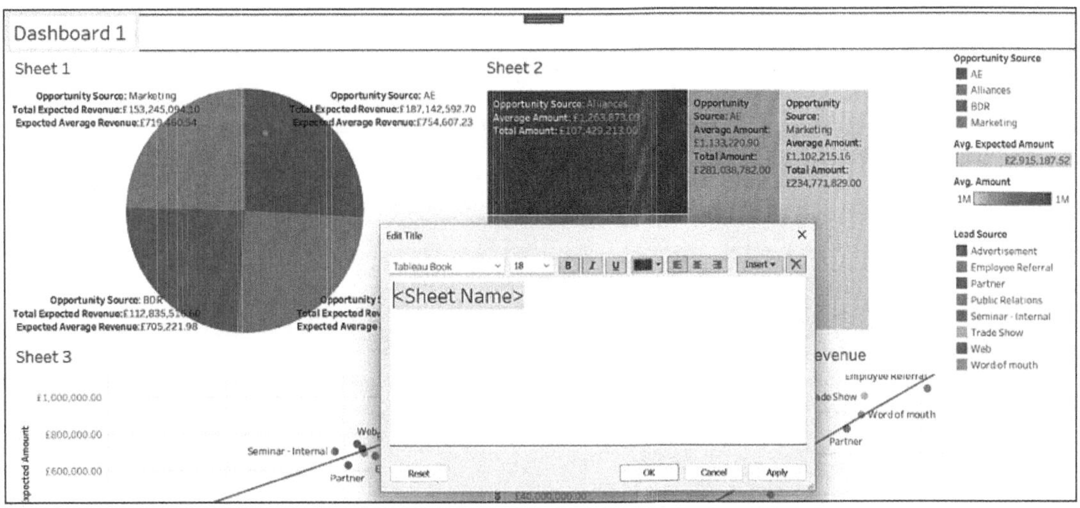

Figure 4.66: *Changing the title of Dashboard 1 using the menu.*

Type in your desired title as shown in *Figure 4.67*:

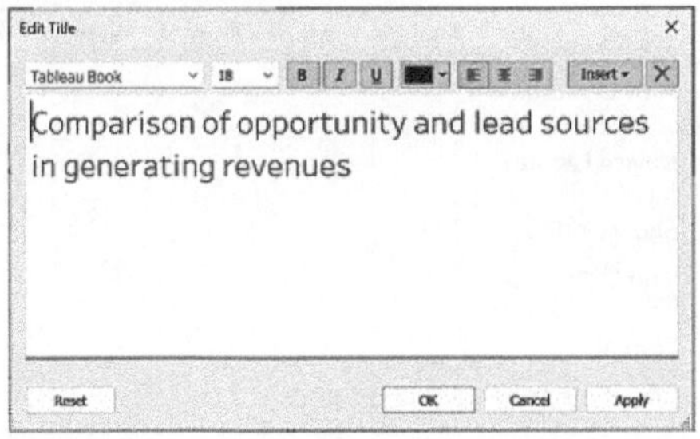

Figure 4.67: *Title input field on a digital screen*

Click on **OK** as shown in *Figure 4.68*:

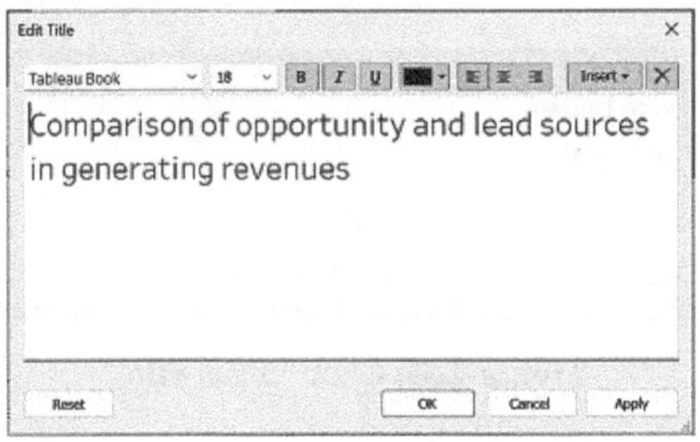

Figure 4.68: *Confirming user action with a simple click of 'OK'*

Following the same method, we will change the titles of each chart as shown in *Figure 4.69*:

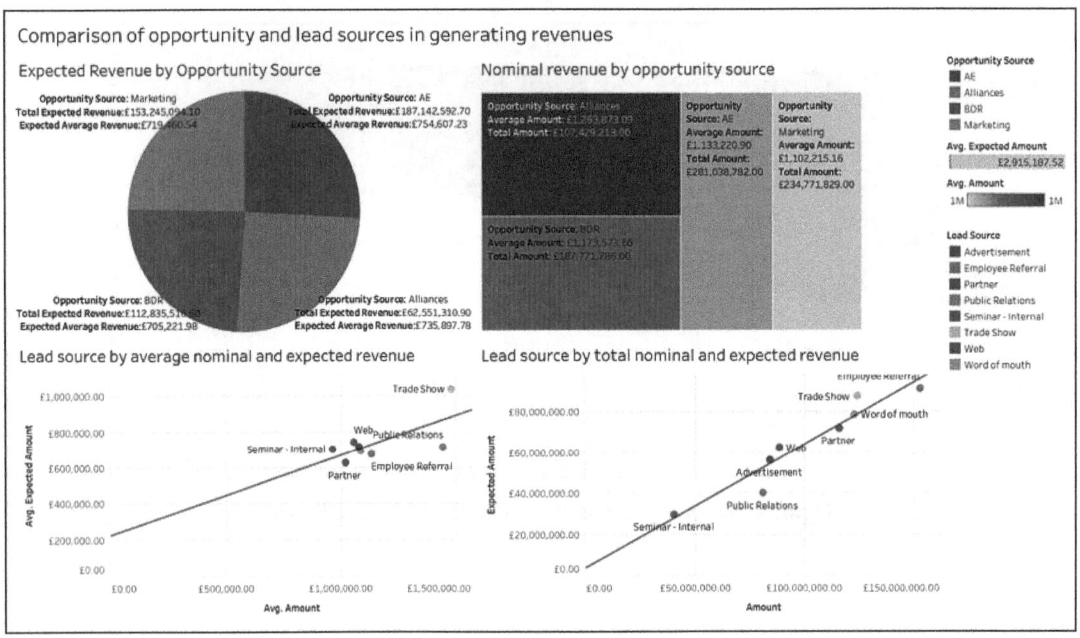

Figure 4.69: *Chart titles undergo transformation with consistent approach*

Since we have added labels to all my charts, the legends are unnecessary, so we will remove them to give more space to my charts. To do so, click on a **legend** as shown in *Figure 4.70*:

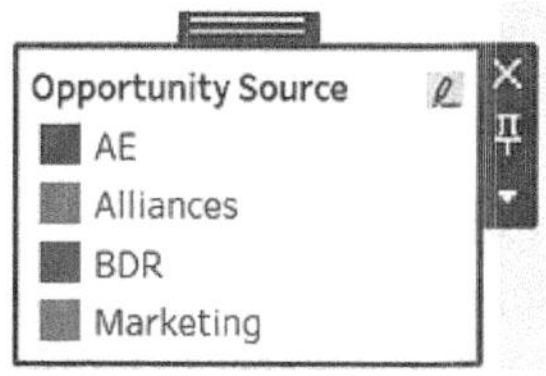

Figure 4.70: *Removing legends to create more space for charts*

Next click on the **x** button in the top right corner, as shown in *Figure 4.71*:

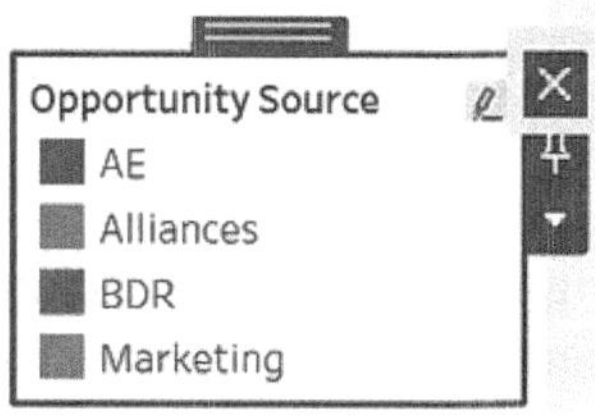

Figure 4.71: *Closing the opportunity score popup*

Repeat for all the legends you do not wish to show. The dashboard looks more professional now, as can be seen below:

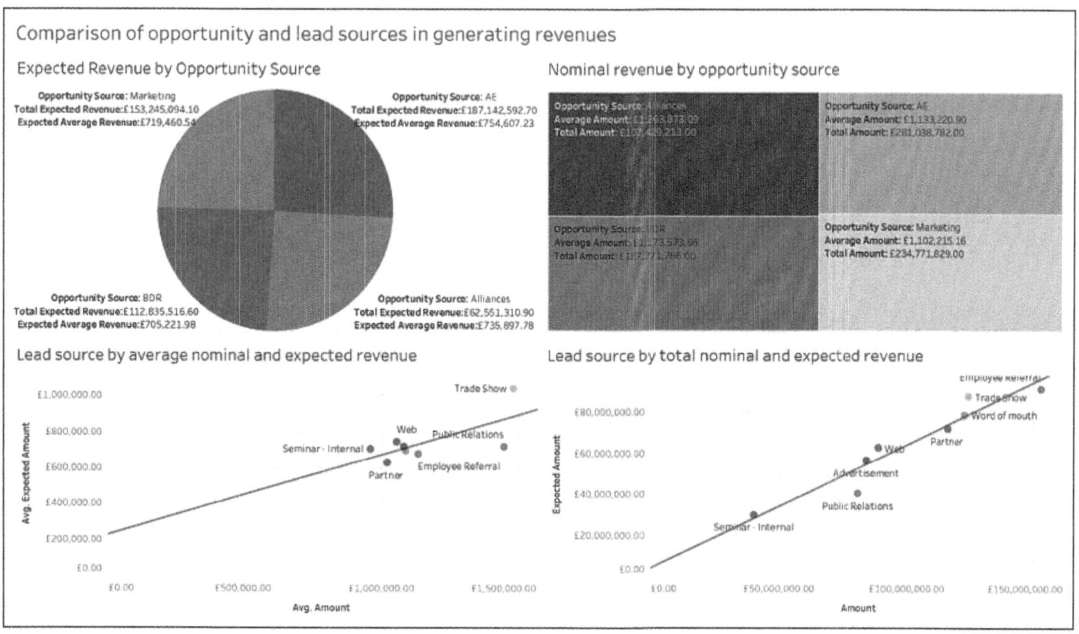

Figure 4.72: *Dashboard with hidden legends*

Your users can now see all your charts at a glance and quickly absorb the knowledge you wish to impart.

Conclusion

In this chapter, we have explored various methods for connecting to data in Tableau and delved into the software's data cleaning and transformation capabilities. We learned how to connect to Salesforce data using the Salesforce Connector and how to authenticate and configure the connection successfully.

We also discussed connecting to data exported to a SQL database and highlighted scenarios where this method may be beneficial. Furthermore, we have equipped you with the skills to manipulate data in Tableau using techniques such as pivot, join, and split once the data is loaded into the software.

In addition, we have covered managing data sources in Tableau, including connecting to multiple data sources, creating data source filters, and crafting calculated fields. With the knowledge and skills gained from this chapter, you are now better prepared to effectively connect to, clean, and transform data in Tableau for enhanced data analysis and visualization. This will ultimately enable you to make more informed decisions and drive impactful insights from your data.

In the next chapter, we will delve into the core functionality that makes Tableau such a powerful visualization tool.

CHAPTER 5

Extracting Deeper Insights with Funnels, Maps, and Hybrid Visualizations

Introduction

In this chapter, we will dive deeper into the world of Tableau visualizations, particularly focusing on intermediate-level charts and features that will help you gain valuable insights from your Salesforce data. We will explore donut charts, funnels, maps, and hybrid visualizations while also learning about filters and calculated fields. By the end of this chapter, you will be well-equipped to create more complex and informative visualizations that can provide powerful insights and help guide business decisions. So, let us get started and take your Tableau and Salesforce skills to the next level!

Structure

The chapter covers the following topics:

- Introduction to deeper insights
- Donut charts
- Filters and calculated fields
- Bar-in-bar charts
- Maps

Objectives

In this chapter, we will get to know how to use different types of charts like donut charts and funnel charts. We will learn what they are good for and what their limits are. You will learn how to make donut charts that show your data clearly. We will also go over how to change your data with filters and special calculated fields to make it just right for your needs.

Next, we will cover how to put together bar-in-bar charts. These let you see two sets of data at the same time in one chart, which can give you better insights. Then, we will explore how to use Tableau's tools to make maps with your data. This can help you see where things are happening in the world.

We will also make sure you know how to tweak these maps so people using them can interact with them easily. You will learn to create filled maps that add color to different areas based on your data. Lastly, we will look at different ways to use maps to spot trends and patterns that have to do with locations. This chapter will give you the skills to turn your data into maps and charts that tell a clear story.

Introducing intermediate visualizations

In the previous chapter, we learned to create several types of visualizations and put them together in a dashboard to help our audience understand our insights more quickly. We will now discuss some more complicated types of charts, use filters, and create calculated fields to bring our ability to gain insight from Salesforce data to the next level.

Donut charts

Donut charts are an alternative to pie charts, which allows for better use of screen space. I would not recommend using donut charts for more than three categories. In this case, we will use it to look at the rate of opportunities closed. To create a donut chart, the steps are as follows:

1. Drag your Dimension (in this case, **Closed**) to the **Color** mark, as shown in *Figure 5.1*:

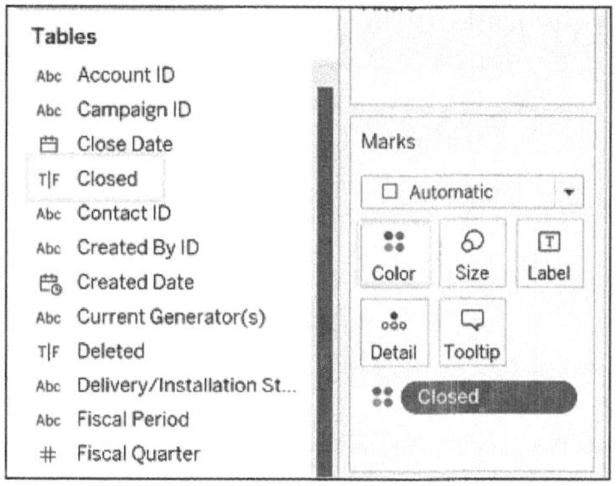

***Figure 5.1:** Dragging Closed field to Color mark to create donut chart*

2. From the **Marks** menu, choose **Pie**, as shown in *Figure 5.2*:

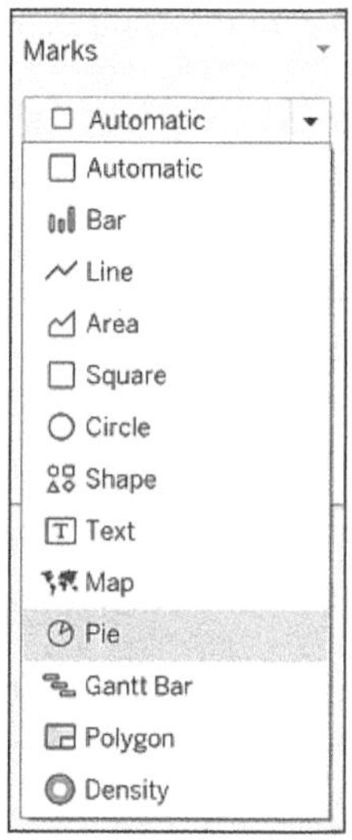

***Figure 5.2:** Changing marks type to Pie to create donut chart*

3. Take your measure (in this case a count distinct of Opportunity ID) and drag it to the **Angle** mark, as shown in *Figure 5.3*:

***Figure 5.3:** Dragging Opportunity ID count to Angle mark for donut chart*

4. Your data should now look like a pie chart, as shown in *Figure 5.4*:

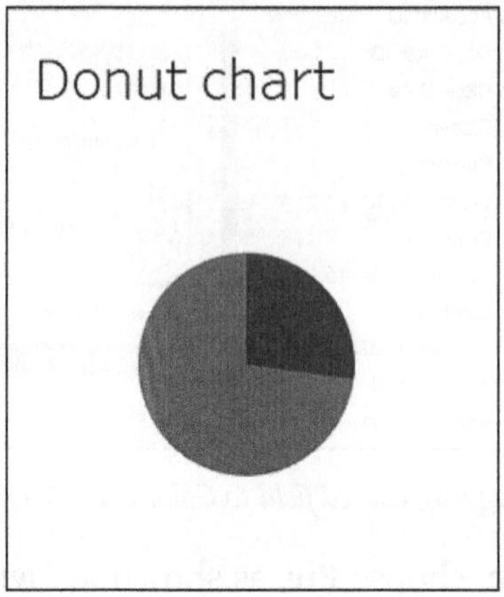

***Figure 5.4:** Initial donut chart created*

5. To create a donut chart we need to 'trick' Tableau into thinking there are two pie charts. To do so, in the **Rows** space, type the following, as shown in *Figure 5.5*:

   AVG(0)

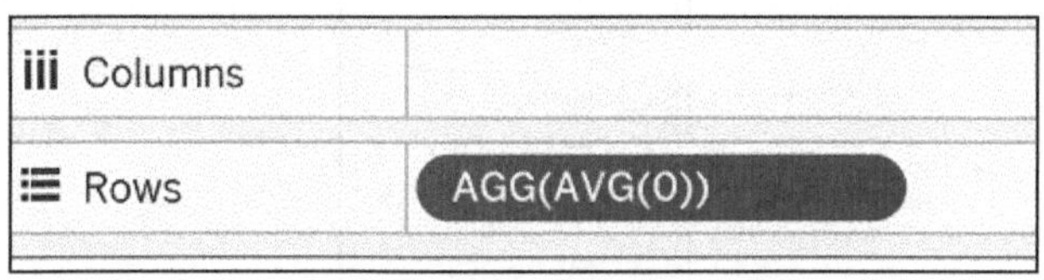

***Figure 5.5:** Adding AVG(0) calculation to rows shelf to create stacked pies*

6. Then, repeat the same step again, as shown in *Figure 5.6*:

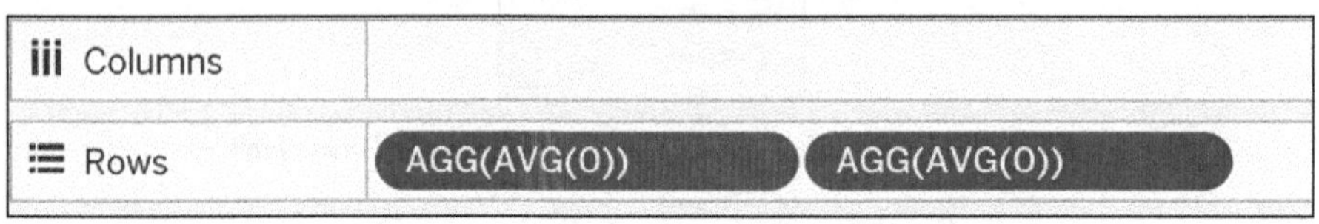

***Figure 5.6:** Adding second AVG(0) calculation to rows shelf*

7. You should now have two pie charts vertically stacked, as shown in *Figure 5.7*:

***Figure 5.7:** Vertically stacked pie charts created*

8. Click on the caret that appears when hovering on either of the measures you have just created. A menu will, now, open, as shown in *Figure 5.8*:

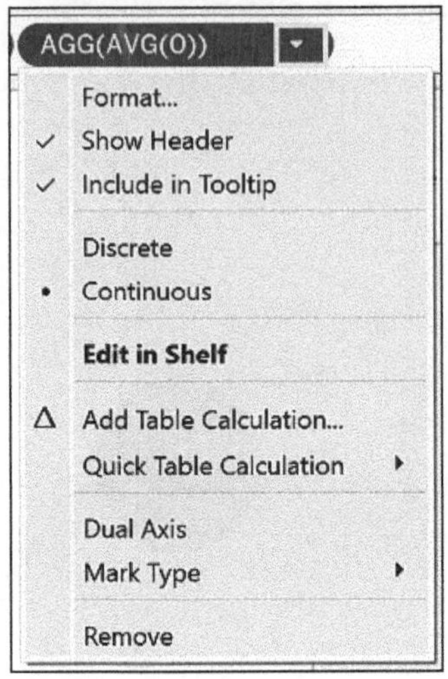

Figure 5.8: *Hovering over measure pill to access menu*

9. Click on the **Dual Axis**, as shown in *Figure 5.9*:

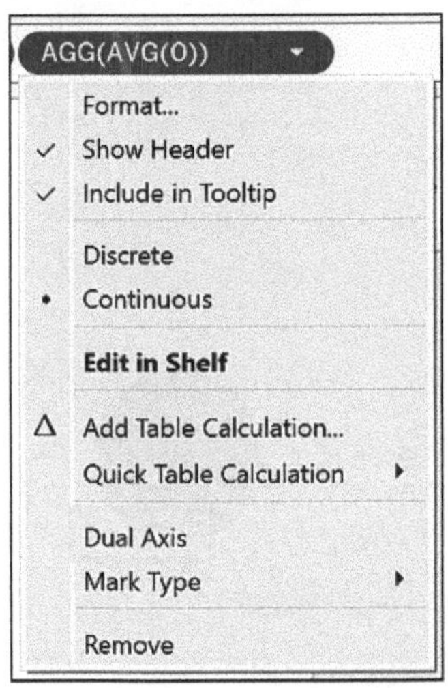

Figure 5.9: *Selecting Dual Axis option*

10. Your pie charts are now on top of each other, so that it looks like you only have one pie chart. You also have 3 Marks menus now; one for each measure and one that controls both, as shown in *Figure 5.10*:

Figure 5.10: *Stacked pie charts now overlapping as one chart*

11. Open one of the measure menus and remove all pills by dragging them away from the menu, as shown in *Figure 5.11*:

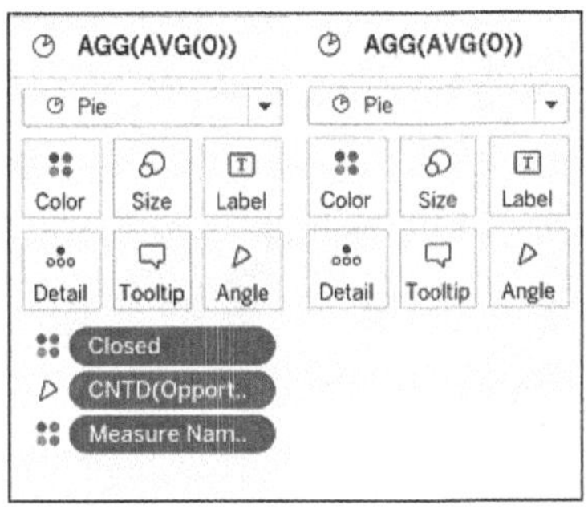

Figure 5.11: *Removing pills from secondary measure*

12. From the same menu, click on the **Color** mark and select the color which matches your background (in this case white), as shown in *Figure 5.12*:

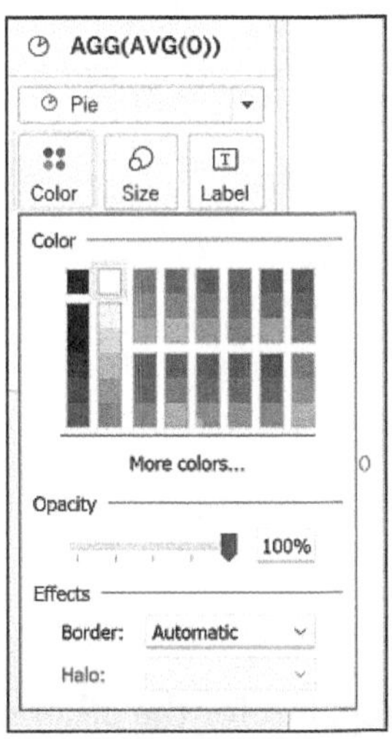

Figure 5.12: *Changing secondary measure's color to match background*

13. Still in the same menu, click on the **Size** mark and drag the indicator left to reduce the size of your chart, as shown in *Figure 5.13*:

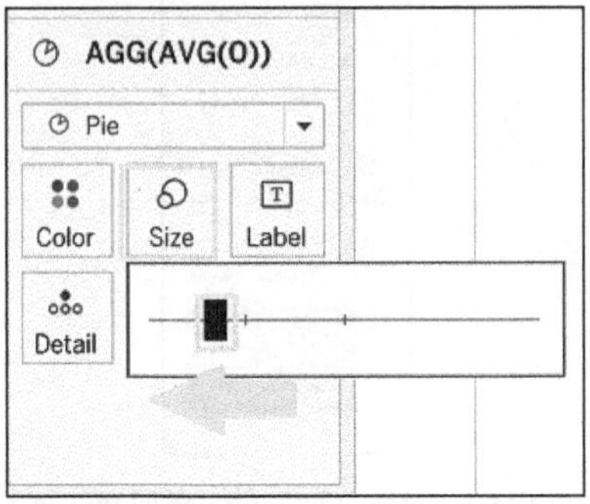

***Figure 5.13:** Reducing secondary measure's size*

14. Your chart should now start to look like a donut chart, as shown in *Figure 5.14*:

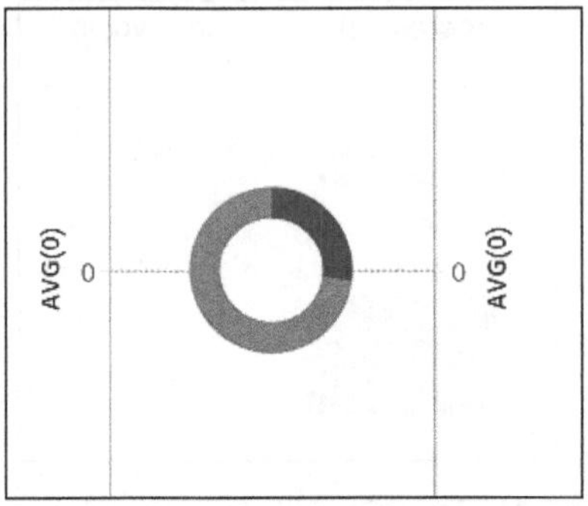

***Figure 5.14:** Donut chart taking shape*

15. As usual we want to make it more informative. We will start by dragging our measure in the **Label** menu for our white pie chart, as shown in *Figure 5.15*:

***Figure 5.15:** Adding measure to label mark of main pie chart*

16. We will repeat the same step, but for the other menu, as shown in *Figure 5.16*:

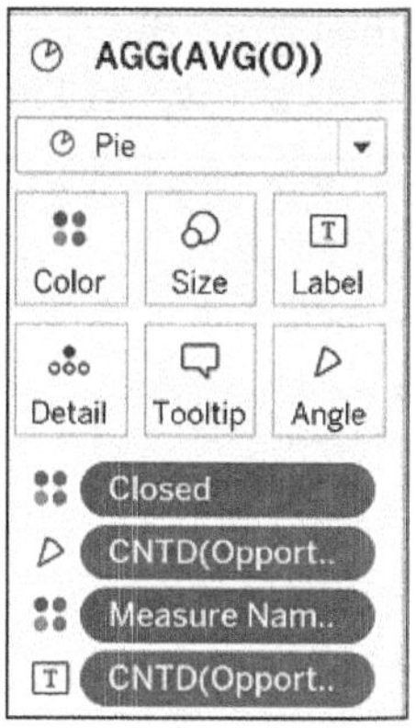

***Figure 5.16:** Adding measure to label mark of secondary pie chart*

17. Next we will hide both axes, as they are not needed for our chart. To do so, right click on your left axis, and a menu will open, as shown in *Figure 5.17*:

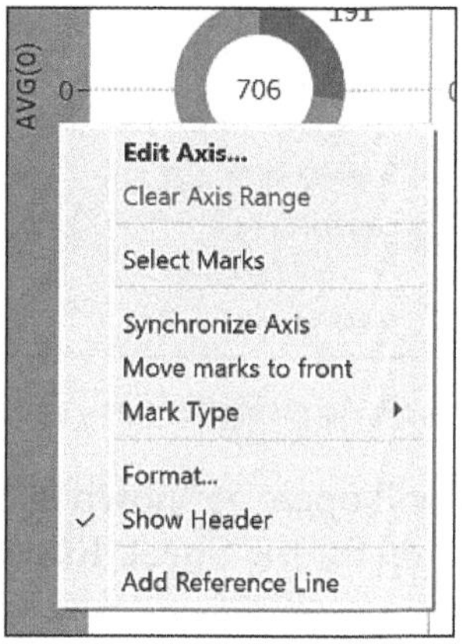

***Figure 5.17:** Right clicking on vertical axis to access menu*

18. Click on **Show Header**, as shown in *Figure 5.18*:

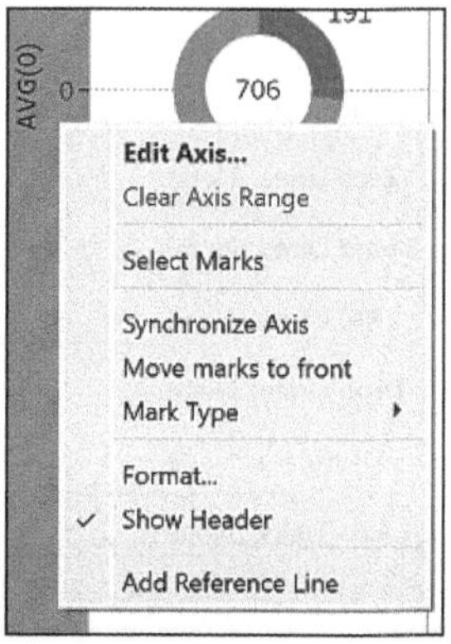

***Figure 5.18:** Selecting "Show Header" option to hide axis*

19. To remove all unnecessary lines from the chart, click on **Format** at the top of your workbook and then on **Lines**, as shown in *Figure 5.19*:

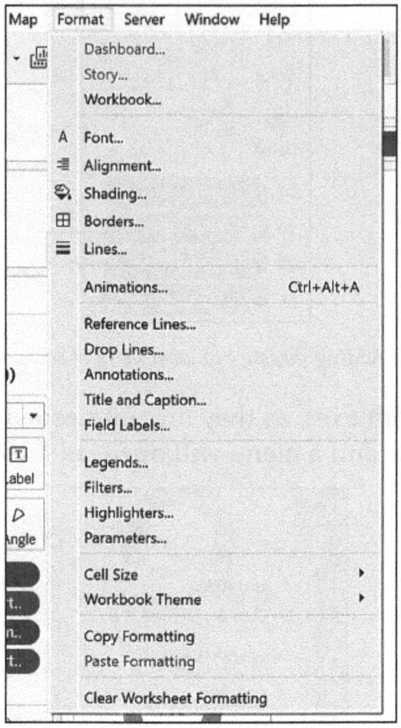

Figure 5.19: *Accessing Format | Lines menu*

20. The **Format Lines** menu will open, as shown in *Figure 5.20*. Open each menu and select None. Repeat this step for the **Sheet**, **Rows** and **Columns** menu:

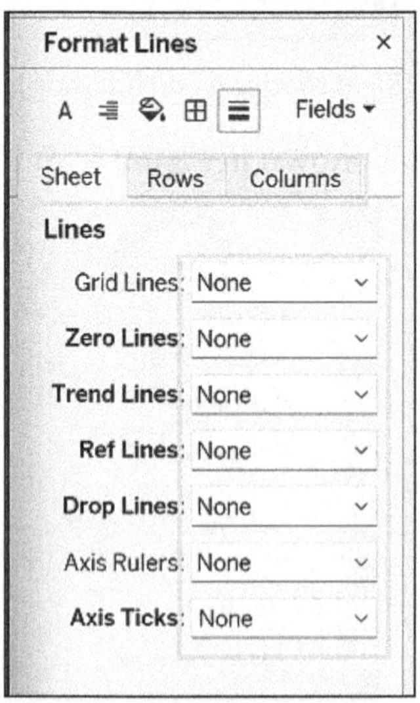

Figure 5.20: *Setting line formatting to None*

21. If you want to also remove the border lines, click on the square icon and select **None**, as shown in *Figure 5.21*, for all the menus in **Sheet**, **Rows** and **Columns**:

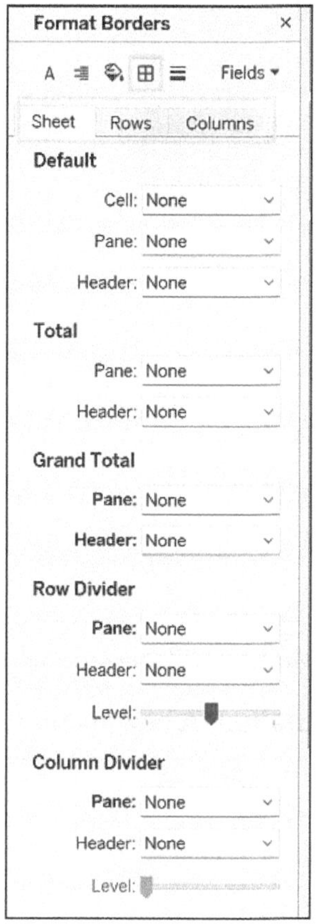

***Figure 5.21:** Removing chart border lines*

22. Your donut chart should look, as shown in *Figure 5.22*. In the center, you can see the full amount and next to each slice, its relative amount.

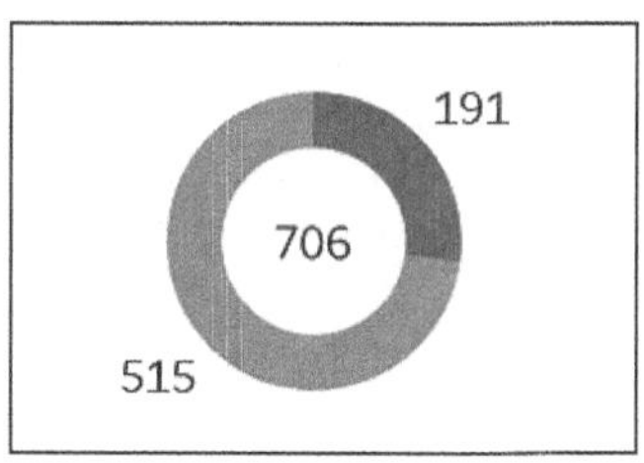

***Figure 5.22:** Final customized donut chart*

23. We can also change the absolute amounts into percentages. To do so, we select the menu for our colorful pie chart and click on the measure we have previously added to the **Labels** mark, as shown in *Figure 5.23*:

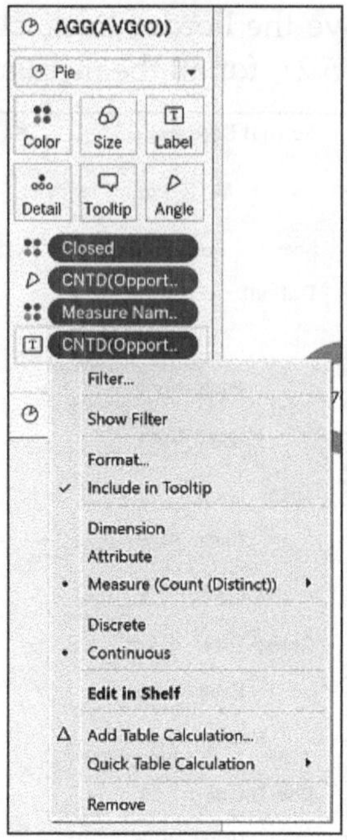

Figure 5.23: *Selecting measure pill*

24. Click on **Add Table Calculation**. A new menu will open, as shown in *Figure 5.24*:

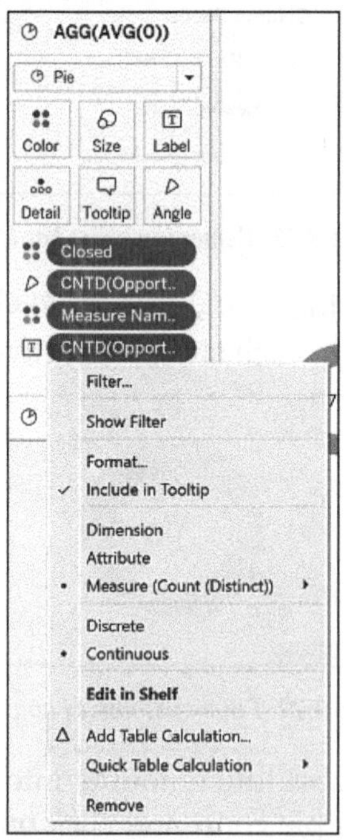

Figure 5.24: *Adding table calculation*

25. In the menu that opens, select **Percent of Total** from the **Calculation Type** menu, as shown in *Figure 5.25*:

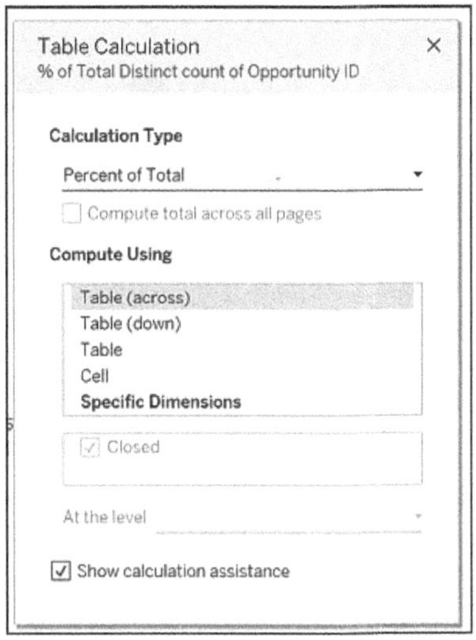

***Figure 5.25:** Setting calculation to Percent of Total*

26. The absolute numbers have now changed into percentages, as shown in *Figure 5.26*:

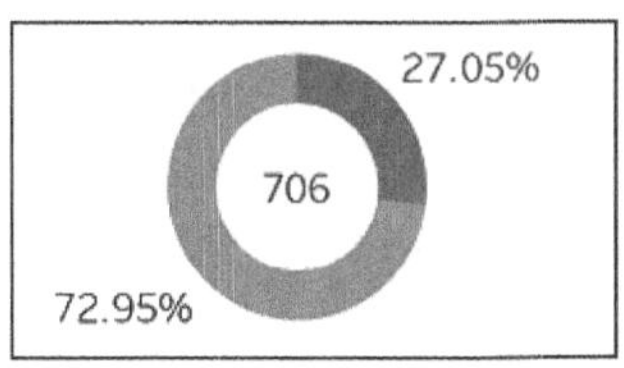

***Figure 5.26:** Measure values converted to percentages*

27. It is possible to have both percentages and absolute numbers by dragging your measure on the **Label** mark in the colored pie menu, as shown in *Figure 5.27*:

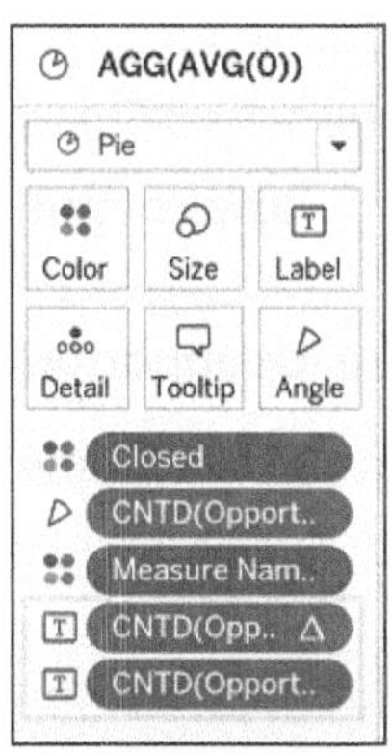

***Figure 5.27:** Adding second measure pill for both values*

28. To further aid comprehension, we will add the dimension to the **Label** as well, and proceeded to format the menu as shown in *Figure 5.28*:

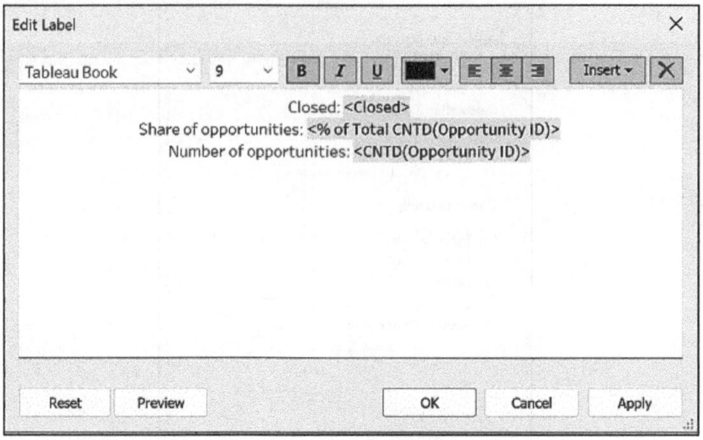

Figure 5.28: Formatting label marks

The final donut chart should look similar to the one in *Figure 5.29*:

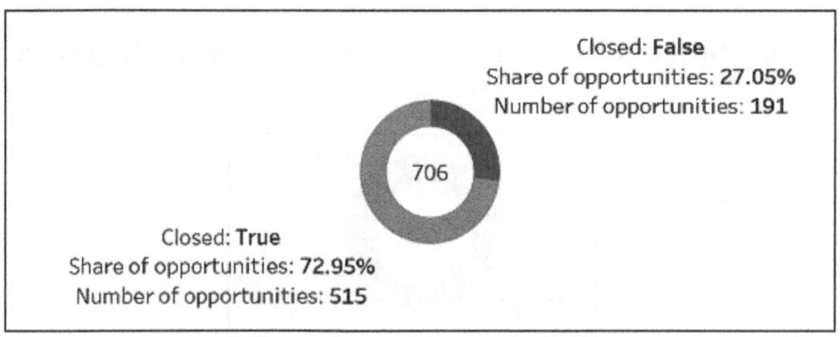

Figure 5.29: Final informative donut chart

Filters and calculated fields

We will again use donut charts to look at the ratio of lost to won opportunities per lead source. To do so, we will have to perform two operations:

- Filter the stage so that it only shows opportunities that have been either Lost or Won.
- Create a new field that labels each opportunity as lost, won, or still open.

From a new sheet, the steps to perform are as follows:

1. Drag **Stage** to the **Filters** card. A menu will open, as shown in *Figure 5.30*:

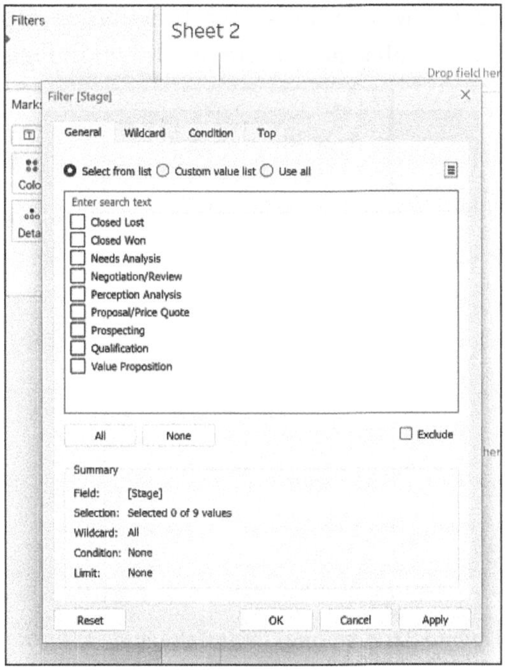

***Figure 5.30:** Adding Stage filter*

2. Select **Closed Lost** and **Closed Won** from the available list and press **OK**, as shown in *Figure 5.31*:

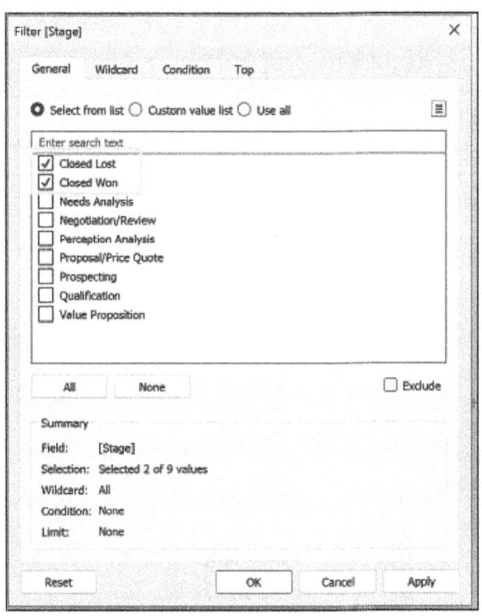

***Figure 5.31:** Selecting specific Stage values to filter*

3. There are several ways to create a calculated field in Tableau. The two most popular ones are the following:

a. Click on the caret next to the search function on top of your dimension list, then select **Create Calculated Field**, as shown in *Figure 5.32*:

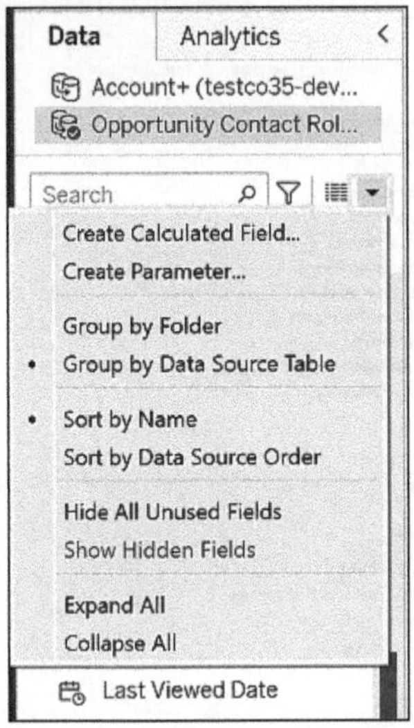

Figure 5.32: Accessing Create Calculated Field option

b. From the **Analysis** menu at the top of your sheet, click on **Create Calculated Field** , as shown in *Figure 5.33*:

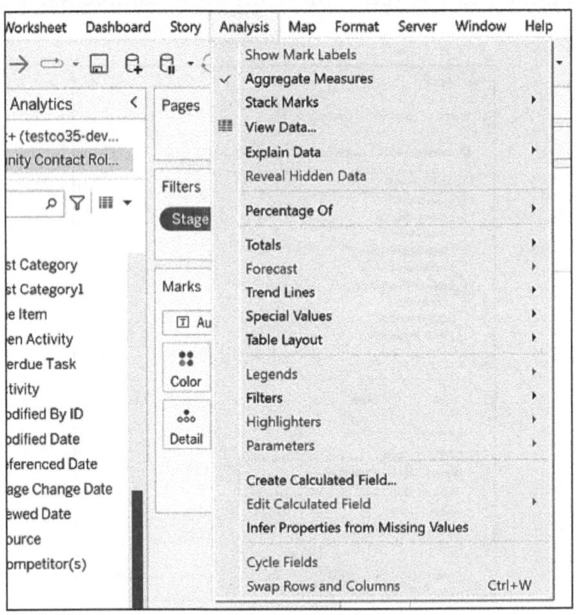

Figure 5.33: Accessing Create Calculated Field via Analysis menu

4. The calculated field window will now open. In this window, you can find five things, as shown in *Figure 5.34*:
    1. **Calculation title:** This is where you can type the name you will give to the new field you are creating.
    2. **Calculation area:** This is where you will write the logic that determines the output of the field you are creating.
    3. **Function list:** This is the list of ready-made functions available to use, which are not too dissimilar from what you can find in Excel or SQL. When you select a function, Tableau shows you what it does and gives you an example of how to use it.
    4. **Apply button:** Clicking this button will create your calculated field or modify your calculated field but will not close the window. It is useful if you are trying different calculations until you set on the final one.
    5. **OK button:** Clicking this button will create your calculated field or modify your calculated field, then close the window. It is useful if you are satisfied with the calculation.

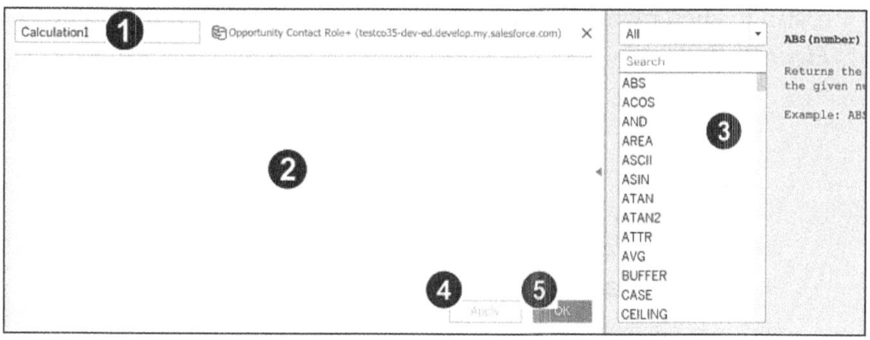

***Figure 5.34:** Calculated Field window overview*

6. Since we want to create a new field based on Stage, we will use an IF function. The formula is as follows:

```
IF [Stage] = 'Closed Lost' THEN 'Lost'
ELSEIF [Stage] = 'Closed Won' THEN 'Won'
ELSE 'Still Open'
END
```

7. As a title, we will write **`Lost, Won or Open`**, then press **OK**, as shown in *Figure 5.35*:

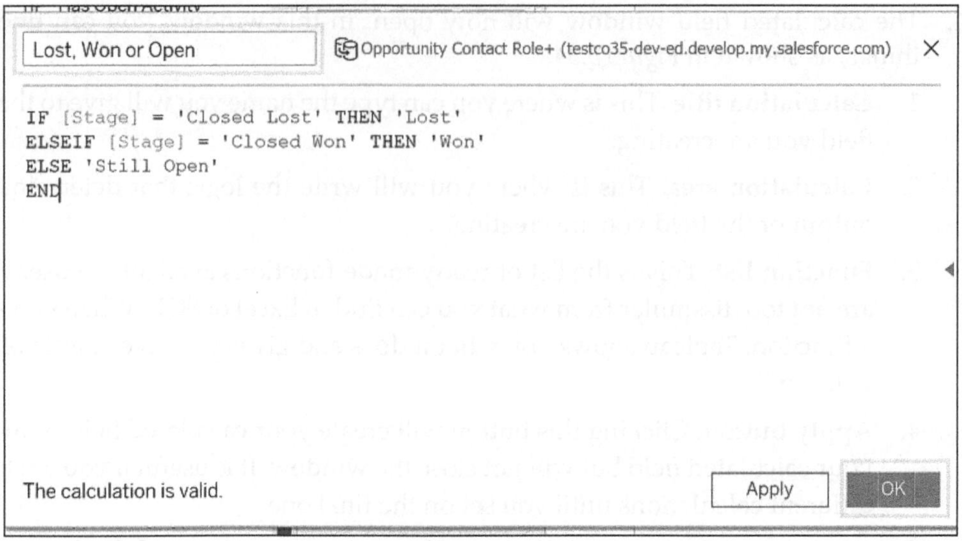

Figure 5.35: Creating Lost, Won or Open calculated field

Calculated fields are automatically added to the list of fields and can be distinguished by the little equal sign that precedes their data type, as shown in *Figure 5.36*:

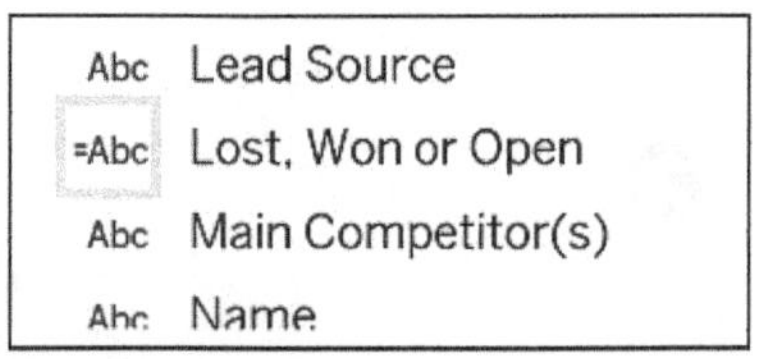

Figure 5.36: New calculated field added to dimensions list

You can always change a calculated field in Tableau, just by right clicking on the name and selecting **Edit** from the menu that opens, as shown in *Figure 5.37*:

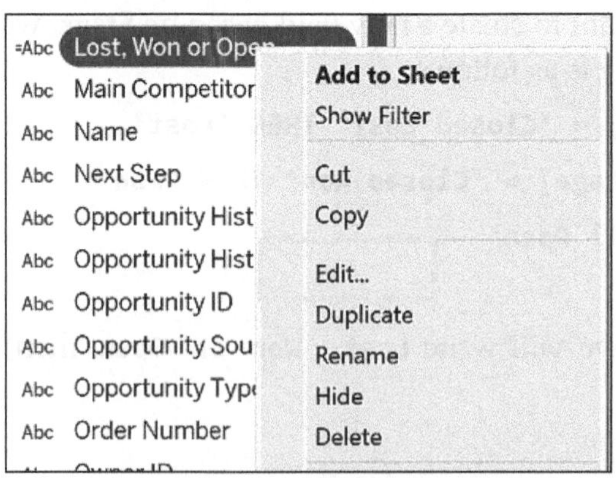

Figure 5.37: Editing a calculated field

5. Now that you have filtered your Opportunities and created a new calculated field, follow the steps in the previous section to create a new donut chart. The final result should look something like *Figure 5.38*:

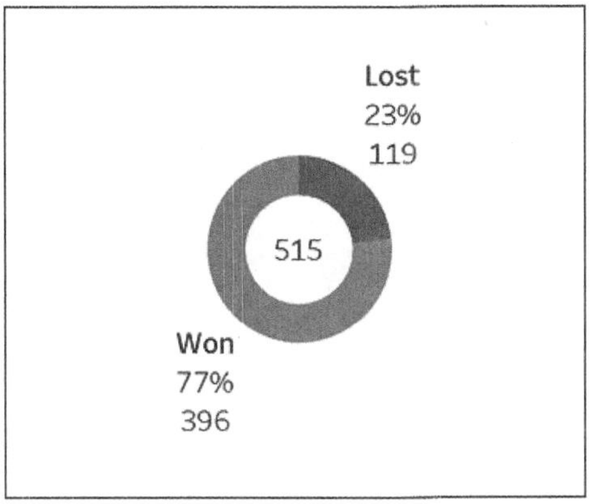

***Figure 5.38:** Final donut chart with calculated field*

6. To compare the share of lost and won opportunities by lead source so we will drag **Lead Source** to **Columns**, as shown in *Figure 5.39*:

***Figure 5.39:** Adding Lead Source to Columns shelf*

7. Tableau has created a series of donut charts, one for each lead source, as shown in *Figure 5.40*:

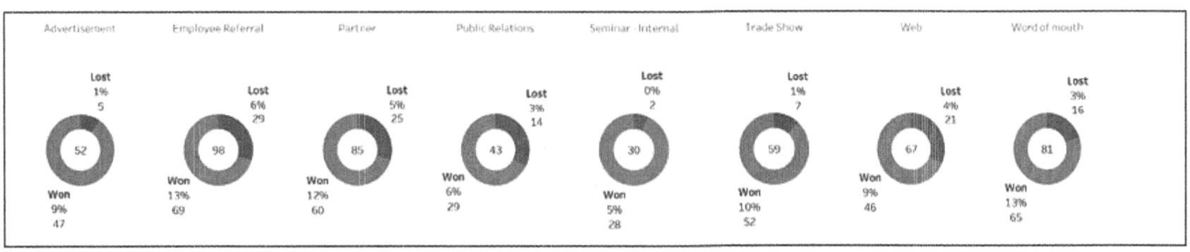

***Figure 5.40:** Donut charts showing breakdown by Lead Source*

8. We can see that some lead sources provide opportunities that are more likely to close, but our calculation does not show the share of lost and won opportunities per lead source.

   To change it, click on the field used for the share calculation. It has a triangle next to its name, as shown in *Figure 5.41*.

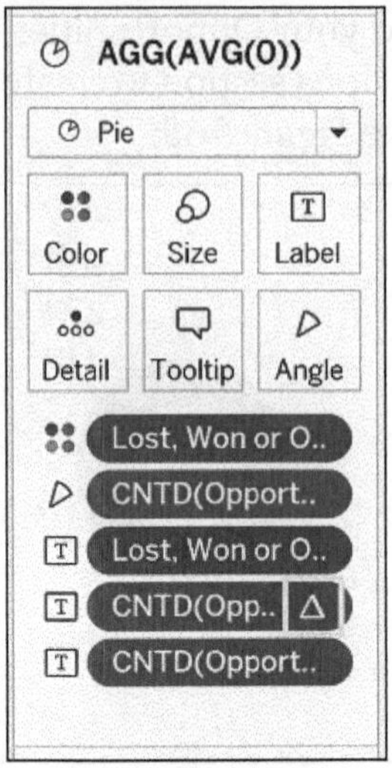

Figure 5.41: Selecting share calculation pill

9. From the menu that opens, click on **Edit Table Calculation**, as shown in *Figure 5.42*:

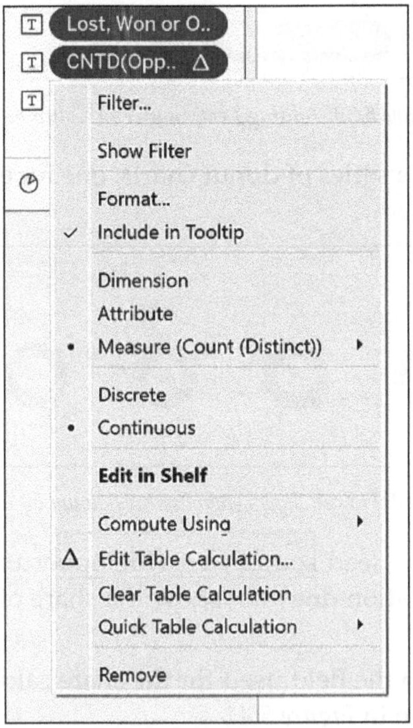

Figure 5.42: Accessing Edit Table Calculation

10. From the menu that opens, click on **Cell**, then click on the x in the top right corner to close the menu, as shown in *Figure 5.43*:

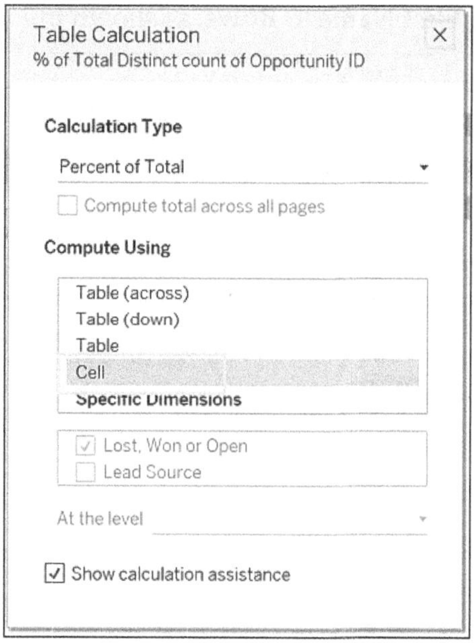

Figure 5.43: *Changing table calculation to Cell level*

Your calculation should now be correct, as shown in *Figure 5.44*:

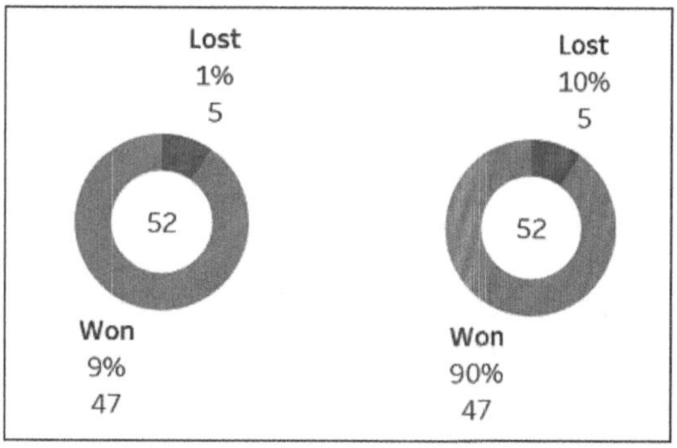

Figure 5.44: *Correct donut chart calculations*

Bar-in-bar chart

A useful case for Salesforce and Tableau is to compare sales performance across time and against a target. To showcase this, we will create a bar-in-bar chart that tracks the Expected Amount for each Opportunity Owner.

In the following example, User table has been added to the Opportunities standard connection in order to show the names, rather than the IDs of the opportunity owners. We will now proceed to build the bar-in-bar chart, using the following steps:

1. To start with, drag **First Name** to **Rows**, as shown in *Figure 5.45*:

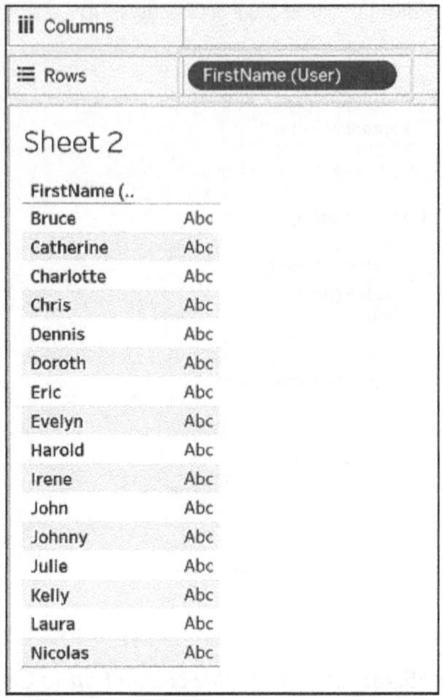

Figure 5.45: *Adding First Name to Rows shelf*

2. Next drag **SUM(Expected Amount)** to **Columns**, as shown in *Figure 5.46*:

Figure 5.46: *Adding Expected Revenue to Columns shelf*

We want to choose only Opportunities that relate to Q1 2022 or Q1 2023. Furthermore, for Q1 2022, we only want to look at Closed Won Opportunities.

We will, therefore, use a calculated field to look only at relevant opportunities. To add the calculated field, follow these steps:

1. First, use one of the methods shown in the previous section to create a new calculated field. In the window that opens, we will write:

```
([Fiscal Year]=2023
AND
[Fiscal Quarter]=1)
OR
([Fiscal Year]=2022
AND
[Fiscal Quarter]=1
AND
[Stage]=”Closed Won”)
```

2. Then we will give it a name, say **Relevant Opportunities**.
3. Finally, we will click on **OK**, the final result is shown in *Figure 5.47*:

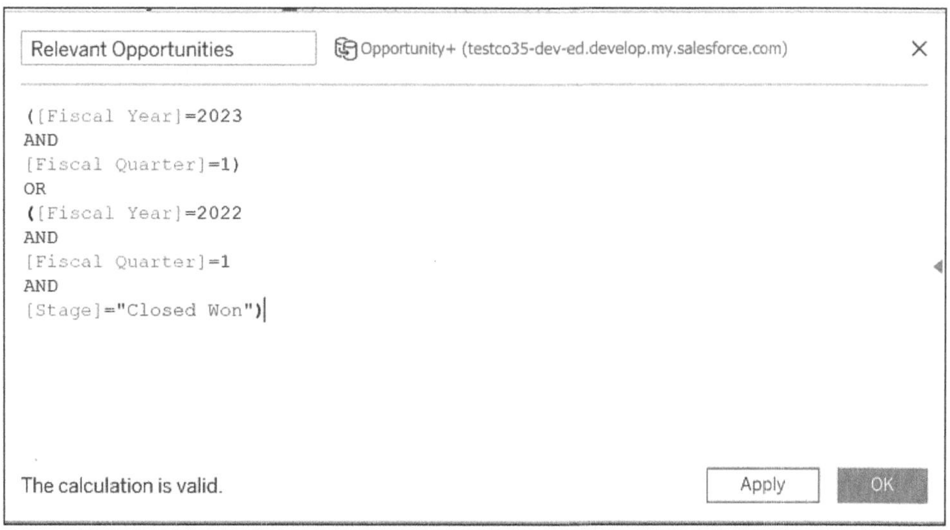

Figure 5.47: *Creating relevant opportunities calculated field*

4. Now that the field has been created, drag it onto the **Filters** card and select **True** from the menu that opens, then click **OK**, as shown in *Figure 5.48*:

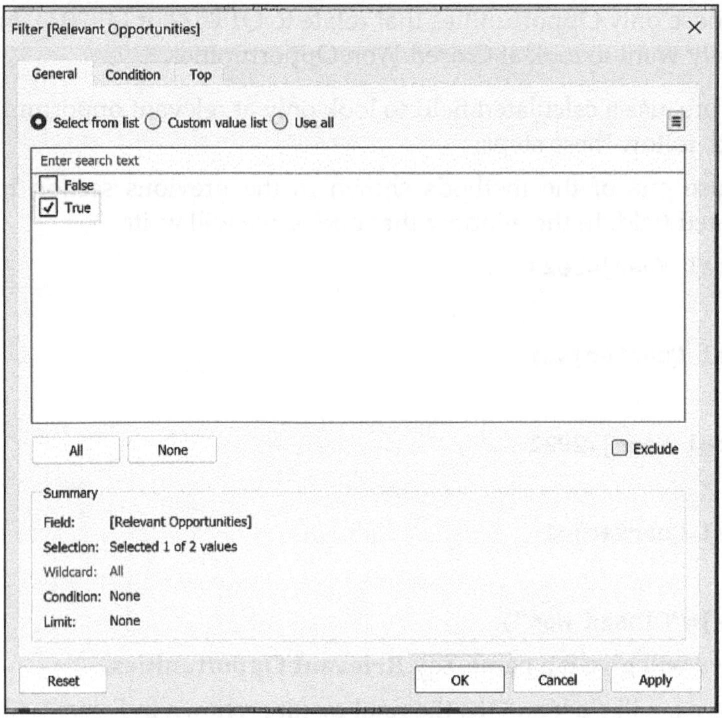

***Figure 5.48:** Filtering data to relevant opportunities*

5. Tableau will now filter all the opportunities to show only the ones that meet our criteria, as shown in *Figure 5.49*:

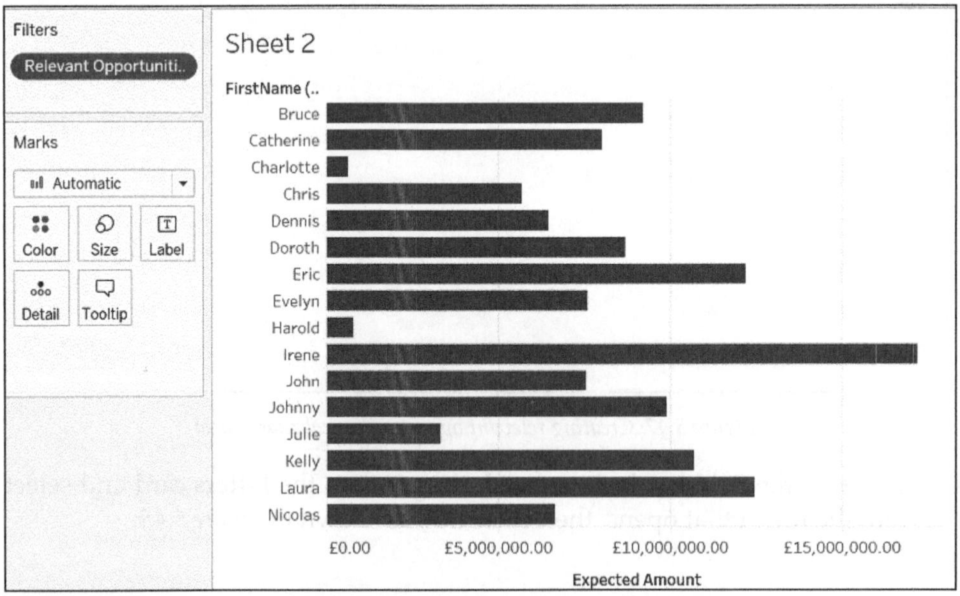

***Figure 5.49:** Data filtered to specified opportunities*

6. Now drag the **Fiscal Year** to the **Size** mark, as shown in *Figure 5.50*:

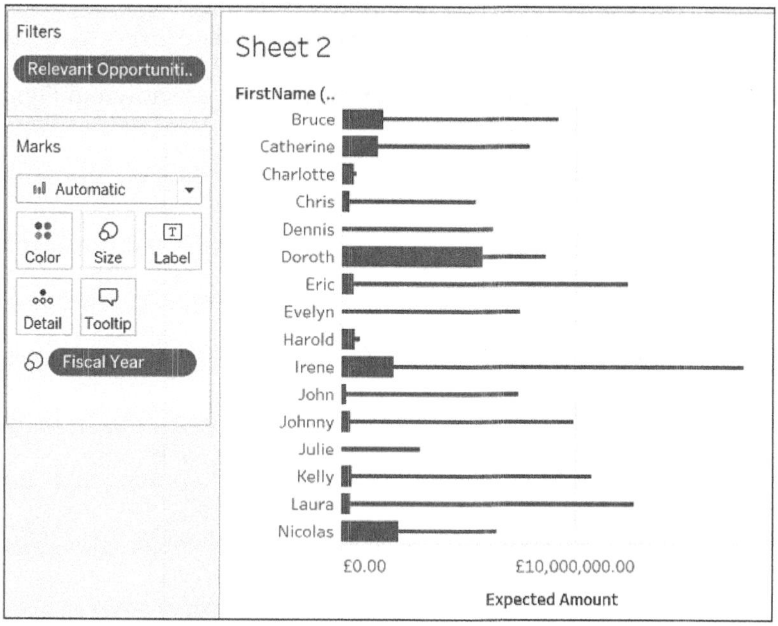

Figure 5.50: *Adding Fiscal Year to Size mark*

7. Drag the **Fiscal Year** to the **Color** mark, as shown in *Figure 5.51*:

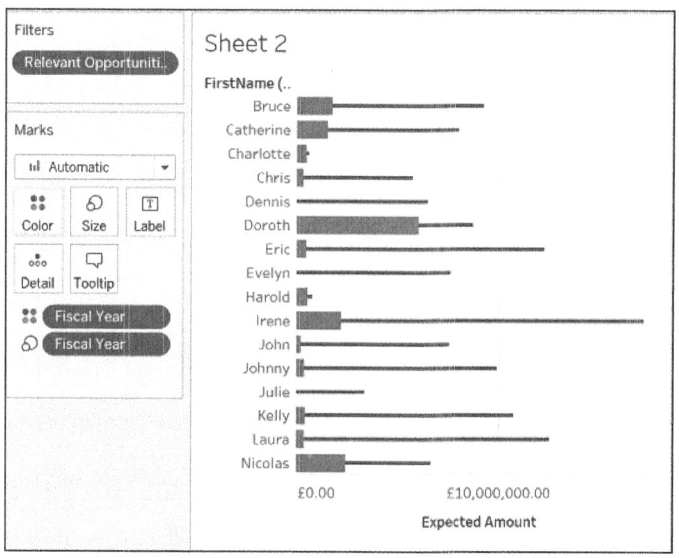

Figure 5.51: *Adding Fiscal Year to Color mark*

8. Right now, Tableau is putting the amount for 2022 after the amount for 2023, but that is not what we want for a bar-in-bar chart. To change that, click on the **Analysis** menu at the top of your screen, as shown in *Figure 5.52*:

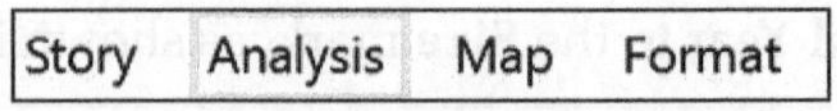

***Figure 5.52:** Accessing Analysis menu*

9. Click on **Stack Marks** in the menu that opens now, as shown in *Figure 5.53*:

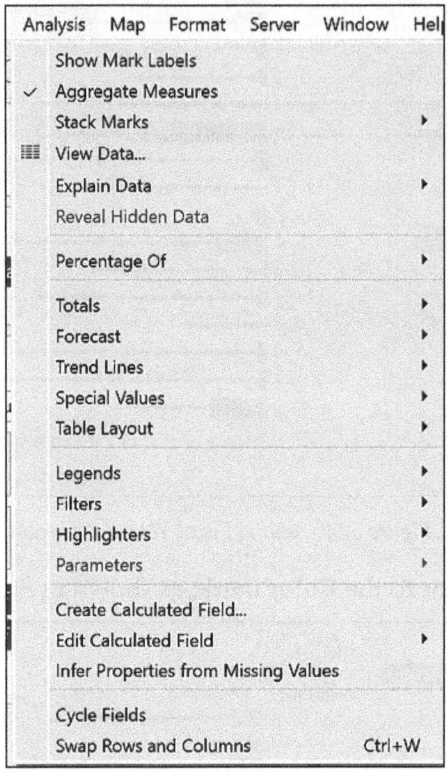

***Figure 5.53:** Turning off Stack Marks option*

10. Select **Off**, as shown in *Figure 5.54*:

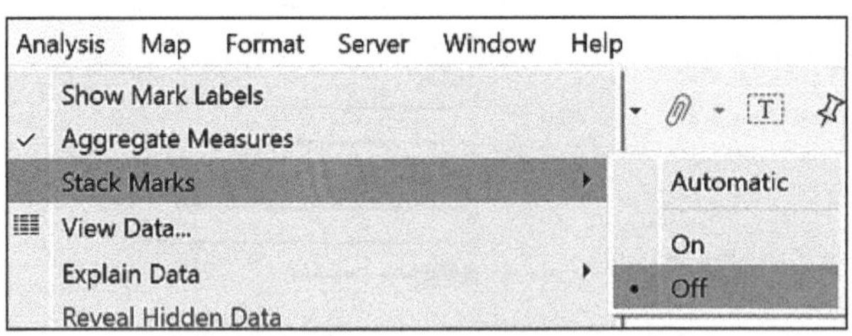

***Figure 5.54:** Stack Marks set to Off*

11. Your bar chart should look something like the chart below, as shown in *Figure 5.55*:

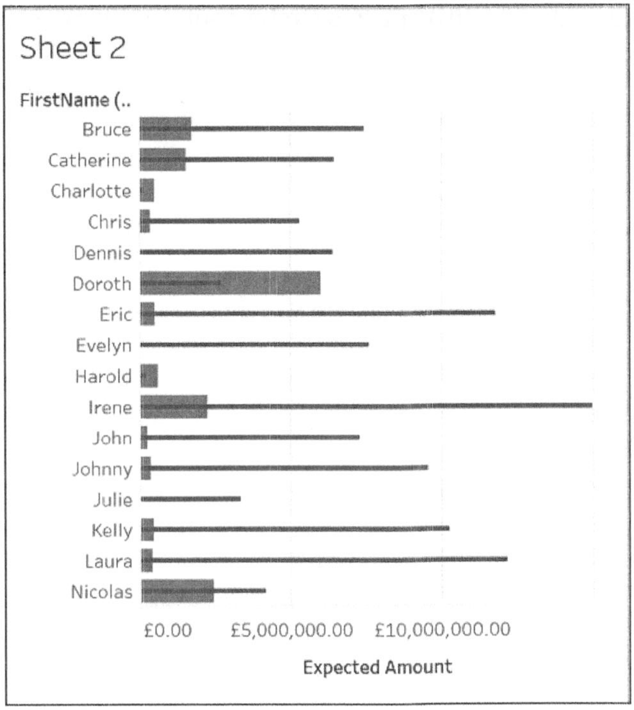

Figure 5.55: Final bar-in-bar chart

12. As you can see, Doroth and Charlotte's performance this year is better than last. Everybody else, however, seems to be having a much tougher time.

Maps

Maps are a convenient way of visualizing geographical information and unlocking insights that may be harder to grasp using other formats. Tableau supports maps out of the box and can showcase information up to zip code and street level. To create a map, follow these steps:

1. The easiest way to create a map is to double-click on the geographical field of your choice. Geographical fields are indicated by a small globe next to their name, as shown in *Figure 5.56*:

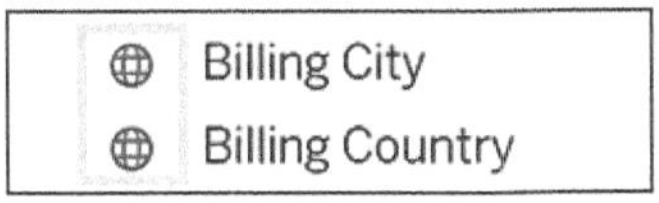

Figure 5.56: Geographical fields marked with globe icon

2. Any field can become a geographical field; the steps to follow have been described in *Chapter 3*.

In this case, the field of choice is **Billing Zip Code**; double clicking on it produces the map you can see in *Figure 5.57*:

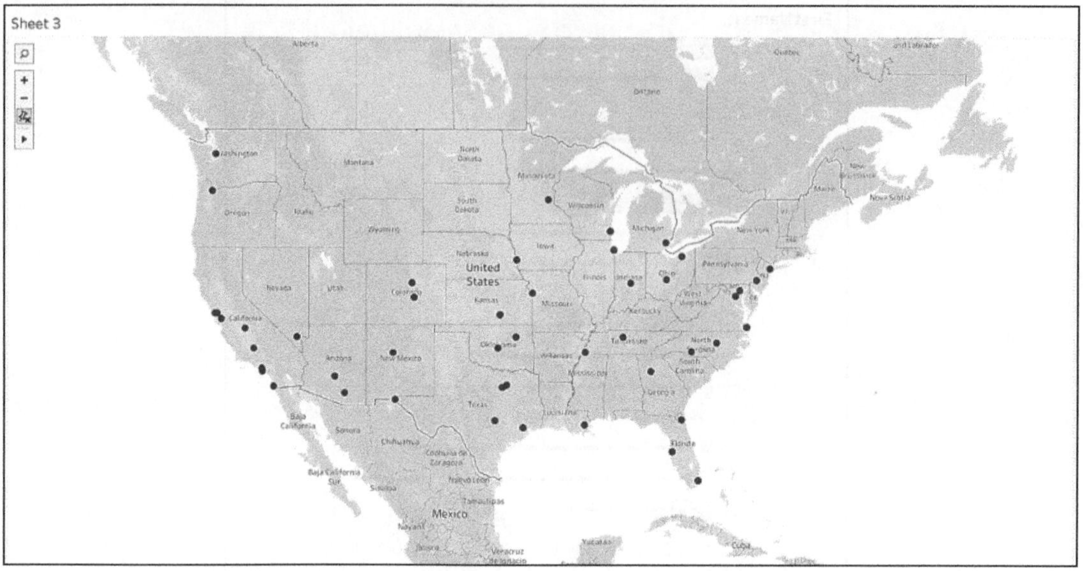

***Figure 5.57:** Initial map created by double clicking geo field*

Before proceeding, you will notice a small set of icons on the top left corner of your map, as shown in *Figure 5.58*:

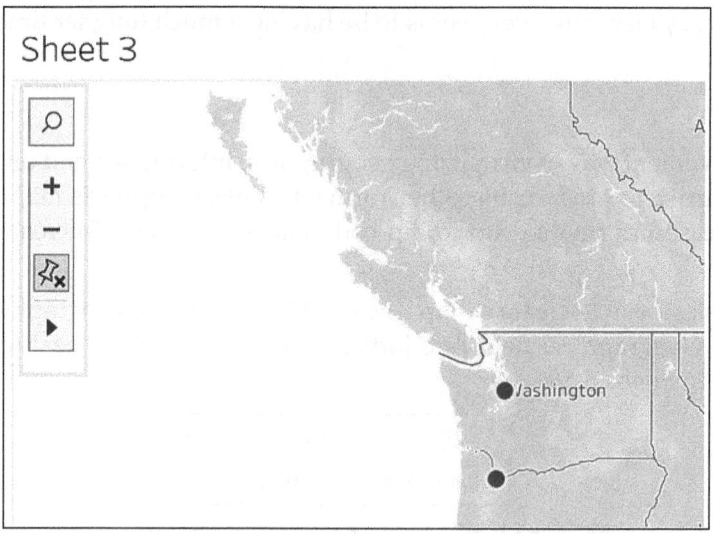

***Figure 5.58:** Map interaction tool icons*

This menu, shown in *Figure 5.59*, lets you interact with the map and customize the user experience.

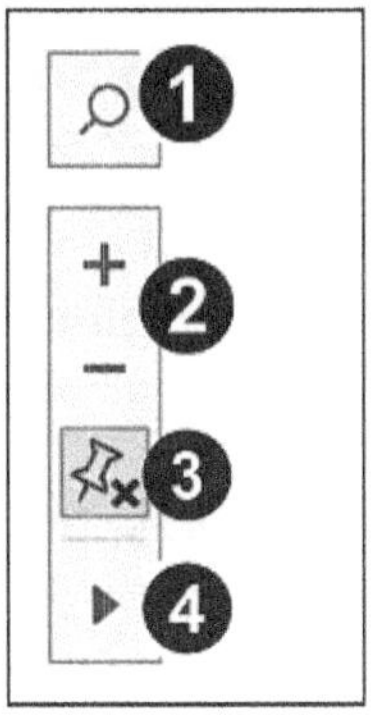

***Figure 5.59:** Additional map tools menu*

Each icon has a function, as follows:

1. **Search**: By clicking on this icon, you can type the name of a specific location you are looking for (that is, London or 09212).
2. **Zoom in and out**: Clicking on the plus sign will zoom into the map, and clicking on the minus sign will zoom out.
3. **Reset button:** Clicking on this button will remove any zoom in or out or any manual adjustments you may have performed on the map.
4. **Tool selection:** Clicking on this icon will open a small sub-menu, from which you can select a variety of tools, as shown in *Figure 5.60*:

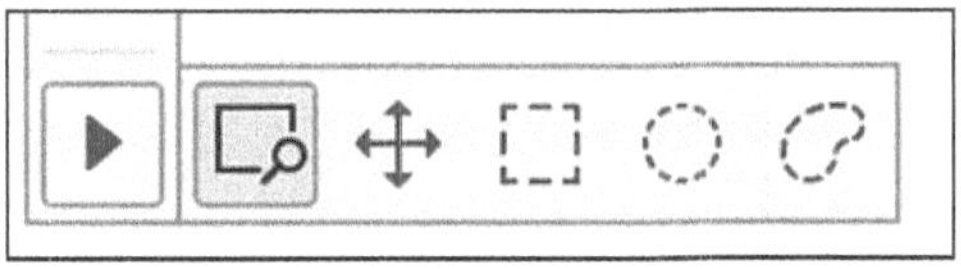

***Figure 5.60:** Map selection tool options*

- **Zoom area**: Selecting this tool will change your cursor to a lens that you can use to zoom in on a specific part of the map.
- **Pan**: Selecting this tool will allow you to rearrange the map manually.
- **Rectangular/Radial/Lasso Selection**: Each tool allows you to select different points in the map according to your needs.

When sharing your map with your end users, you may want to give them access to all these tools or restrict the experience. You may prefer to restrict the tools available for users if you have set up your map to view only a portion. This may be the best display option if that is the area where your insights are concentrated. To do so, follow these steps:

1. Click on the **Map** menu at the top of your Tableau window, as shown in *Figure 5.61*.

***Figure 5.61:** Accessing Map menu*

2. Click on **Map Options**, as shown in *Figure 5.62*:

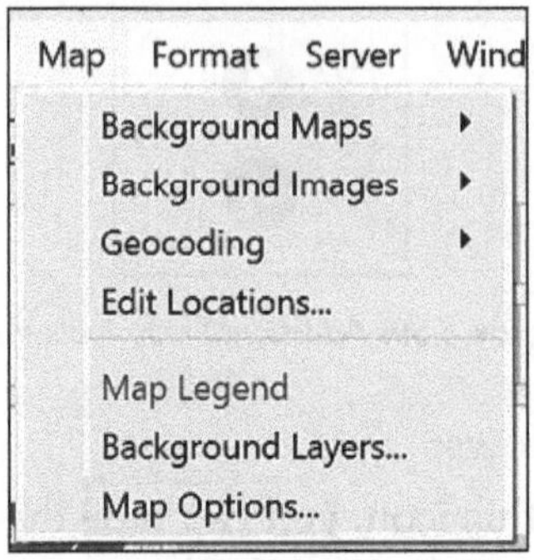

***Figure 5.62:** Opening Map Options dialog*

3. A menu will open on top of the map, as shown in *Figure 5.63*:

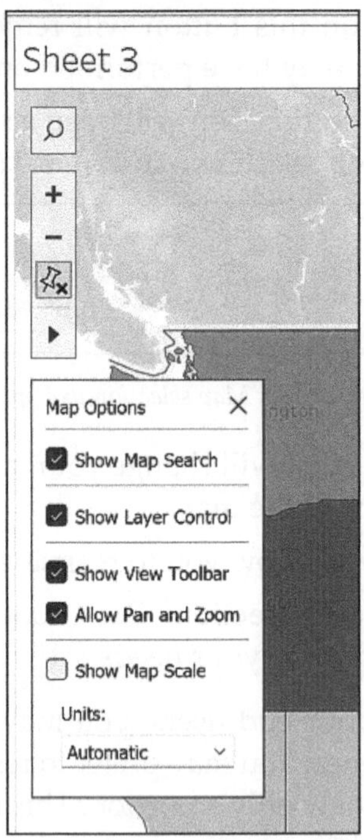

***Figure 5.63:** Map options dialog*

4. Unticking an item will prevent the end user from accessing the tool. As you can see below, this time we do not let the end user customize its interaction with the map, and the map tools have, therefore, disappeared, as shown in *Figure 5.64*:

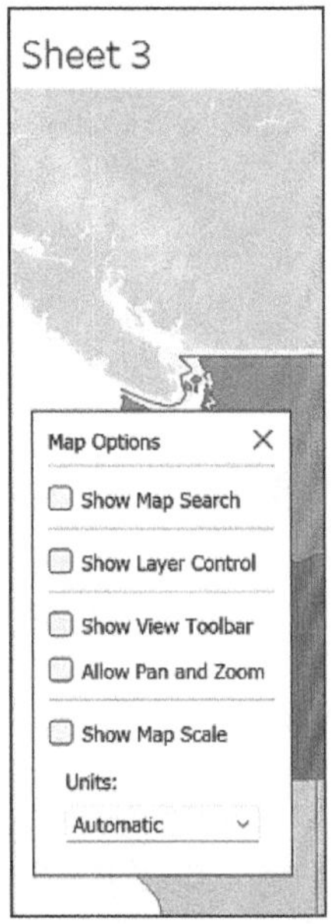

Figure 5.64: Limiting map tools available to user

Filled map

To create a filled map:

1. Double click on the **Billing State/Province** field.
2. Drag **Expected Revenue** on the **Colors** mark.
3. Change the mark type to **Maps**, as shown in *Figure 5.65*.

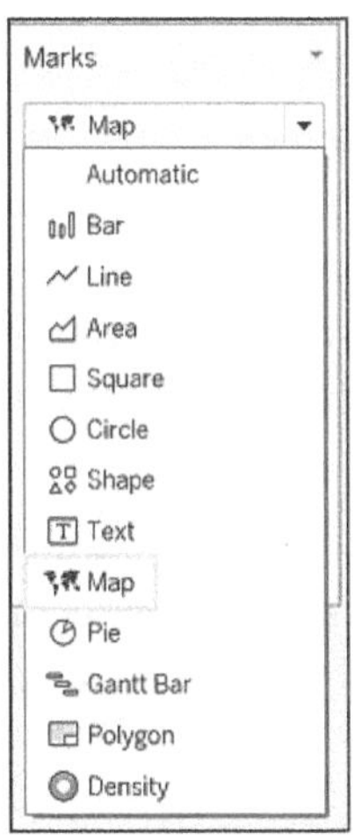

Figure 5.65: Creating filled map

The result should look something like the map in *Figure 5.66*:

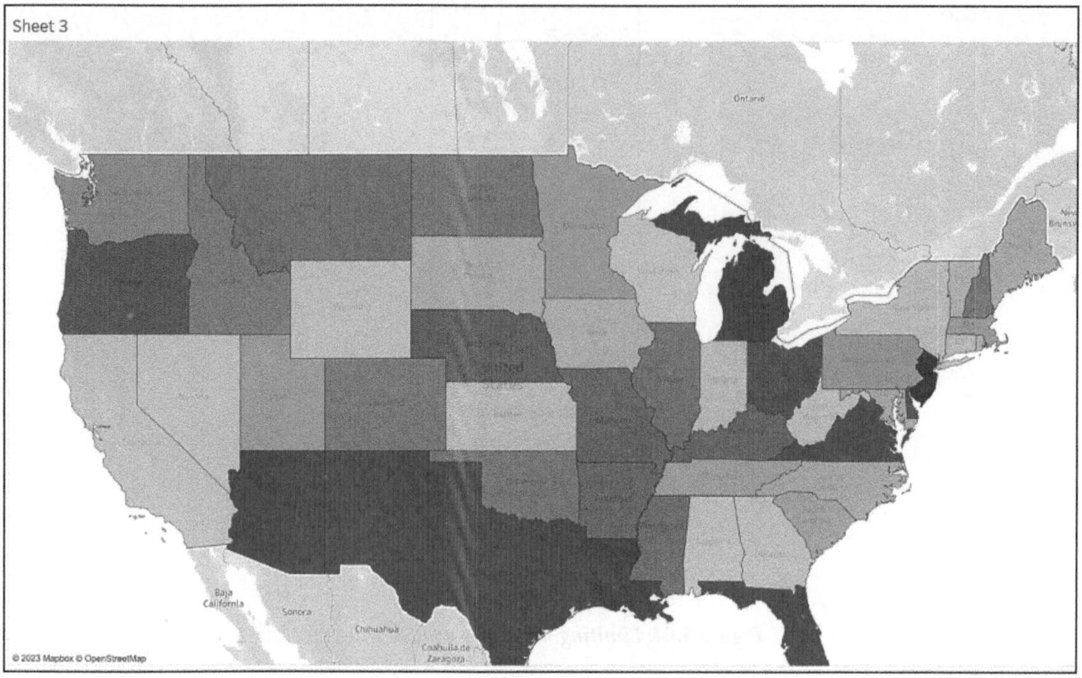

***Figure 5.66:** Final filled map visualization*

We can use the tools mentioned above to zoom in and bring to the center of the view exactly the section of the map we want to show. From here we can see there is a distinct geographic pattern to the revenue we expect, with clusters of states that are close geographically and also present higher revenues.

Conclusion

In conclusion, this chapter has provided you with the knowledge and tools needed to create more advanced visualizations like donut charts, bar-in-bar charts, and maps. You've also learned how to harness the power of filters and calculated fields to customize and improve your data analysis. By following the steps outlined in this chapter, you can now dive deeper into your Salesforce data using Tableau, and more effectively communicate your insights to stakeholders.

Understanding geographical patterns, funnel analysis, and performance tracking are just a few of the many insights you can gain from the techniques discussed in this chapter. With this knowledge in hand, you can leverage the full potential of Tableau and Salesforce to make better-informed decisions for your organization. Keep experimenting with different visualizations and techniques as you continue to explore these powerful tools and uncover new insights into your data.

In the next chapter, we will move on to discussing advanced topics for visualization with Tableau.

CHAPTER 6

Dealing with Complex Visualizations, Customizations, and APIs

Introduction

In this chapter, we explore the untapped potential of Tableau in conjunction with Salesforce CRM data, diving deep into advanced visualizations to unlock richer insights. From a comprehensive look at advanced capabilities, including Sankey charts and calendar-based visualizations, to mastering customized geographical data visualizations, we will take you through the endless customization possibilities that Tableau offers. We will cap it off with a look at third-party integrations, examining how they can enrich your visualizations and optimize decision-making. This chapter aims to inspire you to push boundaries, fostering an innovative and data-curious culture within your organization. Let us embark on this exciting journey together to unravel the full extent of Tableau's power and transform your CRM data into meaningful, actionable information.

Structure

The chapter covers the following topics:

- Introducing the advanced capabilities of Tableau
- Using extensions in Tableau

Objectives

Upon completing this chapter, readers will be able to understand the advanced capabilities of Tableau in visualizing CRM data by learning to create and interpret advanced charts such as Sankey diagrams and calendar visualizations and exploring ways to customize visualizations using geographical data. They will also discover how to utilize third-party integrations to augment data visualization capabilities and develop the necessary skills to uncover deeper insights and patterns from your CRM data. Finally, they will gain proficiency in transforming raw CRM data into meaningful, actionable visual insights and learn to use Tableau features and tools effectively to support data-driven decision-making processes.

Introducing advanced visualizations

At this point, we should feel quite comfortable with creating charts in Tableau, so we will now take it a bit further by looking at creating charts that require to make use of the full range of customization options in Tableau. We will use calculated fields and table calculations and finally bring together several datasets to showcase the possibilities of spatial analysis in Tableau's maps.

Pareto charts

There is a rule in business (and sometimes in other areas of life) that states that 80% of consequences can be attributed to 20% of causes. It is called the *Pareto rule* and can be applied in a business context, too. For example, it is not uncommon for 80% of the revenues to be driven by only 20% of the accounts. Whether your business abides by this rule can be proven with a Pareto chart, which also allows you to identify the accounts driving your sales.

For this chart, we will be using the Account object joined with the Opportunity object in Salesforce, but you can also do it only with the Opportunity object.

We will start by selecting only the data we need and the opportunities that have turned into revenues. To do this:

1. Drag **Stage** into the **Filters** tab, as shown in *Figure 6.1*:

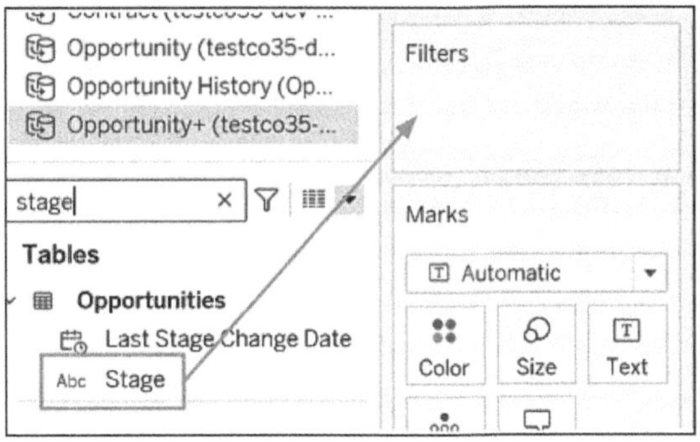

Figure 6.1: *Add Stage filter for Closed Won*

2. Select **Closed Won**, as can be seen in *Figure 6.2*:

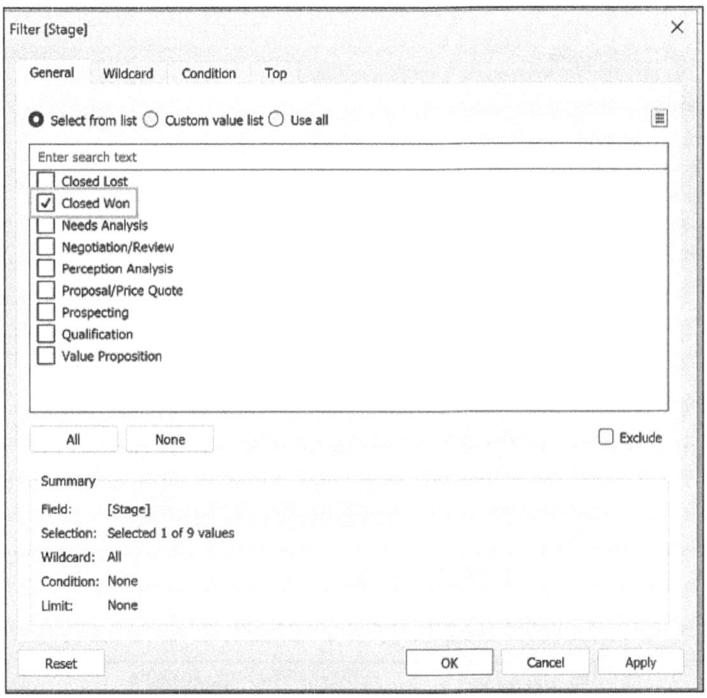

Figure 6.2*: Stage filter set to Closed Won*

3. Click **Ok**.

Now it is time to start creating the chart. The steps are as follows:

1. Drag **Id** from the **Accounts** object to columns, as shown in *Figure 6.3:*

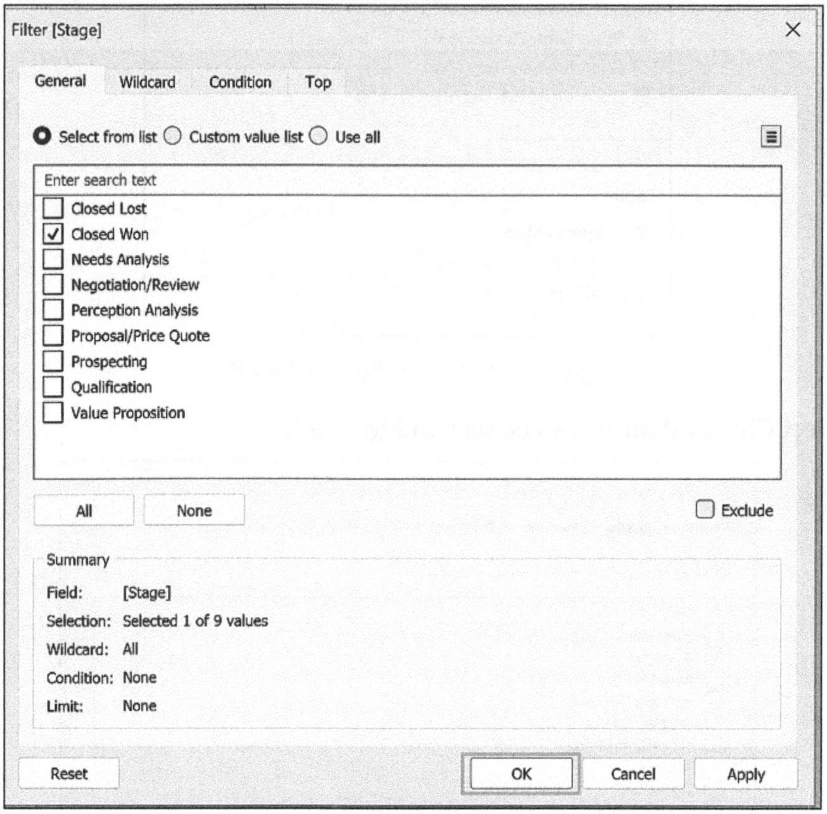

Figure 6.3: *Drag ID to Columns*

2. Drag **Amount** into the **Rows**, as can be seen in *Figure 6.4:*

Figure 6.4: *Drag Amount to Rows*

3. Click on the caret on the ID pill and select **Sort**, as shown in *Figure 6.5*:

Figure 6.5: *Sort the ID field*

4. A new menu will now appear. Follow the steps in the order below:
   a. On this menu, choose to sort by field.
   b. Select **Descending**.
   c. Select **Amount** from **Field Name**.
   d. Select **Sum**, if not already selected.
   e. Close the menu.

5. Your chart should look similar to the one below:

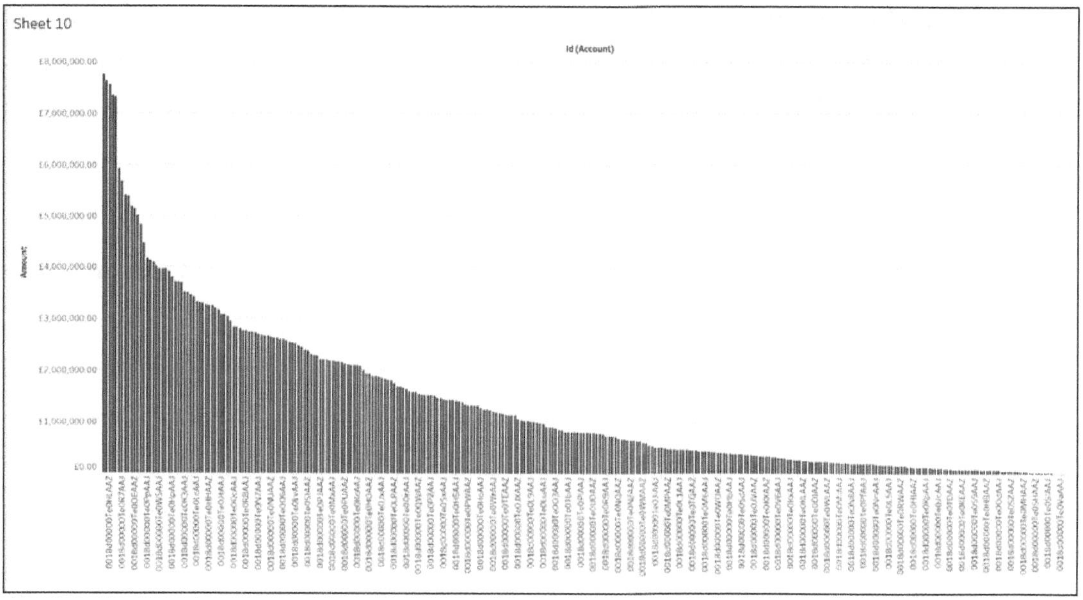

Figure 6.6: *Chart sorted by Amount descending*

6. Click on the caret on the **SUM(Amount)** pill and select **Add Table Calculation.**

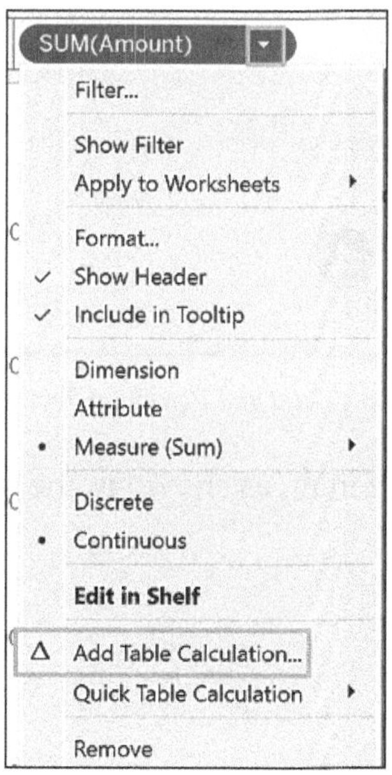

Figure 6.7: *Add Running Total table calculation*

A new menu will appear (*Figure 6.8*), follow the steps in the order below:

1. Select **Running Total** from the **Primary Calculation Type**.
2. Select **Sum**, if not already selected.
3. Select **Specific Dimensions** from the **Compute Using** menu; make sure **Id** is selected.
4. Tick **Add Secondary calculation**.
5. Select **Percent of Total** from the **Secondary Calculation Type**.
6. Select **Specific Dimensions** from the **Compute Using** menu; make sure **Id** is selected.
7. Close the menu.

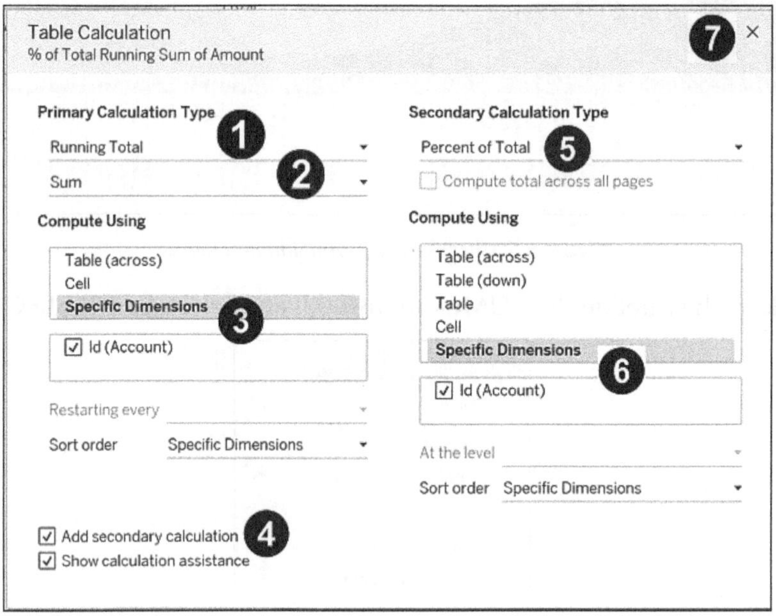

Figure 6.8: *Running Total and Percent of Total calculations added*

Your chart should look much different, as shown in the following figure.

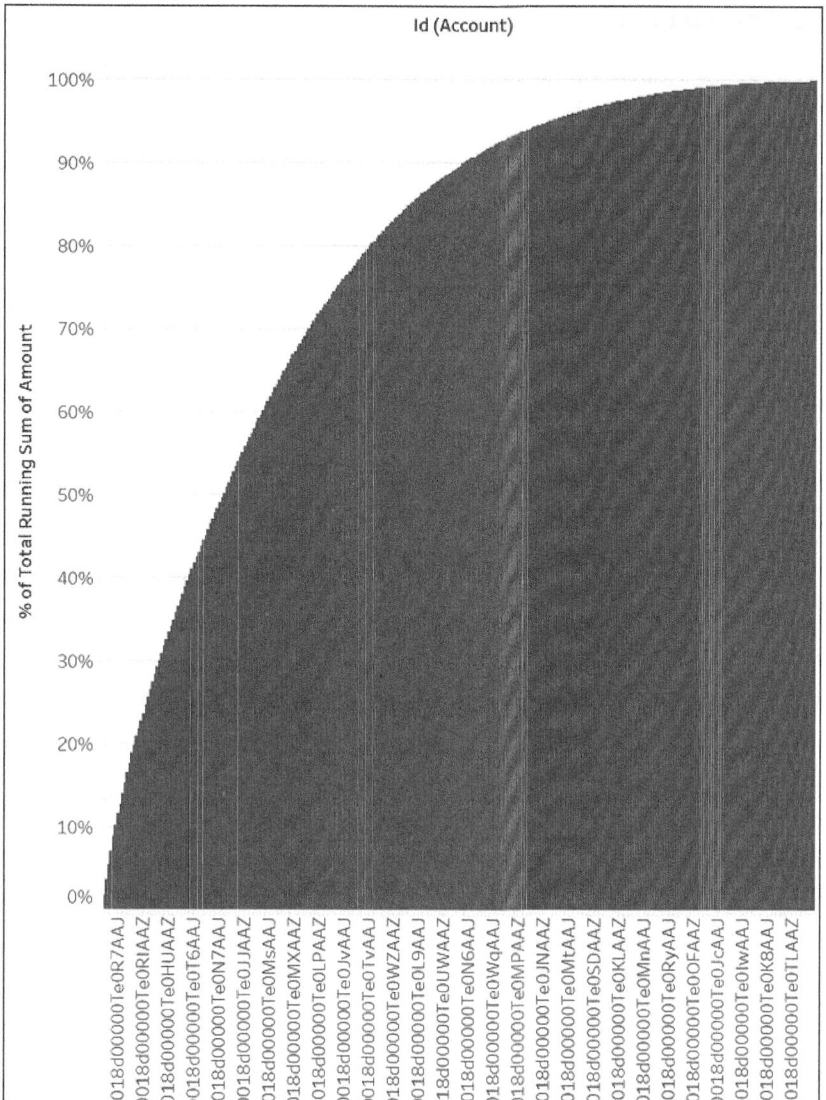

Figure 6.9: *Cumulative chart*

We will use a reference line to understand where 80% of our sales line is. To add a reference line, follow these steps:

1. Click on the **Analytics** tab next to **Data**, as shown in *Figure 6.10*:

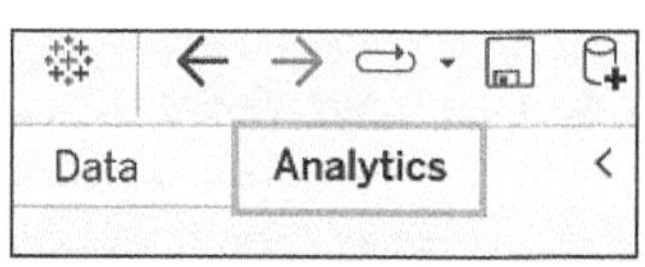

Figure 6.10: *Click on Analytics tab*

2. Select **Constant Line**, as can be seen in *Figure 6.11:*

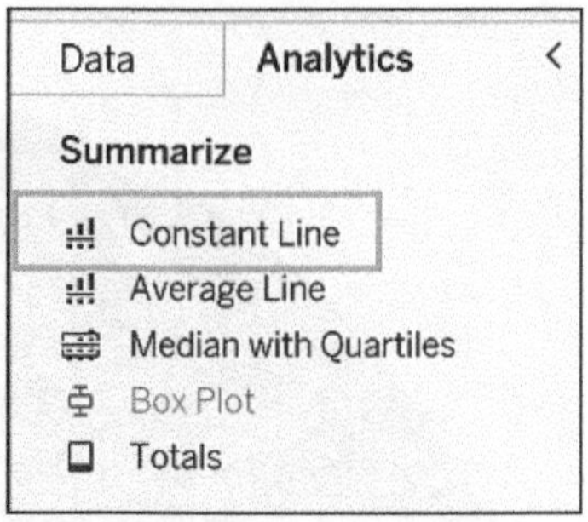

Figure 6.11: *Select Constant Line*

3. Drag it to the **Table** menu which now hovers on your chart, as shown in *Figure 6.12:*

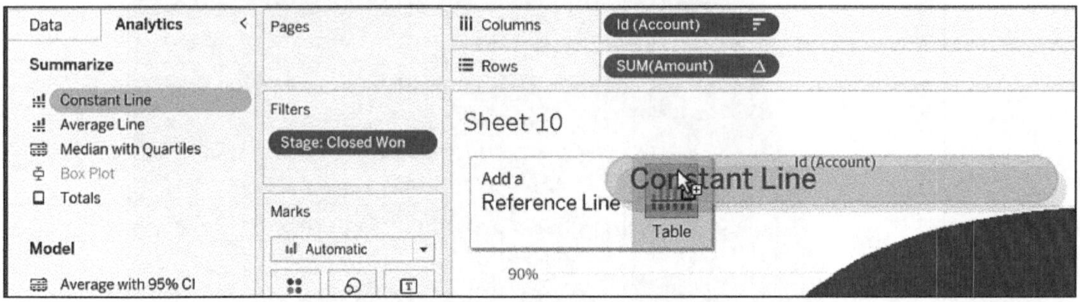

Figure 6.12: *Drag Constant Line to chart*

4. Type **`0.8`** in the menu that opens, as seen below:

Figure 6.13: *Set value to 0.8*

You now have your chart with your reference line, but we can make it a bit clearer. Follow these steps:

1. Right click on the Reference line you just created and click on **Edit**, as seen in *Figure 6.14:*

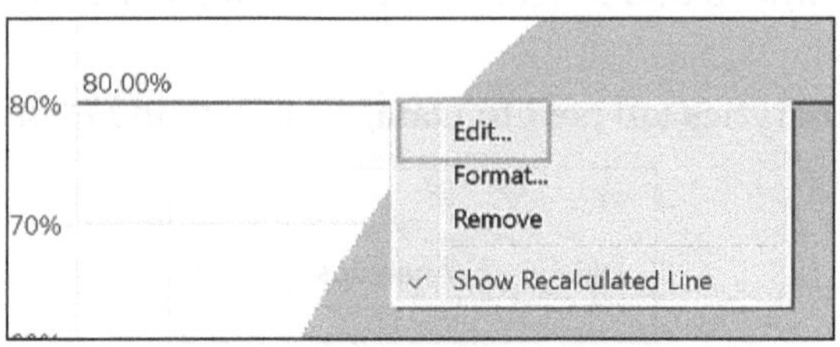

Figure 6.14: *Right click the reference line*

2. In the window that opens, choose **Custom** from the **Label** menu, as can be seen below:

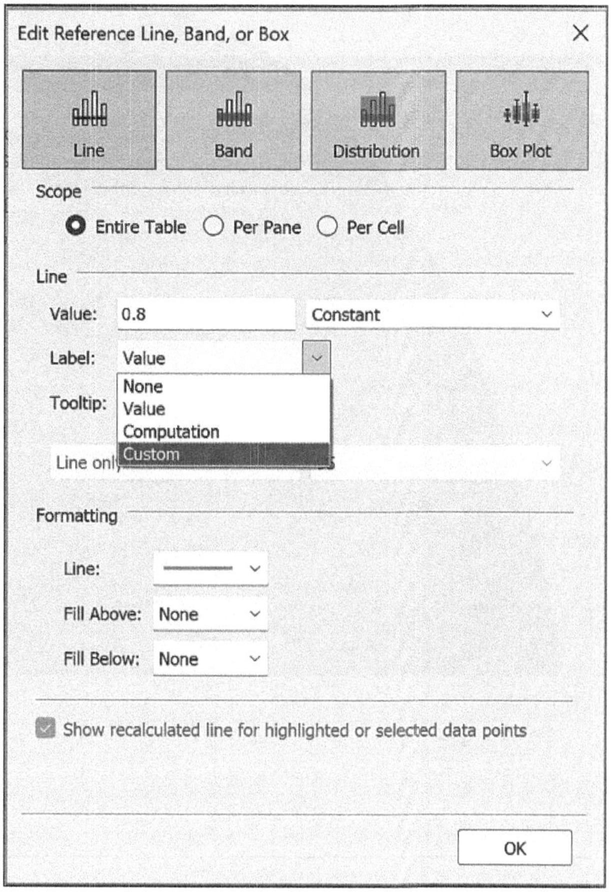

Figure 6.15: *Set custom label*

3. Write something that helps users understand what the line represents, for example, "80% of all sales come from the accounts below this line", as shown below:

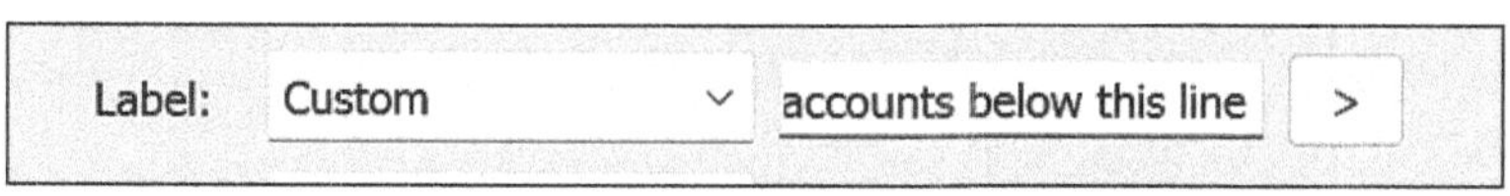

Figure 6.16: *Reference line label*

4. Click on **OK**.

We can see that the 80/20 rule does not apply to our case (*Figure 6.17*), but we cannot yet see clearly where that line is; it seems to be somewhere between 30 and 40%, but is that the case? We can find out exactly and, at the same time, improve our Tableau skills.

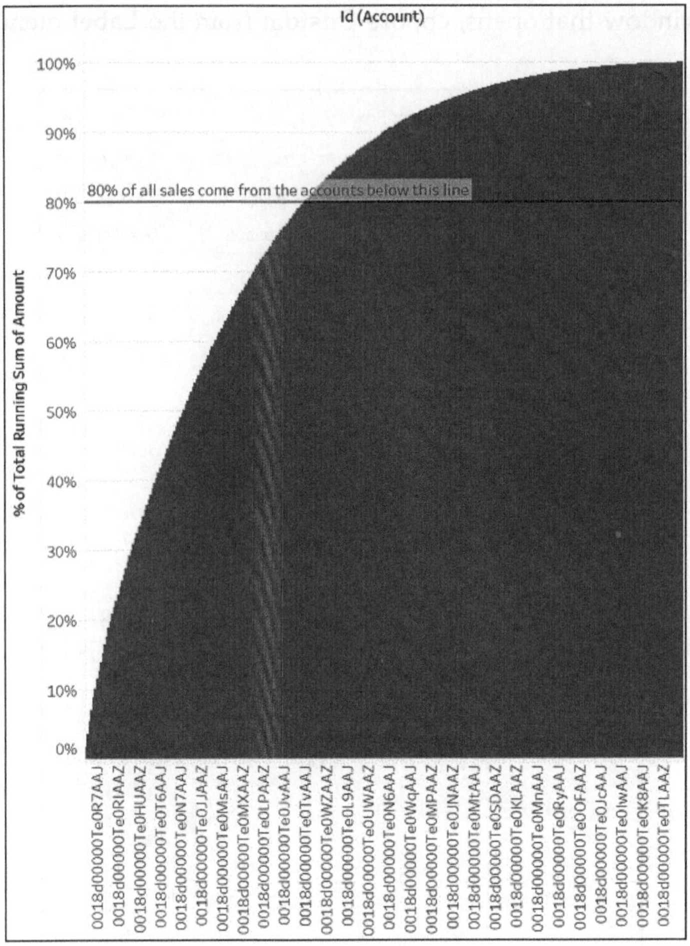

Figure 6.17: Copy Id field

For this next stage, press *CTRL* on your keyboard and drag the **ID** field from **Columns** to the **Detail** mark, as seen in *Figure 6.18*. This should copy not only the field but also the sorting we set up earlier.

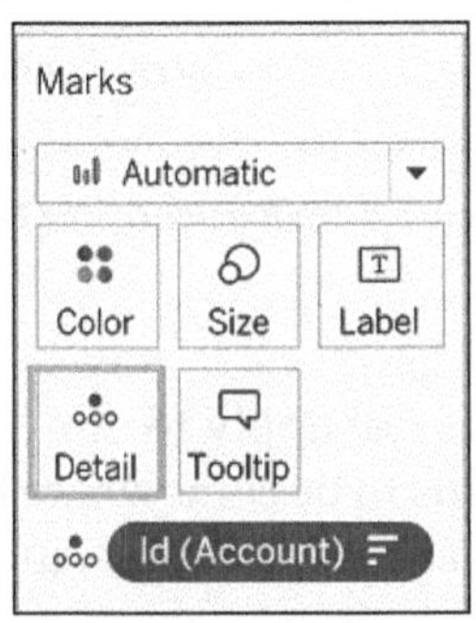

Figure 6.18: Id field copied

From here, follow these steps:

1. Click on the caret on the Id pill, hover on **Measure**, then select **Count (distinct)**, as seen in *Figure 6.19*:

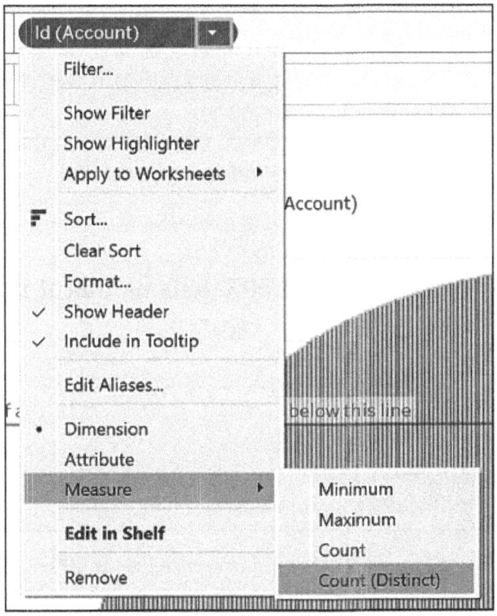

Figure 6.19*: Change Id measure to Count (distinct)*

2. Do not panic if your chart looks broken now; we are about to fix it. Click on the now green **ID** pill and apply the same table calculation we applied on the **SUM (Amount)** pill, with the same options, as shown below:

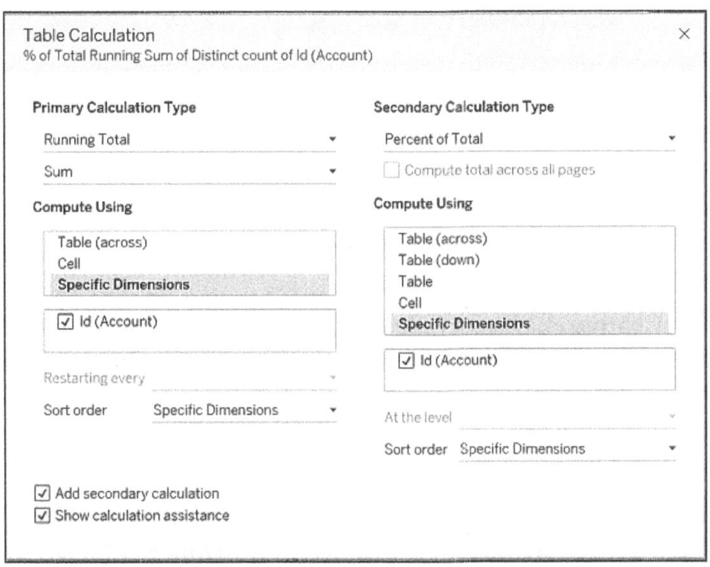

Figure 6.20: *Apply table calculations to copied Id field*

3. You now have a Pareto chart, which tells you that 37% of your accounts drive 80% of your revenues (*Figure 6.21*).

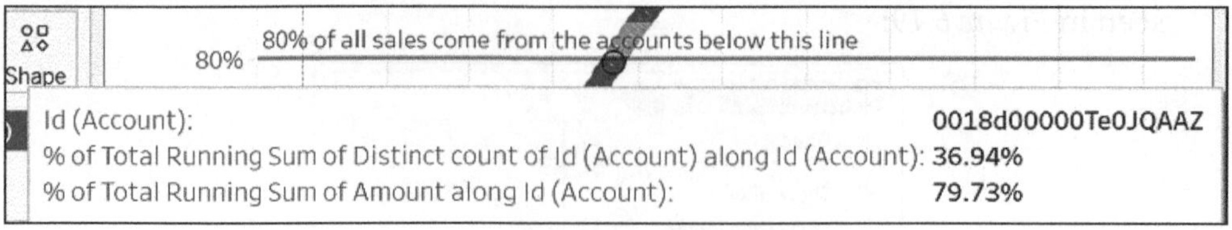

***Figure 6.21:** First reference line at 80%*

Some other insights are:

- Adding a second reference line at 50% tells us that it is 17% of our accounts that drive half of our sales, as shown in *Figure 6.22:*

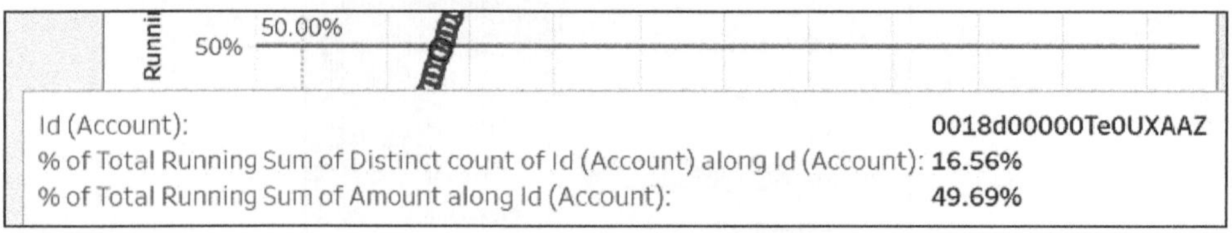

***Figure 6.22:** Second reference line at 50%*

- Adding a third reference line at 10% tells us that it is our sixth-largest account that drives 10% of our sales, as can be seen in *Figure 6.23:*

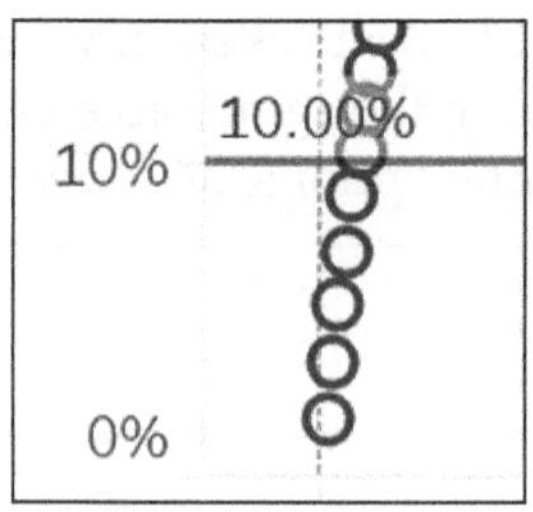

***Figure 6.23:** Third reference line at 10%*

Funnel charts

One of the most indicative charts for Salesforce data is the funnel chart, which is the chart in which we can follow the progression of our sales pipeline from initial contact to final conclusion.

For this chart, we will use the custom dataset Opportunity History that comes with this book. If you are working with real Salesforce data, you should be able to replicate this chart using the Opportunity History object from your Salesforce environment or your data warehouse, following the instructions in *Chapter 3 – Building and Integrating Data Pipelines*.

To create a funnel chart, follow these steps:

1. Filter out "Closed Lost" by using **Stage Name** as a filter and excluding "Closed Lost".
2. Drag **Stage Name** onto **Rows**, as shown in the following figure:

Figure 6.24: *Drag Stage Name to Rows*

3. Right-click on **Opportunity ID** and drag it to **Columns**. In the menu that opens, choose **Count Distinct** (*Figure 6.25*).

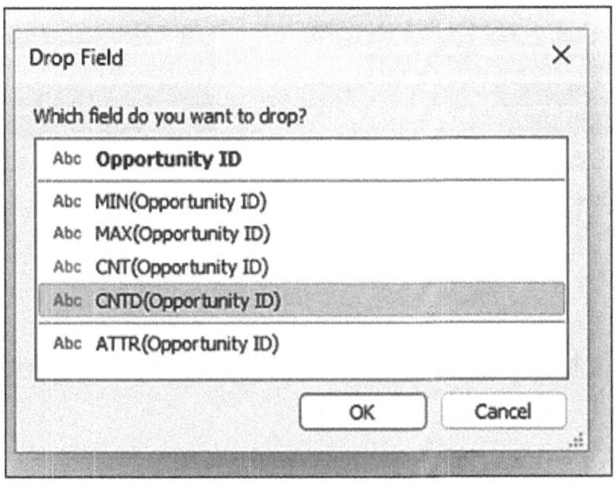

Figure 6.25: *Count distinct Opportunities by Stage*

4. Sort **Stage Names** in descending order according to the number of opportunities.

Figure 6.26: *Sort Stages by count descending*

We now need to *trick* Tableau into creating our funnel chart. To do so:

1. Right-click on **Opportunity ID**, drag it to **Columns**, and drop it next to the green pill you already have there, as shown in *Figure 6.27*:

***Figure 6.27:** Copy Opportunity Id to Columns*

You should now have two identical bar charts which look like the chart below:

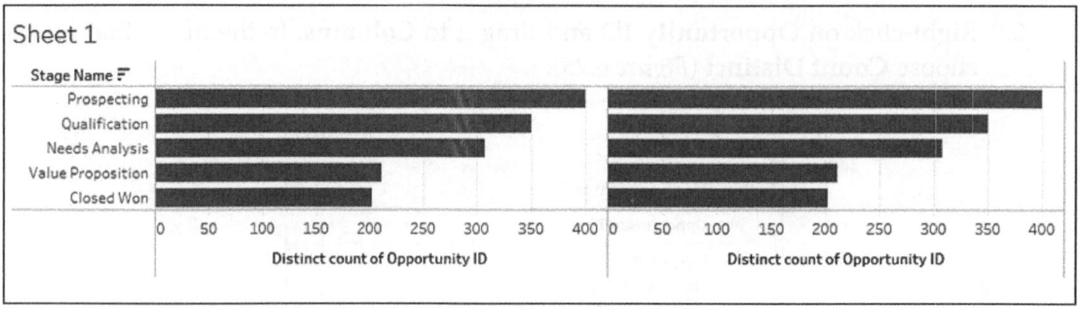

***Figure 6.28:** Two identical bar charts*

2. Right-click on the left axis and click **Edit Axis** from the menu that opens, as shown below:

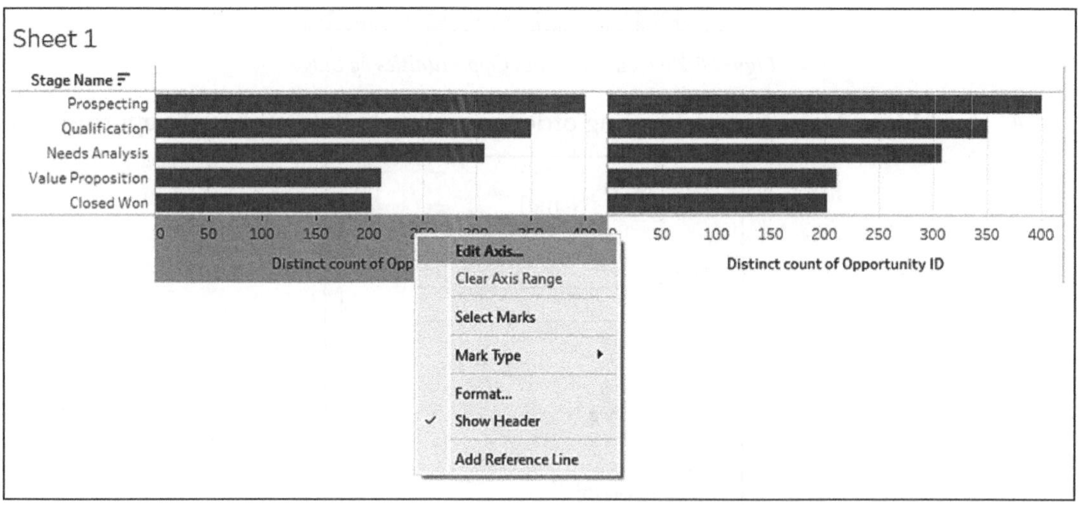

***Figure 6.29:** Copy Opportunity Id to Columns*

3. Select **Reversed**, as shown in *Figure 6.30*:

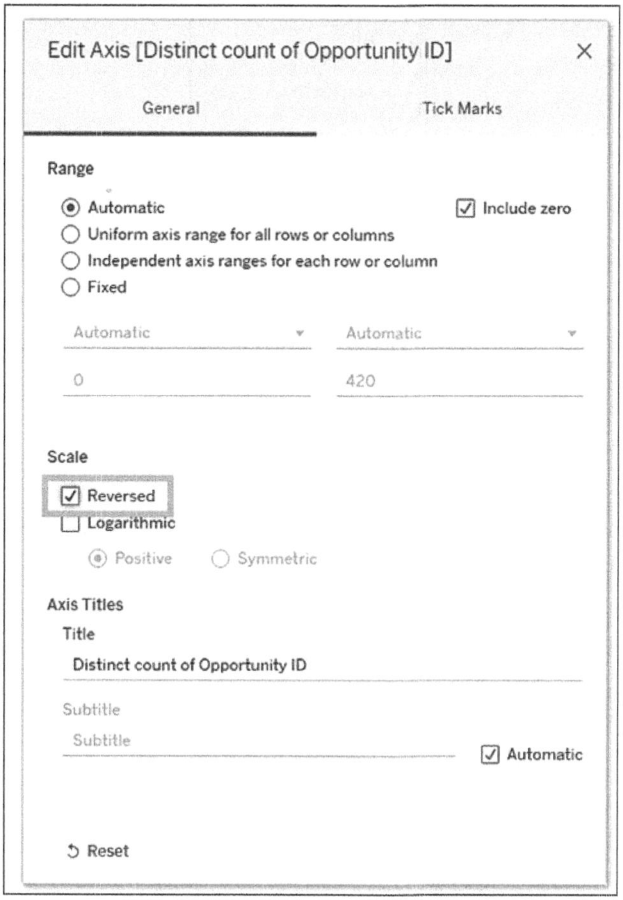

Figure 6.30: *Reverse left axis*

Your chart should now look like the one below, already much more like a funnel.

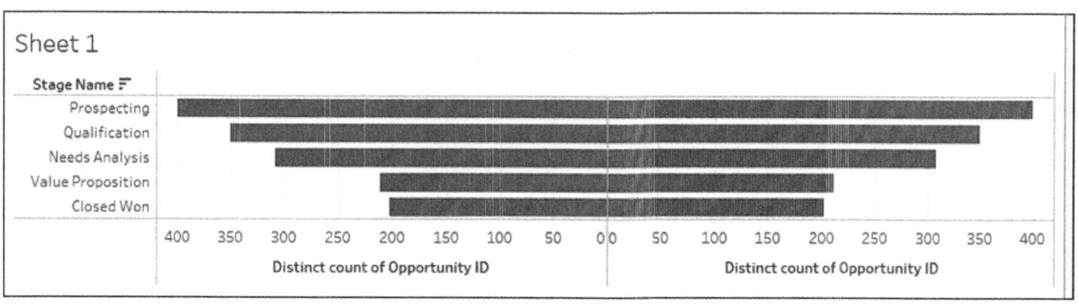

Figure 6.31: *Funnel*

4. Drag **Stage Name** to the **Color** mark in the **All** card, as shown in *Figure 6.32:*

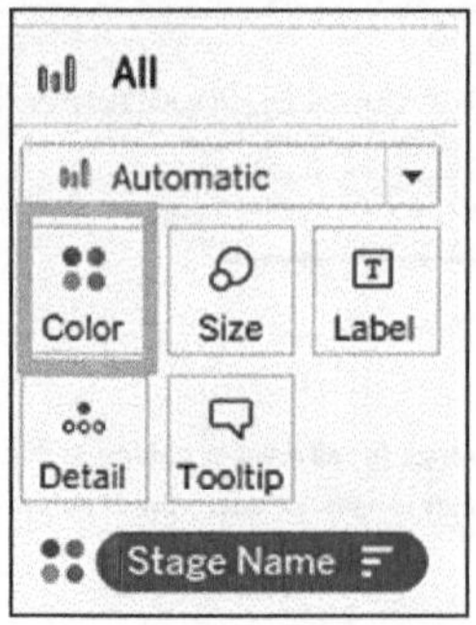

Figure 6.32: *Color Stages*

5. Press *Ctrl* on your keyboard and drag the **CNTD (Opportunity ID)** field to the **Label** mark in the **All** card, as shown in *Figure 6.33:*

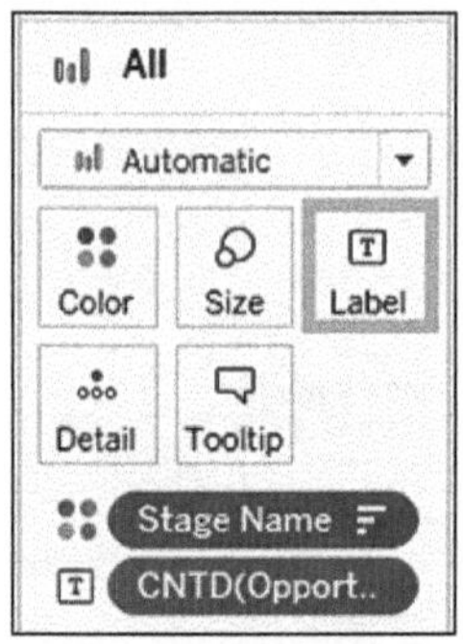

Figure 6.33: *Add label*

6. Click on the **Label** mark on the top **CNTD (Opportunity ID)** card, as shown in *Figure 6.34*:

Figure 6.34: *Select label*

7. In the **Alignment** menu, choose left, as shown in *Figure 6.35*:

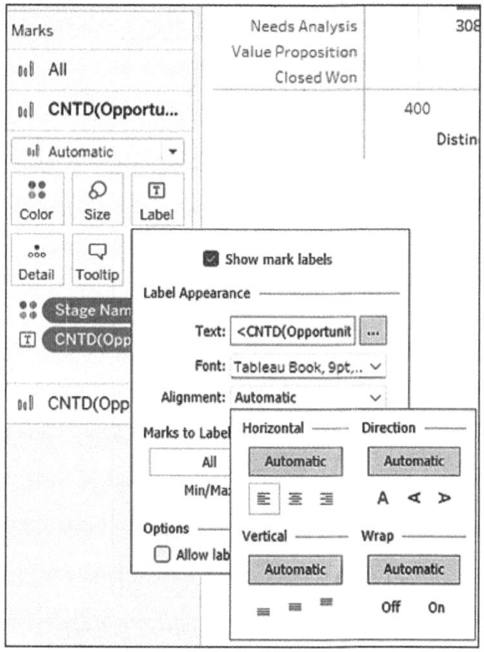

Figure 6.35: Align labels left

A funnel would not be a proper funnel without percentages, so we will create a new calculated field and paste the following formula:

This formula divides the number of opportunities at each stage by the number of opportunities in the first stage, thus giving us a view of the percentage of opportunities that continue to the next stage of our sales pipeline.

8. Give your calculated field a name. The one below, for example, is called "Share of total".

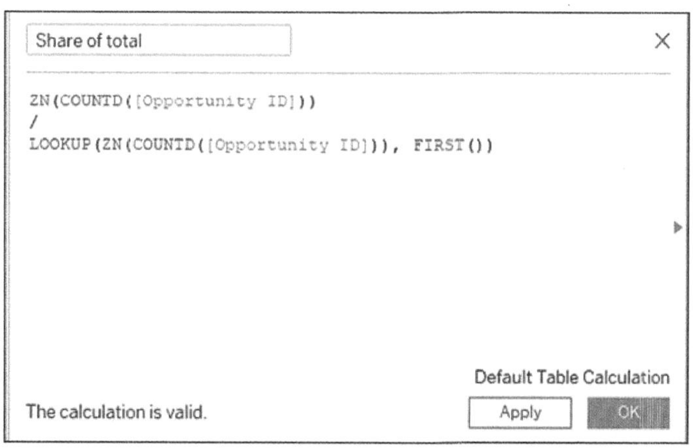

Figure 6.36: Share of total calculation

9. Drag your new calculation onto the **Label** mark in the bottom **CNTD (Opportunity ID)** card, as can be seen in *Figure 6.37:*

***Figure 6.37:** Add calculation to label*

10. Drag **CNTD (Opportunity ID)** away to remove it from the chart, as can be seen in *Figure 6.38:*

***Figure 6.38:** Remove count*

11. Click on the **Label** mark on the bottom **CNTD (Opportunity ID)** mark, as shown in *Figure 6.39*:

Figure 6.39: *Select bottom label*

12. In the **Alignment** menu, choose left, as shown in *Figure 6.40:*

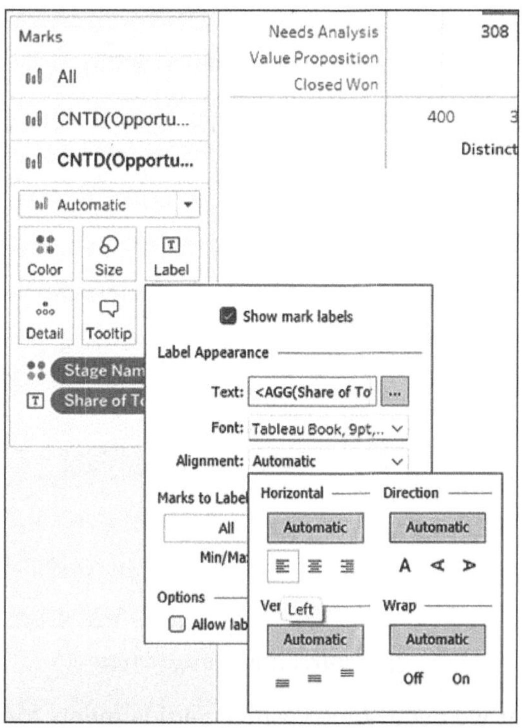

Figure 6.40: *Align bottom labels left*

13. Right click on the calculation you have created and select **Default Properties** from the menu that opens, next click on **Number Format.**

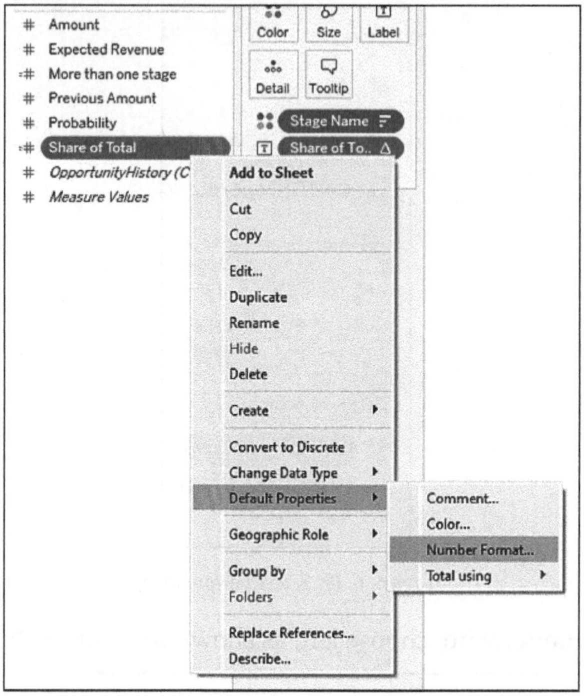

Figure 6.41: Open number formatting

14. In the pane that opens, select percentage, decrease the decimal places to 0, and click on **OK**, as shown in *Figure 6.42:*

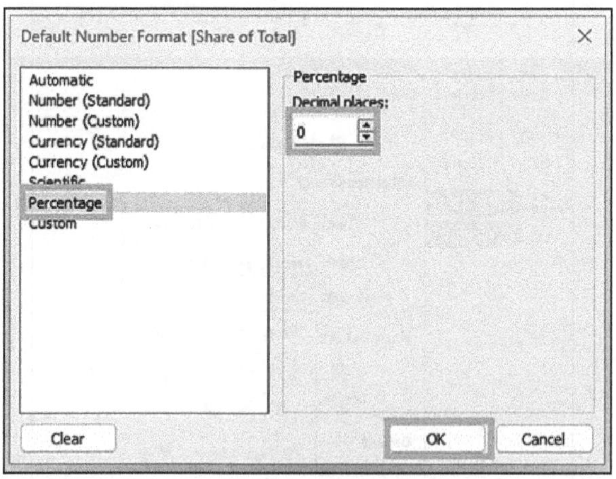

Figure 6.42: Set percentage format

We are almost there, but we need some cosmetic adjustments for this chart to look like a funnel, follow the below steps to do so:

1. From the **Format** menu, click on **Borders,** as can be seen in *Figure 6.43:*

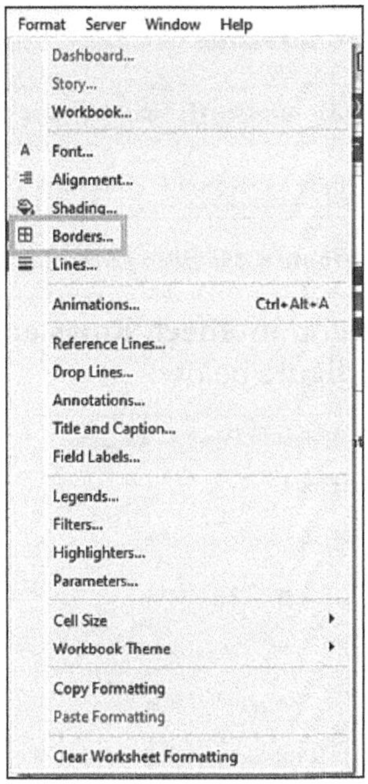

Figure 6.43: *Open Borders menu*

2. Select **None** from each menu in **Sheet**, **Rows** and **Columns** (if it does not say so already), as can be seen in *Figure 6.44:*

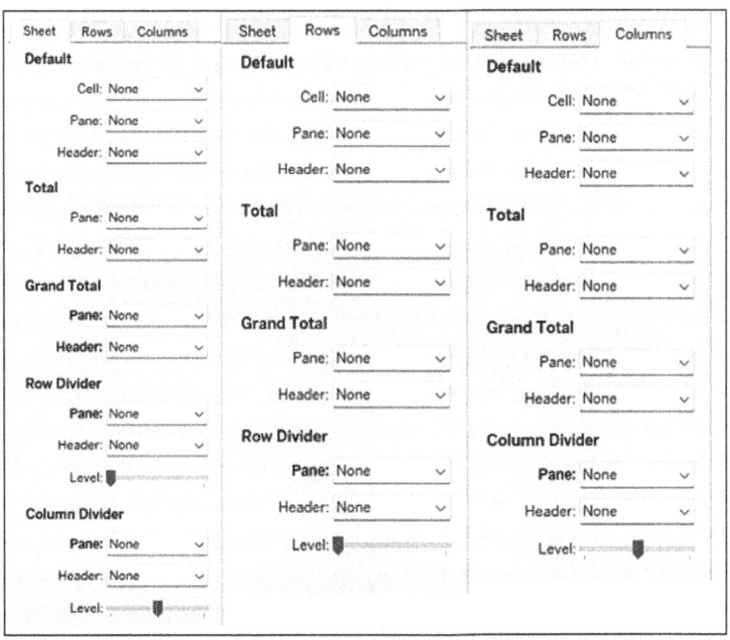

Figure 6.44: *Select no borders*

3. Click on the Lines icon (*Figure 6.45*).

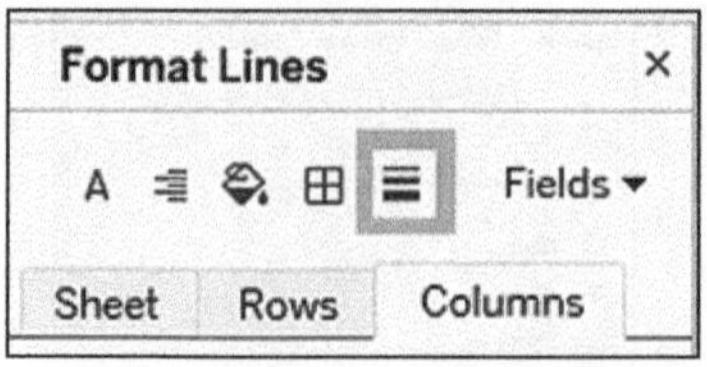

Figure 6.45: *Open Lines menu*

4. Select **None** from each menu in **Sheet, Rows** and **Columns** (if it does not say so already), as shown in the figure below:

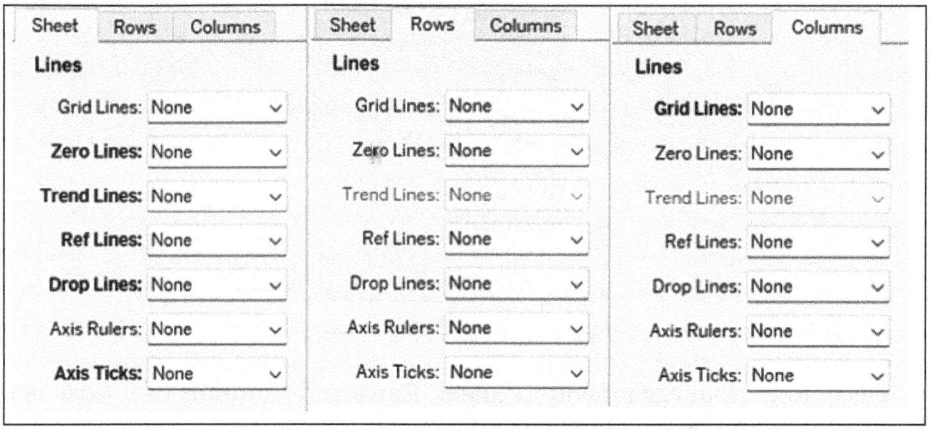

Figure 6.46: *Select no lines*

5. Right click on the left axis and untick "**Show Header**", as shown in *Figure 6.47:*

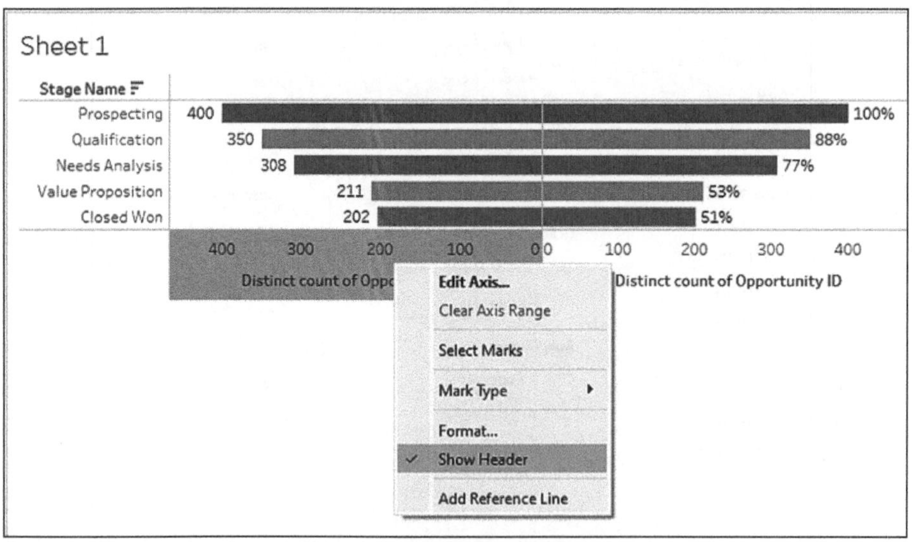

Figure 6.47: *Hide left axis header*

Your chart should look something like the one below:

Figure 6.48: *Funnel final*

Advanced maps

We can convey several layers of information by using maps in Tableau. We started in the previous chapter with a simple filled map, and we will now take it one step forward by looking at the number of accounts and the revenues on the same map.

Before we do so, you will have to upload some additional data to your org that is required for this visualization. First, download the files available at the GitHub repository for the book.

Now follow these instructions to load the opportunities:

1. **Login to Salesforce** and navigate to the 'Setup' area by clicking the gear icon in the upper right corner.
2. In the **Quick Find** box, type and select **Data Import Wizard**.
3. Click on the **Launch Wizard** button within the **Data Import Wizard**.
4. Select the type of object that matches your CSV data, such as **Opportunities** for opportunity data.
5. Click on **Choose a CSV file**, browse to your **tfs_opps.csv** file, and upload it.
6. Review the field mappings. The wizard will try to auto-map CSV columns to Salesforce fields. Adjust manually if necessary.

7. After verifying the field mappings, click **Next**.
8. Review your import settings in the summary page and click **Start Import**.
9. Monitor the import progress. Salesforce will indicate when the import is complete.
10. Once the import is complete, check the relevant object in Salesforce, like Opportunities, to ensure the data is correctly imported.
11. Review any error reports generated by Salesforce and address any issues highlighted.

Repeat this process for the **`tfs_accs.csv`** file, the **`Account`** object, the **`tfs_users.csv`** file, and the **`Users`** object.

For this chart, the Account object was used as a primary data source, and the **`Opportunity`** object as a secondary data source. Please refer to *Chapter 3, Building and Integrating Data Pipelines* for details on how to blend data sources.

To create our map, follow these steps:

1. Double-click on the **Billing State/Province** field (from the Accounts object). This will create a map, as shown in *Figure 6.49:*

***Figure 6.49:** Add Billing State to view*

2. From the **Marks** menu, change the mark type to **Circle**, as shown in *Figure 6.50:*

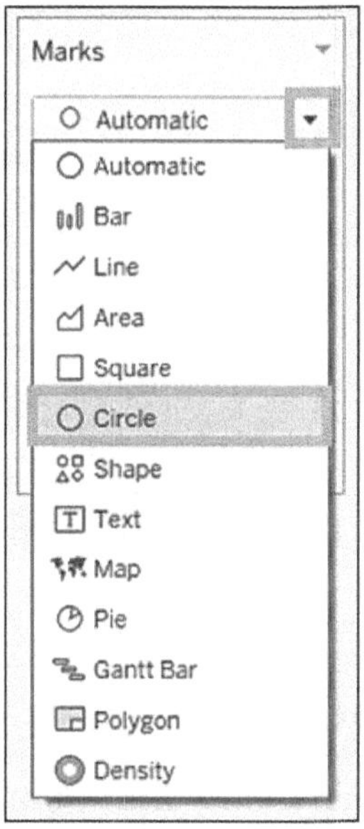

***Figure 6.50:** Change mark type to circle*

3. Right-click on **Account ID** and drag it onto the **Size** card, choose **Count Distinct** from the menu that opens, as shown in *Figure 6.51*:

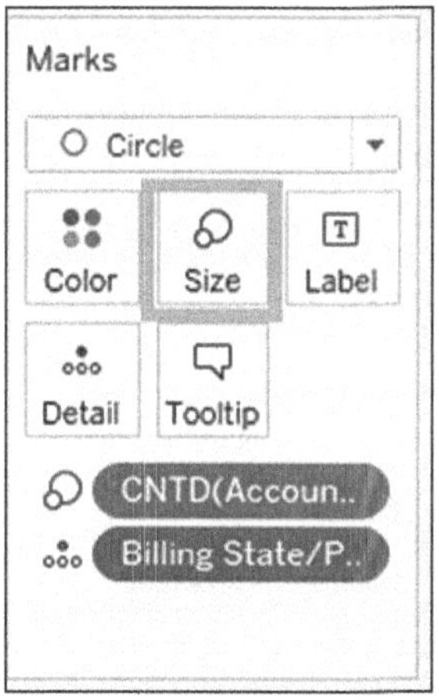

***Figure 6.51:** Size by Account count*

4. From the Opportunity object drag **Expected Amount to Color** (make sure to have set the blend correctly), as shown in *Figure 6.52:*

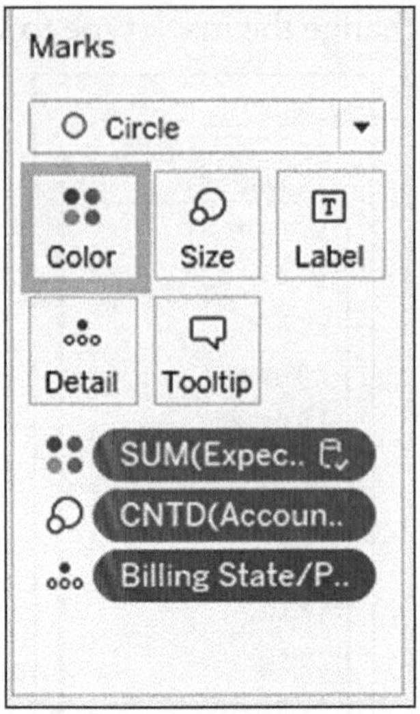

Figure 6.52: Color by Expected Revenue

5. Click on the **Color** card, then choose **Edit Colors**, as can be seen in *Figure 6.53:*

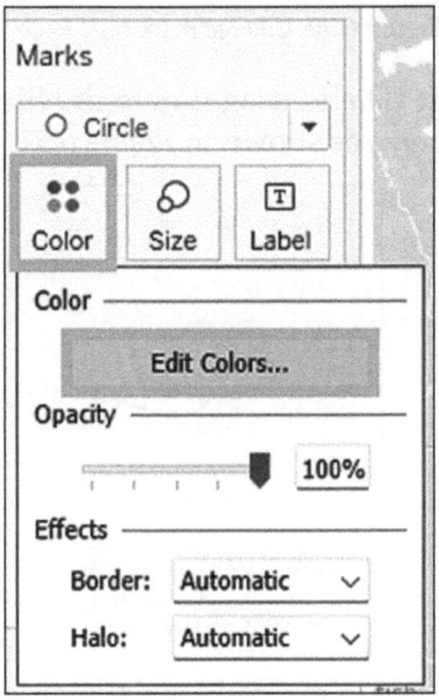

Figure 6.53: Edit colors

6. Choose the **Red - Blue Diverging** palette, as shown in *Figure 6.54:*

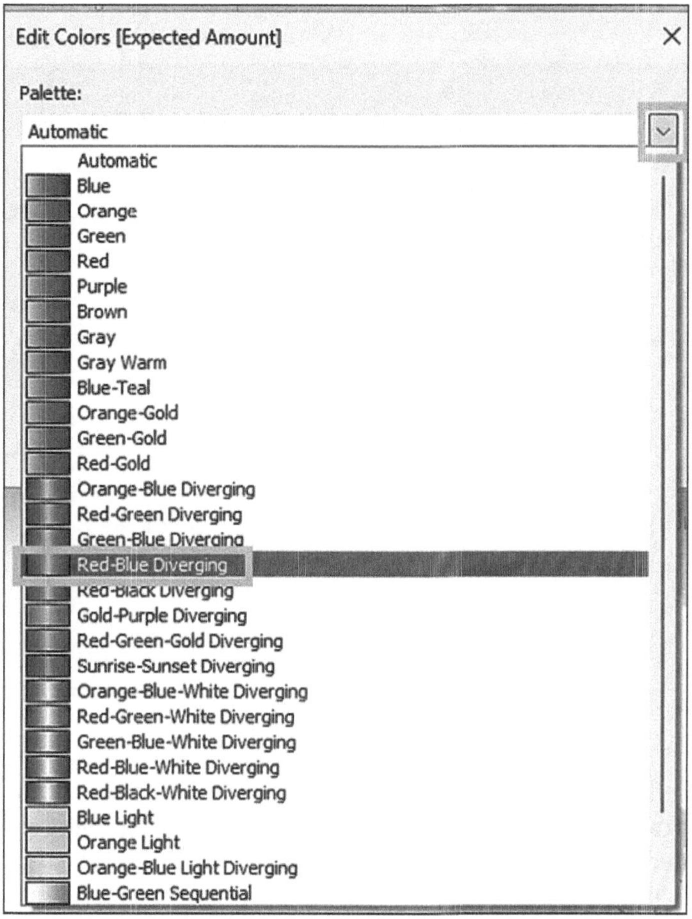

Figure 6.54: *Change color palette*

In one map, we can now see in which states we have the most accounts and the largest revenue. An even more interesting pattern emerges in which the number of accounts and the revenues do not go hand in hand. Rather, we can see even more clearly the clusters where we would expect large revenues (that is California) but are instead seeing poor performances. All of these clusters are close together, so there must be a geographical explanation of what we are seeing (*Figure 6.55*).

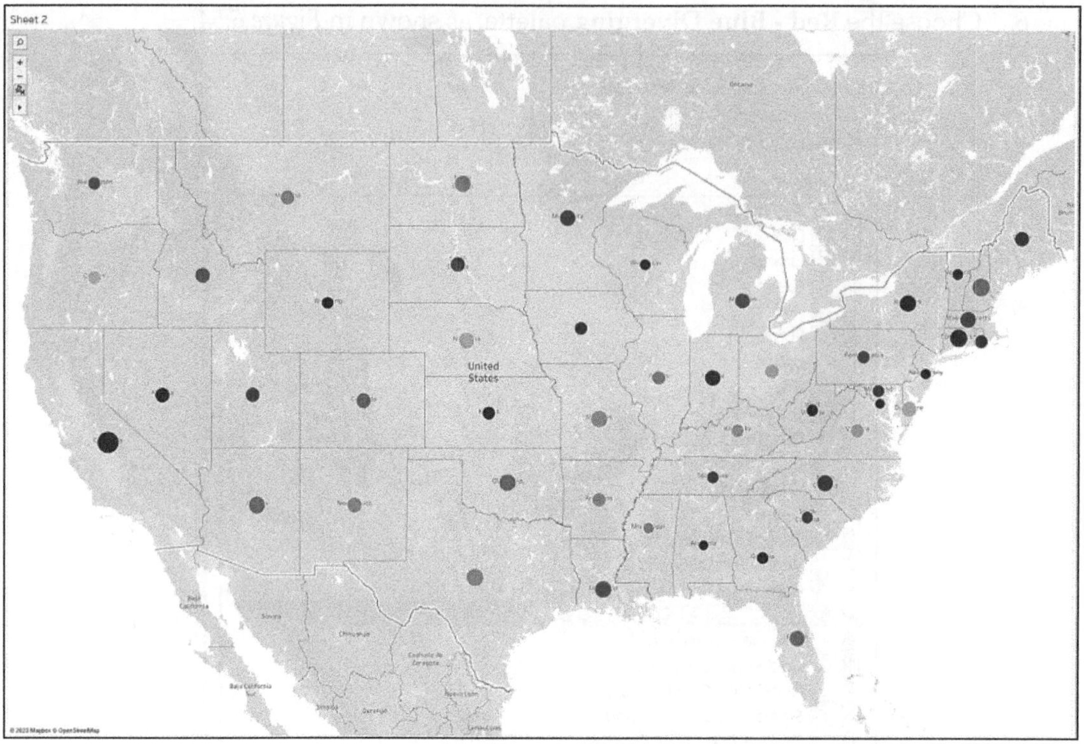

Figure 6.55: *Colored dots*

To proceed with the next step, we need to create a new dataset that joins the objects Accounts, Opportunities, and Users. This will allow us to bring together the geographical information related to the accounts, the financial information tied to opportunities, and the geographical locations pertaining to our sales representatives, which can be found in the User object. Alternatively, you can use the dataset provided in this book.

Since 2019, Tableau has allowed the option to perform spatial analysis even in cases where spatial files are unavailable, as long as information such as latitude and longitude is provided. Luckily, Salesforce provides this information out of the box for both Accounts and Users.

Let us go back to our original map and work from the assumption that since we have spotted a geographical pattern in our data, geography could also present a solution, in this case, by looking at where our sales representatives are located against our accounts and the revenue we expect to generate.

In the previous case, we have built a map at the state level. Now, we will go down to the city level. The process is the same as described before, but this time, we will start with the **Billing City** field rather than the **Billing State**. The final result should look something like the map below:

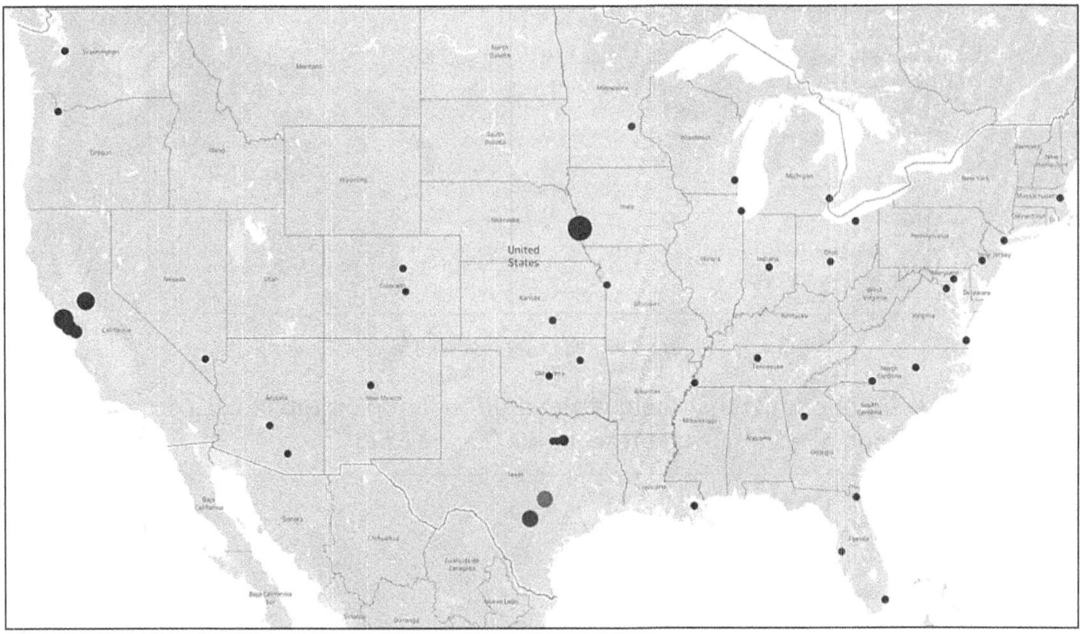

Figure 6.56: *Sized dots*

When we break our data down by cities, the contrast is even starker. We see that California has several accounts but low expected revenues, while revenues in Texas seem to be driven by a specific city. At the border between Nebraska and Iowa, we have our most profitable accounts. How does this compare with the geographical location of our sales representatives?

To answer this question, we will start by creating a spatial object out of the latitude and longitude of our User object. To do so, follow the below-mentioned steps:

1. Create a calculated field and write the following formula:
2. Give a name to your calculation, then press **OK**.
3. Drag the field you have just created to the map and then on top of the **Add a Marks Layer** icon on your map, as shown below.

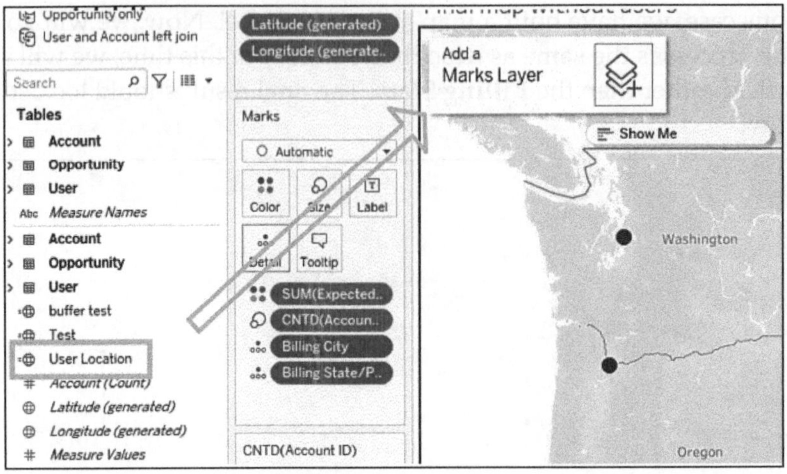

Figure 6.57: Add user locations layer

You will notice now that there is an additional dop on top of each account; this is the location of each sales representative (*Figure 6.58*).

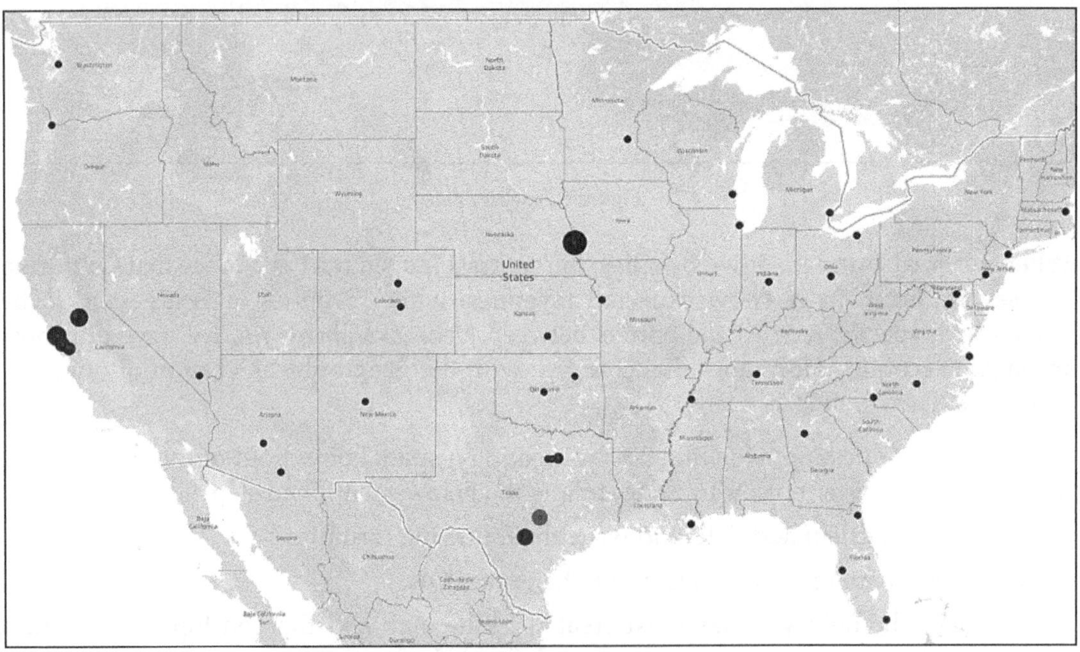

Figure 6.58: Users Layer

4. As usual, we can improve upon this. First, change the kind of mark for the **User Location** field from **Automatic** to **Shape**, as shown in *Figure 6.59:*

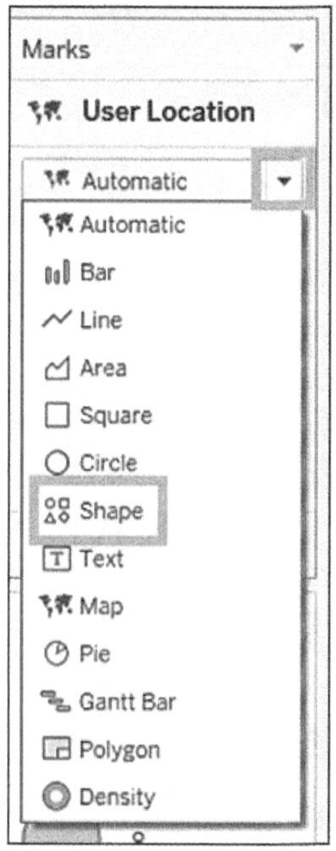

Figure 6.59: Change mark type to shape

5. At this point, your points will disappear to be replaced by a single circle. To fix this, drop the **User ID** onto **Detail** in the **User Location Mark** card, as can be seen in *Figure 6.60:*

Figure 6.60: Add detail

6. All of your circles are now back. But you may want to choose a more evocative shape. Click on **Shape** to open a menu, then click on **More Shapes**, as shown in *Figure 6.61:*

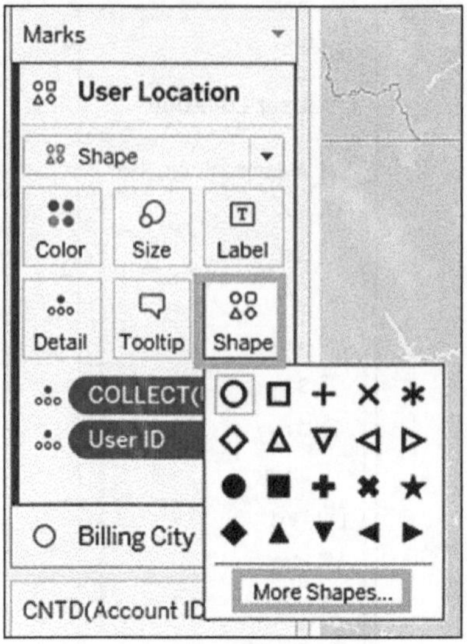

Figure 6.61: Open shape menu

7. From the **Select Shape Palette** menu, click on **Gender**.

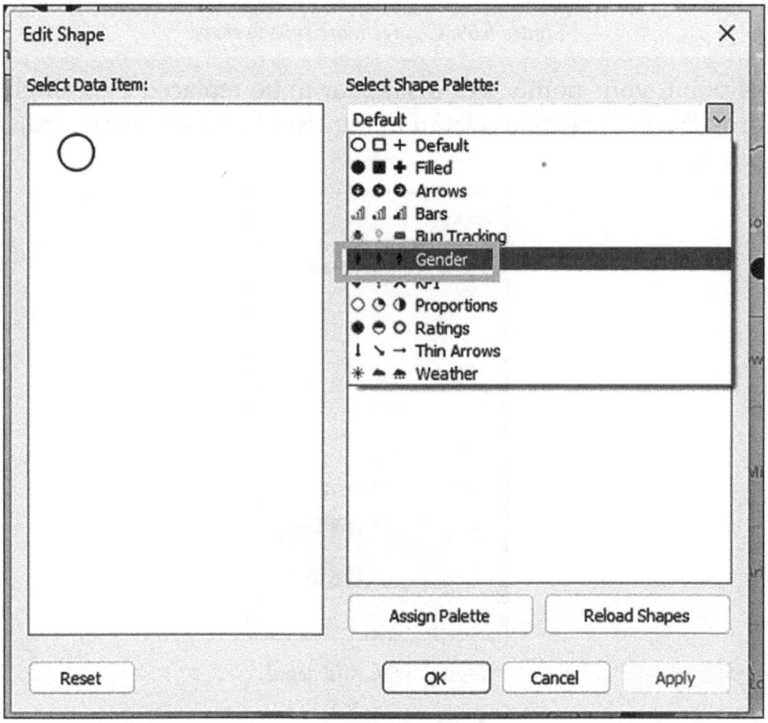

Figure 6.62: Select Gender shapes

8. Click on one of the icon (in this case the first icon has been selected), then press **OK**, as shown in *Figure 6.63:*

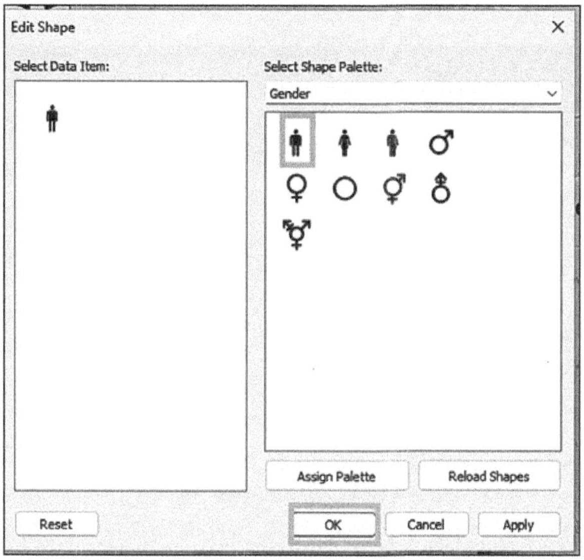

Figure 6.63: *Select first gender icon*

Our map (*Figure 6.64)* now has little human figures showing where our sales representatives are present.

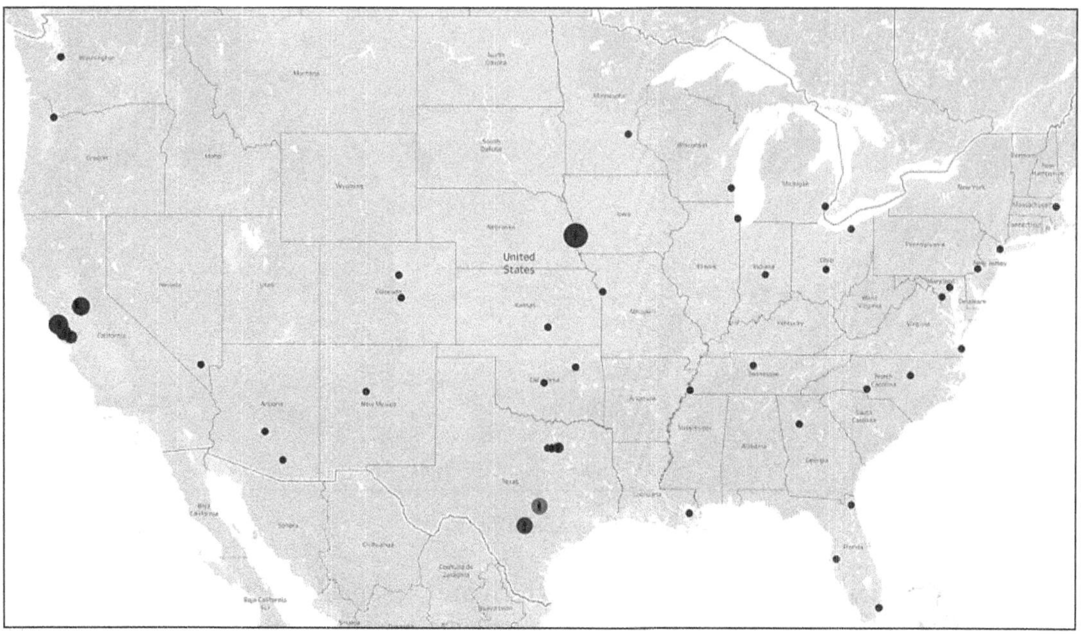

Figure 6.64: *Figures for salespeople*

Once we zoom into some of our states, the reasons for what we see in the data seem clearer. Take Texas, for example, as shown in *Figure 6.65:*

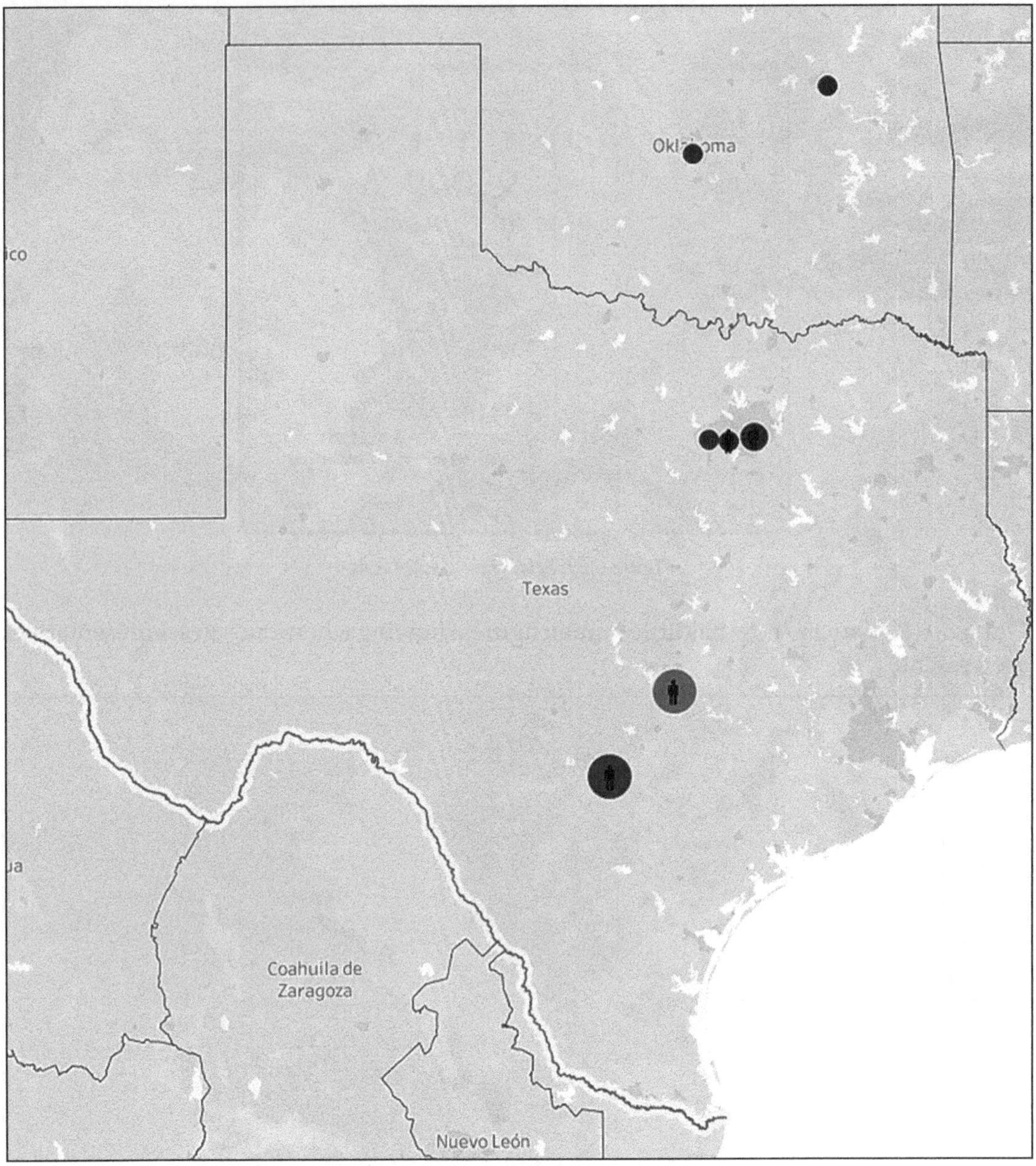

Figure 6.65: *Texas*

We have four sales representatives, two of which are reasonably far from each other and, although the performance of one of them is much worse than the other, it is still not as bad as the performance of the accounts where the sales representatives are close to each other. Looking at California (*Figure 6.66*) reveals a similar pattern.

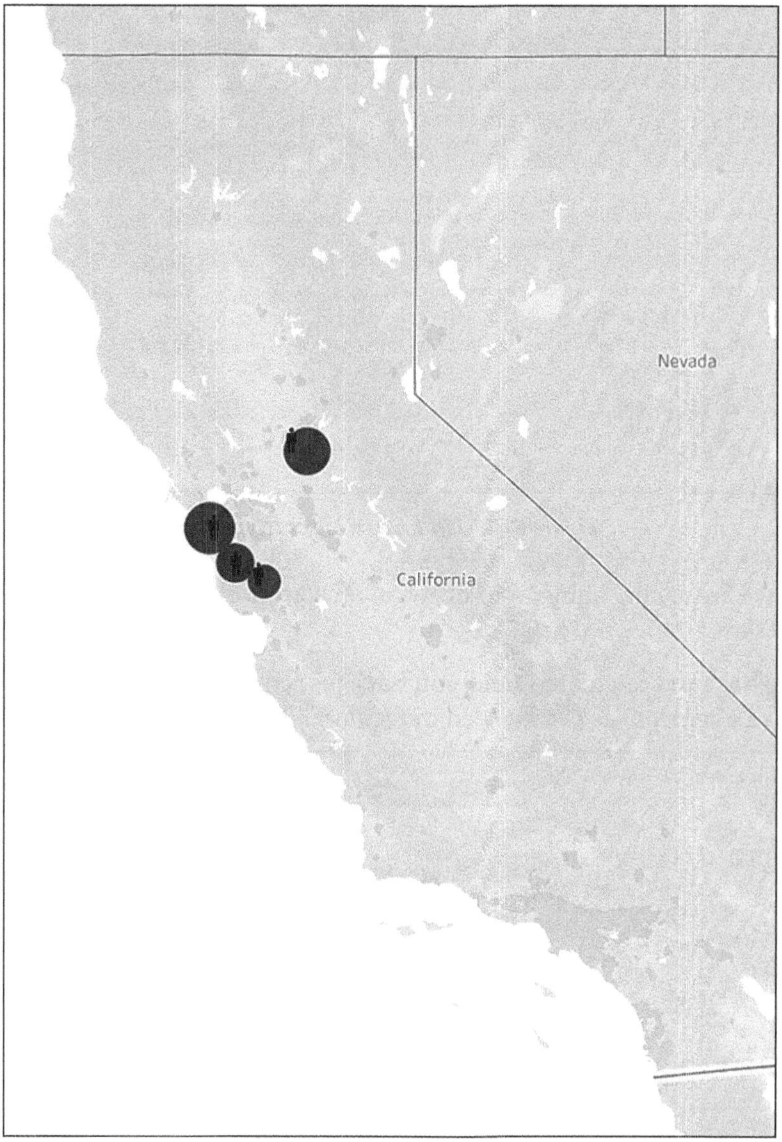

Figure 6.66: California

Again, we see poor performance and sales representatives close to each other. We can show the extent of the problem in a more dramatic way by using the buffer function, which creates a radius around a specified point. In our case, this radius could act as the area we would expect a sales representative to cover.

In order to do so, create a new calculated field and use the following formula, as shown in *Figure 6.67*:

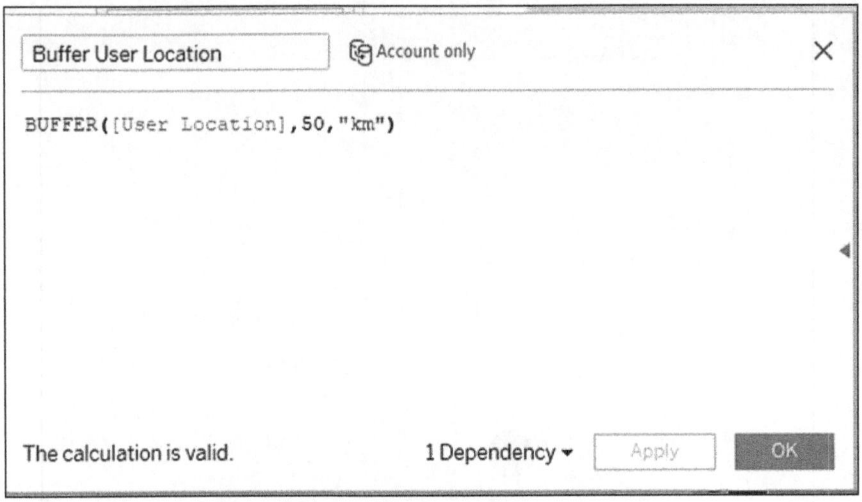

Figure 6.67: User location buffer calculation

In this case, we are asking Tableau to draw an area around each sales representative with a radius of 50 km.

Just as before, take the calculated field you have just created and drag it to the map on the **Add a Marks Layer** icon, as can be seen in *Figure 6.68:*

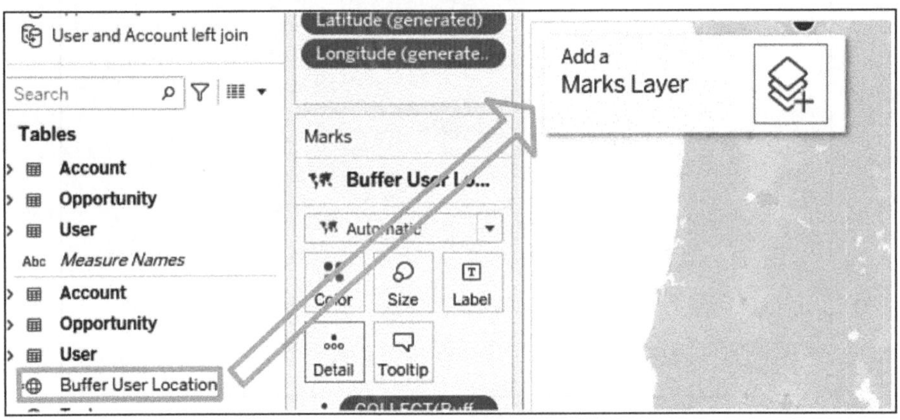

Figure 6.68: Add buffer layer

We can now see the extent of our problem more clearly. Let us start with California. All three sales areas overlap (*Figure 6.69*), which tells us that our sales representatives are pursuing the same accounts, which is possibly leading to frustration in our customers.

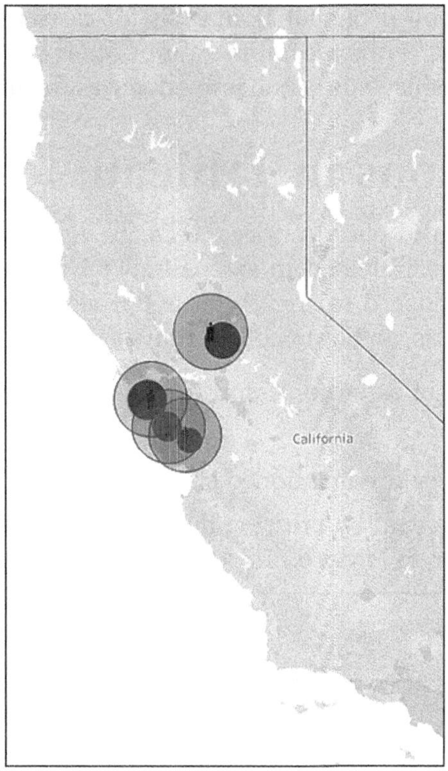

Figure 6.69: *Buffer layer*

Similarly, in Texas, where the sales representatives' areas overlap, we see poor performance in sales.

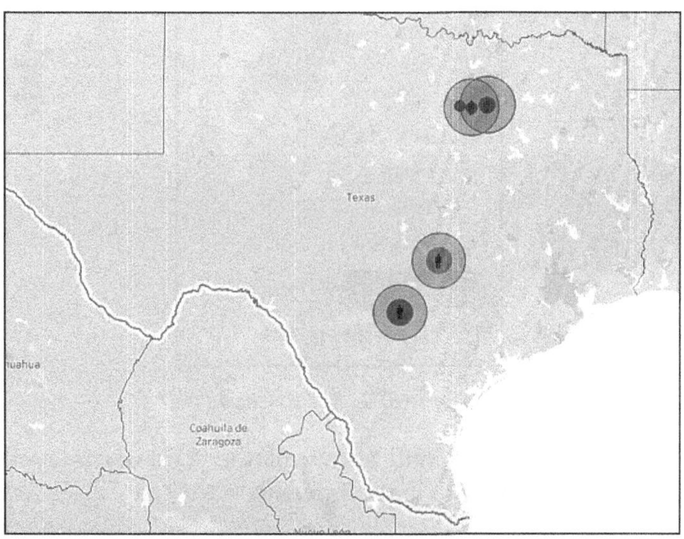

Figure 6.70: *Salespeople with buffer*

This example shows the power of spatial analysis for cases in which geography plays a significant role in the data. While a combination of other charts may have led us to the same result, none would achieve the same immediacy as the map we just built together.

Using extensions in Tableau

It is also possible to use third party services to create visualizations in Tableau. Tableau Exchange (**https://exchange.tableau.com/extensions**) provides an array of objects that can be used in a Tableau dashboard to create charts but also perform spatial analysis, add custom annotations to charts, and even collaborate in Teams.

Salesforce has its own set of extensions, and there is also a set of extensions developed directly by Tableau.

To access them, follow the below-mentioned steps:

1. Create a new dashboard by pressing the New Dashboard button at the bottom of your screen, as seen in *Figure 6.71:*

***Figure 6.71:** New dashboard*

2. Next, drag the **Extension** object on your dashboard.

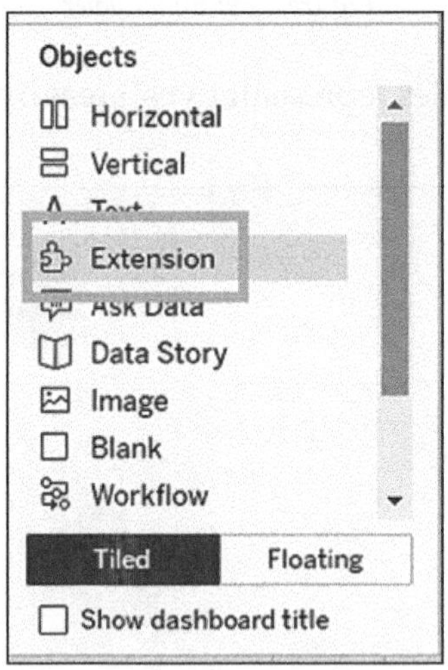

***Figure 6.72:** Add Extension*

3. The interface which opens will show all the Extensions available on Tableau Exchange without needing to leave Tableau.

Each extension has its own set of instructions, and in *Chapter 9 – Exploring Einstein AI and Advanced Analytics*, we will show you how to use the Salesforce Einstein extension, but in the meantime, explore the available range to find the extension that mostly fits your needs. And if you cannot find the perfect one, you are now well-equipped to create every sort of visualization in Tableau.

Conclusion

In conclusion, as we wrap up this insightful journey into the realm of advanced visualizations using Tableau and Salesforce CRM data, it is our hope that you have gained a deeper understanding of the vast capabilities that this visualization tool offers. The power to transform raw, often complex CRM data into meaningful and insightful visual representations lies at your fingertips.

Through this chapter, we aimed to elevate your skills from creating sophisticated Sankey diagrams and calendar-based visualizations to expertly customizing geographical data visualizations. We also discussed the power of third-party integrations, a crucial aspect in today's interconnected technological landscape. The potential for innovation here is vast, and we encourage you to explore further, continually pushing boundaries to uncover deeper insights from your CRM data.

Remember, fostering a data-curious culture within your organization is a journey, not a destination. Every dataset brings new questions, unique insights, and innovative perspectives. The beauty of data visualization is that it brings us closer to the story hidden within the data, enabling data-driven decision-making crucial for business growth.

We will now move back into Salesforce to look at using Tableau Visualizations within the CRM.

CHAPTER 7
Integration, Authentication, and Tableau Viz LWC

Introduction

This chapter will provide a comprehensive guide on integrating Tableau with Salesforce through the Tableau Viz LWC component. It will begin by walking readers through the process of installing the Tableau viz LWC component and configuring it for use in Salesforce. The chapter will then delve into advanced usage of the component, such as creating custom visualizations and modifying the component's settings. Additionally, the chapter will cover setting up **Single Sign-On** (**SSO**) between Salesforce and Tableau to streamline the authentication process. Lastly, the chapter will highlight other ways to connect Salesforce and Tableau dashboards. Overall, this chapter will give readers a detailed understanding of how to utilize the Tableau Viz LWC component to enhance their CRM analytics in Salesforce.

Structure

The chapter covers the following topics:

- Installing and configuring Tableau viz LWC Component
- Configuring and using Tableau viz LWC Component
- Advanced usage of Tableau viz LWC Component

- Setting up Single Sign-On between Salesforce and Tableau
- Alternative ways to connect Salesforce and Tableau dashboards

Objectives

By the end of this chapter, learners will have acquired a comprehensive set of skills and knowledge related to the integration of Tableau with Salesforce. This will include an understanding of the purpose and benefits of using the Tableau Viz LWC component for this integration. They will learn how to install and configure the Tableau Viz LWC component within Salesforce, enabling seamless integration.

Additionally, learners will gain the ability to create custom visualizations and learn how to modify the settings of the Tableau Viz LWC component for more advanced usage. The chapter will also cover the setup of SSO between Salesforce and Tableau, which is crucial for streamlining the authentication process and enhancing security measures.

Moreover, learners will explore alternative methods for connecting Salesforce and Tableau dashboards, such as direct connections and the use of third-party integration tools. Finally, they will be able to apply the knowledge gained to enhance CRM analytics in Salesforce using the Tableau Viz LWC component, thus adding significant value to their Salesforce environment.

Installing the Tableau Viz LWC component

The next few sections, will walk you through installing and configuring the Tableau Viz **Lightning Web Component** (**LWC**) in Salesforce, enabling you to embed Tableau visualizations directly within your Salesforce environment. This integration brings the analytical power of Tableau to the fingertips of Salesforce users, enriching their experience with actionable insights without leaving the Salesforce platform.

The first thing you will need to do to use Tableau visualizations within a Salesforce environment is to install the Tableau Viz LWC component from the Salesforce AppExchange. This component is the most important way to bring Tableau dashboards directly in front of Salesforce business users as they do their work.

To install the Tableau Viz component into your Salesforce Analytics DE Environment, follow these steps:

1. Open your Analytics DE Environment and make a note of its domain, for example, **`testco35-dev-ed.develop.lightning.force.com`**.
2. Now combine that URL with the following path **`/packagingSetupUI/ipLanding.app?apvId=04t5w000005diA4AAI`** and go to the combined URL, for example, **https://testco35-dev-ed.develop.lightning.force.com/packagingSetupUI/ipLanding.app?apvId=04t5w000005diA4AAI**

3. This will bring you to the installation page as shown in the *Figure 7.1:*

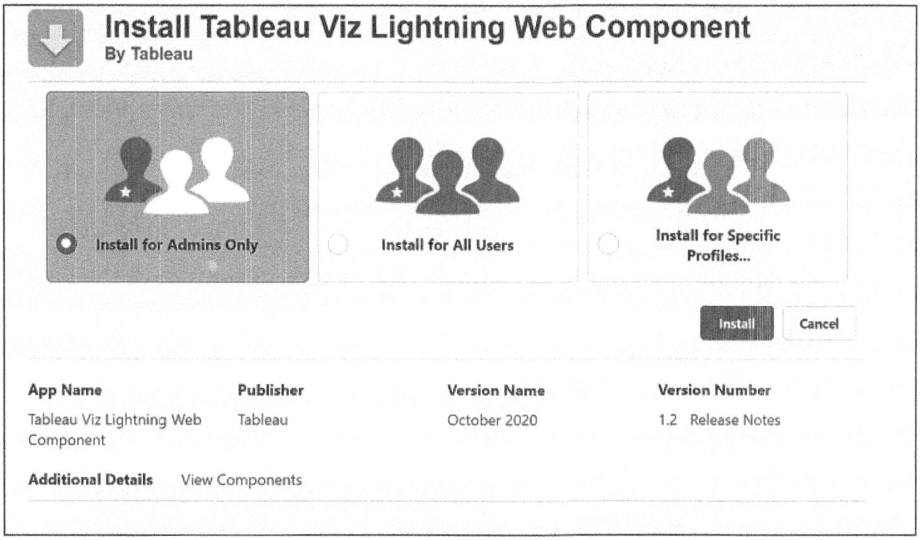

Figure 7.1: *Installation page for Tableau viz LWC component*

4. Now select **Install for All Users** and click **Install**. After this, wait until the installation is completed. This will look like the *Figure 7.2*:

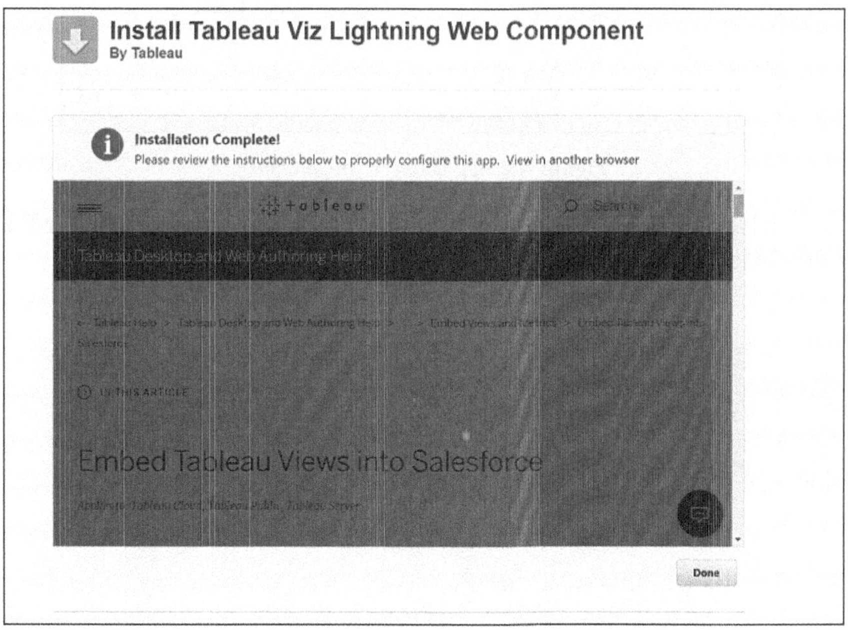

Figure 7.2: *Installation in progress page*

5. You can click **Done** to complete the installation.

Configuring and using the Tableau Viz LWC component

Before we start to play around with the features of the Tableau Viz component, let us check that it is set up correctly. We can do that by simply adding it to an appropriate page and referencing a default dashboard from Tableau Public.

To add the Tableau Viz component to your sales home page, follow these steps:

1. Open the App Launcher and click on the **Sales** app, as shown in the *Figure 7.3:*

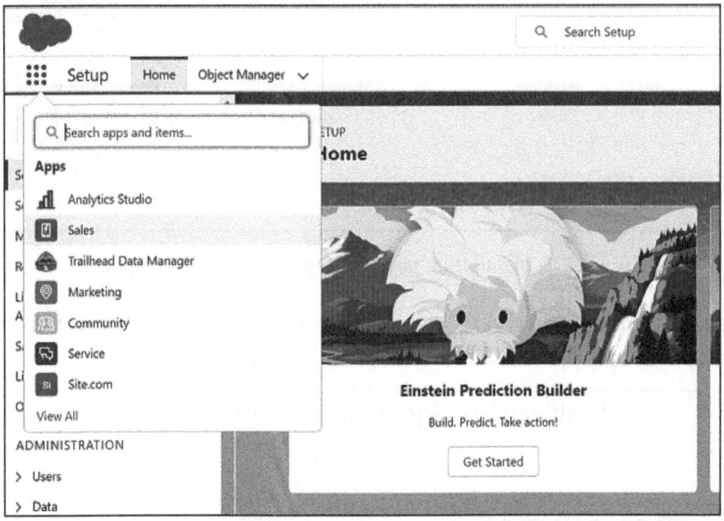

Figure 7.3: App Launcher in Salesforce

2. Now click on the gear icon in the upper right-hand corner and select **Edit Page**, as shown below in *Figure 7.4*.

Figure 7.4: Edit Page option in Sales app

3. From the component list on the left, drag the Tableau Visualization component to the right-hand column, as shown in the following screenshot:

Figure 7.5: Dragging Tableau Visualization components

4. This should result in a default dashboard being loaded, as in the following screenshot:

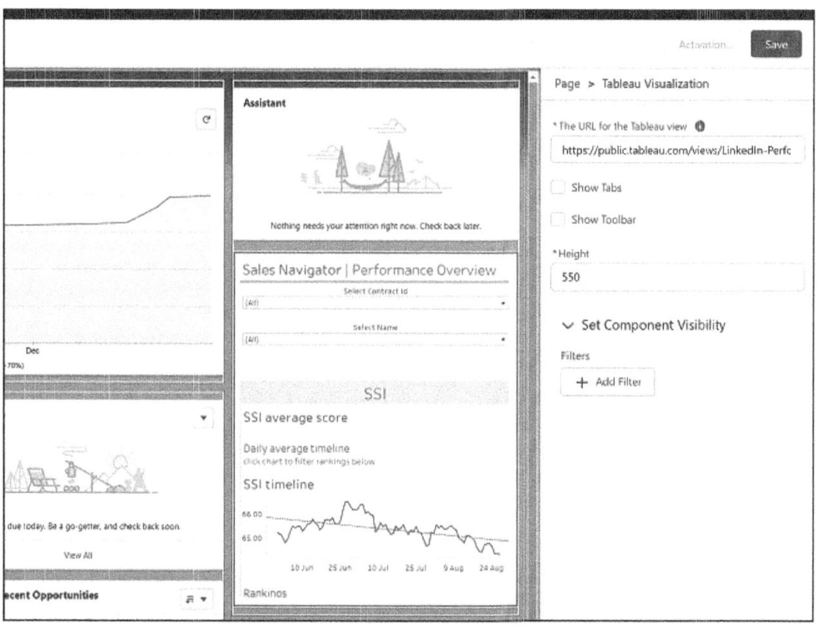

Figure 7.6: Default dashboard loaded

5. You can now save and activate the page by using the org default. This is shown in *Figure 7.7*:

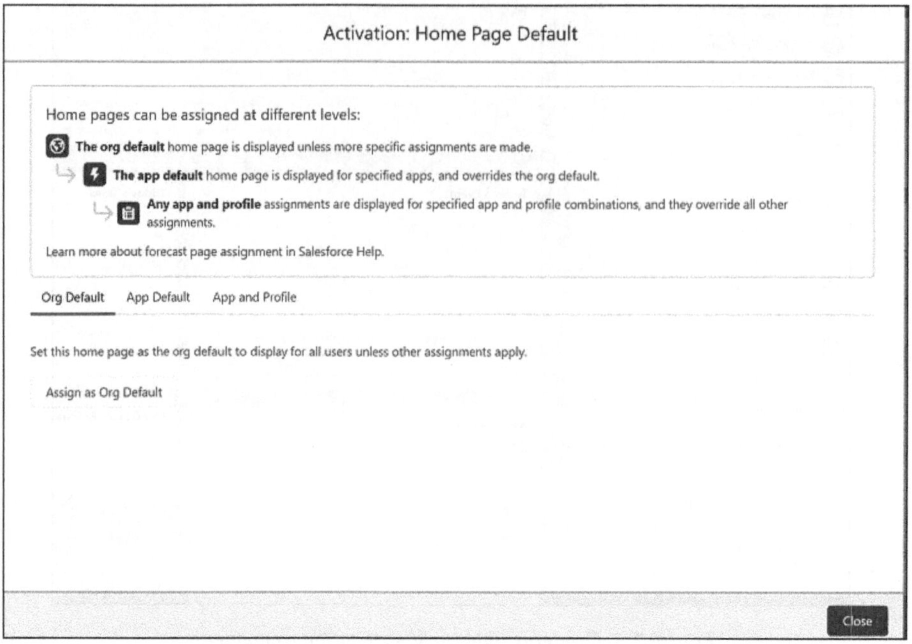

Figure 7.7: *Saving and activating edited page*

6. You can now go back to the Sales Home Page, which should look something like the following screenshot:

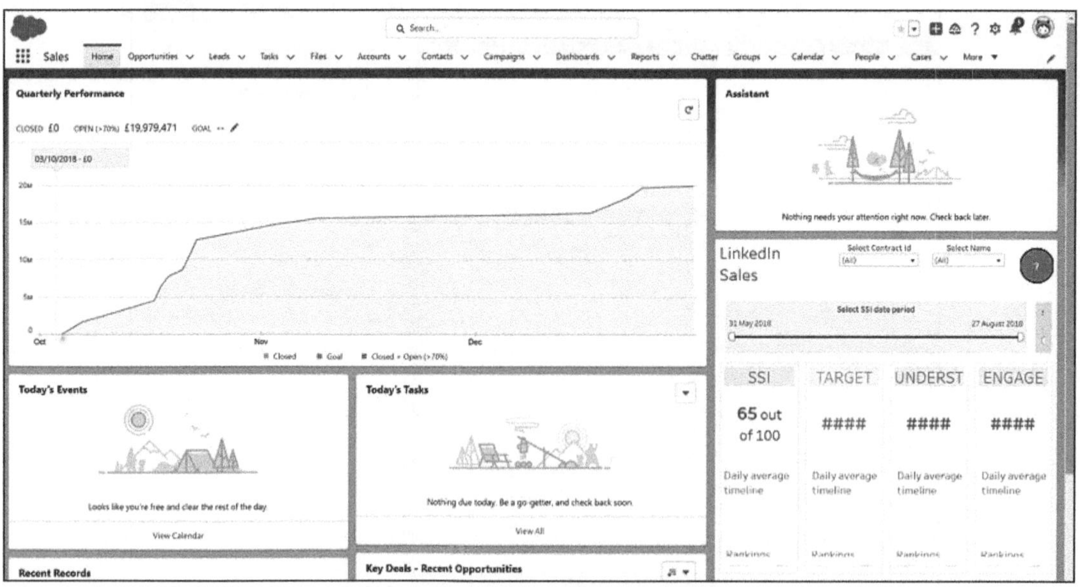

Figure 7.8: *Updated Sales Home Page*

It is worth noting that the Tableau Viz LWC component has limited functionality on the Salesforce side and that most of the power and versatility of the component comes from the interactivity you build in Tableau. However, bringing this into Salesforce and making it part of the end-user context as they do their day-to-day work is incredibly powerful.

In our previous example, we simply accepted the out-of-the-box visualization that is included for demonstration purposes, but we can bring in any visualization we like.

Let us pick another one to demonstrate the basic capabilities of the component. This will show you how to add any visualization from Tableau Public to your Salesforce environment, a very useful function when you are learning how to use the tools and do not always have access to a commercial version.

To add our demonstrator example to your Salesforce org, follow these steps:

1. Go to the URL: **https://public.tableau.com/app/profile/p.padham/viz/SuperstoreDashboard_16709573699130/SuperstoreDashboard.** This is a dashboard based on the Superstore dataset often used to demonstrate Tableau capabilities and is shown in the following screenshot:

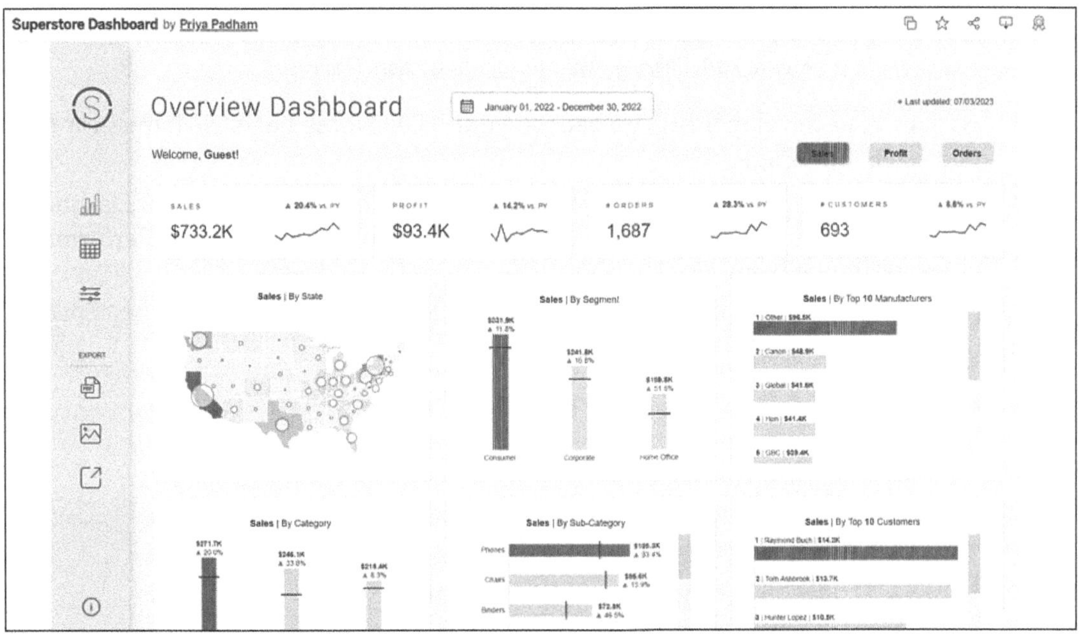

***Figure 7.9:** Superstore Dashboard on Tableau Public*

2. Click on the share icon and copy the public link, as shown in *Figure 7.10:*

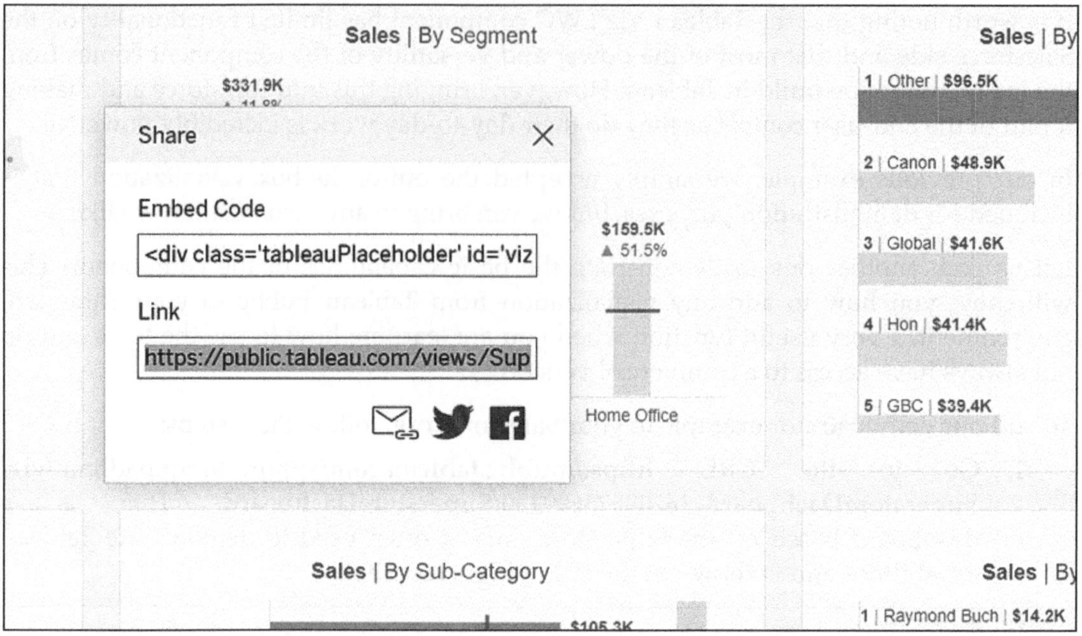

***Figure 7.10:** Sharing public link for Superstore Dashboard*

3. Back in your developer org, go back to your Sales Home Page, click the gear icon, and select **Edit Page**.
4. We will now replace the Quarterly Performance chart with the Sales Dashboard from Tableau Public. Start by clicking the delete icon on the Quarterly Performance chart, as shown below:

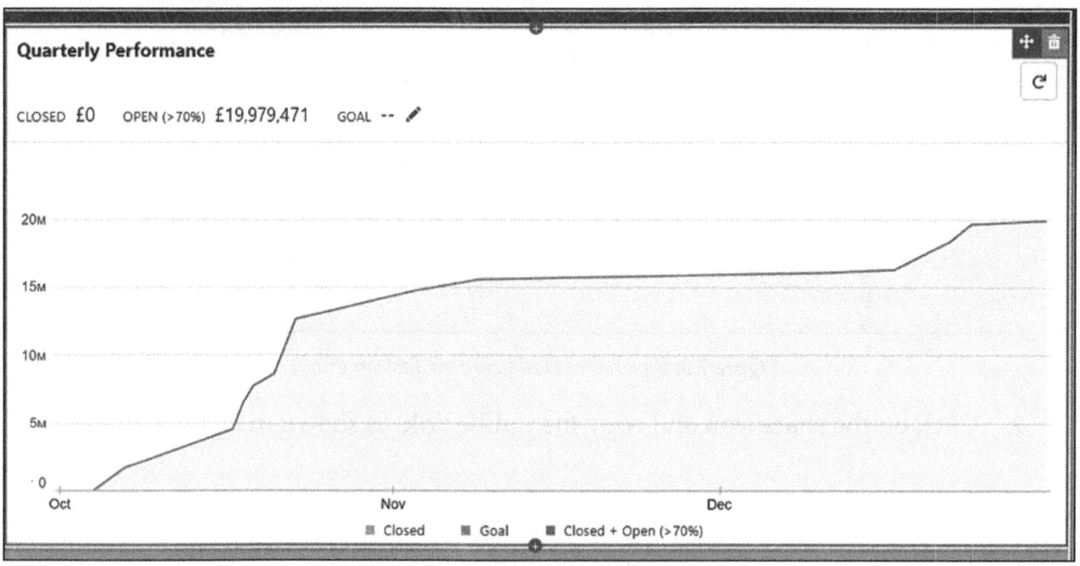

***Figure 7.11:** Deleting existing visualization*

5. Now drag the Tableau Visualization component into the empty slot and replace the URL in the component settings with the URL you copied from Tableau Public. You can see this in the following screenshot:

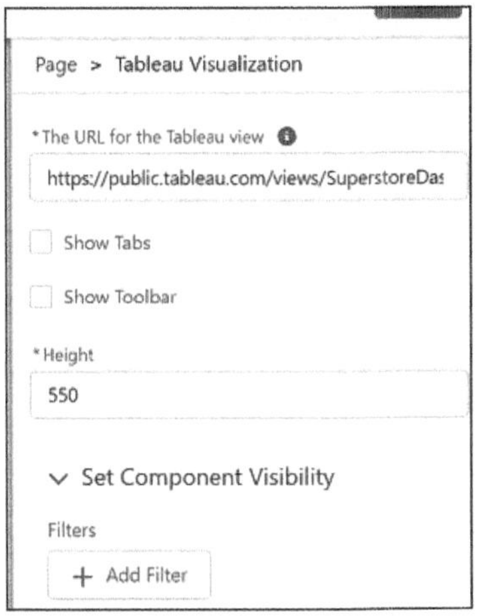

***Figure 7.12:** Configuring new Tableau Visualization component*

6. This should result in a view like the following figure:

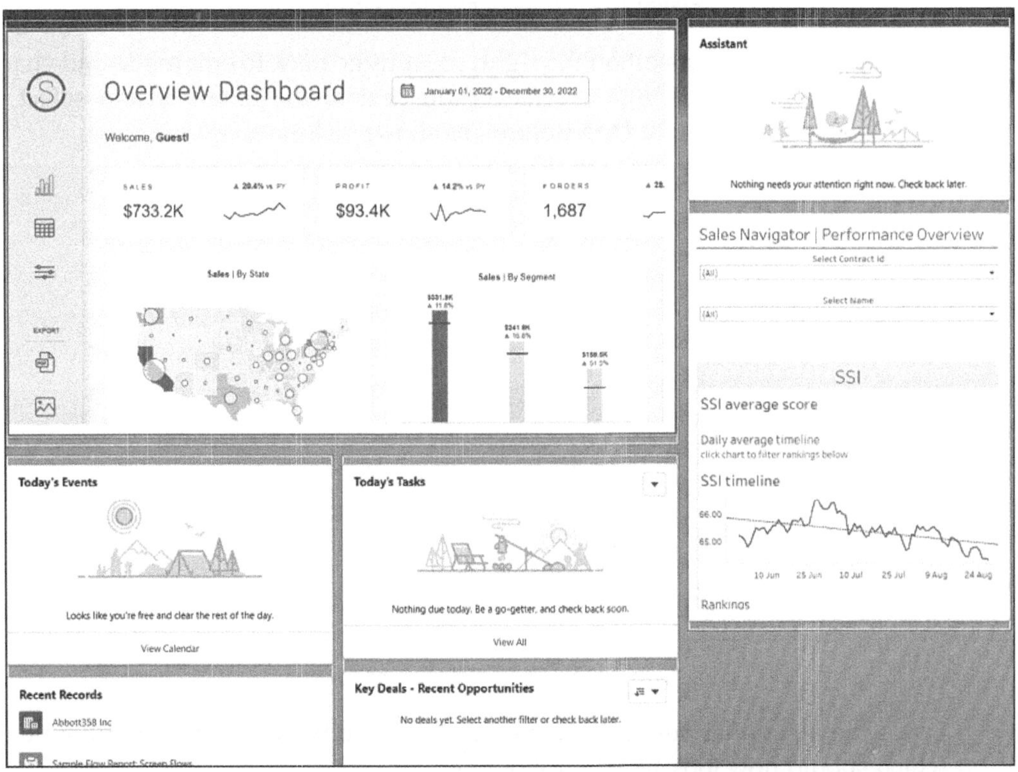

***Figure 7.13:** Superstore Dashboard added*

7. We want to show a larger dashboard, so set the height to 950, save and go back to the Sales Home Page. The view should now look like the following:

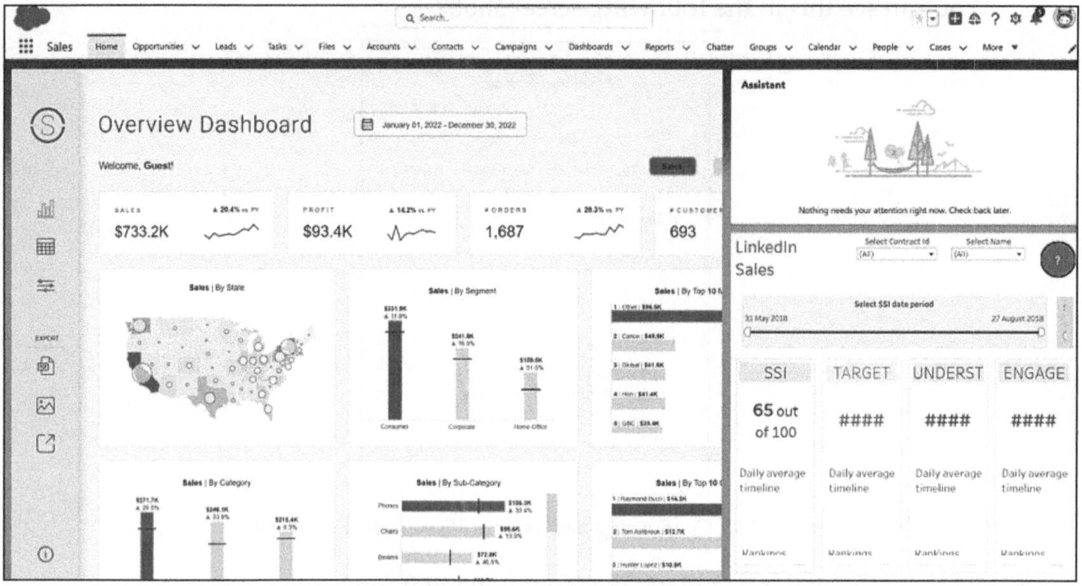

Figure 7.14: Expanded view of dashboard

8. The dashboard still cuts off on the right, so let us go back to edit mode and change the template. Click **Change** on the button next to the template and select the template **Home Template One Region**, as shown below:

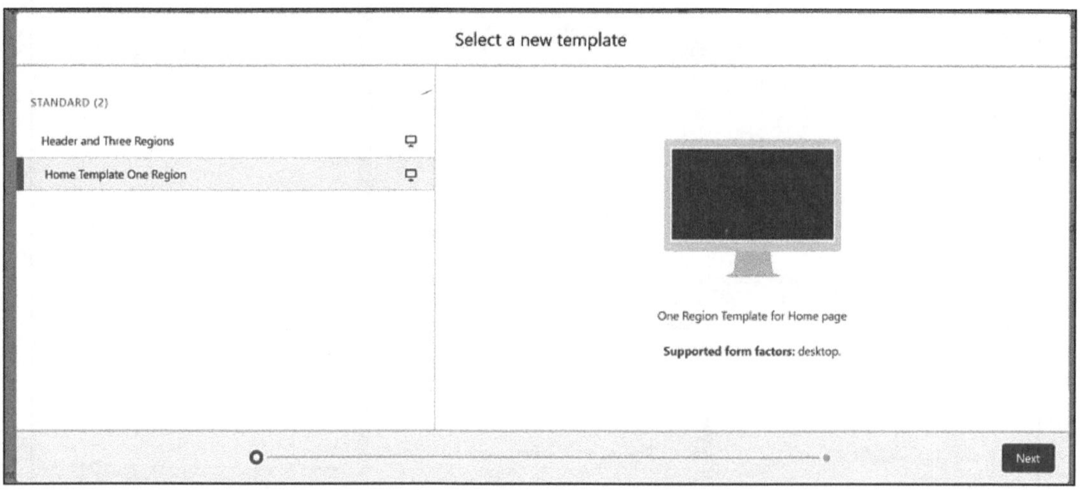

Figure 7.15: Changing page template

9. Leave the default values, click **Done**, save, and go back to the Sales Home Page, which should now look like the following:

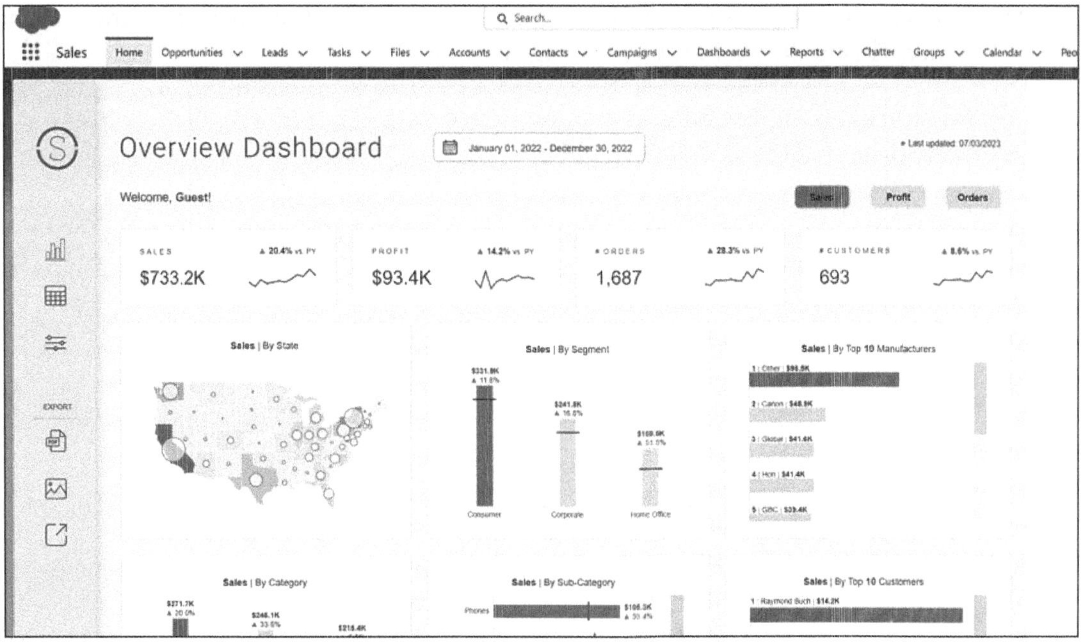

Figure 7.16: *Dashboard with new template*

10. The normal interactive features of the dashboard will work just fine within Salesforce, so try to click the table icon to see order details. This will change the view as per the following screenshot:

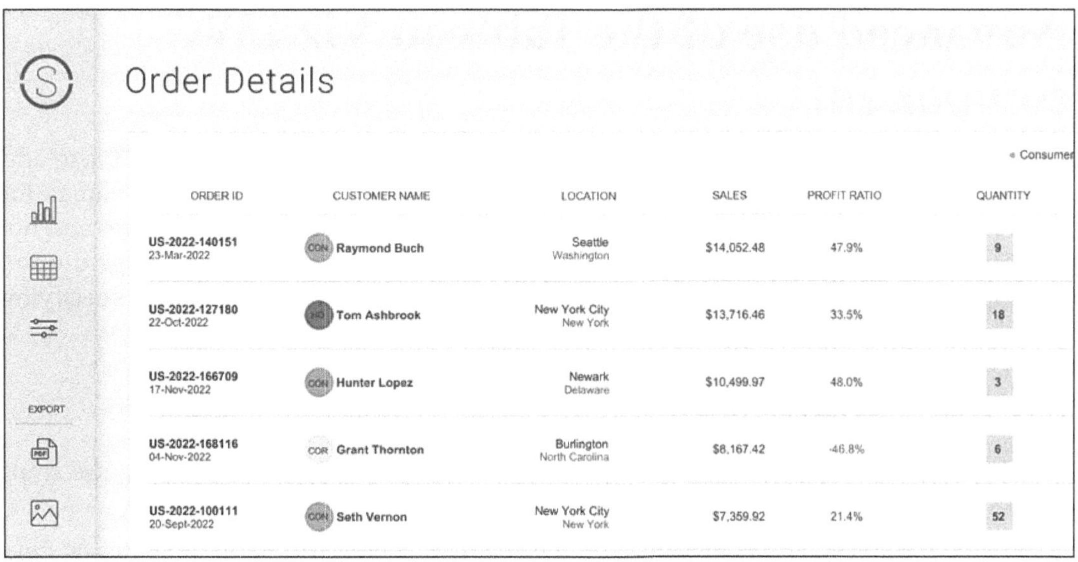

Figure 7.17: *Interactive features of dashboard*

11. You can also go to a full screen view by clicking the button in the lower right corner. This is shown in the following screenshot:

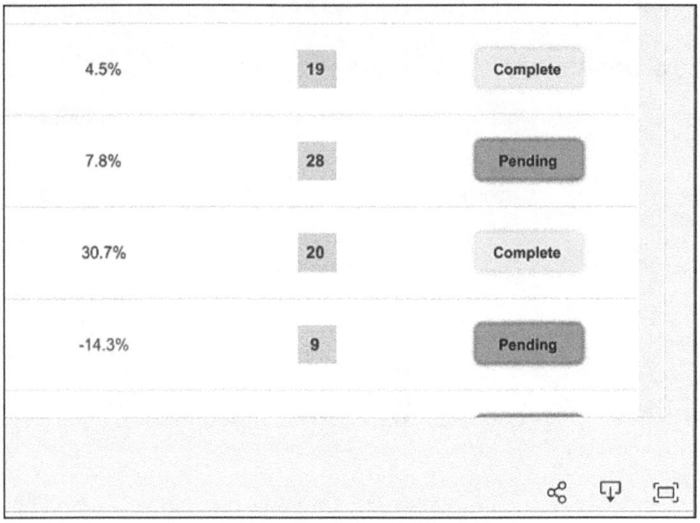

***Figure 7.18:** Full screen view of dashboard*

The process for configuring a visualization is nearly the same whether it is hosted on Tableau Public, on Tableau Online, or on your own Tableau Server. You will, however, be required to log in when accessing protected resources.

Advanced use of the Tableau Viz LWC component

The first and most important advanced use of the Tableau Viz LWC component is to add filtering. The Tableau Lightning Web Component enables two filtering techniques for Tableau visualization, which are exclusively applicable to Lightning record pages and not to Home or App pages. These approaches encompass context filtering, contingent upon the page embedding the visualization, and advanced filtering, which entails specifying corresponding fields in Tableau and Salesforce for more intricate filtering.

Context filtering

You can filter the component to the context of the current page by following the steps below:

1. To implement context filtering, the Tableau visualization necessitates a field corresponding to the record page ID. For instance, to display a sales visualization pertaining to a specific user on their page, the Tableau visualization should encompass a field containing user record IDs.

2. Within your Salesforce organization, choose a record page to embed the visualization (for example, Users or Opportunities).
3. Modify the record page and configure the component by inputting the Tableau visualization URL containing the desired data. The visualization must include a field containing record IDs (for example, user or account IDs).
4. Opt for filtering the Tableau view based on the current Salesforce record and save the alterations to the page.
5. The component applies the filter when the record page ID matches the corresponding field value in the Tableau visualization, such as displaying only the sales data pertinent to the user on their page.

Advanced filtering

For more control over filtering the Tableau visualization on a record page, you can establish a mapping between a Tableau field and a Salesforce field. The Tableau field should be present in the embedded visualization, while the Salesforce field must be a qualified field on the embedding page. The Tableau Lightning Web Component filters the Tableau visualization automatically when these field values match.

To evaluate this filtering, add the Tableau Visualization component to a record page. For example, insert a sales-related Tableau visualization onto your opportunity record pages.

Let us try an example:

1. In your Salesforce organization, access the App Launcher, select **Sales**, and click the **Accounts** tab, like in the following screenshot:

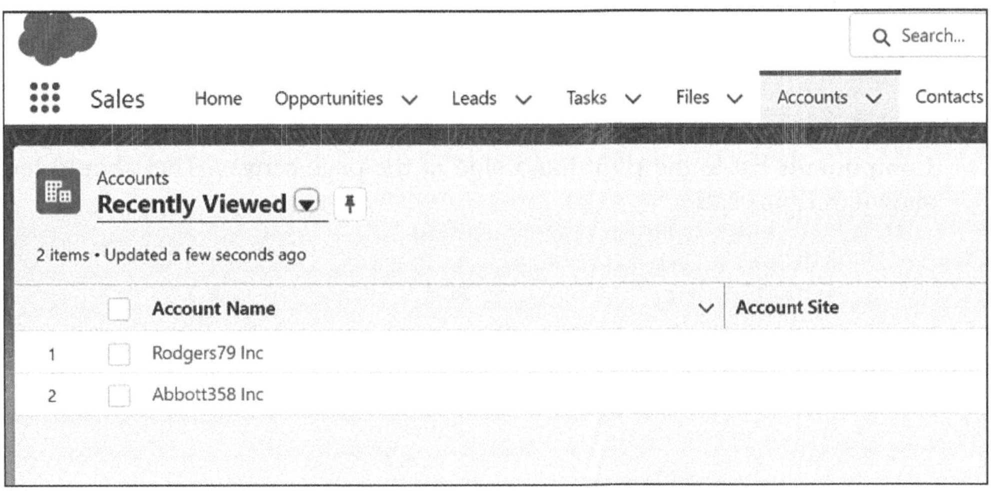

Figure 7.19: *Accounts tab in Sales app*

2. Choose an account from the **All Accounts** list, it does not matter which.
3. Click the **Setup** gear and select **Edit Page**, as shown below.

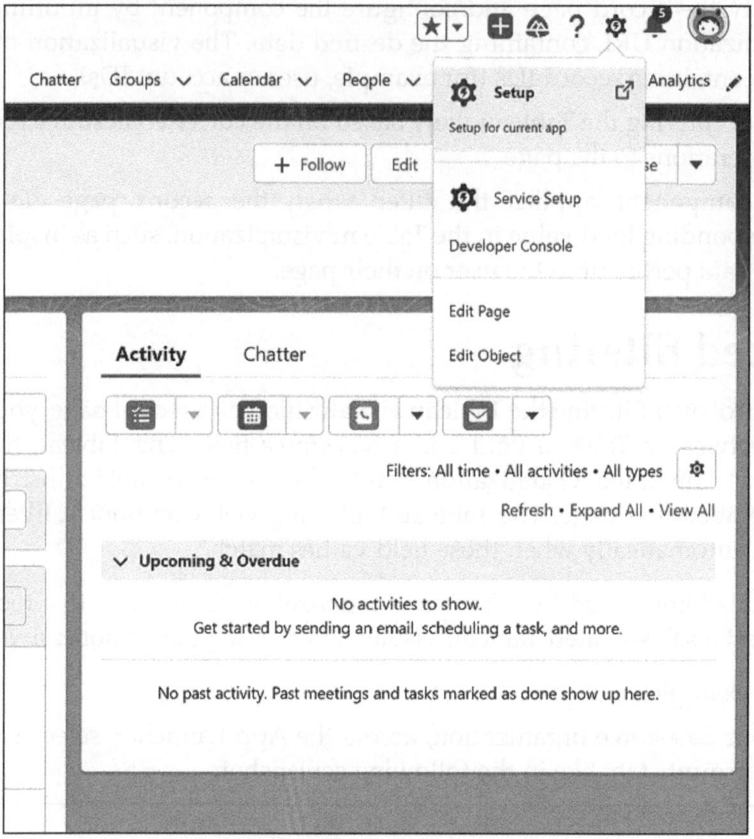

Figure 7.20: Setup menu on Account page

4. Drag the **Tableau Visualization** component from the Custom area of the **Lightning Components** list to the right-hand side of the page canvas. That should look as shown in *Figure 7.21:*

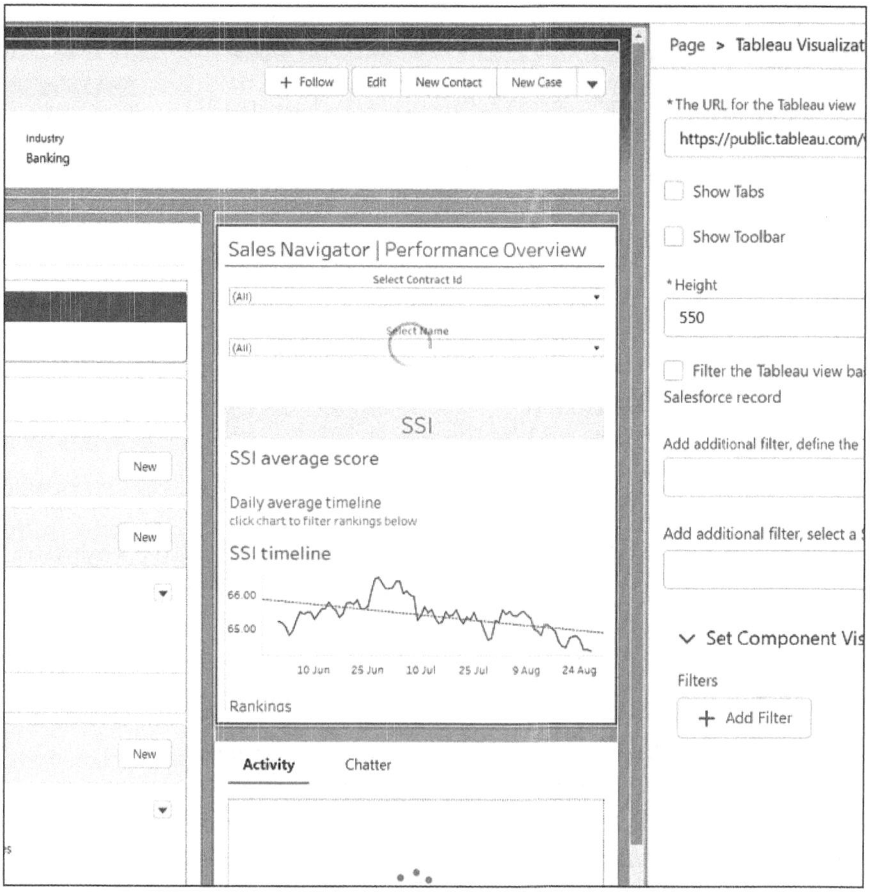

Figure 7.21: *Dragging Tableau Visualization to Account page*

5. Configure the component by entering the Tableau visualization URL containing the desired data. Here you can use: **https://public.tableau.com/views/MarketingActivityCalendar/MarketingActivityCalendar?:language=en&:display_count=y&:origin=viz_share_link**
6. Specify the Tableau field for filtering, which must be a field in the embedded visualization. Here you can type in "City". Now, indicate the Salesforce field for filtering, which can be chosen from the qualified field names drop-down list, here choose "BillingCity"
7. Save the page and return to the account page. The Lightning Web Component now filters the Tableau visualization automatically when the values from the two specified fields match. In the screenshot below, "BillingCity" is set to "Dallas".

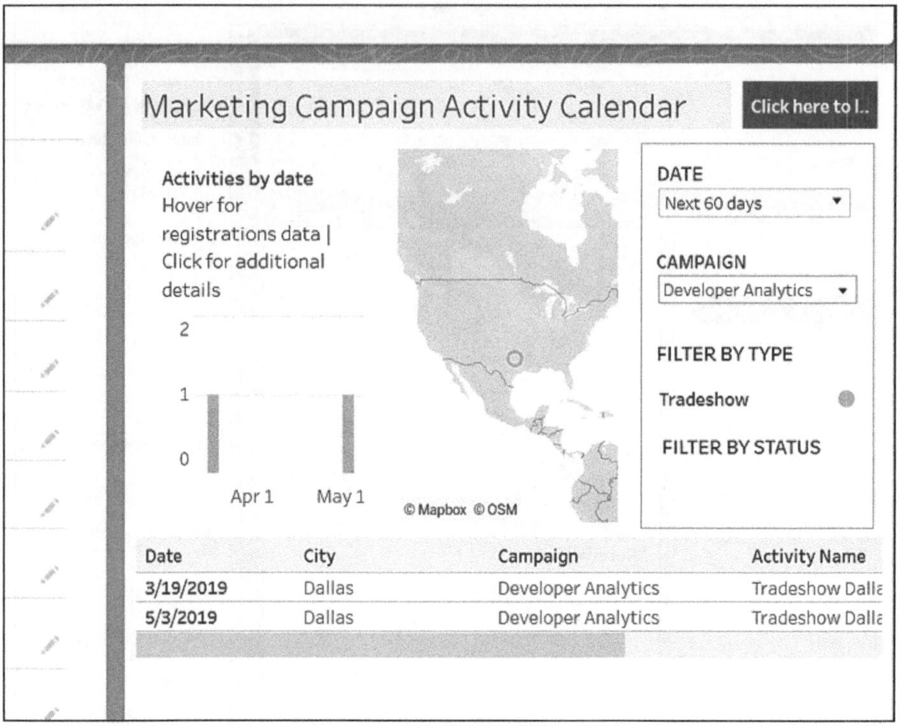

Figure 7.22: *Context filtering based on account field*

If you need an exceptional level of control of the experience, the Tableau Viz LWC is available on GitHub, **https://github.com/tableau/tableau-viz-lwc/** , under an MIT license. This means that you can fork the component and create your own version. This is not advisable under normal circumstances, but it is good to know that it is possible should you experience unique security, performance, or compatibility requirements that cannot be addressed using the standard component.

Setting up SSO between Salesforce and Tableau Online

When you embed dashboards from Tableau Online in Salesforce, you will normally have to log in with your Tableau credentials to see the dashboard, which can be quite annoying to users in the long run. To avoid this, you have the option of setting up SSO between the two environments.

This is a complex process, but worth the effort. To set up a SSO between your organization and Tableau Online, you follow these broad steps:

1. Configure your organization as an identity provider in Salesforce.
2. Adjust SAML settings in Tableau Online.

3. Create a connected app in Salesforce to integrate with Tableau Online.
4. Manage access to the connected app in Salesforce.
5. Download and apply the identity provider metadata from Salesforce in Tableau Online.
6. Test the SSO configuration by launching the application.

As there is no substitute for hands-on practice, let us dive in and set this up:

1. First, we need to configure Salesforce as an IdP. To do this, navigate to **Identity Provider** in **Setup**, as shown in the next screenshot:

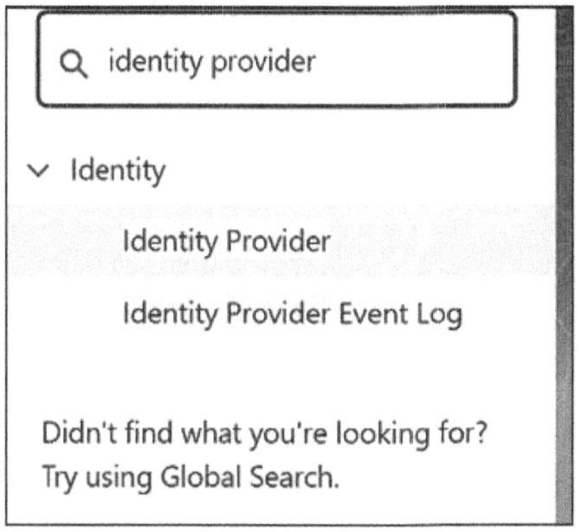

Figure 7.23: *Identity Provider section in Setup*

2. Click **Enable Identity Provider**, shown in the screenshot below, to enable your Salesforce org for identity:

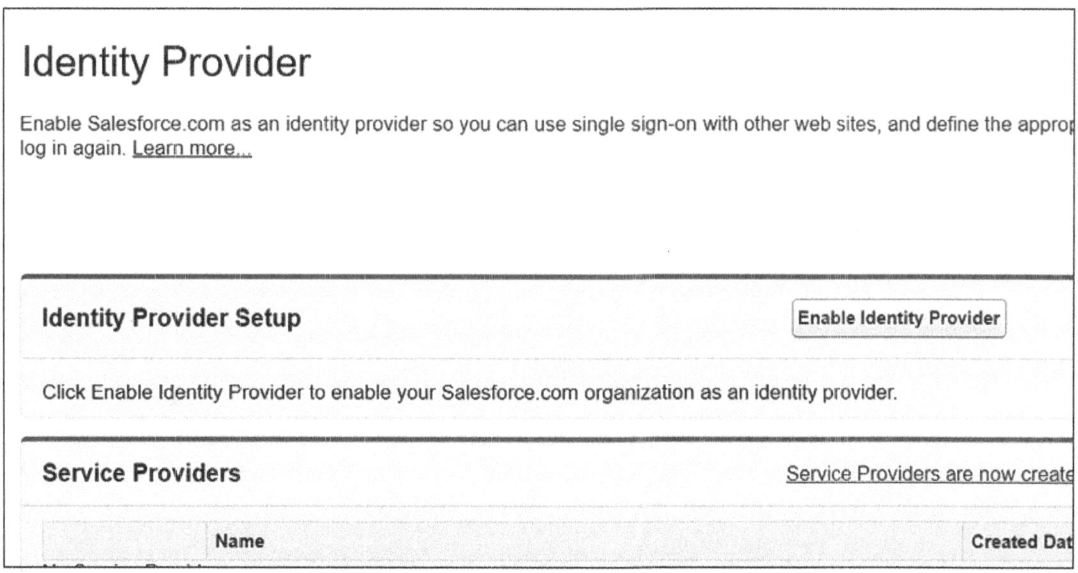

Figure 7.24: *Enabling Identity Provider*

3. Select the default certificate and click **Save**, as shown in *Figure 7.25*. Click **Ok** in the popup.

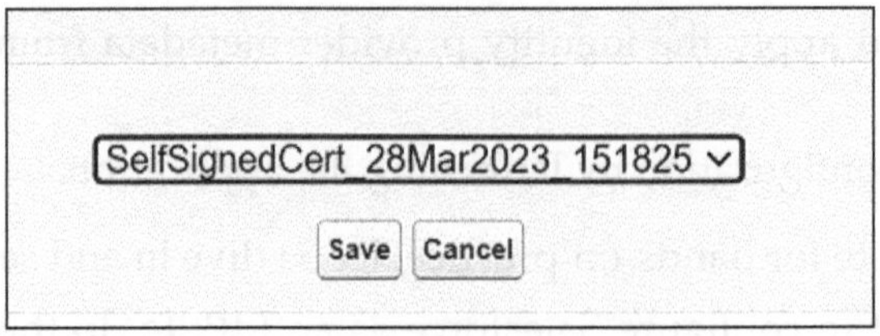

Figure 7.25: Selecting the certificate

4. Your org is now enabled as an identity provider. Click **Download Metadata**, as shown in *Figure 7.26*, and save the file somewhere to get to it later.

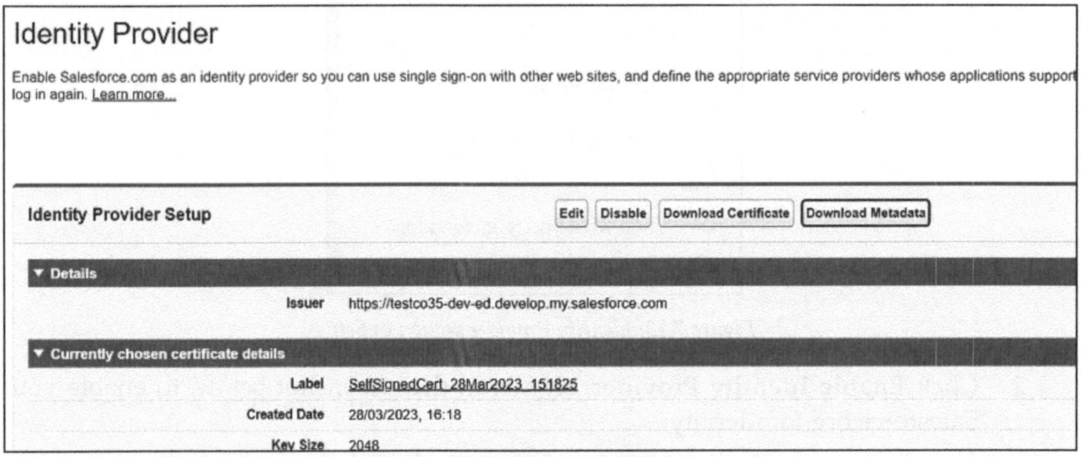

Figure 7.26: Downloading metadata file

The second step involves enabling your Tableau Online site for SSO. You do this by following these steps:

1. Log into your Tableau Online account.
2. Navigate to **Settings | Authentication**, as shown in the following screenshot:

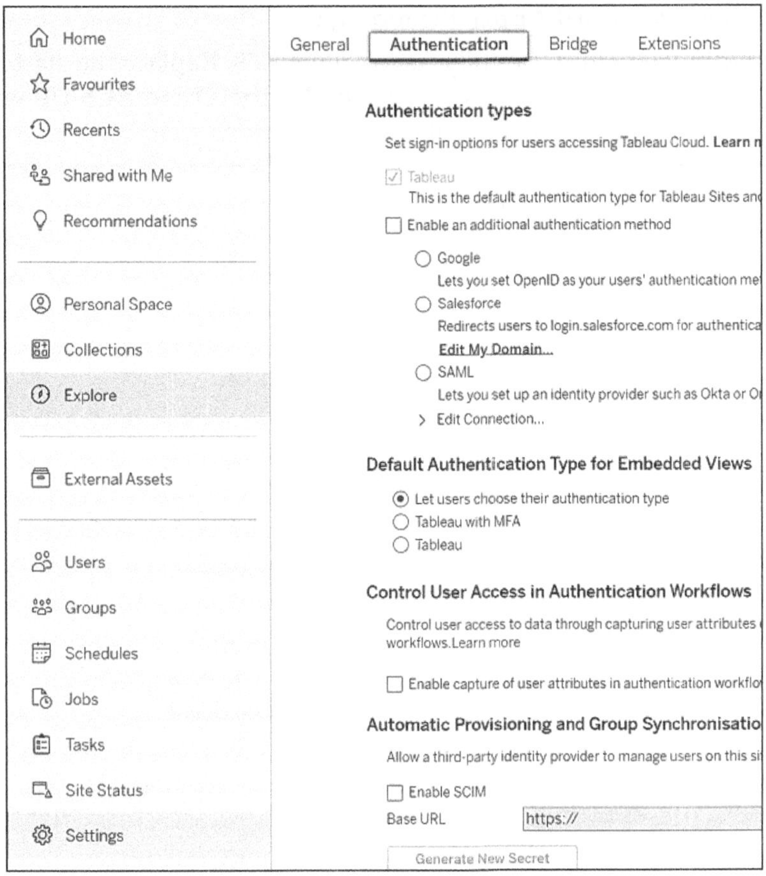

Figure 7.27: Authentication section in Tableau Online

3. Click **SAML** and then **Edit Connection**. Then copy the two URLs **Tableau Cloud entity ID** and **Assertion Consumer Service URL (ACS)** to a text file. You will need these later.

Now you will need to create a connected app in Salesforce for Tableau Cloud:

1. First, navigate to **App Manager** in **Setup**, as shown in the screenshot below.

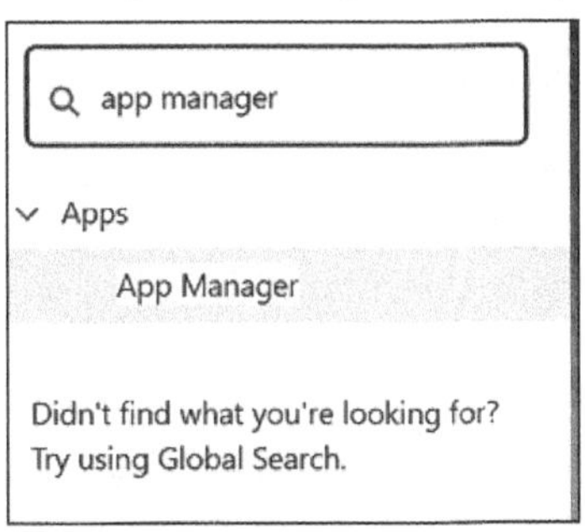

Figure 7.28: App Manager in Setup

2. Click **New Connected App** at the top right.
3. Now fill in the values carefully, as in *Figure 7.29*. Replace the start URL with the URL for your own Tableau Cloud site and **Entity ID** and **ACS UR** with the values you previously copied to a text file.

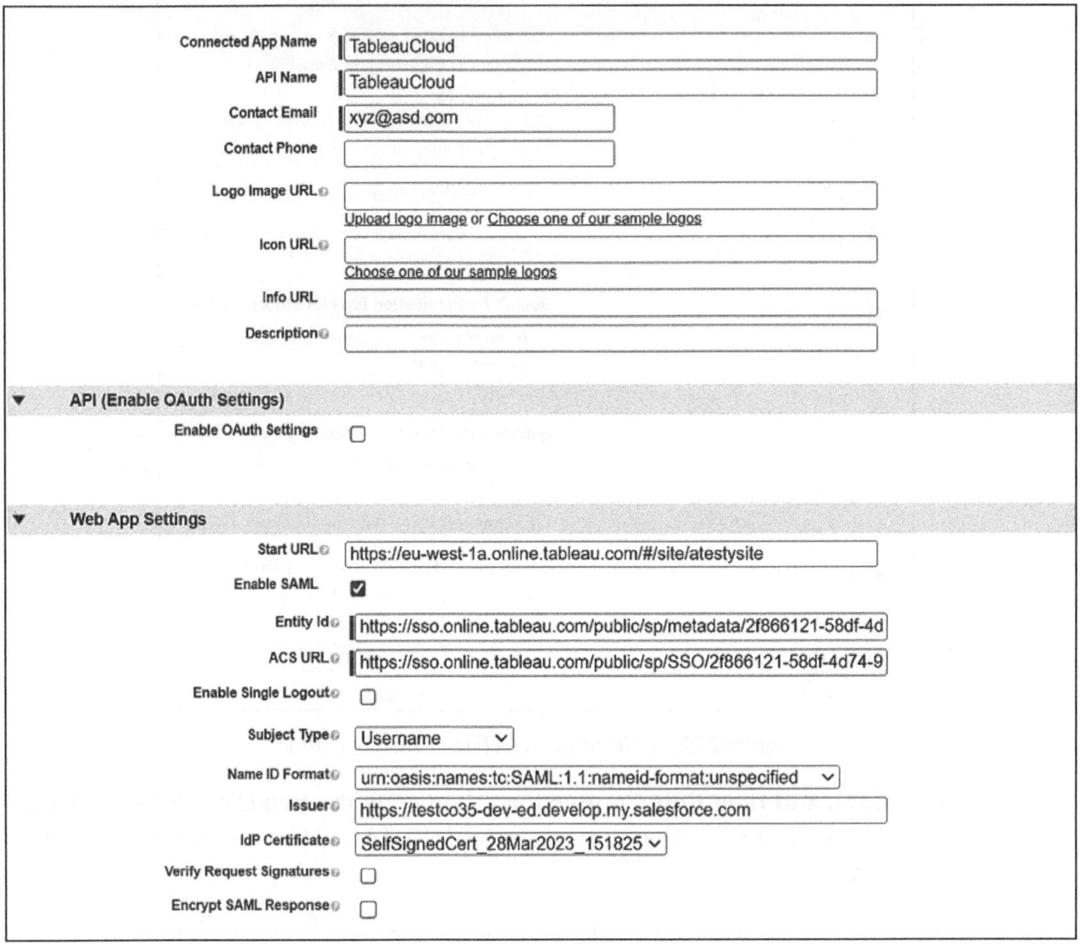

Figure 7.29: *New Connected App configuration*

Now you need to return to Tableau Cloud and import the Salesforce metadata:

1. Navigate to **Settings** | **Authentication**, expand **Edit connection** and go to *Step 4*.
2. Pick the metadata file you downloaded previously and click **Apply** as shown below:

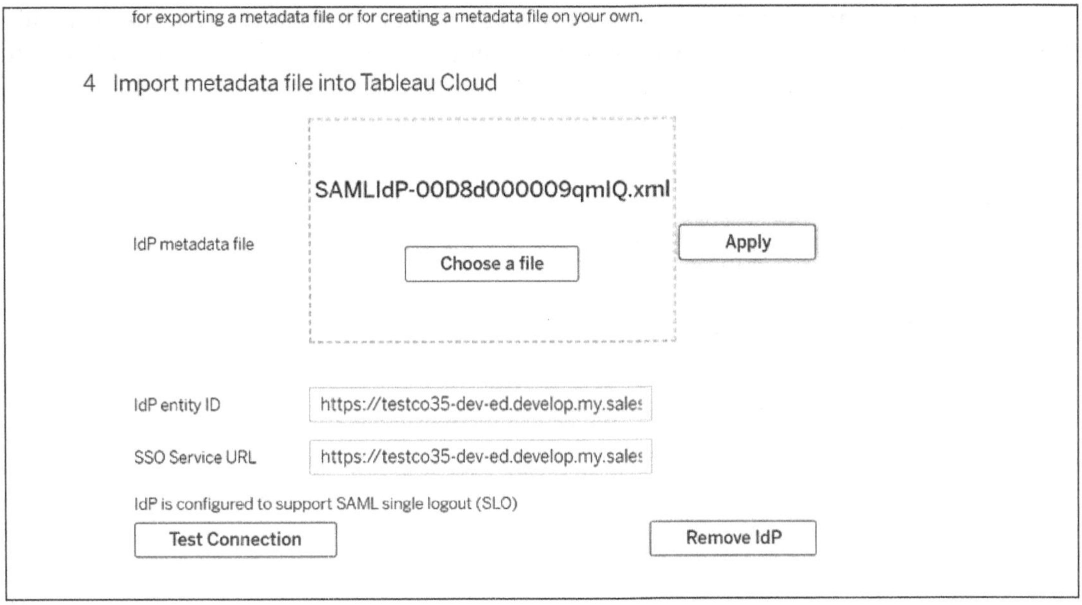

***Figure 7.30:** Importing Salesforce metadata file*

3. In *Step 6*, select **Authenticate using an inline frame**, shown in the screenshot below:

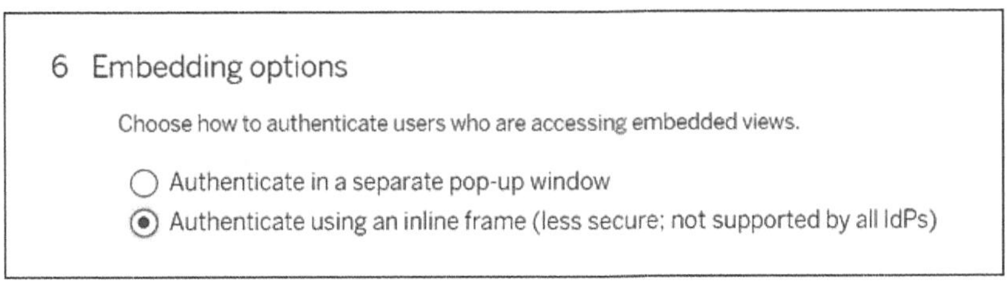

***Figure 7.31:** SAML configuration option*

4. Under **Default Authentication Type for Embedded Views** pick **SAML**, as shown in *Figure 7.32*:

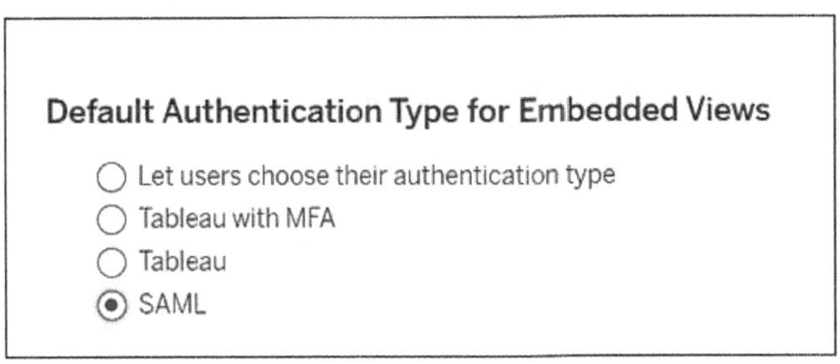

***Figure 7.32:** Default authentication type*

5. Now you can save.

To work, the username (email) of the users using SSO must match between Salesforce and Tableau. So if you have not used the same username on the two systems, you will need to create matching user accounts on either or both systems to make the SSO work. Once you have done that, it will work.

Note that there is now also an option of simply using Salesforce directly for authentication, which is easier to set up, but less general in its applicability. The method we have been through will work with any SAML-based IdP not just Salesforce.

Alternative methods to connect Salesforce and Tableau Dashboards

While the Tableau Viz LWC component is the most common way to link Salesforce and Tableau, there are alternatives that you may want to consider in certain cases. First among these is the humble hyperlink or, alternately, a Salesforce Web Tab, linking to the relevant Tableau destination.

The main reason you would consider using a hyperlink instead of an embedded dashboard is that it is easy to implement and provides a level of control to the user. With a hyperlink, the user can decide when and where to access the Tableau dashboard. They can open it in a separate tab, window, or device and customize the view settings to their liking. Moreover, hyperlinks are easy to create and manage, and they do not require any special integration or maintenance efforts from either the Salesforce or Tableau side.

However, there are many drawbacks to using hyperlinks as well. First, you have to break the context and go to a different interface. It is also more difficult to pass parameters that are specific to the user context, as these will need to be set up in the visualization. Also, the security setup can become more complex by going down this route.

Using a hyperlink to link Salesforce and Tableau can be a viable option in certain cases. Still, it is important to weigh the pros and cons and consider the specific needs and preferences of your users before making a decision.

A second alternate option is to use a Tableau Connected App. Tableau-connected apps are a great way to securely and seamlessly authenticate external applications that embed Tableau content with your Tableau Cloud site. There are two types of connected apps: direct trust and OAuth 2.0 trust.

- Direct trust allows you to restrict access to content that can be embedded and where it can be embedded. With direct trust, users can access embedded content using SSO without having to integrate with an IdP. You can also programmatically authorize access to the Tableau REST API and manage the Tableau REST API capabilities that users or applications can perform.

- OAuth 2.0 trust also allows you to control access to embedded content and enable users to access it through SSO via your IdP. You can provide access using the standard OAuth 2.0 protocol, programmatically authorize access to the Tableau REST API, and manage Tableau REST API capabilities that users or applications can perform.

It is important to note that Tableau-connected apps and Salesforce-connected apps are different and offer distinct functionalities. Currently, Tableau connected apps are intended for embedding Tableau views and metrics in external applications and authorizing access to the Tableau REST API.

Generally, you should not use a Connected App with Salesforce. The one exception might be if you are planning to use the same app across several target systems that need to embed information from Tableau and should be managed in a consistent way. You would just be creating more trouble for yourself.

Finally, there is the option of embedding Tableau Dashboard as a canvas app using the Sparkler framework. This used to be the preferred way of embedding Tableau Dashboards into Salesforce, but it has now been superseded by the Tableau Viz LWC Component. The setup for this option is very complex. It involves a Java-based application, *Sparkler*, which can be used to embed Tableau dashboards in Salesforce using Salesforce's canvas framework.

To set up Sparkler, you must download the adapter, create a virtual machine to run it, install Java 8, install Tomcat, enable HTTPS for Tomcat, install Sparkler, configure secure communication between Sparkler and Tableau Online, and configure a connection between Salesforce and Sparkler.

Finally, you must embed and filter the dashboard on a record in Lightning Experience by creating a new Visualforce page and customizing the record page. All in all, not something you want to do, given other options. However, you should know it as you could see it in a legacy environment.

Conclusion

In this chapter, we have provided a comprehensive guide on integrating Tableau with Salesforce using the Tableau Viz LWC component. You have learned the purpose and benefits of this integration, as well as the process of installing and configuring the Tableau Viz LWC component for seamless integration in Salesforce.

Furthermore, we have delved into advanced usage techniques, including the creation of custom visualizations and modifying the component's settings. We have also covered the implementation of **Single Sign-On (SSO)** between Salesforce and Tableau to streamline the authentication process and enhance security.

Additionally, we have explored alternative methods for connecting Salesforce and Tableau dashboards, such as direct connections and third-party integration tools. With the knowledge gained from this chapter, you are now well-equipped to enhance your CRM analytics in Salesforce using the Tableau Viz LWC component and make more data-driven decisions to drive business success.

In the next chapter, we will dive deeper into how you can combine Tableau with CRM Analytics to create game-changing analytical use cases.

Join our book's Discord space

Join the book's Discord Workspace for Latest updates, Offers, Tech happenings around the world, New Release and Sessions with the Authors:

https://discord.bpbonline.com

CHAPTER 8
Blending Tableau with Traditional CRM Analytics

Introduction

This chapter will introduce CRM Analytics and its importance in understanding and improving customer relationships. It will begin by providing an overview of CRM analytics and its key features, including creating datasets and lenses to analyze customer data. Additionally, the chapter will explain how to create an Einstein Discovery model within Salesforce and use it from within the CRM Analytics platform. Lastly, the chapter will detail the use of the CRM Analytics Tableau Output Connector, which allows for the seamless integration of Salesforce data into Tableau for further analysis. Overall, this chapter will provide a comprehensive understanding of the capabilities and benefits of CRM Analytics within Salesforce and its integration with Tableau.

Structure

The chapter covers the following topics:

- Introducing CRM Analytics
- Creating Datasets, Lenses, and Dashboards in CRM Analytics
- Building a lens
- Creating an Einstein Discovery Model and using it from CRM Analytics
- Using the Tableau Online Output Connection

Objectives

In this chapter, learners will develop a thorough understanding of CRM Analytics and its crucial role in managing and enhancing customer relationships. They will delve into the key features of CRM analytics, including how to create datasets and lenses for effective customer data analysis.

The chapter guides learners through creating an Einstein Discovery model within Salesforce and demonstrates how to utilize it within the CRM Analytics platform. A significant focus is placed on employing the CRM Analytics Tableau Output Connector, which facilitates the seamless integration of Salesforce data into Tableau. This includes learning how to export Salesforce data for use in Tableau and maximizing the capabilities of the CRM Analytics Tableau Output Connector.

Learners will gain a comprehensive understanding of the functionalities and benefits of CRM Analytics within Salesforce, particularly in its integration with Tableau. By the end of the chapter, they will be equipped to apply their knowledge of CRM Analytics and Tableau in a way that significantly improves the quality of customer relationships and enhances business decision-making.

Introducing CRM Analytics

CRM Analytics, formerly known as Tableau CRM and Einstein Analytics, is a powerful data analysis and business insights platform that provides users with a comprehensive way to analyze customer data and derive actionable insights. Integrated seamlessly with Salesforce CRM, CRM Analytics leverages the power of machine learning from Einstein Discovery to deliver intelligent analytics for businesses.

One of the key features of CRM Analytics is its native two-way integration with the rest of the Salesforce platform. This integration allows users to easily access and analyze data from their CRM system, creating a unified platform for managing customer relationships and analyzing customer data. Additionally, CRM Analytics offers on-platform data extraction and transformation, enabling businesses to process and prepare their data for further analysis.

CRM Analytics also provides external connectivity to various platforms and cloud storage providers, facilitating data ingestion from multiple sources. The platform enables users to visualize and explore their data through interactive dashboards, enhancing their ability to identify trends and patterns. Moreover, the data action framework allows users to make data-driven decisions based on the insights generated.

Embedded intelligence from Salesforce Einstein further enriches the analytical capabilities of CRM Analytics. This integration allows businesses to benefit from features such as Einstein Sentiment Analysis, providing deeper insights into customer data.

Another notable aspect of CRM Analytics is its integration with Tableau. By connecting CRM Analytics to Tableau, users can create interactive visualizations and insights using data from their CRM system. This enhances their ability to analyze and understand customer data, ultimately leading to improved customer relationships, increased sales, and enhanced overall business performance.

CRM Analytics offers businesses a powerful and comprehensive tool for analyzing customer data and making data-driven decisions. Through the creation of custom datasets and lenses, CRM Analytics empowers businesses to gain a deeper understanding of their customers and improve their relationships, all while leveraging the capabilities of Salesforce CRM.

The addition of CRM Analytics, therefore, adds another puzzle piece in the larger analytics picture for organizations that are invested in the Salesforce platform. We cannot cover this tool in detail in this book, but we will touch on some of the key places where it intersects with Tableau to give additional capabilities. First, however, we will look at how to do some basic analysis in CRM Analytics.

Creating Datasets, Lenses, and Dashboards in CRM Analytics

In CRM Analytics, the most basic concepts are app, dataset, lens, and dashboard. These are the basic building blocks to understand to be able to work in the system, although, of course, they are just the beginning.

Before we dive into the practical steps of creating a dashboard in CRM Analytics, let's briefly familiarize ourselves with the fundamental concepts of app, dataset, lens, and dashboard. Understanding these components is crucial as they form the backbone of CRM Analytics.

- **App**: In CRM Analytics, an app serves as a container for your analytical projects. It's a workspace where you can organize your datasets, lenses, and dashboards. Think of it as a folder on your computer where you keep related files together for easy access and organization.
- **Dataset**: A dataset is a collection of data that CRM Analytics can process. This data can come from various sources, including Salesforce records, external databases, or files like CSVs. Datasets are the raw materials from which you extract insights.
- **Lens**: A lens is a tool for exploring a dataset. It allows you to visualize data in different formats (such as charts or tables), filter the data to focus on specific aspects, and perform basic analyses. You can think of a lens as a magnifying glass that helps you examine the details of your dataset.

- **Dashboard**: A dashboard is a visual representation of your data analyses, often comprising multiple widgets (charts, tables, etc.) that display data from one or more datasets. Dashboards are designed to provide at-a-glance insights and support decision-making.

Now that we have a basic understanding of these concepts, let's proceed to create a simple dashboard in CRM Analytics to give you a feel for what you might be able to achieve if you were to dig deeper into the topic.

We will do this in a few steps:

1. Create an app to hold your unique analytical assets.
2. Import a dataset into the system.
3. Explore this dataset through a lens.
4. Build a simple dashboard to visualize the data.

Doing this will also teach you some of the key differences between creating dashboards in Tableau and doing so in CRM Analytics and why you might prefer one over the other in particular cases.

Let us begin!

Creating an analytics app

A CRM Analytics app is a comprehensive collection of analyses, data exploration paths, and powerful tools designed for in-depth, real-time data examination. CRM Analytics relies on apps to organize data projects, run presentations directly from dashboards, and manage asset sharing.

To get started with creating an app in your CRM Analytics-enabled Developer Edition org, follow these steps:

1. Open your CRMA Developer Edition org.
2. Access the App Launcher and search for Analytics Studio. Select it to open **Analytics Studio** in a new tab. Keep both tabs open, as you will need to work on the original tab later in the project. This is shown in the following screenshot:

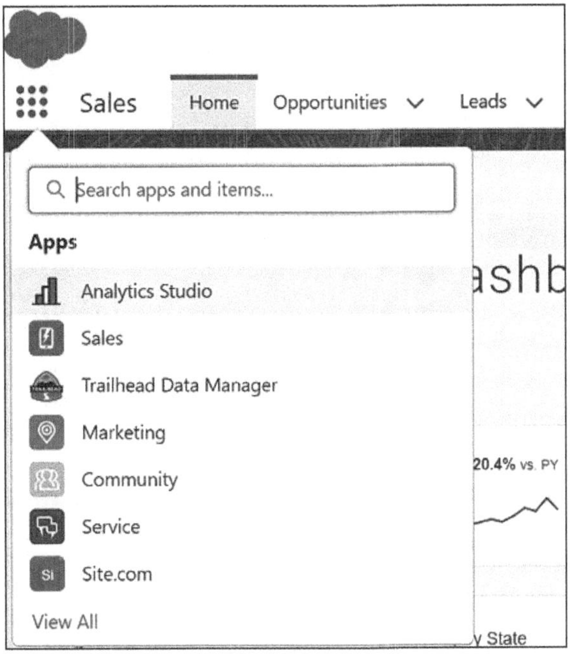

Figure 8.1: App Launcher showing Analytics Studio

3. In Analytics Studio, click the **Create** button and select **App** from the dropdown menu, as shown below:

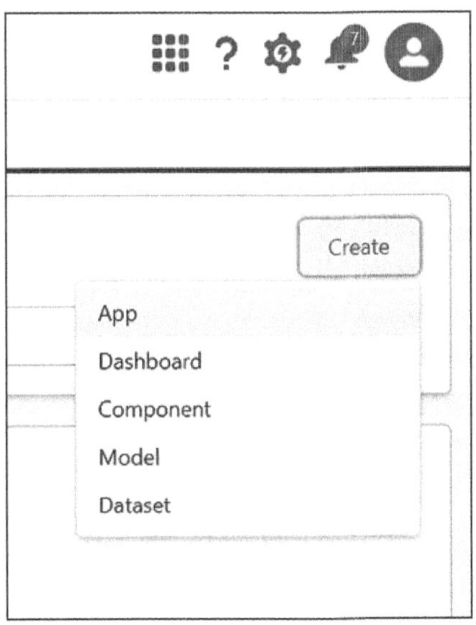

Figure 8.2: Create menu dropdown showing App option

4. Choose **Create Blank App** to start with a clean slate, as shown in the following screenshot:

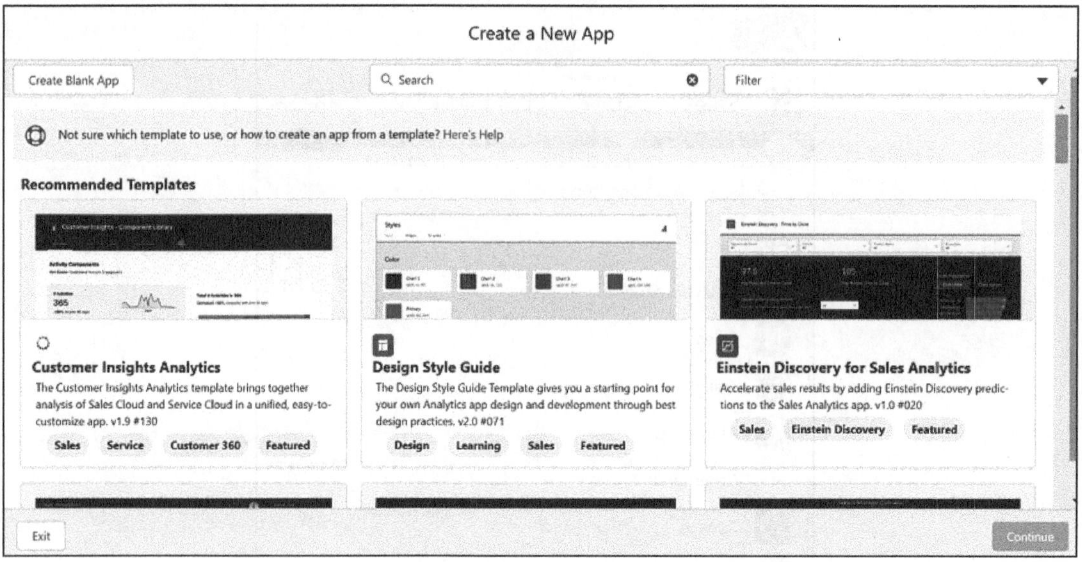

Figure 8.3: Blank App creation dialogue

5. Click **Continue** to proceed to the next step. Enter **My Test App** as the name of your new app, as shown below:

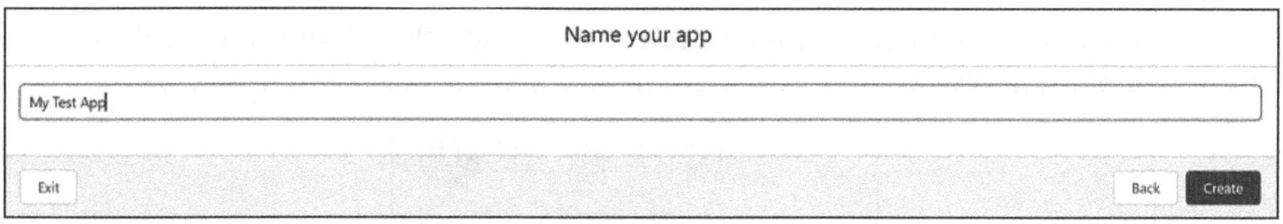

Figure 8.4: My Test App creation dialogue

6. Click **Create** to finalize the app creation process.

Congratulations! You have successfully created an app in CRM Analytics. We will now move on to importing a dataset.

Importing a dataset

CRM Analytics can work with many different kinds of data, both internal to the Salesforce platform and external, such as in a Snowflake data warehouse. To keep things simple, we will simply get our data from a CSV file. Start by downloading the file: **https://developer.salesforce.com/files/opportunity_history.csv**. This file is used for several Salesforce tutorials, and we will make use of it as well, for instance: **https://trailhead.salesforce.com/content/learn/modules/einstein-discovery-basics/build-your-crm-analytics-dataset**.

Our next step is, therefore to import the data from the CSV file into a CRM Analytics dataset, which can be done using the following steps:

1. On the Analytics Studio home tab, click **Create**, select **Dataset**, and then choose **CSV File**, as shown in *Figure 8.5*:

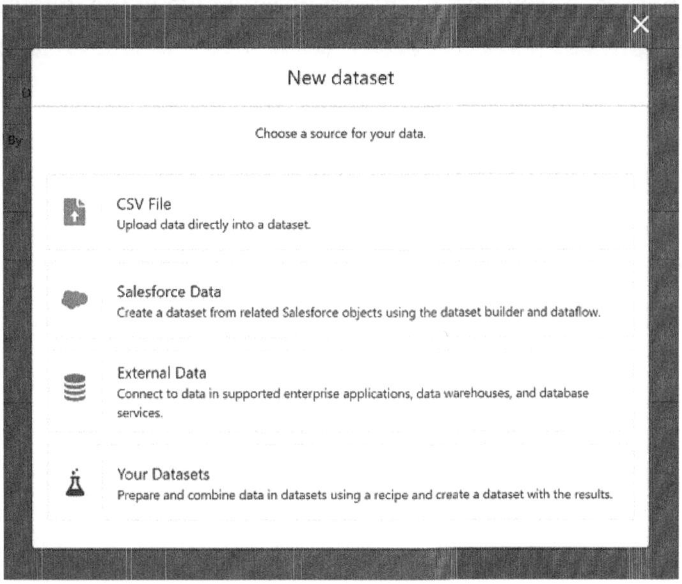

***Figure 8.5:** Dataset creation menu showing CSV file option*

2. In the file-selection window that opens, locate the CSV file you downloaded, **`opportunity_history.csv`**, select it and then click **Next**. You can see this in the following screenshot:

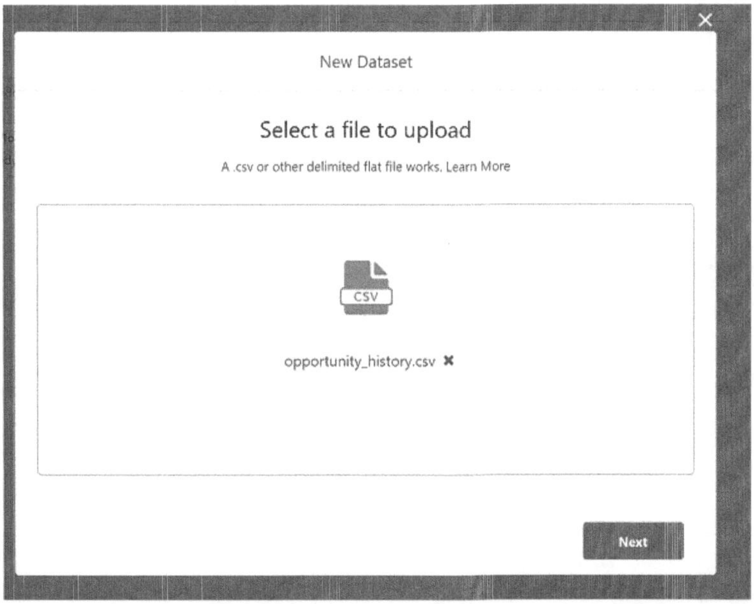

***Figure 8.6:** File selection dialogue*

3. In the **Dataset Name** field, you can change the default name (opportunity_history), as shown below. By default, Analytics Studio uses the file name as the dataset name, which cannot exceed 80 characters as shown in the following figure:

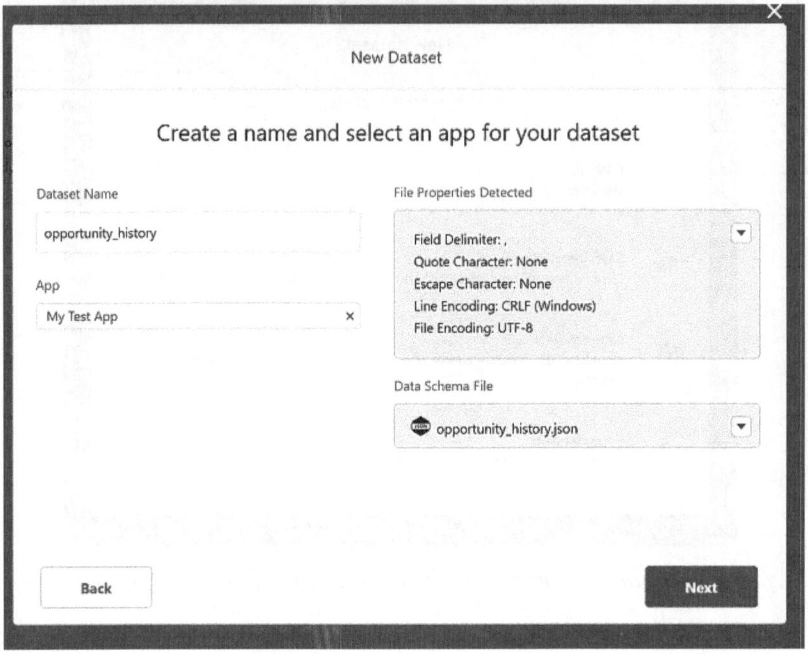

Figure 8.7: Dataset name field

4. Choose the app where you want to create the dataset. By default, Analytics Studio selects **My Test App**.
5. Click **Next**. The **Edit Field Attributes** screen appears, shown in *Figure 8.8*, where you can preview the data and view or edit the attributes for each field.

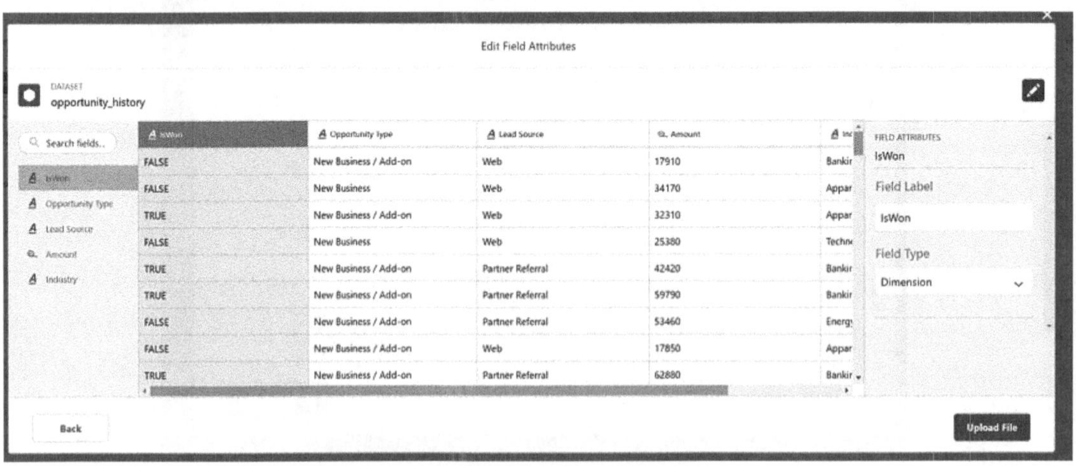

Figure 8.8: Edit field attributes screen

6. For now, accept the defaults and click **Upload File**. Analytics Studio uploads the data, prepares, and creates the dataset while showing progress as it occurs. You can see this in the following screenshot:

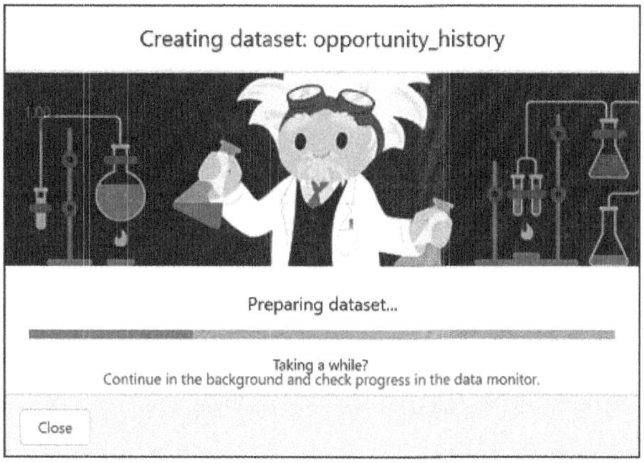

Figure 8.9: *File upload progress*

Once finished, you will see details about the dataset you created. If you do not see the dataset details, check your **Datasets** or search for **opportunity_history** in Analytics Studio.

Building a lens

A lens is a visual representation of the data within a dataset, allowing you to explore data graphically and construct queries for a dashboard. To build a lens, follow the steps below:

1. Click on the **Analytics Studio** tab to return to the CRM Analytics Home page.
2. Click **Browse** and then select **Datasets.**
3. Choose the **`opportunity_history`** dataset, which will open a new tab, shown below, with a lens for exploring the dataset.

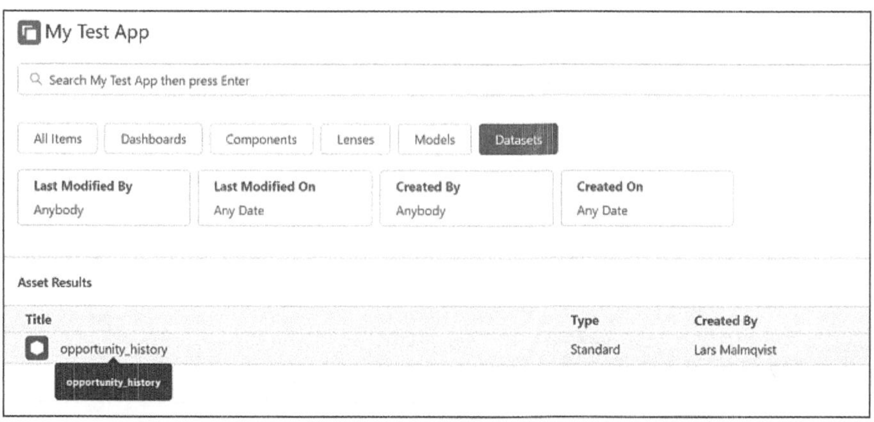

Figure 8.10: *Opportunity_history dataset details*

2. In the **New Lens** tab, click on **Count of Rows** located beneath **Bar Length**, as shown in the following screenshot:

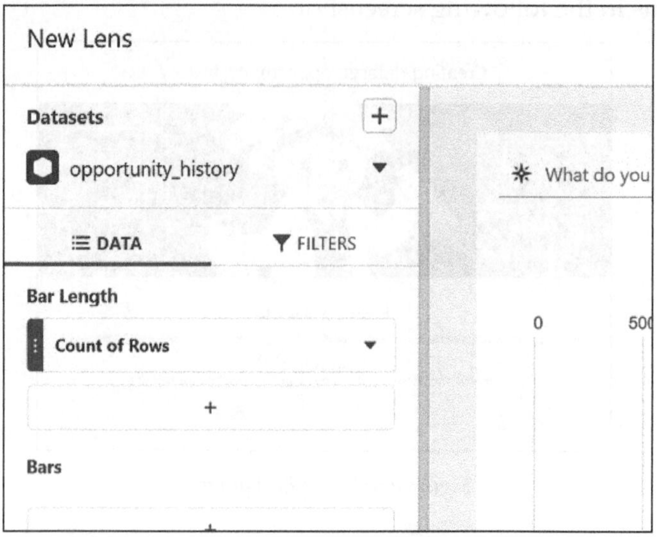

Figure 8.11: Lens builder with Count of Rows highlighted

4. Select **Sum** and then choose **Amount** from the dropdown menu, as shown in the next screenshot:

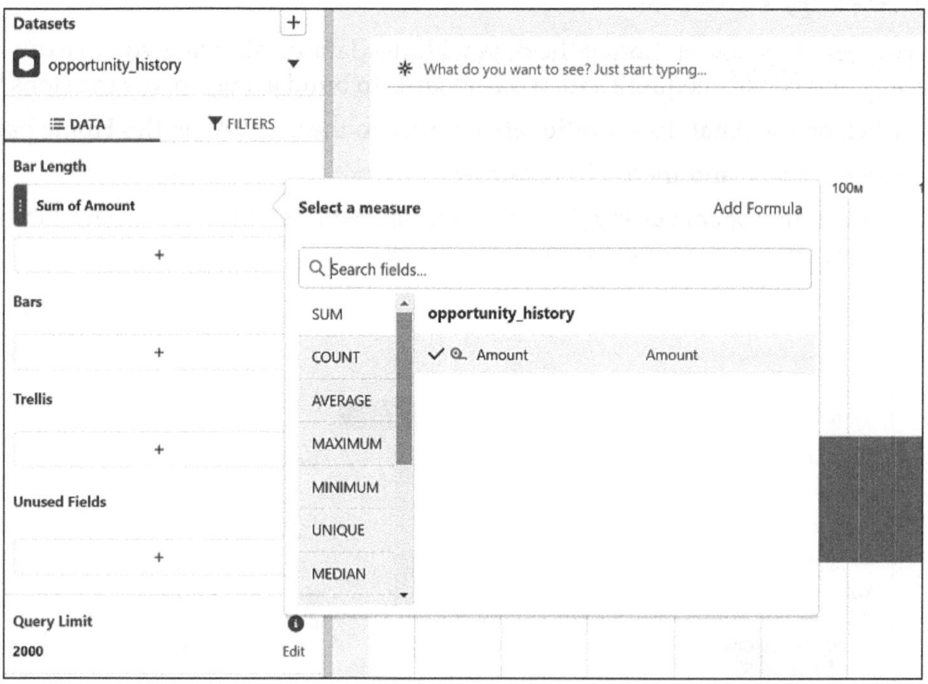

Figure 8.12: Sum Amount selected

5. Under **Bars**, click the plus sign (+) and select **Industry**, as shown below:

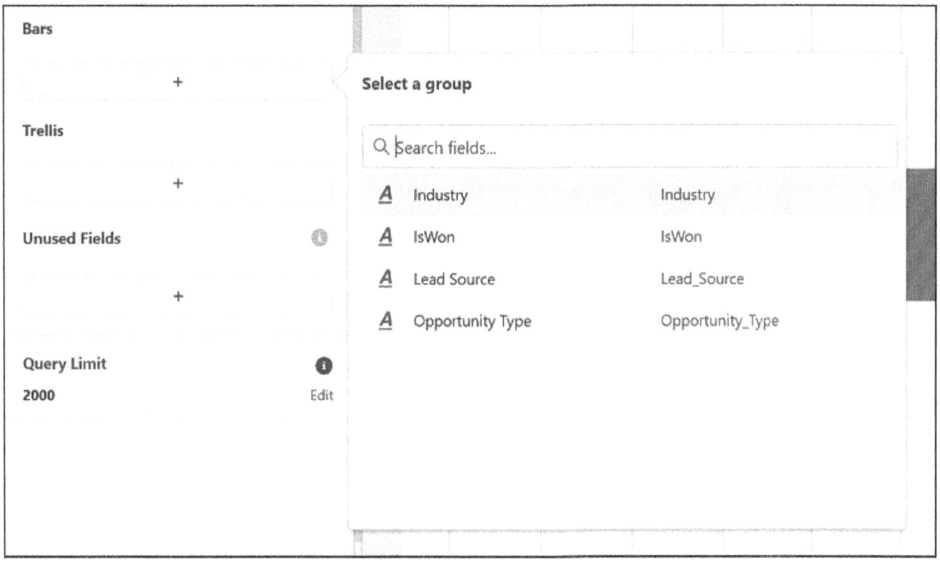

Figure 8.13: *Industry field added to lens*

6. Click the plus sign (+) under **Bars** again, and choose **Opportunity Type**, as shown below:

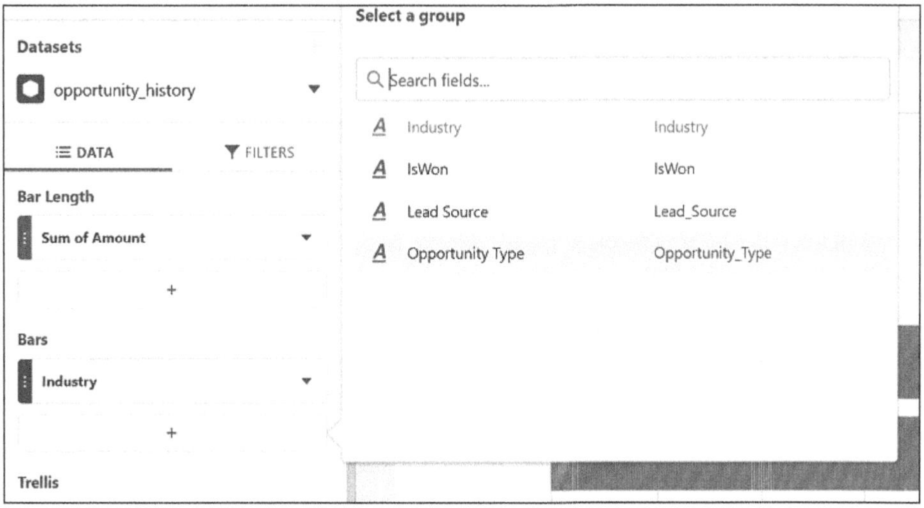

Figure 8.14: *Opportunity Type added to lens*

7. Under **Bar Length**, click the arrow next to **Sum of Amount** and select **Sort Descending**, shown in *Figure 8.15*:

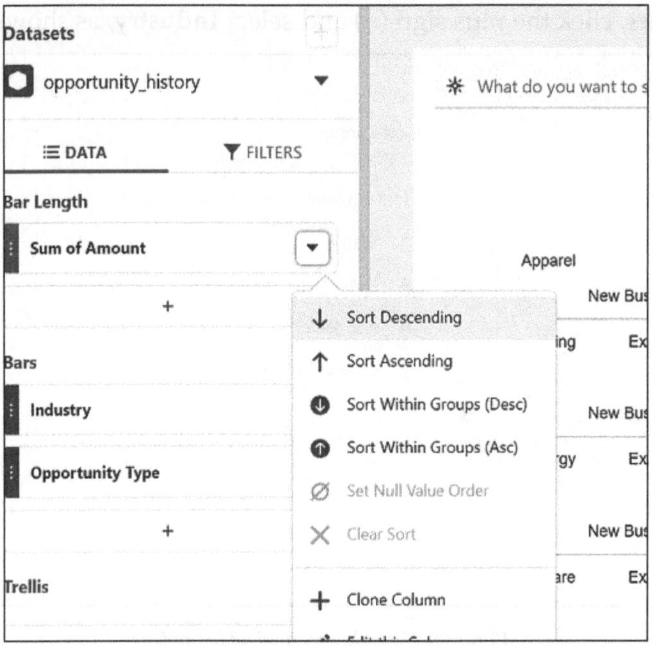

Figure 8.15: Sort descending selected

8. Click the **Charts** icon to access different chart options, shown in the following screenshot:

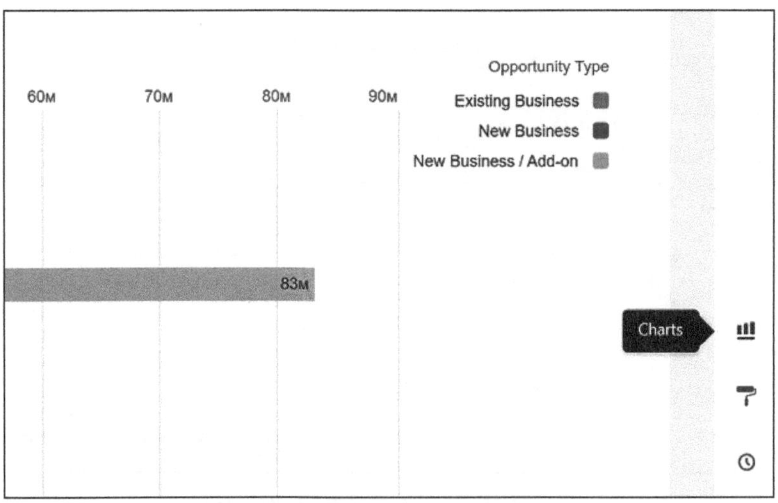

Figure 8.16: Charts icon highlighted

9. Select the **Stacked Column** chart icon, shown in the screenshot below, to create a Stacked Column chart, which will display the sum of the amount according to the industry.

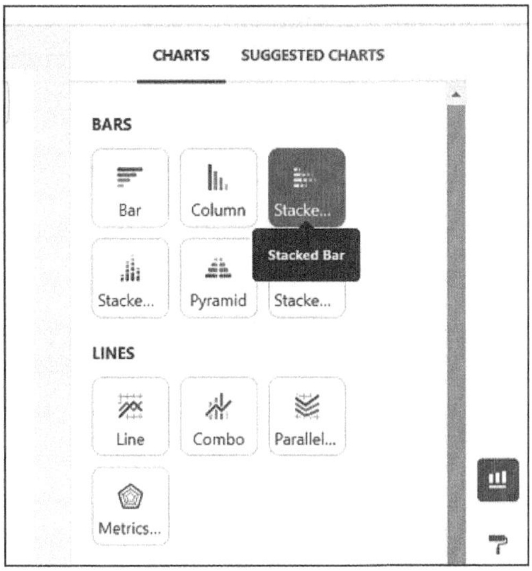

Figure 8.17: Stacked column chart selected

10. Save your lens by clicking the **Save** button.
11. Enter **My Test Lens**, indicated in the following screenshot, as the title of your new lens, and then choose **App** | **My Test App** from the dropdown menu.

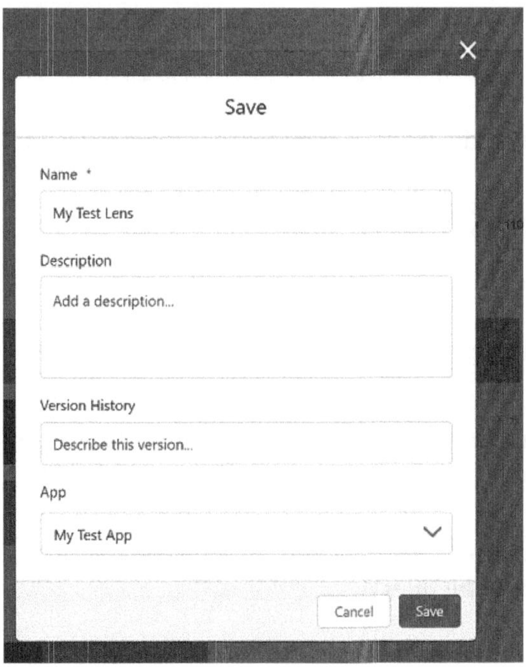

Figure 8.18: Save lens dialogue

12. Click **Save** to complete the process.

Your final product should look like the following:

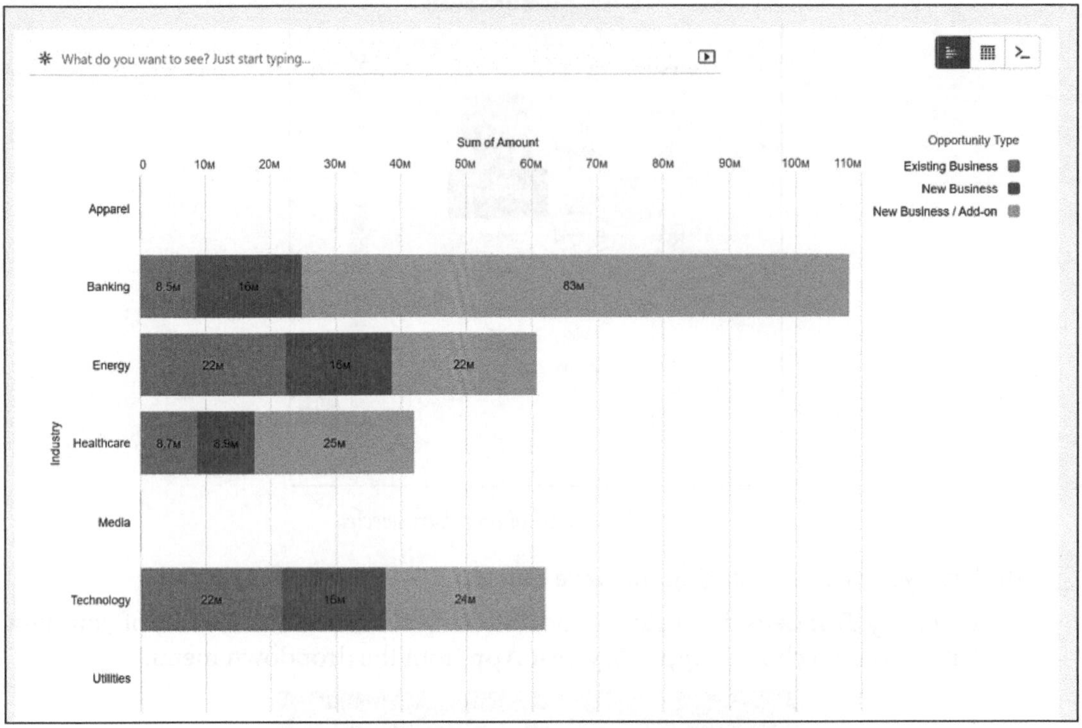

***Figure 8.19:** Completed stacked column lens visualization*

With your app, dataset, and lens now created, you can proceed to create a dashboard.

Making a dashboard

A dashboard is an engaging compilation of widgets that display the results of data queries. In this section, you will create a dashboard with an interactive chart and a list widget. You will incorporate the lens from the previous step and explore tools in the dashboard designer.

To incorporate a lens into a dashboard, you need to clip it. Clipping the lens allows CRM Analytics to add the query as a step in a new dashboard (or the most recently used open dashboard).

1. In your newly created lens, click the **Clip to Designer** icon, marked in the following screenshot, to clip the query.

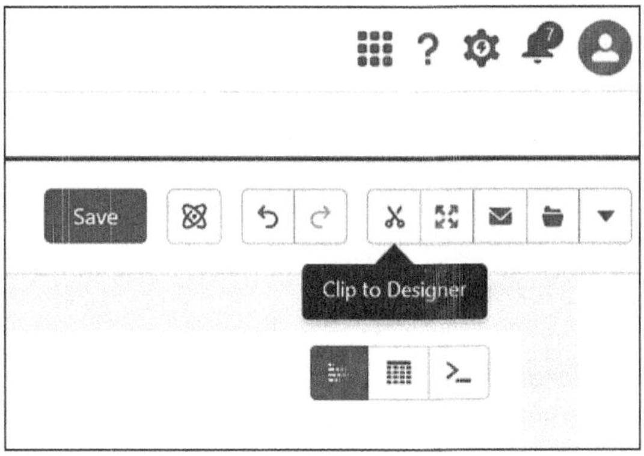

***Figure 8.20:** Clip to designer icon*

2. Under **Display Label**, enter **Breakdown by Industry** and click **Clip to Designer**.
3. CRM Analytics will open the dashboard designer and add the query in the query panel. **Breakdown by Industry** will be displayed under the **opportunity_history** dataset.

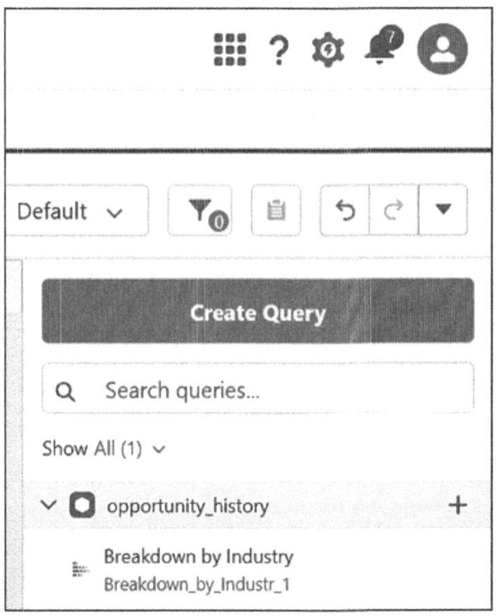

***Figure 8.21:** Lens added to designer with query name showing*

4. Drag the **Breakdown by Industry** query onto the new dashboard grid.
5. Resize the chart by dragging its corner to make it larger. The result should look like the following screenshot:

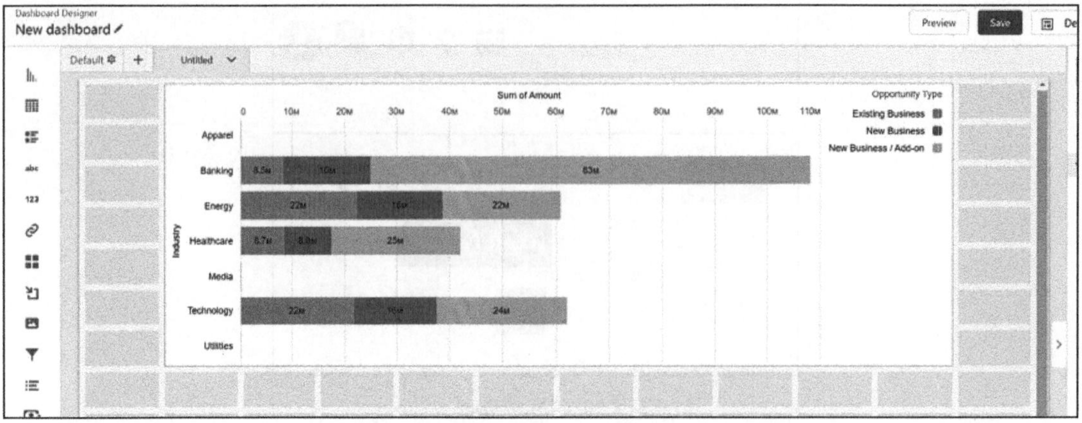

Figure 8.22: Query chart resized on dashboard

Widgets are the basic building blocks of a dashboard, providing various functions such as displaying key performance indicators, filtering dashboard results, visualizing data using interactive charts, or showing record-level details in tables. In this step, you will add a list widget to enable dashboard users to facet all the charts in the dashboard.

1. Drag the **List** widget icon, shown in the screenshot, from the left side onto an empty space on the dashboard underneath the chart.

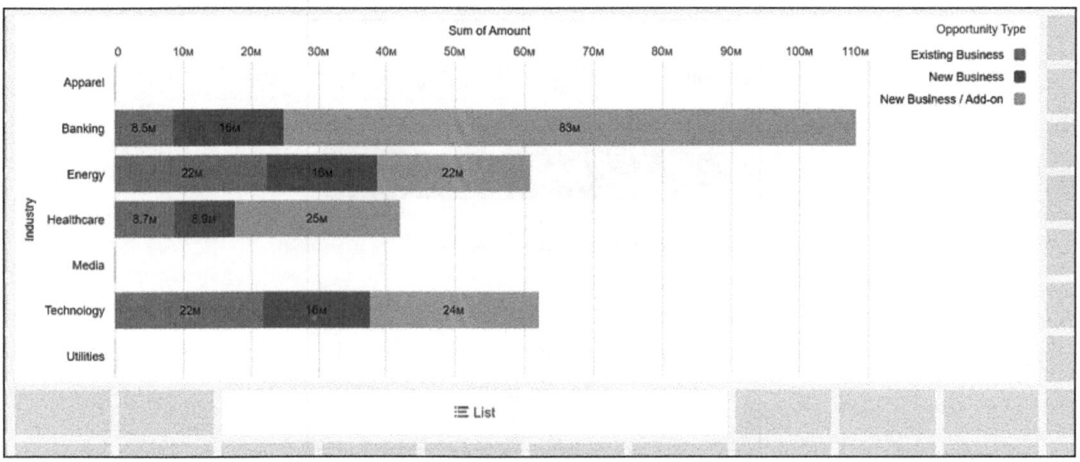

Figure 8.23: List widget being added to dashboard

2. Click on the **List** widget and select **Industry**.
3. Click **Create** in the window shown in the next screenshot:

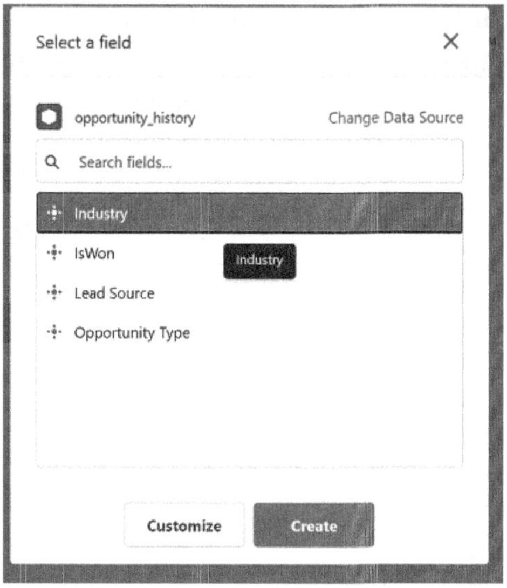

***Figure 8.24:** Industry field selected for list*

4. Select the list widget by clicking on it.
5. In the **Properties** panel on the right, click the **Query** tab.
6. Ensure that both **Apply global filters** and **Broadcast selections as facets** are selected.
7. Under **Selection Type**, choose **Multiple Selection**, shown in *Figure 8.25:*

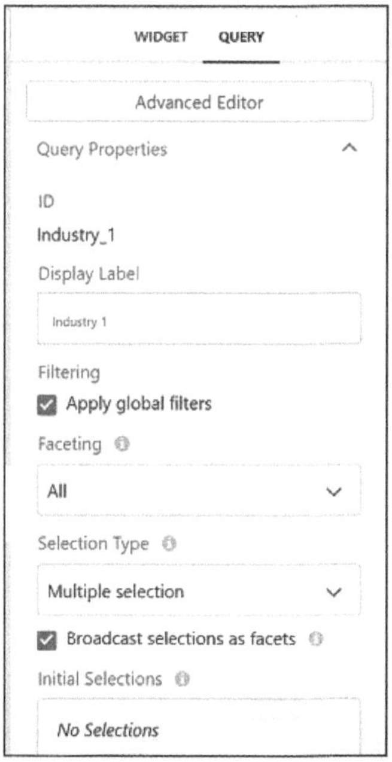

***Figure 8.25:** List widget properties*

8. Save your dashboard by clicking the **Save** button.
9. Enter **My Test Dashboard** as the title of your new dashboard, and select **App** | **My Test App** from the dropdown menu, as shown below:

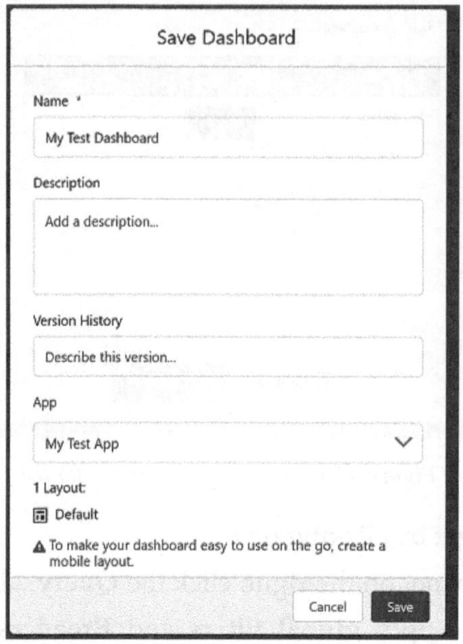

***Figure 8.26:** Save dashboard dialogue*

10. Click **Save** to complete the process. You can preview your dashboard, which should look like this:

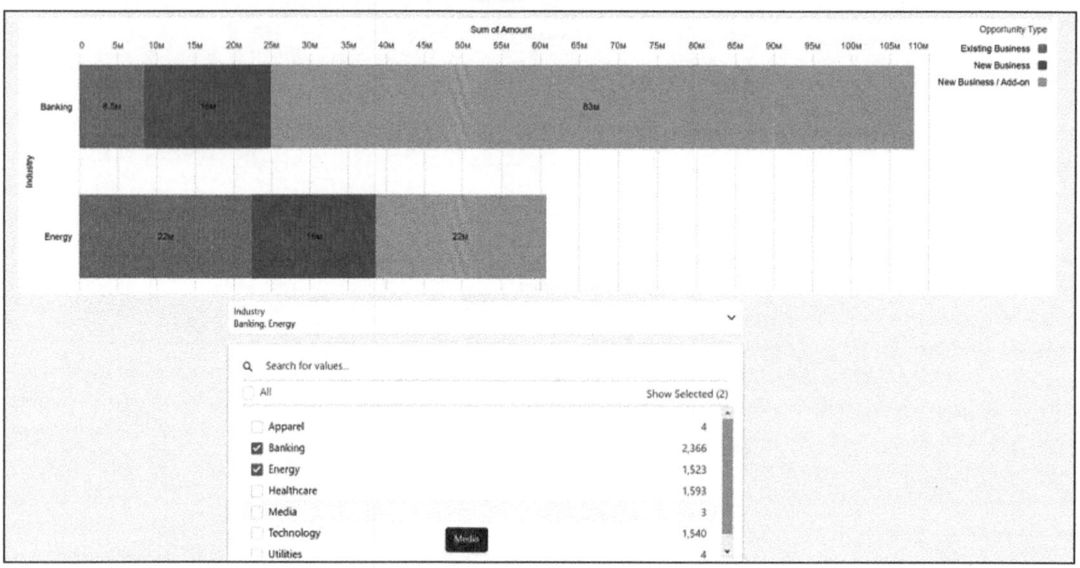

***Figure 8.27:** Completed test dashboard*

You have now created a basic dashboard. We hope you will explore the potential of CRM Analytics much further on your own, but for now we will move on to Einstein Discovery, the machine learning engine that powers CRM Analytics.

Creating an Einstein Discovery Model and using it from CRM Analytics

Einstein Discovery, a cutting-edge machine learning platform developed by Salesforce, is designed to bring transparent predictions and recommendations to users within Tableau workflows and in Salesforce CRM. This powerful tool enables data scientists, analysts, and business users to create predictive models without writing any algorithms. With its intuitive, no-code environment, Einstein Discovery empowers individuals and organizations to make smarter, more informed decisions guided by ethical and transparent AI.

In this section, we will create an Einstein Discovery model based on our opportunity history data and investigate it within CRM Analytics. In *Chapter 9 – Exploring Einstein AI and Advanced Analytics*, we will examine how to use this model from within Tableau.

To create a model and investigate its parameters, use the following steps:

1. Go to Analytics Studio and click **Create** | **Model**, as demonstrated in the following screenshot.

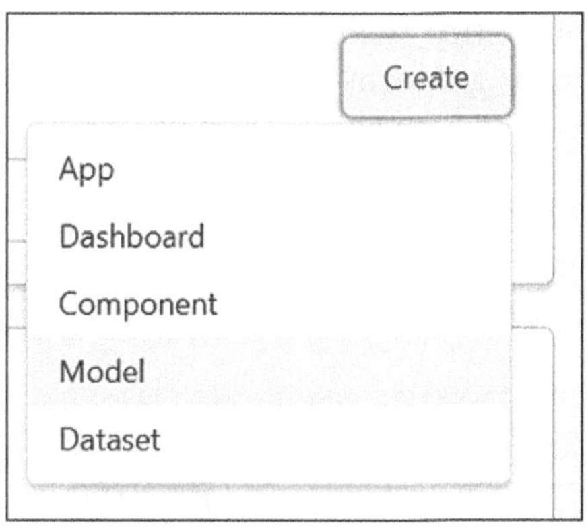

Figure 8.28: *Model creation dialogue*

2. Choose **Create from Dataset** in the dialogue that appears, shown below:

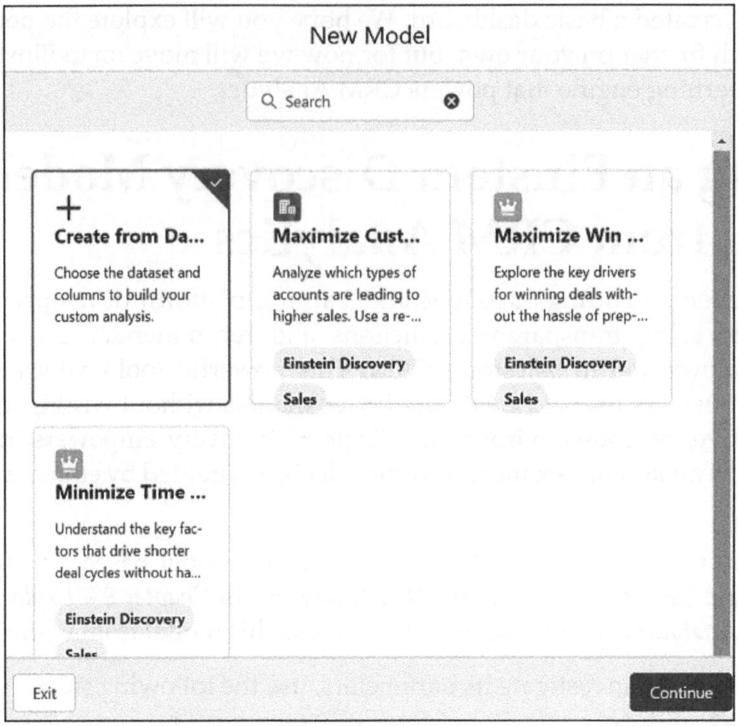

Figure 8.29: Create from dataset dialogue

3. Now select the **opportunity_history** dataset that we have previously created, as indicated in the following screenshot:

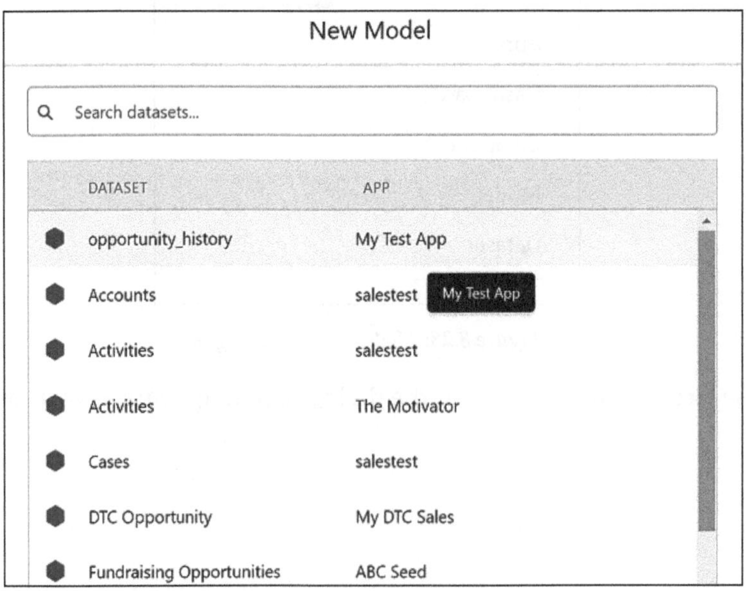

Figure 8.30: opportunity_history dataset selected

4. As the goal, follow the settings in the following screenshot to maximize the amount of the opportunity:

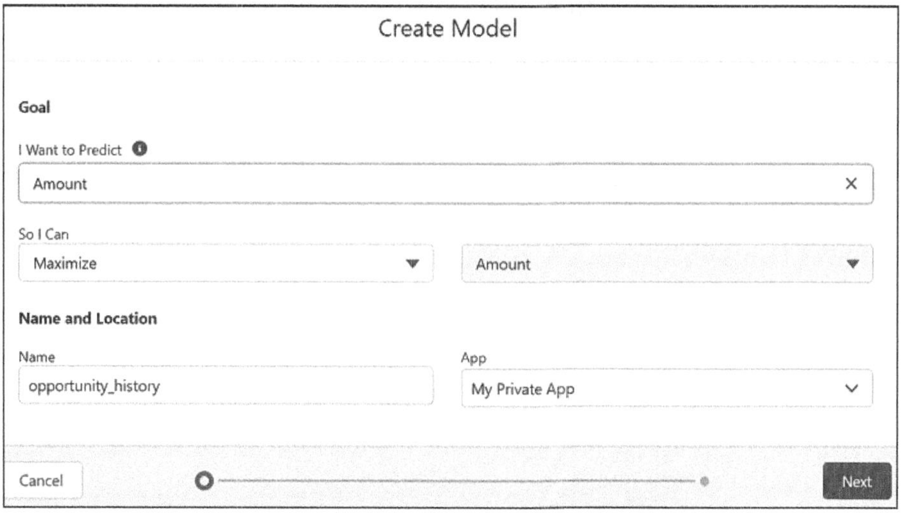

Figure 8.31: Model goal configuration

Einstein Discovery allows for considerable freedom in manually configuring the model that you want. However, for the purposes of this exercise, we will simply allow it to make the decisions itself. Therefore, select **Automated** in the **Configure Model Columns** dialogue. Note that this does mean we will take into account whether the opportunity was won or not, which you may want to exclude in a real scenario. However, in this scenario, the influence is not huge, so keeping it in does not materially change the result. You can see this in the following screenshot:

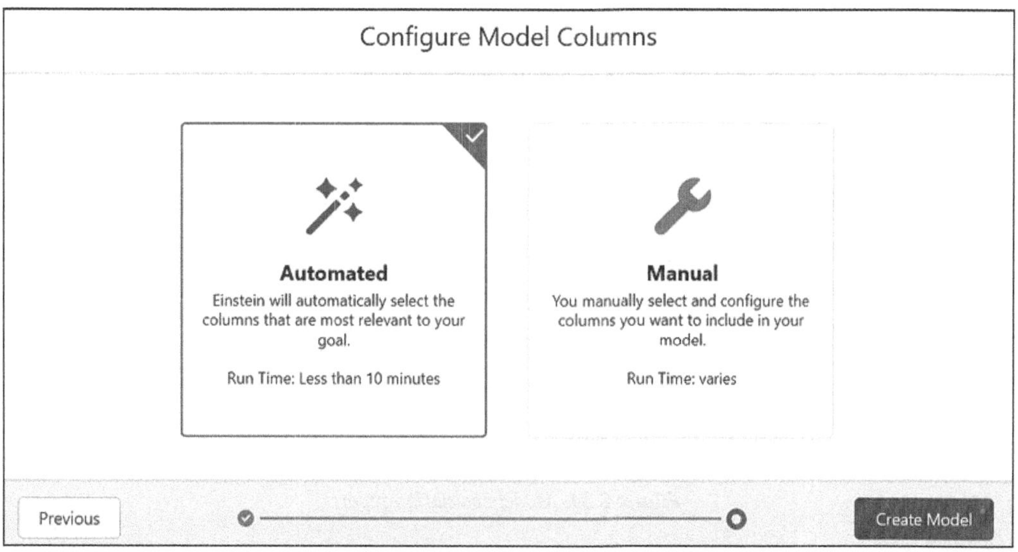

Figure 8.32: Automated configuration selected

The system will now build your model, which usually takes 5 to 10 minutes. When it is done, you should see the following overview. You can check the alert and also note that at the highest level, shown in the screenshot below, the model's prediction seems fairly good.

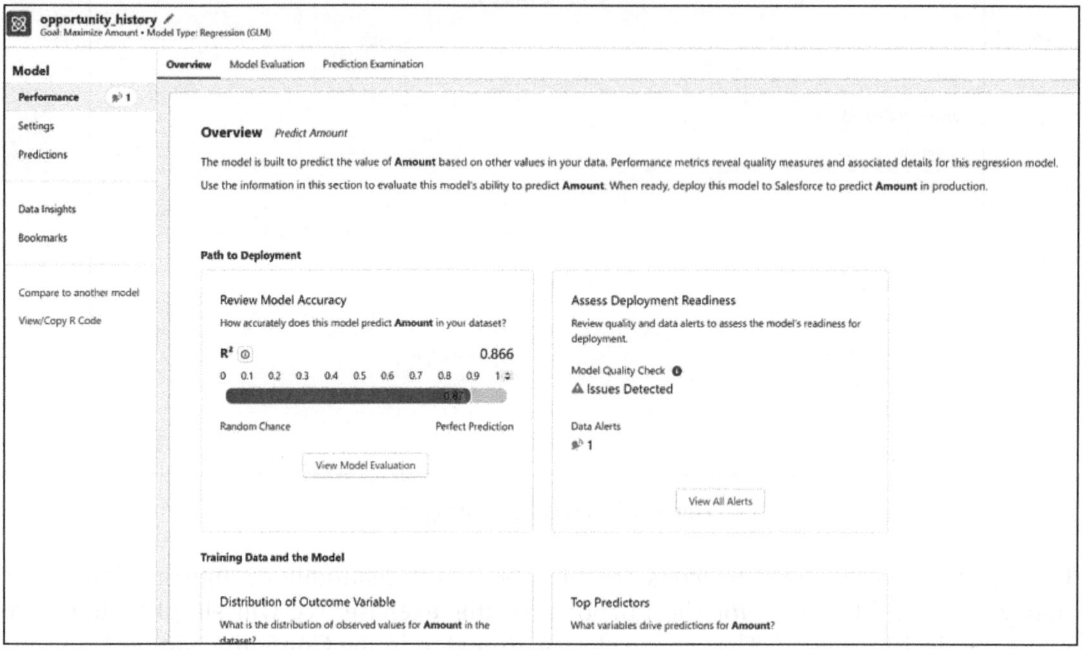

Figure 8.33: Model overview showing performance

If you now click on the **Model Evaluation** tab, you can see more detail about the model performance. This is shown in *Figure 8.34*:

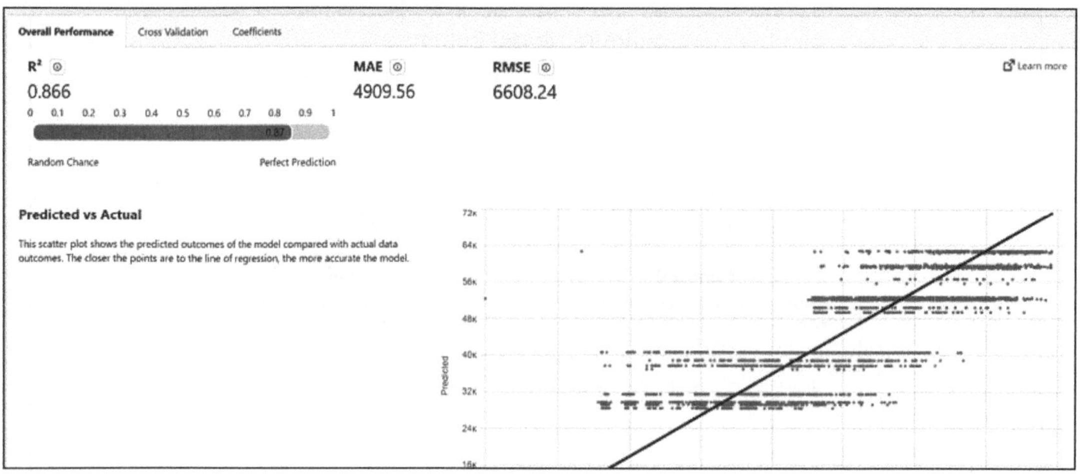

Figure 8.34: Model evaluation report

It is also worth going into the **Model Coefficients** tab, shown below, where you can see the most important variables in the model for predicting the opportunity amount.

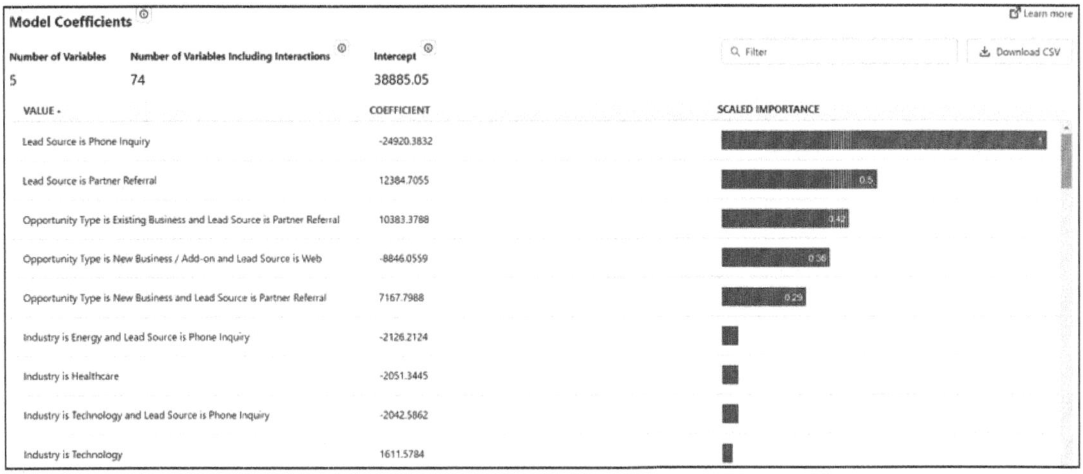

Figure 8.35: Model coefficients tab

Now go into the **Prediction Examination** tab, shown in the following screenshot, where you can see how the model classified actual data from the training dataset. This can give you a good sense of how it will work in practice.

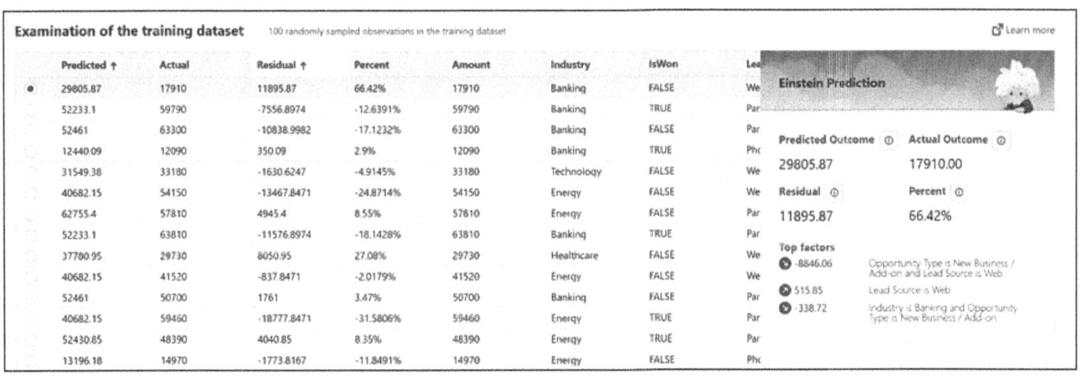

Figure 8.36: Prediction examination tab

On the **Data Insights** tab, shown in *Figure 8.37*, accessible from the sidebar, you get an overview of what factors play the biggest role in making the amount high or low.

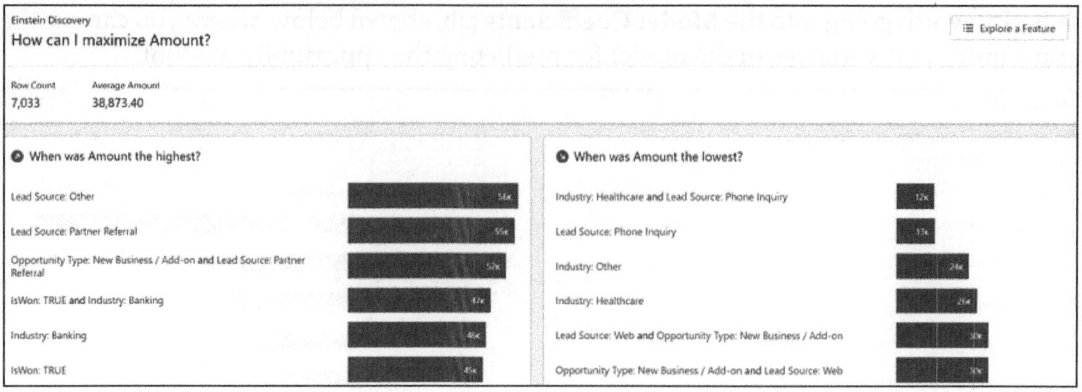

Figure 8.37: Data insights overview

Finally, on the **Predictions** tab, shown in *Figure 8.38*, you can actually test out different values and see what the model predicts.

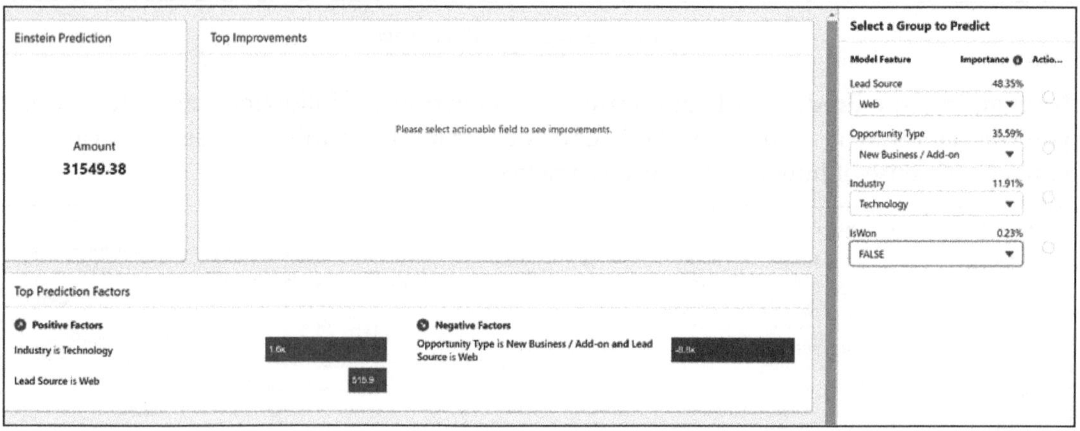

Figure 8.38: Predictions tab

Have a good play with the different aspects of the model, and now, we will move on to look at the Tableau Online Output Connection.

Using the Tableau online output connection

The Tableau Online Output Connector is a powerful tool that enables you to seamlessly push your prepared data from CRM Analytics into Tableau Online for further analysis. By transforming, merging, and cleaning your data in CRM Analytics, you can easily create a `.hyper` file that can be analyzed using Tableau Online's advanced analytics tools. This connector is designed to work with Data Prep recipes and requires a Creator license for the Tableau Online account. In this section, we will walk you through the process of enabling the Tableau Online Output Connector, configuring connection settings, and pushing data to Tableau Online.

In this example, we will write the **`opportunity_history`** dataset that we have been using all through this chapter to our Tableau Cloud environment, using the Tableau Online Output Connector.

To do so follow the instructions below:

1. First, go to setup and search for analytics in the **Quick Find** box. Click **Settings**.
2. Under settings, shown in the following screenshot, enable the Tableau Online output connection and save:

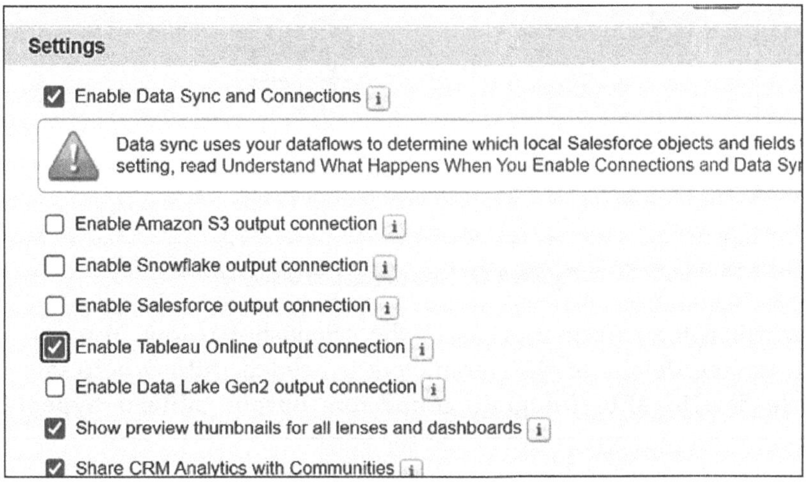

Figure 8.39: Analytics settings showing Tableau connector

3. Go to **Analytics Studio** and click **Data Manager**, then from the page that appears, click **Connections**. This should look like the following screenshot:

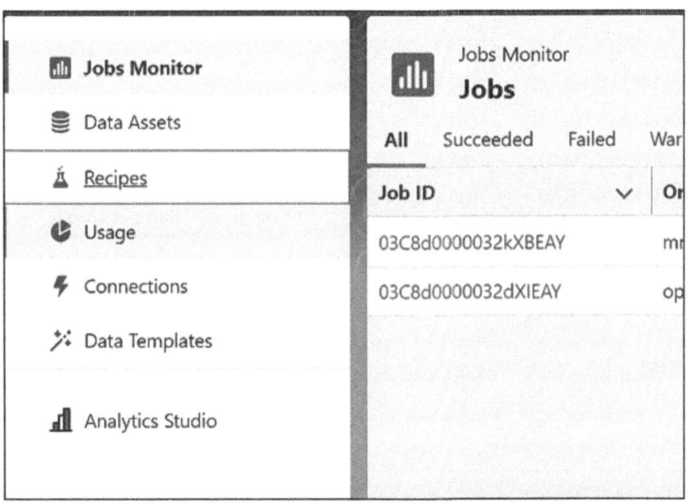

Figure 8.40: Data manager showing connections

4. Click **New Connection**, select **Output** under **Connector Type** and click **Tableau Online Output Connector**, as shown below:

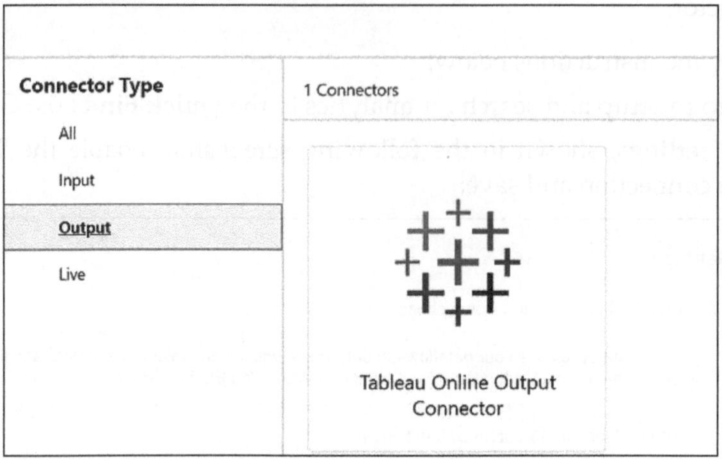

Figure 8.41: *New connection dialogue*

5. Now fill in the information as in the screenshot below. You can refer to this URL for the details of the parameters if needed: **https://help.salesforce.com/s/articleView?id=sf.bi_integrate_connectors_output_tableau_hyper.htm&type=5**

Figure 8.42: *Tableau Online connector configuration*

6. Now you have established the connection. Time to test it. To do so, go back to **Data Manager** and click on **Recipes**, as shown in the following screenshot:

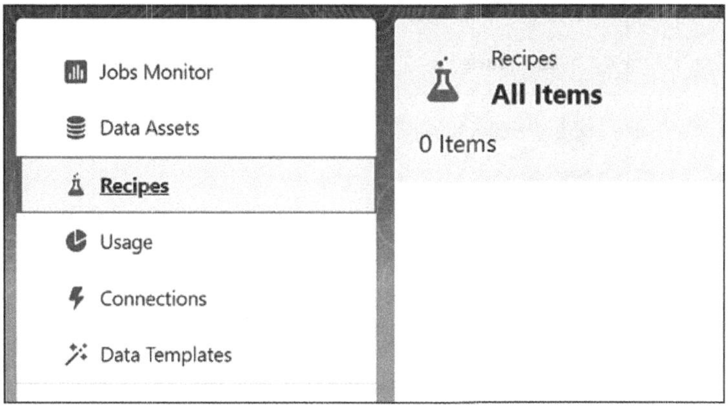

Figure 8.43: *Data manager recipes tab*

7. On the Canvas that appears, click **Add Input Data**, shown in the following screenshot:

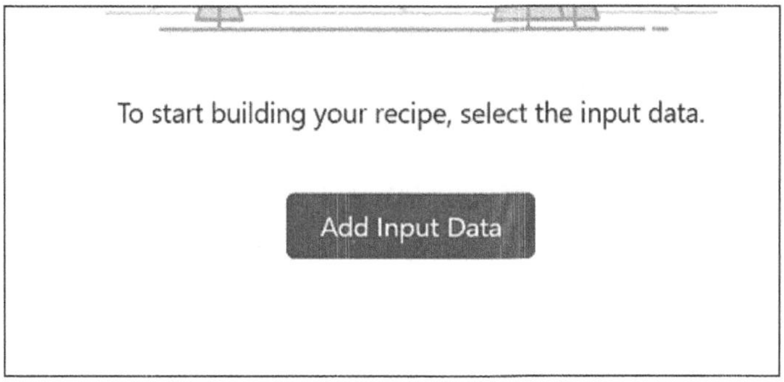

Figure 8.44: *Add input data button*

8. Select the **opportunity_history** dataset, as shown in the following figure:

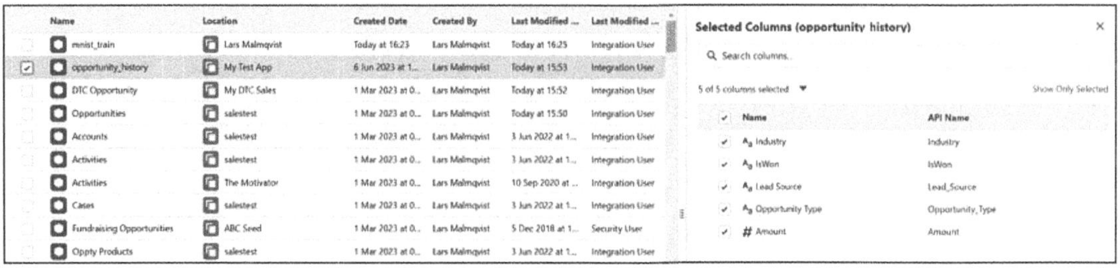

Figure 8.45: *opportunity_history dataset selected as input*

9. Now add a node by clicking on "+". Select **Output**, shown below:

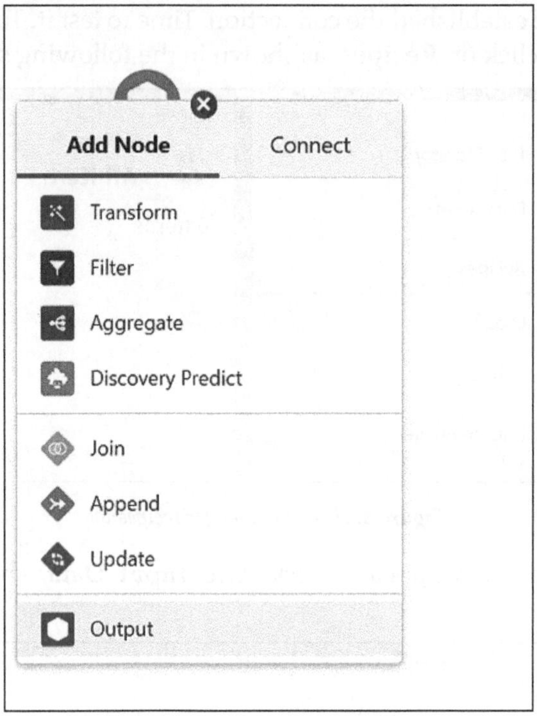

***Figure 8.46:** Output node being added*

10. Fill out the form as per the screenshot below:

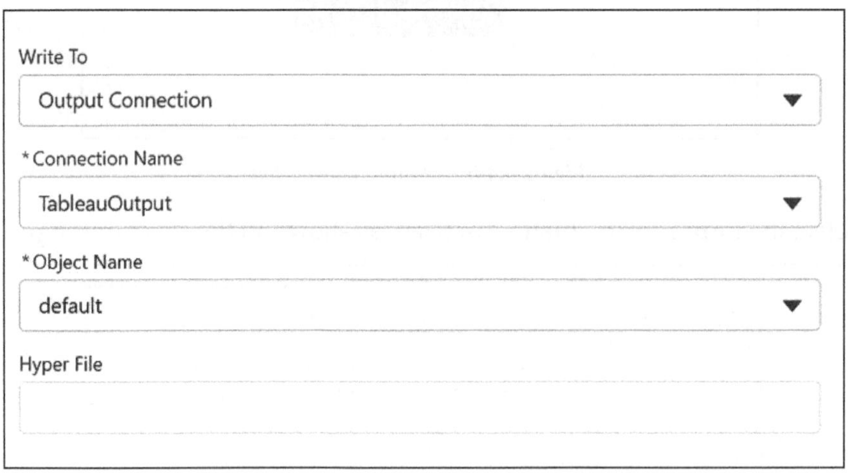

***Figure 8.47:** Output node configuration*

11. *Save and Run* the Recipe by clicking on the button and giving it a name, for instance as in the following screenshot:

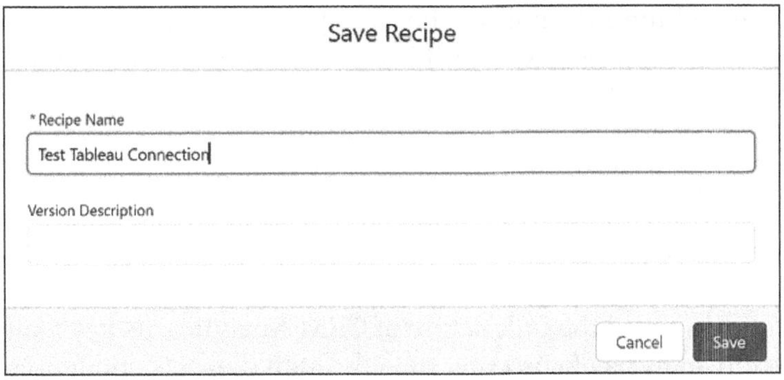

***Figure 8.48:** Save and run recipe dialogue*

12. The job will now run, so wait until it has been completed. You can monitor this in **Jobs Monitor**, shown in *Figure 8.49*:

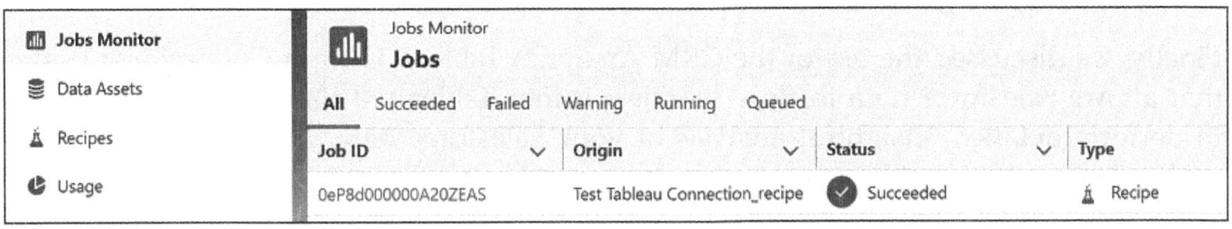

***Figure 8.49:** Jobs monitor showing recipe run*

When the job is complete, you can find and explore the dataset in Tableau Cloud by clicking **Explore**, selecting **default**, and then clicking on **Extract**, which is the extract you have just created. This will look as in the following screenshot:

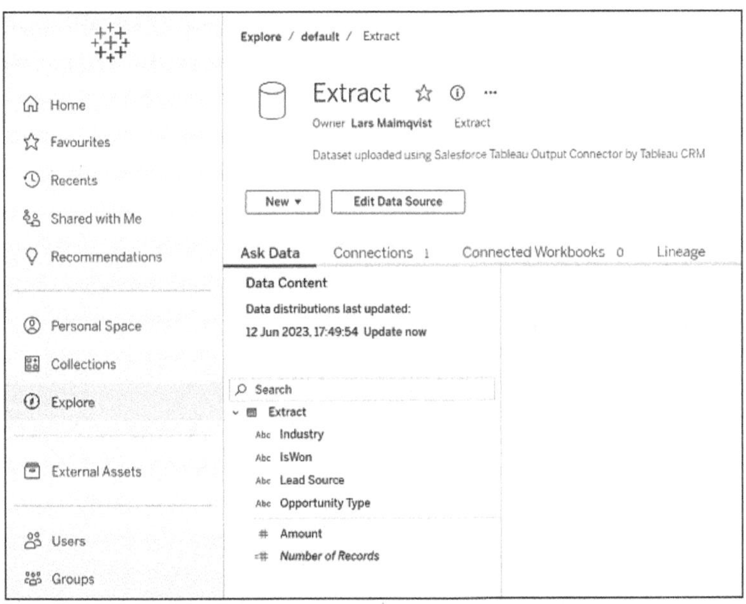

***Figure 8.50:** Explore dataset in Tableau dialogue*

We have now covered the material for this chapter. Well done! However, we have even further heights to scale as we explore the world of advanced analytics in *Chapter 9 – Exploring Einstein AI and Advanced Analytics*.

Conclusion

In this chapter, we have journeyed through the crucial domain of CRM Analytics and its paramount role in understanding, managing, and improving customer relationships. You should now be able to grasp the full picture of CRM Analytics, its key features, and how it facilitates thorough analysis of customer data through datasets and lenses.

The concept of Einstein Discovery within Salesforce, and its application in the CRM Analytics platform, was another essential part of our journey. Now, you should be capable of creating and utilizing Einstein Discovery models to enhance your data interpretation and decision-making processes.

Finally, we discussed the use of the CRM Analytics Tableau Output Connector, a bridge that allows Salesforce data to flow seamlessly into Tableau. This key tool enables you to perform detailed, insightful analysis of your Salesforce data, further enriching your understanding and enabling you to derive practical benefits.

In sum, we have armed you with a comprehensive understanding of CRM Analytics within Salesforce, its integration with Tableau, and the immense value these tools bring to your organization. Now, you should feel confident to apply these skills in your own work, harnessing the power of CRM Analytics and Tableau to transform raw data into strategic actions, and thereby improve your business operations and customer relationships.

We will now move on to putting our hard work on setting up CRMA to use inside Tableau for advanced analytics use cases, while also covering the basics of what advanced analytics are really all about in the process.

Join our book's Discord space

Join the book's Discord Workspace for Latest updates, Offers, Tech happenings around the world, New Release and Sessions with the Authors:

https://discord.bpbonline.com

CHAPTER 9

Exploring Einstein AI and Advanced Analytics

Introduction

This chapter will focus on the concept of advanced analytics and its applications in Tableau and Salesforce. The chapter will begin by defining advanced analytics and its capabilities in providing deeper insights and predictions from data. The chapter will then cover the use of advanced analytics in Tableau, highlighting relevant features. Additionally, the chapter will delve into advanced analytics in Salesforce, including its Einstein platform and its capabilities for machine learning and AI-powered insights. Lastly, the chapter will guide how to create a combined analytical use case across Tableau and Salesforce, leveraging the strengths of both platforms for enhanced data analysis and decision-making.

Structure

The chapter covers the following topics:

- Advanced analytics
- Using advanced analytics in Tableau
- Using advanced analytics in Salesforce
- Combining Tableau and Salesforce for advanced Analytics

Objectives

This chapter provides learners with a comprehensive understanding of advanced analytics and its significant role in interpreting data and aiding decision-making. It explores the potential of advanced analytics to yield deeper insights and more accurate predictions. Learners will discover how to harness the capabilities of advanced analytics in Tableau, leading to robust data visualization and exploration. The chapter also imparts knowledge about Salesforce's Einstein platform, which incorporates machine learning and artificial intelligence to facilitate advanced analytics. Additionally, it explains how Salesforce utilizes advanced analytics to enhance customer relationship management and other business functions.

A key focus of the chapter is teaching learners how to create a combined analytical use case that leverages the strengths of both Tableau and Salesforce for improved data analysis. This involves understanding the integration and synergies between these platforms, which is crucial for optimizing their use in a business context. Finally, learners are encouraged to apply the techniques and knowledge acquired to real-world problems. This application not only enhances their data analysis skills but also bolsters their strategic decision-making capabilities, equipping them with the tools to make informed, data-driven decisions in various business scenarios.

Advanced analytics

Advanced Analytics involves the independent or partially independent analysis of data or content using complex methods and tools. These often surpass the capabilities of standard **Business Intelligence** (**BI**), allowing for the uncovering of more profound insights, the making of predictions, or the provision of suggestions. Techniques employed in advanced analytics encompass data or text mining, machine learning, pattern identification, forecasting, visual representation, semantic and sentiment analysis, network and cluster analysis, multivariate statistics, graph analysis, simulation, complex event processing, and neural networks.

Advanced analytics applications in businesses are broad and varied, covering areas such as customer acquisition and retention, marketing efforts enhancement, risk management, and product development and innovation.

With the aid of advanced analytics, businesses can identify customer preferences, target their marketing efforts, foresee potential risks, and innovate in product development. Let us delve deeper into these applications:

- **Customer acquisition and retention**: Advanced analytics can process customer interaction data, market research, and feedback to identify customer preference trends. Salesforce's intelligent Customer 360 platform can be used here to provide a unified customer view, allowing businesses to meet and exceed customer expectations effectively.

- **Enhancing marketing efforts**: Machine learning, business intelligence, and predictive modeling can enable companies to develop sophisticated marketing campaigns. Salesforce Marketing Cloud can assist in delivering personalized experiences to customers, tracking real-time behavior changes, and making data-driven decisions.
- **Improving risk management**: Advanced analytics tools can model scenarios and forecast risks, guiding enterprises toward strategic risk management plans. Salesforce Shield provides a set of integrated services for managing business risks, from archiving sensitive data to implementing fine-grained user permissions.
- **Product development and innovation**: By analyzing customer needs, advanced analytics tools can identify areas of improvement and potential new product niches. Salesforce's Product Development Cloud can manage the entire lifecycle of product development, from ideation to launch.

Real-world applications of advanced analytics

Various global brands have harnessed the power of advanced analytics to drive their success. For instance, Amazon uses advanced analytics to provide personalized customer experiences. Starbucks optimizes its menu and product offerings through data analytics. American Express uses predictive modeling to anticipate potential customer churn and optimize marketing efforts.

Tableau, with its powerful data visualization capabilities, can be used to replicate these successes by presenting complex data in an understandable and actionable format. Whether it is predicting customer behavior like Amazon, optimizing product offerings like Starbucks, or forecasting customer churn like American Express, Tableau is a versatile tool in the hands of data scientists and analysts.

Advanced analytics is crucial for fostering innovation and improving business operations. By utilizing predictive analytics, businesses can make better-informed decisions and model outcomes beforehand. This capability allows businesses to craft strategic plans for all areas of operations, from customer service to digital marketing.

With technology's evolution, the potential applications and capabilities of data science tools, like Salesforce and Tableau, are continually expanding. This advancement has reflected in the growing number of organizations planning to integrate advanced analytics into their decision-making models.

The future of advanced analytics will likely see more complex algorithms, more data science, and more process automation. Both Salesforce and Tableau, with their robust and continually improving features, are well-positioned to support this evolution.

Tableau: Advanced analytics capabilities

Tableau and Salesforce provide powerful analytics capabilities that cater to both business users and data scientists. This comprehensive platform offers a wide range of features, including segmentation and cohort analysis, what-if and scenario analysis, sophisticated calculations, time-series and predictive analysis, and external services integration. By combining advanced analytics features with an intuitive interface, Tableau enables users to perform complex analyses and gain valuable insights from their data quickly and efficiently. Here are the applications:

- **Segmentation and cohort analysis** Tableau enables quick, iterative analysis and comparison of segments to generate initial hypotheses and validate them. This section covers various capabilities in Tableau, such as:
- **Clustering:** Tableau's clustering feature uses unsupervised machine learning to segment data based on multiple variables.
- **Sets and set actions:** Sets in Tableau allow defining collections of data objects either by manual selection or programmatic logic. Set Actions enable storing a selection of data points within a set, allowing for use cases like proportional brushing.
- **Groups:** Groups in Tableau support creating ad-hoc categories and establishing hierarchies, which can help with basic data cleaning needs and structuring data intuitively for analysis tasks.
- **What-if and scenario analysis**: Tableau enables users to experiment with inputs of their analysis and share scenarios while keeping data fresh using parameters and story points.
- **Parameters:** Parameters in Tableau allow changing input values into a model or dashboard, driving calculations, altering filter thresholds, and selecting data.
- **Story points:** Story points in Tableau enable constructing presentations that update with data changes and retain parameter values.
- **Sophisticated calculations:** Tableau offers powerful capabilities to support complex logic using calculated fields. Two types of calculated fields that enable advanced analysis are:
    - o **Level of detail expressions:** LOD Expressions in Tableau are an extension of the calculation language, enabling answering questions involving multiple levels of granularity in a single visualization.
    - o **Table calculations:** Table calculations in Tableau enable relative computations applied to all values in a table and are often dependent on the table structure itself.
- **Time-series and predictive analysis**: Tableau simplifies time-series analysis and offers predictive capabilities such as trending and forecasting.

- **Time-series analysis:** Tableau's flexible front end and powerful back end make time-series analysis a simple matter of asking the right questions.
- **Forecasting:** Tableau's forecasting functionality runs several different models in the background and selects the best one, automatically accounting for data issues such as seasonality.
- **External services integration:** Tableau integrates with external services like Python, R, and MATLAB to expand functionality and leverage existing investments in other solutions.
- **Python, R, and MATLAB integrations:** Tableau integrates directly with Python, R, and MATLAB, allowing users to call any function available in R or Python on data in Tableau and manipulate models created in these environments using Tableau.

In conclusion, Tableau's advanced analytics capabilities make it a versatile and valuable tool for users at all levels of expertise. By offering a wide range of features, such as clustering, calculated fields, forecasting, and integration with Python, R, and MATLAB, Tableau empowers users to perform complex analyses and derive actionable insights from their data.

Salesforce: Advanced analytics capabilities

The following sections will dive into the advanced analytics capabilities within Salesforce and CRMA._This will teach you the options for working with advanced analytics within Salesforce prior to diving into the hands-on case.

Deeper dive in Einstein discovery

Einstein Discovery is a powerful tool within the context of advanced analytics. It can seamlessly incorporate **Artificial Intelligence** (**AI**) and machine learning into a business user's workflow, allowing for the creation of predictive models without the need for data scientists or advanced developers. To truly leverage this platform's potential, users must understand their data, interpret model outcomes, and correctly configure training datasets.

Advanced analytics involves sophisticated techniques and tools that delve beyond the traditional realm of BI to uncover deeper insights, make predictions, and offer recommendations. Einstein Discovery aligns with several aspects of advanced analytics, such as machine learning, pattern matching, and forecasting. Utilizing a no-code AI approach, the platform embeds algorithms to train its models, eliminating the need for manual coding.

Choosing the right features and incorporating business knowledge is an important process in utilizing Einstein Discovery effectively. Business representatives and data analysts need to collaborate from the start of the model development process. This collaboration ensures that the most relevant predictors are chosen and that the model's outputs are aligned with business needs and goals.

Some key practices for model enhancement in Einstein Discovery include segmenting datasets into different models, handling multicollinearity, managing diverse inputs, detecting and handling outliers, and choosing the optimal bucketing method for every use case. It is essential to balance the accuracy that the model delivers with the need for understanding why the prediction was made, with business requirements often guiding these decisions.

Segmentation can improve prediction quality by creating separate models for different data segments, accommodating the behavior of each segment in the model. Tests such as examining distributions of input variables can be used to determine when segmentation is a viable strategy.

Multicollinearity occurs when dependent variables can be linearly predicted from each other, causing potential issues in model quality. Methods to address multicollinearity include a thorough investigation of data, understanding business relations between variables, and using Einstein Discovery to highlight problematic relationships.

Outliers can impact the accuracy and explainability of models. Detecting and managing outliers can improve model quality by reducing noise. Einstein Discovery can recommend an approach for handling outliers, but business input is crucial in the decision-making process.

Bucketing is an essential consideration in model quality and explainability. The right balance between optimal model metrics and clear explanations can be achieved by using different bucketing methods such as bucket by count, manual bucketing, bucket by width, or Einstein Discovery's recommended buckets.

Lastly, adding explicit second-order variables representing interactions between different features can also improve model accuracy. However, this method should be used with caution, taking into account potential limitations such as the number of possible column value combinations and the variety of data reflecting those combinations.

Einstein Discovery provides a powerful means of advanced analytics by incorporating machine learning, pattern matching, and forecasting techniques seamlessly into the business user's workflow. Close collaboration between business users and data analysts ensures that the right features are chosen and that the model is both accurate and relevant to the company's goals. Adopting various model enhancement practices, such as strategically segmenting datasets and fine-tuning bucketing methods, can help perfect the insights provided by Einstein Discovery and maximize its value as an advanced analytics solution.

Einstein prediction builder

Einstein Prediction Builder is a powerful tool within the Salesforce Einstein platform that enables users to create custom predictions for specific business use cases. It simplifies the process of predictive analytics by automating most technical aspects, such as algorithms, parameter tuning, and infrastructure management. In the context of advanced analytics, Einstein Prediction Builder's capabilities streamline the process of building, analyzing, and deploying machine learning models, resulting in deeper insights and better decision-making.

Advanced analytics goes beyond traditional business intelligence to discover deeper insights, make predictions, or generate recommendations using techniques such as data mining, machine learning, pattern matching, forecasting, visualization, semantic analysis, and more. Einstein Prediction Builder's capabilities align with advanced analytics as it involves the use of machine learning to make predictions based on historical data and analyze the performance of these predictions to drive better business outcomes.

The Einstein Prediction Builder simplifies the entire prediction workflow by breaking it down into six steps: defining the use case, identifying the data that supports the use case, creating the prediction, reviewing and iterating the prediction, monitoring the prediction, and deploying and using the prediction.

The following steps can be used when implementing predictions with Einstein Prediction Builder:

1. Define your use case.

   The process begins by identifying a business outcome that needs improvement, such as increasing lead conversion rates, improving customer satisfaction scores, or reducing churn.

2. Identify the data that supports your use case.

   With a clear use case, users can frame their prediction using the "Avocado Framework", which helps segment the data, identify examples of outcomes, and distinguish between historical data for training and new data for making predictions.

3. Create your prediction.

   Einstein Prediction Builder's wizard enables users to set up predictions quickly by selecting the data object, specifying the question to be answered (binary or numeric), configuring positive and negative examples, and selecting the fields to be included or excluded from the analysis.

4. Review, iterate and enable your prediction.

   Once the prediction is created, a scorecard is generated that provides information on the quality of the prediction. Users can review and revise their prediction based on the scorecard metrics and insights, remove any potential biases, and enable the prediction.

5. Monitor your prediction.

   After enabling the prediction, it is recommended to let it run for a period of time behind the scenes so that its performance can be assessed on new data. Users can verify the model's accuracy using Salesforce reports or by utilizing the Einstein Prediction Builder Model Accuracy Template.

6. Deploy and use your prediction.

   Finally, the prediction can be integrated into the business processes using list views, lightning components, Process Builder, or Einstein Next Best Action strategies. Monitoring KPIs, performing a phased rollout, and periodically reviewing the model's assumptions and performance are essential for success.

In summary, Einstein Prediction Builder simplifies the complex process of creating machine learning models and applying advanced analytics concepts to deliver actionable insights. By streamlining the prediction workflow, users can quickly generate predictions, analyze their performance, and efficiently integrate them into business processes. This tool makes advanced analytics more accessible and easier to use for driving better business decisions.

Other Einstein features

There are many other features that are part of the Salesforce Einstein offering that could fall under the rubric of advanced analytics. Here we will consider the following:

- **Einstein lead scoring**: This advanced analytics product utilizes machine learning techniques to assign a lead score to each lead based on their likelihood of converting. The score ranges from 1-99 and helps prioritize the leads for sales teams. It also provides insights into the factors that contribute to a lead's score. By analyzing historical data and identifying patterns, Einstein Lead Scoring makes data-driven predictions, enabling sales teams to focus on the most promising leads.
- **Einstein opportunity scoring**: Like Einstein lead scoring, this advanced analytics product uses machine learning techniques to score opportunities based on their likelihood of becoming *Closed Won*. The scoring system ranges from 1-99, and the scores are available as a field on the opportunity record, in list views, reports, and on the forecast page. By identifying conversion patterns, Einstein Opportunity Scoring helps sales teams concentrate on high-priority opportunities while making data-backed predictions.
- **Einstein opportunity insights**: This advanced analytics product draws on machine learning and data analysis techniques to provide predictions about which deals are likely to be won, reminders to follow up, and key moments in a deal process. By examining historical data and patterns, Einstein Opportunity Insights helps sales teams make informed decisions and prioritize their efforts.
- **Pipeline inspection (Einstein deal insights + Tiered Einstein opportunity scores)**: Pipeline inspection assists sales managers in monitoring their team's forecast for a given time period by providing a consolidated view of pipeline metrics, opportunities, week-to-week changes, AI-driven insights, close date predictions, and activity information. With Einstein Deal Insights, the product predicts the

likelihood of winning deals within the current month and provides additional insights from Einstein Opportunity Scoring and Cases. The tiered Einstein Opportunity Scores categorize scores into *High*, *Medium*, and *Low* tiers, making it easier for sales managers to track the progress and prioritize efforts effectively.

- **Einstein forecasting**: Leveraging artificial intelligence technology, Einstein Forecasting brings more certainty and visibility to sales forecasts. It helps improve forecasting accuracy, provides forecast predictions, and offers suggestions for taking a better approach if projected performance is suboptimal. By examining historical data and trends, Einstein Forecasting can support sales teams with more accurate and data-driven forecasts.
- **Einstein account insights**: This product uses advanced analytics techniques, such as sentiment analysis and text mining, to provide valuable information about accounts. account insights can help sales teams stay on top of news affecting their businesses, including account expansion or cost-cutting, changes in company leadership, and involvement in merger and acquisition talks. By identifying these insights, Einstein account insights helps teams make more informed decisions and take advantage of new opportunities.
- **Einstein automated contacts**: This advanced analytics product uses email and event activity to find new contacts and opportunity contact roles to add to Salesforce, making the process more efficient for sales teams and admins. The product can either suggest new contacts to be added by sales team members or automatically associate opportunity contact roles in the background. By utilizing machine learning techniques, Einstein's automated contacts streamline the process of managing contacts and opportunities in Salesforce.
- **Recommended connections**: Although the word *Einstein* is not used in the product name, recommended connections is an AI-driven feature that provides suggestions for connecting with leads and contacts based on existing relationships within the company. The product showcases colleagues with the strongest connections to an individual, helping facilitate conversations with prospects. This intelligent feature can help sales teams make more meaningful connections by tapping into their colleagues' networks and leveraging existing relationships.

Combining Salesforce and Tableau for Advanced Analytics

To give an example of how you might combine Tableau and Salesforce to achieve advanced analytical use cases, we will bring the Einstein Discovery prediction model that you created in *Chapter 8, Blending Tableau with Traditional CRM Analytics* into Tableau Desktop. If you have not already completed the setup of this Einstein Discovery model, now is the time to do so.

We will employ the Tableau Einstein Discovery connector to bring the predictions into our Tableau environment, and thereby we will learn one of the most important ways of combining CRM Analytics with Tableau Desktop to get more out of both.

To start with, let us get the connection set up. Please follow the steps below to set up the connection between Tableau Desktop and Einstein Discovery:

1. Go to your model from *Chapter 8* in Analytics Studio. It can be reached via **Browse | Models**, as shown in *Figure 9.1*:

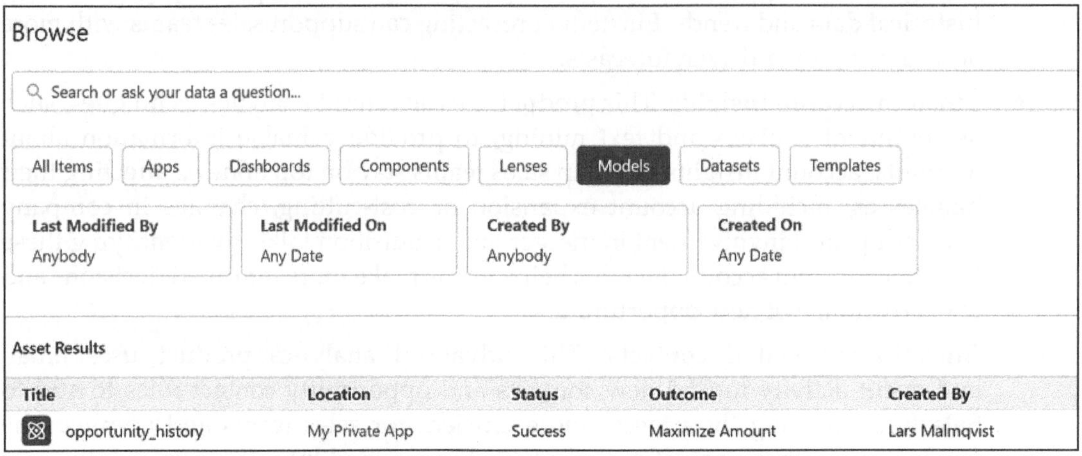

Figure 9.1: Deploy model screen in Analytics Studio

2. Now open your model and deploy it by clicking **Deploy Model**; this will make it usable from Tableau Desktop, among other places. You can see this in the *Figure 9.2:*

Figure 9.2: Model deployment options

3. Leave the defaults as is and ignore any model warnings; they are not relevant to the example. See the warning in the *Figure 9.3:*

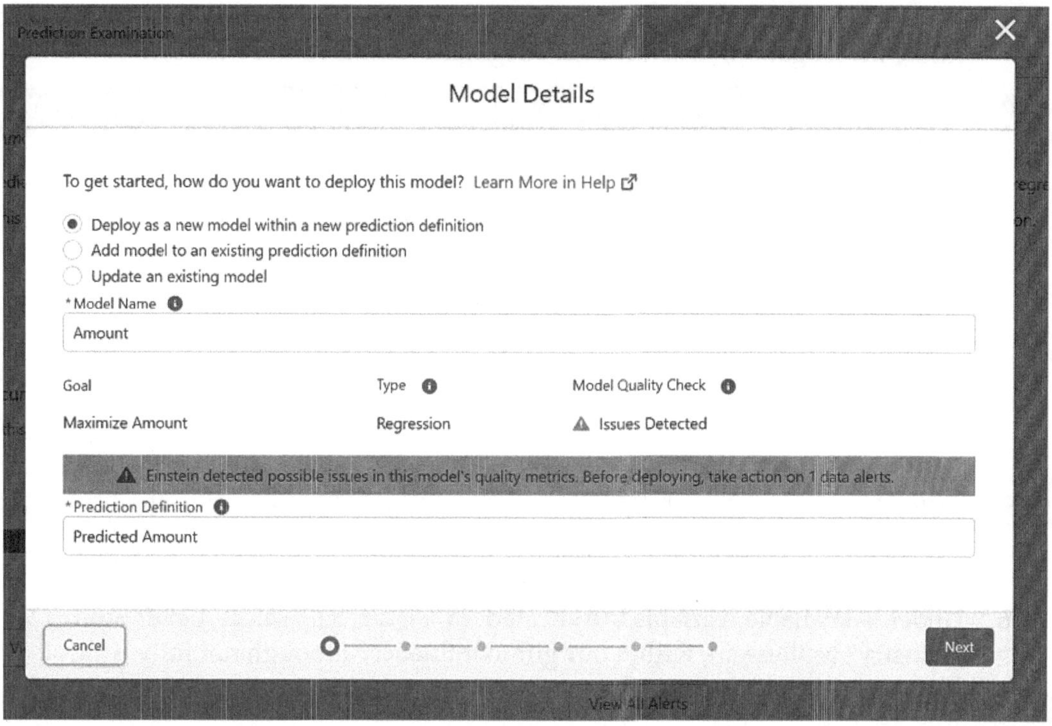

Figure 9.3: *Ignore warnings*

4. On the following screen, select **Deploy without connecting to a Salesforce object**, as we are not writing back to the CRM but using it from Tableau. You can see this in *Figure 9.4*:

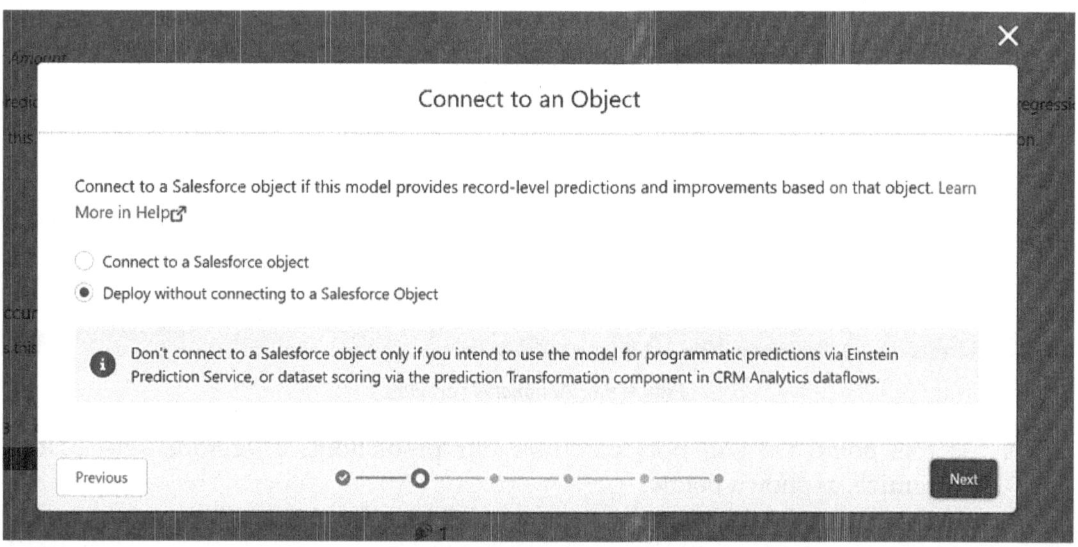

Figure 9.4: *Deployment settings*

5. We will not be segmenting our data, although it is worth noting this capability for future investigation, so select **Don't segment**, as shown in *Figure 9.5:*

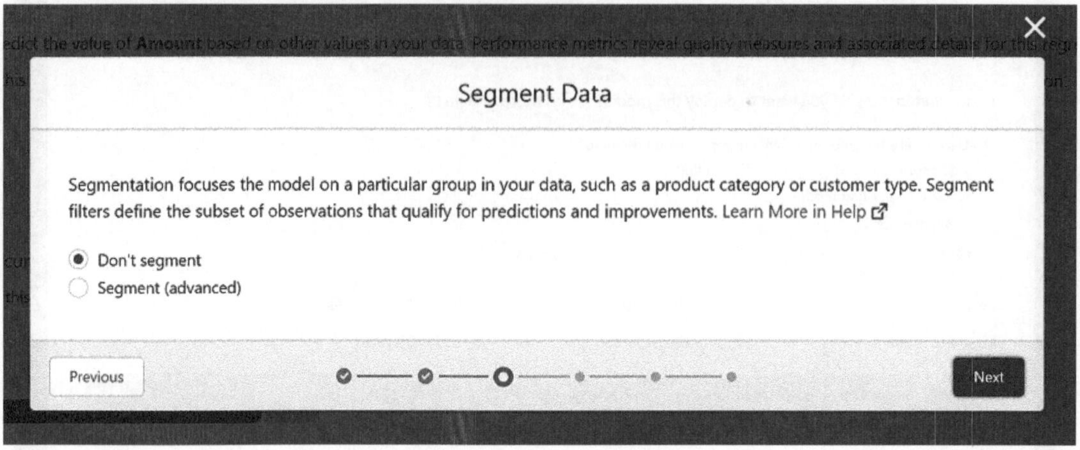

Figure 9.5: *Segmentation options*

6. Under Actionable variables, indicated in *Figure 9.6*, select **Lead Source** and **Industry**" as these are within our gift to influence, although not fully control.

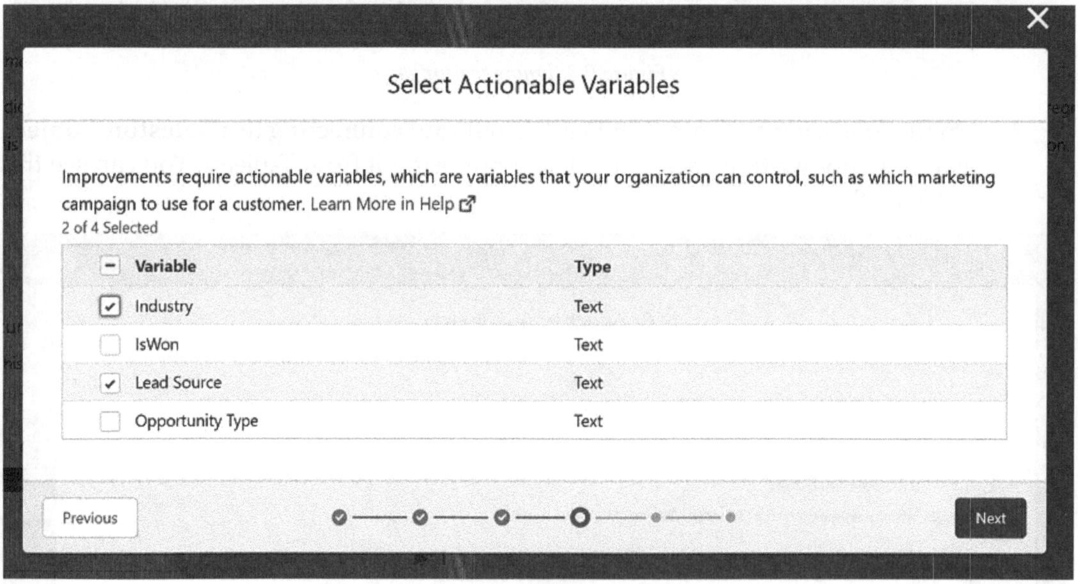

Figure 9.6: *Actionable variables*

7. At this point, we will not customize our predictions. Therefore, select **Don't customize**, as shown below.

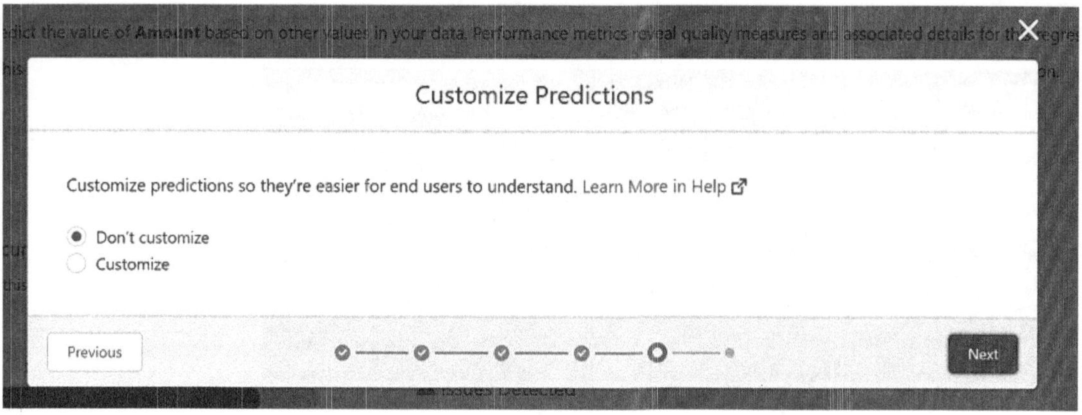

Figure 9.7: Customization options

8. Click **Deploy** to deploy the model, as shown in *Figure 9.8:*

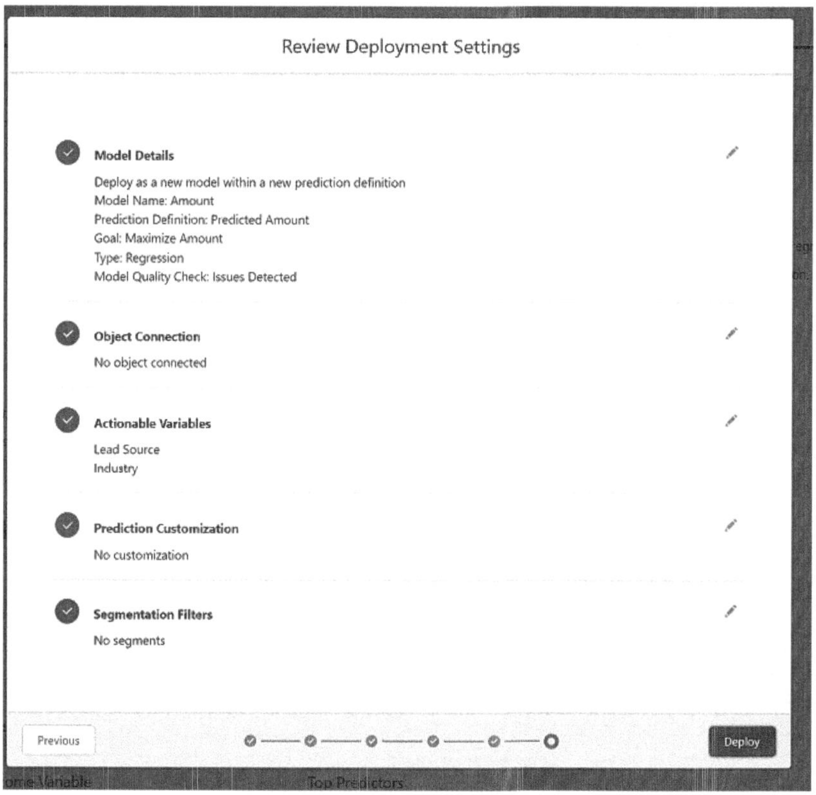

Figure 9.8: Deploy model

9. When you are redirected to a screen as shown *Figure 9.9*, you are ready to proceed to the next stage.

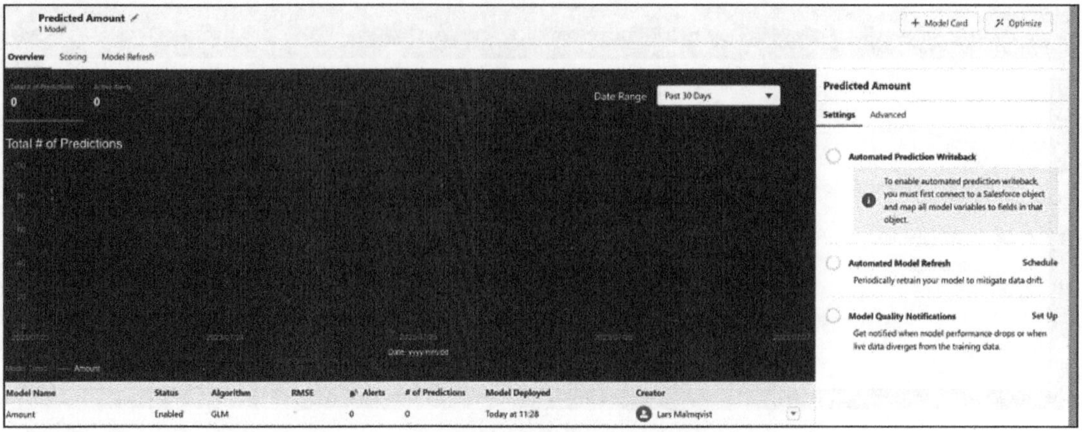

Figure 9.9: Model deployed

We will test our Einstein Discovery model on the raw CSV that we used to create the model in the first place, follow the below mentioned steps:

1. Start by creating a new Tableau workbook and connect to the **opportunity_history.csv** file you downloaded. You can see how this should look in *Figure 9.10*:

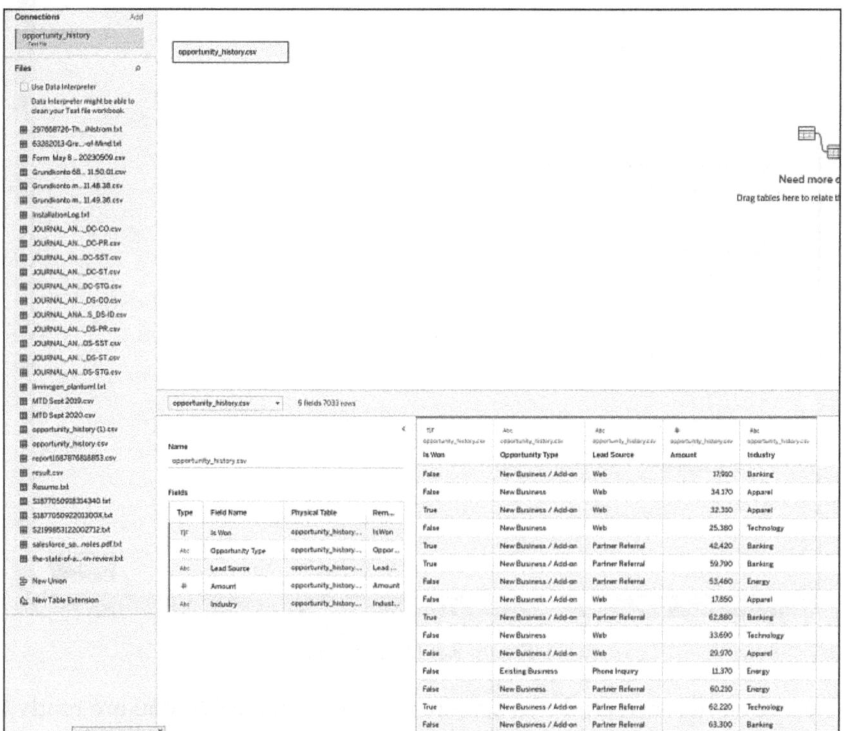

Figure 9.10: Connect Tableau to CSV

2. Create a worksheet, like the one shown in *Figure 9.11*, with the four fields **Is Won, Industry, Lead Source,** and **Opportunity Type.** You can format this worksheet as you like, as long as the fields are present.

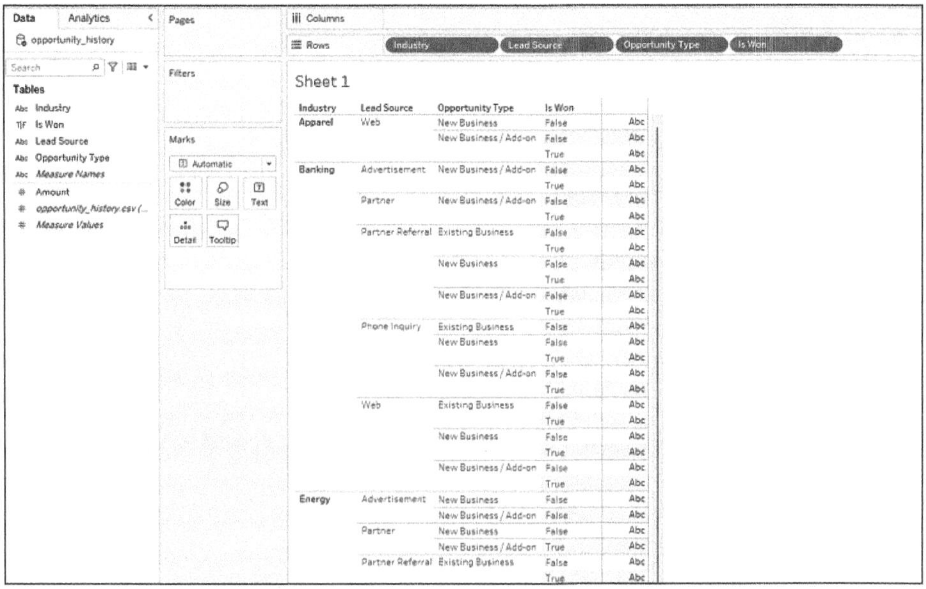

***Figure 9.11:** Create worksheet*

3. Now add a dashboard to the workbook and add the worksheet you have just created to it. You can see how this should look in *Figure 9.12*:

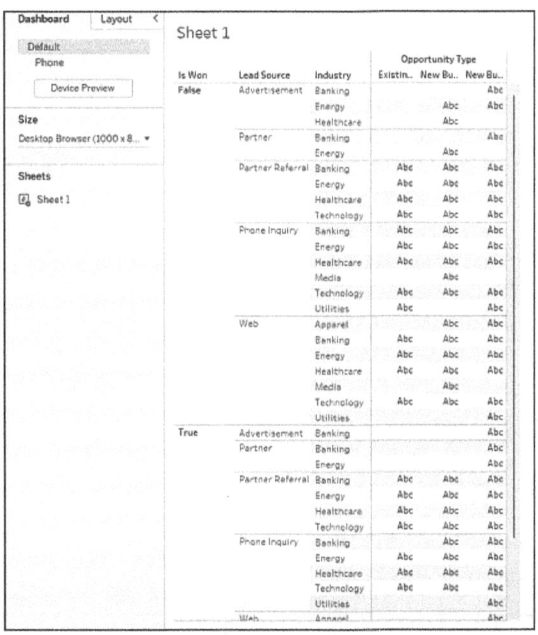

***Figure 9.12:** Add dashboard*

4. On the dashboard, add an **Extension** of type **Einstein Discovery**, as shown in *Figure 9.13*:

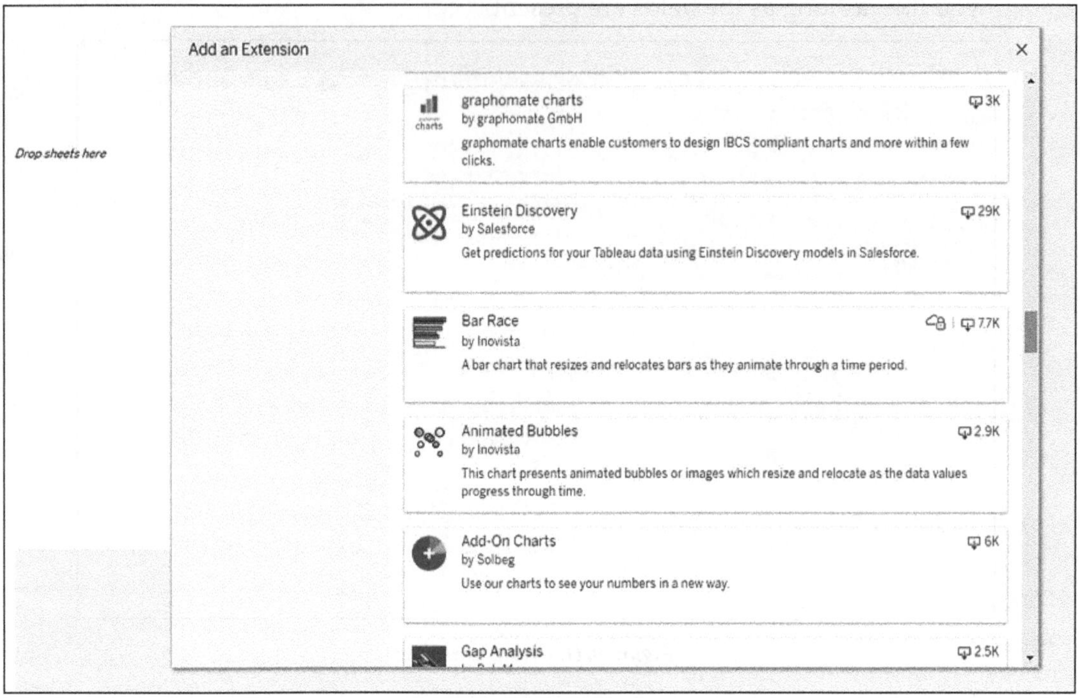

Figure 9.13: *Add Einstein Discovery extension*

5. Click add to **Dashboard**, as shown in *Figure 9.14:*

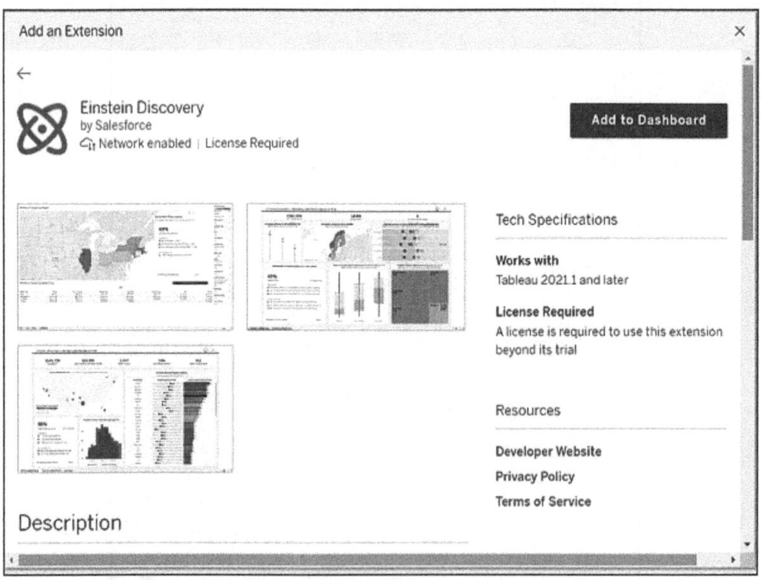

Figure 9.14: *Add extension to dashboard*

6. You will now have to authenticate against your Salesforce org and allow your Tableau Desktop installation to access it. You can see this screen in *Figure 9.15*:

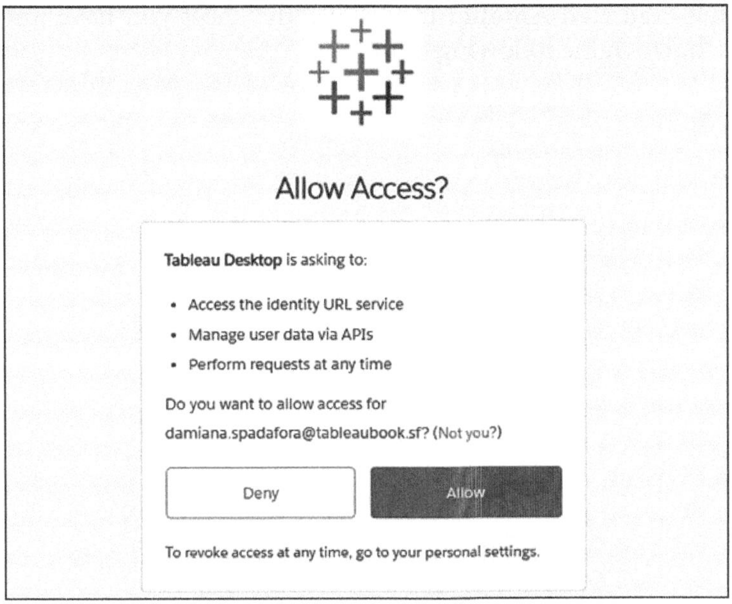

***Figure 9.15:** Authenticate Salesforce access*

7. The extension will now need to be configured, so click **Open Settings**, shown in *Figure 9.16:*

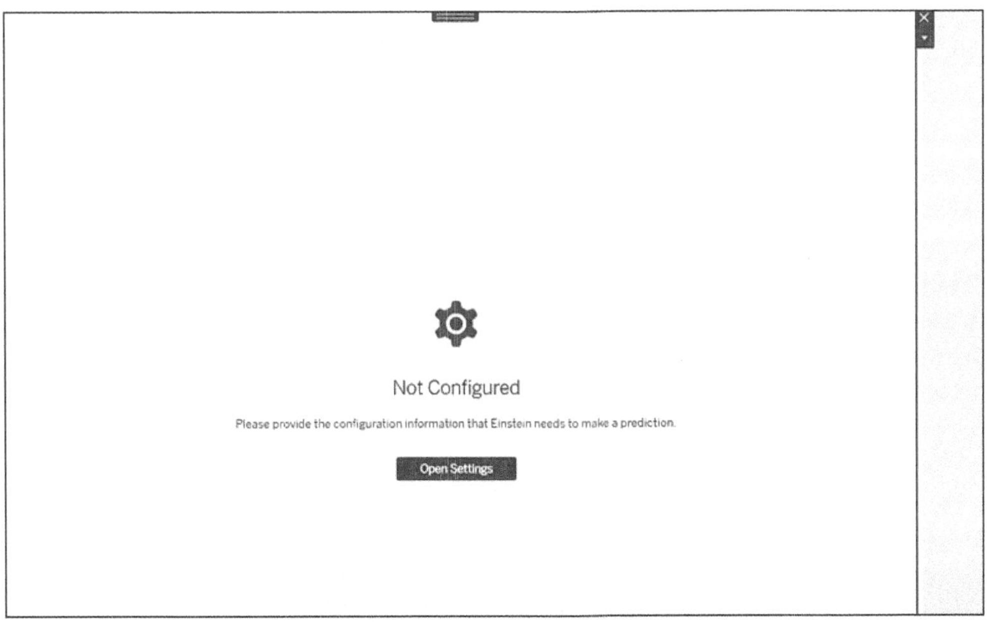

***Figure 9.16:** Open extension settings*

8. If you get an error at this point, you probably need to add the CRM Analytics Admin permission set to the user you are logged in as.
9. Select the **Predicted Amount** model and the sheet you have just created in the dialog, shown in the following figure:

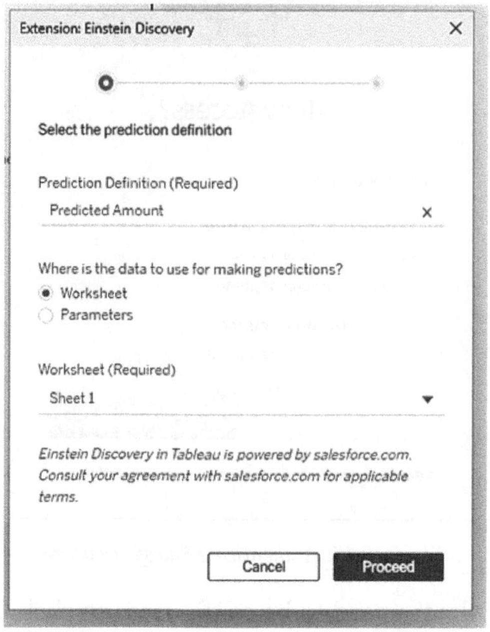

Figure 9.17: *Select model and worksheet*

10. Map the fields to their worksheet equivalents, following the example in *Figure 9.18*:

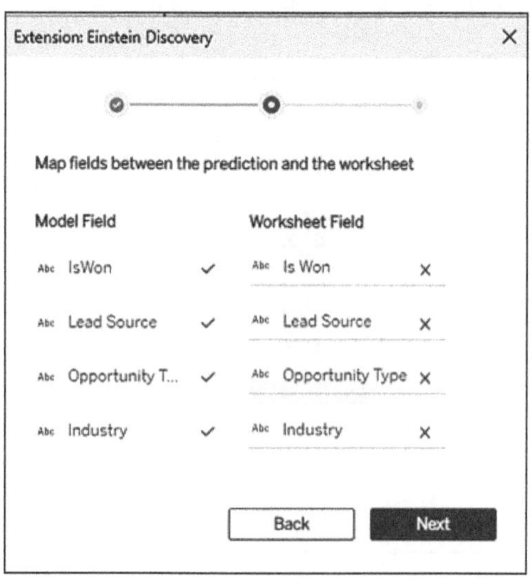

Figure 9.18: *Map fields*

11. Leave all fields at their default values in the final screen, as shown in *Figure 9.19:*

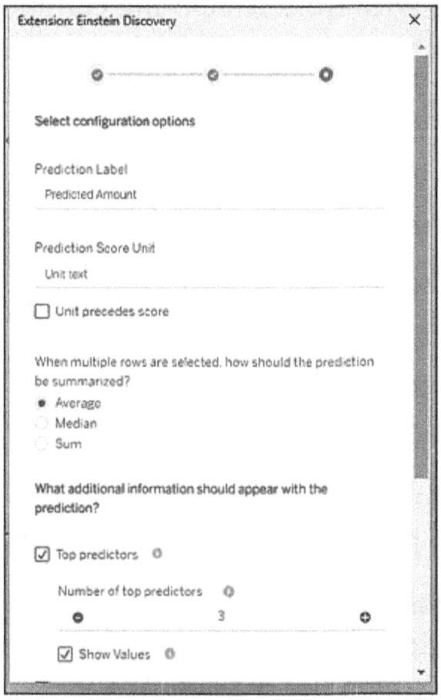

Figure 9.19: *Extension settings*

12. You can now see your Einstein Discovery model directly in the worksheet and use standard worksheet controls to navigate and filter it. This should look like the *Figure 9.20:*

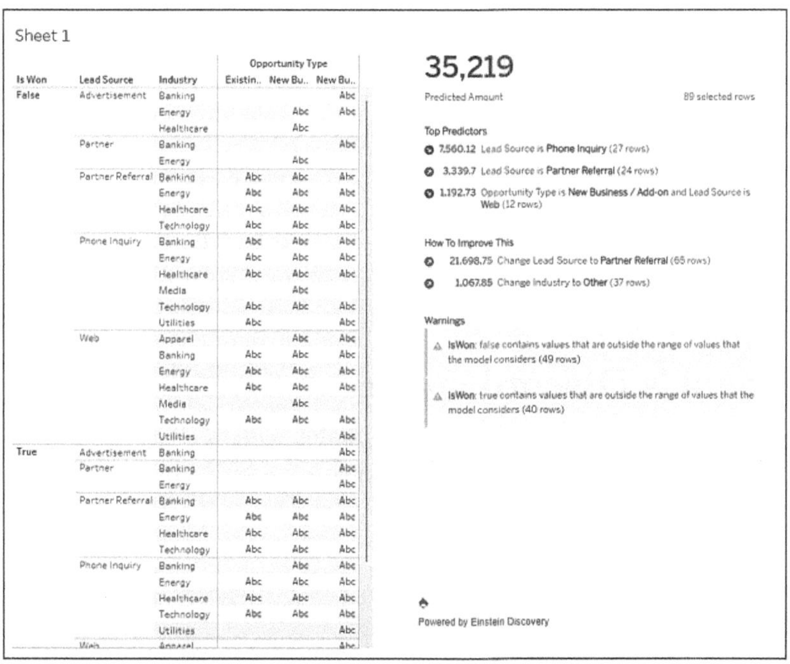

Figure 9.20: *View predictions in worksheet*

Congratulations, that was a hard task. Now, take a little break before going onto the final chapter in this book that deals with troubleshooting common issues and where to go from here.

Conclusion

Congratulations on reaching the conclusion of this rich journey into advanced analytics with Tableau and Salesforce! By now, you should have a solid understanding of the concept of advanced analytics and how it can elevate our data exploration to provide deeper insights and predictions.

Throughout this chapter, we have unlocked the power of Tableau's advanced analytics, admired the intelligence of Salesforce's Einstein platform, and learned how they can be harnessed to make data-driven decisions. We have also explored the synergy of these two platforms and their combined potential in enhancing your data analysis capabilities.

Remember, the field of advanced analytics is ever evolving, with new techniques and technologies constantly emerging. What you've learned here serves as a robust foundation, but there's always more to discover and master. As we continuously strive for better data comprehension and predictive prowess, these tools will prove to be invaluable assets. Keep practicing, experimenting, and pushing the boundaries.

We will now move on to the final chapter of our book.

CHAPTER 10

Troubleshooting, Tricks, and Best Practices

Introduction

This chapter will summarize why Tableau and Salesforce are such a powerful combination, with an emphasis on their capabilities for data analysis, visualization, and decision-making. Additionally, the chapter will provide tips on how to get started using Tableau and Salesforce in practice, with guidance on best practices and useful resources. It will also contain guidance on troubleshooting common issues. The chapter will also explain how to continue the learning journey, including recommended further reading. Lastly, the chapter will help you start using the knowledge gained to improve your data analysis and decision making skills.

Structure

The chapter covers the following topics:

- Tableau and Salesforce: a powerful combination
- Trouble shooting guidance
- Troubleshooting guidance
- Continuing the learning journey

Objectives

This chapter is designed to provide learners with a thorough understanding of the combined use of Tableau and Salesforce for data analysis and visualization, highlighting their unique strengths and synergies. It delves into the reasons why integrating Tableau with Salesforce can significantly enhance business decision-making capabilities.

Learners will also be equipped with essential tips and best practices for effectively starting with Tableau and Salesforce in practical, real-world scenarios. Furthermore, the chapter includes strategies for troubleshooting common issues that may arise in the Tableau and Salesforce environments.

It also guides learners to discover a range of useful resources, tools, and platforms that can support their journey in mastering these technologies. The importance of continuous learning is emphasized, with strategies provided for staying current with the latest trends and developments in Tableau and Salesforce.

Additionally, learners will find recommendations for further reading that can deepen their understanding and proficiency in using these tools. Finally, the chapter aims to encourage and empower learners to confidently apply the knowledge and skills acquired from this book in their data analysis and decision-making tasks.

Tableau and Salesforce: a powerful combination

In the previous chapters, we delved into the incredible power the combination of Salesforce and Tableau offers to organizations. By pulling together these world-class solutions, businesses can not only access a wide array of features but also unlock unique synergies that boost their operational efficiency and decision-making prowess.

Let us take a moment to reflect on the insights we have gathered so far.

Tableau's advanced visualization tools make the wealth of data stored in Salesforce readily understandable and actionable. By crafting intuitive dashboards, teams across your organization can leverage Salesforce's rich customer data to gain insights previously hidden in the complexity of raw data. Merging Salesforce data with information from other business sources also allows for a more holistic view of your business and its customers, enabling you to make decisions with confidence and precision.

We also discussed how bringing Tableau dashboards into the Salesforce CRM environment enhances user efficiency. Having visualized data within the same workspace where business activities take place saves precious time and prevents potential information loss that can occur during context switching. The power of Tableau's Dashboard Starters and the seamless integration within Salesforce CRM workflows translate into convenience and deeper understanding, equipping your teams with the tools to make smarter, more informed decisions.

We delved into the fascinating world of Einstein AI and how its advanced insights can propel your Tableau dashboards to another level. Einstein AI's easy-to-set-up models connect your analytics to actionable next steps. Coupled with Data Cloud for Tableau, this enables your organization to tap into unified data sources, providing a wide field of view of your customer's journey.

And finally, we explored the full integration of Tableau CRM (previously referred to as CRM Analytics) within the Salesforce platform. This native solution amalgamates Salesforce's comprehensive sales, service, and marketing data with Tableau's visualization prowess, allowing businesses to detect trends, anticipate outcomes, identify anomalies, and enhance customer experiences.

In short, the marriage of Salesforce and Tableau is more than just the sum of its parts. It is a potent blend that unlocks the full potential of customer data, empowers users to work more efficiently, and uncovers advanced insights. By leveraging this powerful combination, organizations can make data-driven decisions with greater ease and accuracy, thereby boosting their overall performance. And this is the power of harnessing two world-class solutions to enhance your business's strategic decision-making capabilities.

Using Tableau and Salesforce in practice

Now that you have gained a solid understanding of the synergistic power of Salesforce and Tableau, it is time to convert this newfound knowledge into practice. Here are some practical steps to guide you in this exciting journey:

- **Think in terms of business needs**: Always frame your application of Salesforce and Tableau in terms of what your business needs. Remember, technology should serve your business goals, not the other way around. Begin by identifying key business questions or challenges, then determine how Salesforce and Tableau can help address them.
- **Start small and scale**: It can be tempting to apply your new knowledge across the entire business straight away. However, it is often beneficial to start small. Choose a specific project or team to pilot your initiatives, then gradually scale based on your successes.
- **Practice data visualization**: Spend time honing your data visualization skills with Tableau. Data visualization is an art, and just like any art, it improves with practice. Explore different charts and dashboards, play with customization options, and learn what types of visualization best communicate different kinds of information.
- **Dive into Salesforce CRM**: Make sure to get your hands dirty with Salesforce's CRM functionalities. It is one thing to understand it theoretically, but experiencing

it firsthand will cement your understanding and help you find ways to enhance your organization's workflows.

- **Embrace the power of Einstein AI**: Do not shy away from the advanced capabilities offered by Einstein AI. While AI might seem intimidating, remember that Einstein AI models require no coding and can greatly boost your analytic capabilities. Do not hesitate to experiment and explore how AI can benefit your organization.
- **Join the community**: Salesforce and Tableau have vast, passionate communities full of experts willing to share their experiences and insights. Join forums, participate in webinars, and attend user group meetings. The knowledge and support you can find within these communities is invaluable.
- **Iterate and learn from mistakes**: You are likely to face challenges as you begin implementing Salesforce and Tableau. Do not be disheartened. Use these challenges as learning opportunities. Adopt a mindset of continuous improvement, adjusting and refining your approach as you progress.
- **Stay up-to-date**: Salesforce and Tableau are dynamic, evolving platforms. Make sure to stay updated with the latest features and improvements. Regularly check official blogs, attend product webinars, and subscribe to newsletters.

Remember, the journey from learning to practice is a marathon, not a sprint. Be patient with yourself, continue learning, and keep refining your skills. With time, you will become proficient in harnessing the combined power of Salesforce and Tableau to drive your organization forward.

Troubleshooting guidance

Through the course of this book, you have gained a robust understanding of Salesforce and Tableau and how they can work in unison. However, as with all technology deployments, there are certain quirks and caveats you should be aware of to ensure a smooth implementation. In this chapter, we will share some hands-on tips to help you navigate your Salesforce-Tableau journey.

Connecting to Salesforce

Here are the top tips for avoiding issues when connecting to Salesforce:

- **Tip 1: Salesforce authentication**

  Tableau Cloud supports Salesforce authentication, which allows users to enter their credentials directly on the Salesforce sign-in page, with the credentials stored and managed by Salesforce. This setup is beneficial for scenarios where Salesforce federates authentication with another **Identity Provider (IdP)**.

- **Tip 2: Mismatched usernames**

  Suppose existing Tableau Cloud users have usernames that don't match their Salesforce usernames; first, change the existing Tableau Cloud user to an Unlicensed site role to prevent license consumption. Then, add the new Tableau Cloud user for Salesforce authentication, making sure the username matches the Salesforce organization's username. If necessary, migrate content owned by the old username in Tableau Cloud to the new user.

- **Tip 3: Unsuccessful login with OAUTH_APP_BLOCKED in return URL**

  This issue arises when a user configured with Salesforce authentication attempts to sign in but is not redirected, indicating that the connected application within Salesforce is being blocked by your organization. To resolve this, ensure the Tableau Cloud - Salesforce User Login via OIDC-connected application is installed and has the appropriate user profiles and permission sets applied.

Embedding Tableau dashboards in Salesforce

Here are the top tips for embedding Tableau dashboards inside Salesforce:

- **Tip 1: Mind the gap with Salesforce formula fields:**

  An important point to note is that formula fields in your Salesforce deployment do not automatically transfer when using Tableau's Salesforce connector. You might have to rebuild these formulas in Tableau using calculated fields. For more information on this, please refer to **https://kb.tableau.com/articles/Issue/salesforce-formulas-do-not-import?userSource=1**. There is an ongoing community idea to bring this feature. Consider supporting it if this is important for your organization.

- **Tip 2: Prioritize your sign-in:**

  When you start testing embedding without synchronizing authentication between platforms, remember to sign in to your Tableau Server or Online site first. This order of operations can prevent potential issues down the line.

- **Tip 3: Embedding done right:**

  When it comes to embedding, the code you might need can be slightly different from the conventional Apex code. Instead of an iFrame, it is beneficial to use a "script" tag. Using the "iframe" tag embeds an iFrame inside another iFrame, which can slow down the loading times. The "script" tag is also beneficial in bypassing Tableau Server's clickjacking protections, which might otherwise flag your Salesforce embed as potentially malicious.

- **Tip 4: Navigating URLs in Tableau:**

  While navigating to a view in Tableau, your URL might look something like this: **https://<server>/#/views/Superstore/Performance**. However, when embedding, be sure to replace the "#" with "t", so your URL becomes **https://<server>/t/views/Superstore/Performance.** This slight alteration makes a significant difference when it comes to embedding.

- **Tip 5: Navigating parameters and filters:**

  Tableau has two types of URL parameters: Display and Viz. The Display parameters include settings like "toolbar=no" or "embed=y," whereas Viz parameters might specify "region=West" or "Sub-Category=Tables." The way you call these in your URL differs. Display parameters should be preceded by "&:, "whereas Viz parameters should be preceded by "&" only.

  Additionally, if a field has a space in it, replace that space with a "+" sign when calling it in the URL. For instance, the field "Sales Type" will become "Sales+Type."

  Please refer to this link for the source of these tips: **https://thedataism.wordpress.com/2020/02/19/5-tips-for-embedding-tableau-in-salesforce/**

Using CRMA

Here are the top tips for working with CRMA:

- **Tip 1: Dataflow failures during app creation:**

  Do not modify the dataflow definition before its first successful run to prevent the app creation from finalizing. Only customize the data after the stock version has run at least once.

- **Tip 2: Failures due to field availability or org configuration:**

  If the failure can be resolved by changing the org configuration (such as field availability, user roles, or running replication dataflow), then correct the org configuration, manually start the dataflow via the Data Manager, then click **Reset** in the App and complete the reset process without changing any options.

- **Tip 3: Failures due to data sync:**

  If failure is due to data sync issues, run Data Sync for any SFDC Local connections in Data Manager, open the **App** folder for the failed app, click **Reset**, and complete the reset process without changing any options.

- **Tip 4: Failures due to app configuration:**

  If failure is due to incorrect configuration (such as wrong field reference), either delete the app and create a new version or reset the app and choose different answers in the app wizard.

- **Tip 5: Warning messages:**

  Warnings could indicate data quality issues even when dataflow has been completed, and all datasets have been registered. Investigate the root cause of the warning by understanding which nodes are responsible and, if necessary, consult with Salesforce Support.

- **Tip 6: Error messages:**

  Errors could indicate serious issues where none of the data flow's datasets are registered. If a dataflow has failed, re-running it may overcome a transient issue. If the failure persists, an administrator needs to investigate further, and it may be necessary to engage Salesforce Support.

- **Tip 7: Error messages related to remote connection:**

  If you get error messages related to the configuration settings for the object while saving or testing the configuration for a CRM Analytics remote connection, ensure the settings are correct by comparing them to the configuration in the remote database. If the issue persists, input the same connection settings into another database client. If the database client cannot connect, the settings are likely incorrect, and you may need to reach out to the database provider's support team.

Tableau dashboard

Here are the top tips working with dashboards in Tableau:

- **Tip 1: When blending, remember to check that your blend is set up correctly.**

  Your primary data source should be the one from which you will be using most of your fields. To tell your primary from your secondary data sources, remember your primary data source has a blue tick next to its name, while secondary data sources have a yellow tick. Also, make sure that Tableau is using the right field in the blend by checking that there is an unbroken chain link symbol next to the field name.

- **Tip 2: You can resize charts within the dashboard to aid visibility.**

  After you have dragged your chart into your dashboard, you can click on the caret in the top right corner to choose whether you want the chart to take the entire view, fit only its width or height, or make no adjustment at all.

- **Tip 3: Use containers within your dashboard to finetune the way your dashboard looks down to the pixel.**

  Putting charts into containers rather than directly into the dashboard allows you to choose exactly where to place each chart and what its size should be, down to the pixel. For a guide on containers in Tableau, please use this: **https://www.thedataschool.co.uk/harry-cooney/dashboard-formatting-with-containers-in-tableau/#:~:text=Containers%20allow%20you%20to%20essentially,position%20relative%20to%20each%20other.**

- **Tip 4: You can always add a blank.**

  If your dashboard is looking too packed, adding a small blank (10 - 20 pixels) will help the eye digest all the good content you have worked so hard to convey.

- **Tip 5: Tableau's filters act in a specific order.**

  If your dashboard shows some strange behavior, like your top 10 being the only top 6 or table calculations that do not add up, this could be due to the way Tableau computes filters. Tableau's filters are rendered in this order:

  - Extract Filters
  - Data Source Filters
  - Context Filters
  - Dimensions Filters
  - Measures Filters
  - Table Calculation Filters

  Note that all the filters in the same category are computed together, which may give rise to the behavior you are experiencing. If you want some filters to be computed before others, add them as context filters. A guide on how to do so can be found at **https://help.tableau.com/current/pro/desktop/en-us/filtering_context.htm**.

- **Tip 6: Your data will not refresh if it is stored as a file in a packaged workbook.**

  If your data, for example, comes from Excel and you save your workbook as a packaged workbook, Tableau will no longer read from your Excel file but from a copy that is saved in your **AppData** folder. Therefore, changes to your original Excel will not be reflected in your workbook. To check if you are working with a packaged workbook, look at the extension; a packaged workbook's extension is **`.twbx`**. To fix this issue, remove the extract and save your workbook again as a **`.twb`** file.

- **Tip 7: Your custom color scheme will change to Tableau's default one when changing data source.**

  This is a known behavior in Tableau and the cause of many frustrations. The best advice is to leave the color and shape customization as the very last step once you are sure you will not change your datasource. A workaround can be found at **https://kb.tableau.com/articles/issue/colors-change-after-replacing-data-source**, but it can be a cumbersome one according to your number of calculated fields.

- **Tip 8: If your connection is slow, consider creating an extract before you start working or pausing the data update.**

  Creating an extract at the beginning may mean you will have to wait longer before you can start creating your visualization, but it will save you from having to wait for each query to be sent back to your data to complete. Similarly, pressing the pause update button will allow you to make a series of changes to your work and then send them all in at once by refreshing the data.

- **Tip 9: If Tableau is not creating maps, make sure you have given your fields a geographical reference.**

  For guidance on how to do so, please refer to *Chapter 3 - Building and Integrating Data Pipelines*.

- **Tip 10: MEDIAN or COUNTD() functions not working:**

  This may be due to the type of data you are using, or it may happen because you are blending your data. If the issue is with MEDIAN, it may be because you are not using an Extract. Creating a data extract will solve your problem. If you are using a data blend, it is still possible to find a solution, but the process is less straightforward. For a complete guide to this and a few other data blend issues, please refer to **https://theinformationlab.nl/2023/03/17/tableau-blending-common-problems-and-workarounds/**.

Continuing the learning journey

As you deepen your knowledge and expertise in Salesforce and Tableau, it is essential to know that both platforms are vast, with a wealth of resources to support you on your learning journey. Below are some avenues for continued learning:

- **Salesforce Trailhead**: Salesforce Trailhead is an online learning platform designed specifically for Salesforce. It offers interactive learning paths, called trails, divided into modules. Each module contains units that include a quiz at the end. You'll learn everything from beginner basics to advanced admin and developer skills. Trailhead also offers preparation for Salesforce certification exams.
- **Salesforce certifications**: Obtaining Salesforce certifications can significantly enhance your credentials and demonstrate your proficiency in different areas of the platform. There are certifications for administrators, developers, architects, marketers, consultants, and more. Each certification requires passing an examination, and some certifications have prerequisites.
- **Tableau learning resources**: Tableau offers numerous resources for learning, including free training videos, instructor-led training, e-learning courses, webinars, and documentation. Topics cover everything from basic functionality and features to advanced techniques for data visualization, data management, and more.
- **Tableau public**: Tableau public is a platform where users can publish, share, and explore data visualizations created by people worldwide. It is a fantastic resource for seeing what's possible with Tableau and gaining inspiration for your work.
- **Tableau user groups and community**: The Tableau community is a vibrant network of users who collaborate, share knowledge, and support each other. Join

a Tableau user group, participate in the Tableau Community forums, or participate in the Tableau public community.

- **Tableau certifications**: Like Salesforce, Tableau also offers a range of certifications to validate your skills and expertise. From Tableau Desktop Specialist to Certified Data Analyst, there's a certification for every level of Tableau proficiency.
- **Online courses and tutorials**: Many online platforms offer Salesforce and Tableau courses. These courses often include hands-on exercises and projects to give you practical experience.
- **Conferences and events**: Events like Salesforce's Dreamforce and Tableau's Conference provide great opportunities to learn from experts, network with other users, and stay up-to-date with the latest product updates and features.

Remember, the learning journey with Salesforce and Tableau is ongoing. As both platforms continue to evolve and introduce new features, it is essential to stay updated with these changes and continue learning. Good luck with your journey!

Conclusion

Congratulations! You have reached the end of this learning journey, and you should be incredibly proud of the progress you have made. By delving into this material and dedicating yourself to understanding and implementing these practices, you have made significant strides in mastering Salesforce and Tableau.

This book was designed to equip you with the knowledge and tools needed to leverage the powerful capabilities of Salesforce and Tableau, two of the most advanced and widely used platforms in the world of data management and visualization. We have explored a lot of ground, from basic functionalities to complex, real-world applications. Your new skills are an asset that will benefit not only you but also your team, organization, or clients.

However, remember that mastery is an ongoing process. The world of technology is dynamic, with new features, best practices, and standards continually emerging. Keep on learning, stay curious, and never stop improving your skills. Take advantage of the many resources available to you, engage with the Salesforce and Tableau communities, and continue to build on the foundation you have established here.

The journey you have embarked on with Salesforce and Tableau is one filled with opportunities for growth and innovation. As you move forward, take the time to reflect on what you have learned, apply these insights in real-world situations, and don't be afraid to experiment and push the boundaries of what you think is possible.

Thank you for investing your time and effort into this learning journey. Your dedication and hard work have paid off, and you are now well-equipped to navigate the exciting world of Salesforce and Tableau.

Best of luck on your continued journey in harnessing the power of data, and once again, congratulations on your achievement!

Index

A

B

C

P

R

S

T

U

V